profilers

LEADING INVESTIGATORS
TAKE YOU INSIDE
THE CRIMINAL MIND

EDITED BY JOHN H. CAMPBELL
AND DON DeNEVI

Prometheus Books

59 John Glenn Drive
Amherst, New York 14228-2197

Published 2004 by Prometheus Books

Inquiries should be addressed to
Prometheus Books
59 John Glenn Drive
Amherst, New York 14228–2197
VOICE: 716–691–0133, ext. 207
FAX: 716–564–2711
WWW.PROMETHEUSBOOKS.COM

08 07 06 05 04   5 4 3 2 1

Library of Congress Cataloging-in-Publication Data

Profilers : leading investigators take you inside the criminal mind / edited by John H.
    Campbell and Don DeNevi.
        p. cm.
    Includes bibliographical references and index.
    ISBN 1–59102–266–5 (hardcover : alk. paper)
    1. Criminal psychology. 2. Criminal profilers. 3. Criminal behavior, Prediction of.
4. Criminal investigation. I. Campbell, John H. (John Henry) II. DeNevi, Don 1937–

HV6080.P66 2004
363.25—dc22

                                                                    2004014513

CONTENTS

INTRODUCTION

Violent serial crime significantly affected American society during the 1970s and continues to do so well into the millennium. Due in part to nation-gripping trials, the public's interest in such crimes has risen each year, and the media have been quick to publish provocative articles and produce documentaries for television and fictional feature-length films on the subject. Celebrated TV series such as *The Profiler* and *CSI*—to say nothing of mesmerizing movies such as *Manhunter, Silence of the Lambs*, and *Hannibal*—have awakened our awareness and stimulated our imaginations regarding the art and science of criminal profiling those among us capable of unbelievable depravity and cruelty. Unfortunately, the artistic license taken in such dramas has resulted in simplistic and sensationalistic images of the true and tedious work of profilers engaged in what Robert Ressler, former director of the FBI's Violent Criminal Apprehension Program, refers to as the "psychological autopsy of murder."

One of the more fortunate consequences of the 2003 publication of our *Into the Minds of Madman: How the FBI's Behavioral Science Unit Revolutionized Crime Investigation* is that the book served as the fountainhead for a new, almost effortless collaboration among current bureau profilers to share their individual and unique insights in tracking down specific predator personalities who commit horrendous crimes.

Our sequel, *Profilers: Leading Investigators Take You Inside the Criminal Mind*, is the first-ever collection of law enforcement profiling articles assembled for the general public that describe critical behind-the-scenes thinking and how old-fashioned detective work generally cracks difficult cases. Written between 1976 and 2004 by internationally recognized FBI profilers and city homicide investigators, virtually all pioneers in the development of investigative analysis, the compilation was culled from more than five hundred similar articles. More suspenseful than detective thrillers, several of the chapters deliver punches so dramatic that few novels can match. True crime is always more terrifying than fiction, especially when the reader is transported to the scene of the often grisly crime and presented enough clues to immerse the self in the head of the perpetrator.

One sees in the contributions of the investigators—such as former and current Behavioral Science Unit (BSU) members Conrad Hassel, Robert Ressler, Roy Hazelwood, Russell Vorpagel, Alan Brantley, Jim Fitzgerald, and Mary Ellen O'Toole, among others—a combination of not only long familiarity with the growth and development of investigative analysis but also a strong theoretical grasp, thanks in part to extensive criminal experiences, in profiling autoerotic murderers and killers who enucleate to serial fire-starting firefighters and rapist-mutilators of elderly women. Intrinsic throughout these chapters is the continuing challenge of creating a psychological profile for a specific crime.

Each of the BSU authors of this anthology has distilled the complexities of both his expertise and its associated profiling theory and technique into a style that is eminently readable, remarkably concise, and admirably clear. Such literary skill and knowledge are the result of an intensive multidisciplinary learning approach to a wide variety of investigative problems faced by the FBI's legendary National Center for the Analysis of Violent Crime (NCAVC). Established as a pilot program in 1984 and funded by the National Institute of Justice, the center became a law enforcement–oriented behavioral science and data-processing center designed to consolidate research, training, and investigative-operating support functions for the purpose of providing information and know-how to all law enforcement agencies confronted with unusual, bizarre, or repetitive crimes. The authors learned from FBI and visiting crime analysts, psychologists, sociologists, criminologists, political scientists, computer scientists, and police specialists. Virtually all the writers were supervisory special agents, experienced police officers, or scholars with advanced degrees in the behavioral science disciplines of psychology, criminology, and sociology.

All fourteen chapters were requested by and written under the auspices of either the NCAVC or the BSU to establish a new body of knowledge, no matter how slight, in a specialty area to improve the operational effectiveness of local police agencies and for use in training, consultation, and federal operational matters.

We believe that what follows is an invaluable book of enlightening readings for those who want to understand the nature of serial crime and fine-tune their sense of detective logic. Via the profilers' words, the reader works alongside of some of the most venerated profilers in America as they open up the often-mystifying procedural forensic techniques.

By following these profilers' ingenious trails from the crime scenes, analyzing the victims, and engaging in mental duels with the unknown assailants who attacked them, readers find themselves in both a superb introduction and an integral part of the real thing—the deadly, desolate landscape of the serial criminal mind.

PART 1:

THE ORIGINAL BEHAVIORAL SCIENCE ARTICLES ON CRIMINAL PROFILING

CRIMINAL PROFILING FROM CRIME SCENE ANALYSIS

John E. Douglas, Robert K. Ressler, Ann W. Burgess, and Carol R. Hartman

Since the 1970s, investigative profilers at the FBI's Behavioral Science Unit (now part of the National Center for the Analysis of Violent Crime) have been assisting local, state, and federal agencies in narrowing investigations by providing criminal personality profiles.[1] An attempt is now being made to describe this criminal-profile-generating process. A series of five overlapping stages lead to the sixth stage, or the goal of apprehension of the offender: (1) profiling inputs, (2) decision-process models, (3) crime assessment, (4) the criminal profile, (5) investigation, and (6) apprehension. Two key feedback filters in the process are (a) achieving congruence with the evidence, with decision models, and with investigation recommendations and (b) the addition of new evidence.

"You wanted to mock yourself at me! . . . You did not know your Hercule Poirot." He thrust out his chest and twirled his moustache.

I looked at him and grinned . . . "All right then," I said. "Give us the answer to the problems—if you know it."

"But of course I know it."

Hardcastle stared at him incredulously. "Excuse me. Monsieur Poirot, you claim that you know who killed three people. And why? . . . All you mean is that you have a hunch."

Published in a slightly different form in *Behavioral Sciences and the Law* 4 (1986): 401–21. Copyright © 1986 by Wiley. Reprinted with the permission of Wiley.

"I will not quarrel with you over a word . . . Come now, Inspector. I know—really know . . . I perceive you are still sceptic. But first let me say this. To be sure means that when the right solution is reached, everything falls into place. You perceive that in no other way could things have happened."

(Christie 1963, pp. 227–28)

The ability of Hercule Poirot to solve a crime by describing the perpetrator is a skill shared by the expert investigative profiler. Evidence speaks its own language of patterns and sequences that can reveal the offender's behavioral characteristics. Like Poirot, the profiler can say, "I know who he must be."

This chapter focuses on the developing technique of criminal profiling. Special agents at the FBI Academy have demonstrated expertise in crime scene analysis of various violent crimes, particularly those involving sexual homicide. This section discusses the history of profiling and the criminal-profile-generating process and provides a case example to illustrate the technique.

INTRODUCTION: HISTORY OF CRIMINAL PROFILING

Criminal profiling has been used successfully by law enforcement in several areas and is a valued means by which to narrow the field of investigation. Profiling does not provide the specific identity of the offender. Rather, it indicates the kind of person most likely to have committed a crime by focusing on certain behavioral and personality characteristics.

Profiling techniques have been used in various settings, such as hostage taking (Reiser 1982). Law enforcement officers need to learn as much as possible about the hostage taker in order to protect the lives of the hostages. In such cases, police are aided by verbal contact (although often limited) with the offender and possibly by access to his family and friends. They must be able to assess the subject in terms of what course of action he is likely to take and what his reactions to various stimuli might be.

Profiling has been used also in identifying anonymous letter writers (Casey-Owens 1984) and persons who make written or spoken threats of violence (Miron and Douglas 1979). In cases of the latter, psycholinguistic techniques have been used to compose a "threat dictionary," whereby every word in a message is assigned, by computer, to a specific category. Words as they are used in the threat message are then compared with those words as they are used in ordinary speech or writings. The vocabulary usage in the message may yield "signature" words unique to the offender. In this way, police may be able not only to determine that several letters were written by the same individual but also to learn about the background and psychology of the offender.

Rapists and arsonists also lend themselves to profiling techniques. Through careful interview of the rape victim about the rapist's behavior, law enforcement personnel begin to build a profile of the offender (Hazelwood 1983). The rationale behind this approach is that behavior reflects personality, and by examining behavior the investigator may be able to determine what type of person is responsible for the offense. For example, common characteristics of arsonists have been derived from an analysis of the data from the FBI's *Crime in the United States* (Rider 1980). Knowledge of these characteristics can aid the investigator in identifying possible suspects and in developing techniques and strategies for interviewing them. However, studies in this area have focused on specific categories of offenders and are not yet generalizable to all offenders.

Criminal profiling has been found to be of particular usefulness in crimes such as serial sexual homicides. These crimes create a great deal of fear because of their apparently random and motiveless nature, and they are also given high publicity. Consequently, law enforcement personnel are under great public pressure to apprehend the perpetrator as quickly as possible. At the same time, these crimes may be the most difficult to solve, precisely because of their apparent randomness.

While it is not completely accurate to say that these crimes are motiveless, the motive may all too often be one understood only by the perpetrator. D. T. Lunde (1976) demonstrates this issue in terms of the victims chosen by a particular offender. As Lunde points out, although the serial murderer may not know his victims, their selection is not random. Rather, it is based on the murderer's perception of certain characteristics of his victims that are of symbolic significance to him. An analysis of the similarities and differences among victims of a particular serial murderer provides important information concerning the "motive" in an apparently motiveless crime. This, in turn, may yield information about the perpetrator himself. For example, the murder may be the result of a sadistic fantasy in the mind of the murderer, and a particular victim may be targeted because of a symbolic aspect of the fantasy (Ressler et al. 1985).

In such cases, the investigating officer faces a completely different situation from the one in which a murder occurs as the result of jealousy or a family quarrel, or during the commission of another felony. In those cases, a readily identifiable motive may provide vital clues about the identity of the perpetrator. In the case of the apparently motiveless crime, law enforcement may need to look to other methods in addition to conventional investigative techniques in its efforts to identify the perpetrator. In this context, criminal profiling has been productive, particularly in those crimes where the offender has demonstrated repeated patterns at the crime scene.

THE PROFILING OF MURDERERS

Traditionally, two very different disciplines have used the technique of profiling murderers: mental health clinicians, who seek to explain the personality and actions of a criminal through psychiatric concepts, and law enforcement agents, whose task is to determine the behavioral patterns of a suspect through investigative concepts.

PSYCHOLOGICAL PROFILING

In 1957, the identification of George Metesky, the arsonist in New York City's Mad Bomber case (which spanned sixteen years), was aided by psychiatrist-criminologist James A. Brussel's staccato-style profile: "Look for a heavy man. Middle-aged. Foreign born. Roman Catholic. Single. Lives with a brother or sister. When you find him, chances are he'll be wearing a double-breasted suit. Buttoned."

Indeed, the portrait was extraordinary in that the only variation was that Metesky lived with two single sisters. Brussel, in a discussion about the psychiatrist acting as Sherlock Holmes, explains that a psychiatrist usually studies a person and makes some reasonable predictions about how that person may react to a specific situation and about what he or she may do in the future. What is done in profiling, according to Brussel, is to reverse this process. Instead, by studying an individual's deeds one deduces what kind of a person the individual might be (Brussel 1968).

The idea of constructing a verbal picture of a murderer using psychological terms is not new. In 1960, Palmer published results of a three-year study of fifty-one murderers who were serving sentences in New England. Palmer's "typical murderer" was twenty-three years old when he committed murder. Using a gun, this typical killer murdered a male stranger during an argument. He came from a low social class and achieved little in terms of education or occupation. He had a well-meaning but maladjusted mother, and he experienced physical abuse and psychological frustrations during his childhood.

Similarly, Rizzo (1982) studied thirty-one accused murderers during the course of routine referrals for psychiatric examination at a court clinic. His profile of the average murderer listed the offender as a twenty-six-year-old man who most likely knew his victim, with monetary gain the most probable motivation for the crime.

CRIMINAL PROFILING

Through the techniques used today, law enforcement seeks to do more than describe the typical murderer, if in fact there ever was such a person. Investigative profilers analyze information gathered from the crime scene for what it may reveal about the type of person who committed the crime.

Law enforcement has had some outstanding investigators; however, their skills, knowledge, and thought processes have rarely been captured in the professional literature. These people were truly the experts of the law enforcement field, and their skills have been so admired that many fictional characters (Sergeant Cuff, Sherlock Holmes, Hercule Poirot, Mike Hammer, and Charlie Chan) have been modeled on them. Although Lunde (1976) has stated that the murders of fiction bear no resemblance to the murders of reality, a connection between fictional detective techniques and modern criminal profiling methods may indeed exist. For example, it is attention to detail that is the hallmark of famous fictional detectives; the smallest item at a crime scene does not escape their attention. As stated by Sergeant Cuff in Wilkie Collins's *The Moonstone*, widely acknowledged as the first full-length detective study: "At one end of the inquiry there was a murder, and at the other end there was a spot of ink on a tablecloth that nobody could account for. In all my experience . . . I have never met with such a thing as a trifle yet."

However, unlike detective fiction, real cases are not solved by one tiny clue but the analysis of all clues and crime patterns.

Criminal profiling has been described as a collection of leads (Rossi 1982), as an educated attempt to provide specific information about a certain type of suspect (Geberth 1981), and as a biographical sketch of behavioral patterns, trends, and tendencies (Vorpagel 1982). Geberth (1981) has also described the profiling process as particularly useful when the criminal has demonstrated some form of psychopathology. As used by the FBI profilers, the criminal-profile-generating process is defined as a technique for identifying the major personality and behavioral characteristics of an individual based upon an analysis of the crimes he or she has committed. The profiler's skill is in recognizing the crime scene dynamics that link various criminal personality types who commit similar crimes.

The process used by an investigative profiler in developing a criminal profile is quite similar to that used by clinicians to make a diagnosis and treatment plan: data are collected and assessed, the situation is reconstructed, hypotheses are formulated, a profile is developed and tested, and the results are reported back. Investigators traditionally have learned profiling through brainstorming, intuition, and educated guesswork. Their expertise is the result of years of accumulated wisdom, extensive experience in the field, and familiarity with a large number of cases.

A profiler brings to the investigation the ability to make hypothetical formulations based on his or her previous experience. A formulation is defined here as a concept that organizes, explains, or makes investigative sense out of information and that influences the profile hypotheses. These formulations are based on clusters of information emerging from the crime scene data and from the investigator's experience in understanding criminal actions.

A basic premise of criminal profiling is that the way a person thinks (i.e., his or her patterns of thinking) directs the person's behavior. Thus, when the investigative profiler analyzes a crime scene and notes certain critical factors, he or she may be able to determine the motive and type of person who committed the crime.

THE CRIMINAL-PROFILE-GENERATING PROCESS

Investigative profilers at the FBI's Behavioral Science Unit (now part of the National Center for the Analysis of Violent Crime [NCAVC]) have been analyzing crime scenes and generating criminal profiles since the 1970s. Our description of the construction of profiles represents the off-site procedure as it is conducted at the NCAVC, as contrasted with an on-site procedure (Ressler et al. 1985). The criminal-profile-generating process is described as having five main stages, with a sixth stage or goal being the apprehension of a suspect (see fig. 1.1).

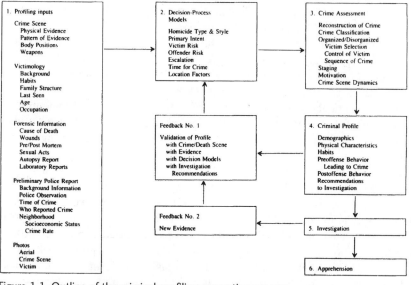

Figure 1.1. Outline of the criminal-profiling-generating process.

1. PROFILING INPUTS STAGE

The profiling inputs stage begins the criminal-profile-generating process. Comprehensive case materials are essential for accurate profiling. In homicide cases, the required information includes a complete synopsis of the crime and a description of the crime scene, encompassing factors indigenous to that area to the time of the incident such as weather conditions and the political and social environment.

Complete background information on the victim is also vital in homicide profiles. The data should cover domestic setting, employment, reputation, habits, fears, physical condition, personality, criminal history, family relationships, hobbies, and social conduct. Forensic information pertaining to the crime is also critical to the profiling process, including an autopsy report with toxicology/serology results, autopsy photographs, and photographs of the cleansed wounds. The report should also contain the medical examiner's findings and impressions regarding estimated time and cause of death, type of weapon, and suspected sequence of delivery of wounds.

In addition to autopsy photographs, aerial photographs (if available and appropriate) and eight-by-ten color pictures of the crime scene are needed. Also useful are crime scene sketches showing distances, directions, and scale, as well as maps of the area (which may cross law enforcement jurisdiction boundaries).

The profiler studies all this background and evidence information, as well as all initial police reports. The data and photographs can reveal such significant elements as the level of risk of the victim, the degree of control exhibited by the offender, the offender's emotional state, and his criminal sophistication.

Information the profiler does not want included in the case materials is that dealing with possible suspects. Such information may subconsciously prejudice the profiler and cause him or her to prepare a profile matching the suspect.

2. DECISION PROCESS MODELS STAGE

The decision process begins the organizing and arranging of the inputs into meaningful patterns. Seven key decision points, or models, differentiate and organize the information from stage 1 and form an underlying decisional structure for profiling.

Homicide Type and Style

As noted in table 1.1, homicides are classified by type and style. A single homicide is one victim, one homicidal event; double homicide is two victims, one event, and in one location; and a triple homicide has three victims in one location during one event. Anything beyond three victims is classified a mass murder; that is, four or more victims in one location and within one event.

TABLE 1.1. Homicide Classification by Style and Type

Style	Single	Double	Triple	Mass	Spree	Serial
Number of Victims	1	2	3	4+	2+	3+
Number of Events	1	1	1	1	1	3+
Number of Locations	1	1	1	1	2+	3+
Cool-Off Period	N/A	N/A	N/A	N/A	No	Yes

There are two types of mass murder: classic and family. A classic mass murder involves one person operating in one location at one period of time. That period of time could be minutes or hours and might even be days. The classic mass murderer is usually described as a mentally disordered individual whose problems have increased to the point that he acts against groups of people unrelated to these problems. He unleashes his hostility through shootings or stabbings. One classic mass murderer was Charles Whitman, the man who armed himself with boxes of ammunition, weapons, ropes, a radio, and food; barricaded himself on a tower in Austin, Texas; and opened fire for ninety minutes, killing sixty people and wounding over thirty others. He was stopped only when he was killed during an assault on the tower. James Huberty was another classic mass murderer. With a machine gun, he entered a fast-food restaurant and killed and wounded many people. He also was killed at the site by responding police. More recently, Pennsylvania mass murderer Sylvia Seegrist (nicknamed Ms. Rambo for her military-style clothing) was sentenced to life imprisonment for opening fire with a rifle at shoppers in a mall in October 1985, killing three and wounding seven.

The second type of mass murder is family member murder. If more than three family members are killed and the perpetrator takes his own life, it is classified as a mass murder/suicide. Without the suicide and with four or more victims, the murder is called a family killing. Examples include John List, an insurance salesman who killed his entire family on November 9, 1972, in Westfield, New Jersey. The bodies of List's wife and three children (ages sixteen, fifteen, and thirteen) were discovered in their front room, lying side by side on top of sleeping bags, as if in a mortuary. Their faces were covered, and their arms were folded across their bodies. Each had been shot once behind the left ear, except one son, who had been shot multiple times. A further search of the residence discovered the body of List's mother in a third-floor closet. She had also been shot once behind the left ear. List disappeared after the crime, and his car was found at an airport parking lot.

In another family killing case, William Bradford Bishop beat to death his wife, mother, and three children in the family's Bethesda, Maryland, residence in March 1976. He then transported them to North Carolina in the family station wagon where their bodies, along with the family dog's, were buried in a shallow grave. Bishop was under psychiatric care and had been prescribed antidepressant medication. No motive was determined. Bishop was a promising mid-level diplomat who had served in many overseas jobs and was scheduled for higher level office in the US Department of State. Bishop, like List, is a federal fugitive. There is strong indication both crimes were carefully planned, and it is uncertain whether the men have committed suicide.

Two additional types of multiple murder are spree and serial. A spree murder involves killings at two or more locations with no emotional cooling-off time period between murders. The killings are all the result of a single event, which can be of short or long duration. On September 6, 1949, Camden, New Jersey, spree murderer Howard Unruh took a loaded German luger with extra ammunition and randomly fired the handgun while walking through his neighborhood, killing thirteen people and wounding three in about twenty minutes. Even though Unruh's killings took such a short amount of time, they are not classified as a mass murder because he moved to different locations.

Serial murderers are involved in three or more separate events with an emotional cooling-off period between homicides. This type killer usually premeditates his crimes, often fantasizing and planning the murder in every aspect with the possible exception of the specific victim. Then, when the time is right for him and he is cooled off from his last homicide, he selects his next victim and proceeds with his plan. The cool-off period can be days, weeks, or months and is the main element that separates the serial killer from other multiple killers.

However, there are other differences between the murderers. The classic mass murderer and the spree murderer are not concerned with who their victims are; they will kill anyone who comes in contact with them. In contrast, a serial murderer usually selects a type of victim. He thinks he will never be caught, and sometimes he is right. A serial murderer controls the events, whereas a spree murderer, who oftentimes has been identified and is being closely pursued by law enforcement, may barely control what will happen next. The serial killer is planning, picking and choosing, and sometimes stopping the act of murder.

A serial murderer may commit a spree of murders. In 1984, Christopher Wilder, an Australian-born businessman and race car driver, traveled across the United States killing young women. He would target victims at shopping malls or would abduct them after meeting them through a beauty contest setting or dating service. While a fugitive as a serial murderer, Wilder was investigated, identified, and tracked by the FBI and almost every police department in the country. He then went on a long-term killing spree throughout the country and eventually was killed during a shoot-out with police.

Wilder's classification changed from serial to spree because of the multiple murders and the lack of a cooling-off period during his elongated murder event lasting nearly seven weeks. This transition has been noted in other serial/spree murder cases. The tension due to his fugitive status and the high visibility of his crimes gives the murderer a sense of desperation. His acts are now open and public and the increased pressure usually means no cooling-off period. He knows he will be caught, and the coming confrontation with police becomes an element in his crimes. He may place himself in a situation where he forces the police to kill him.

It is important to classify homicides correctly. For example, a single homicide is committed in a city; a week later a second single homicide is committed, and the third week, a third single homicide. Three seemingly unrelated homicides are reported, but by the time there is a fourth, there is a tie-in through forensic evidence and analyses of the crime scenes. These three single homicides now point to one serial offender. It is not mass murder because of the multiple locations and the cooling-off periods. The correct classification assists in profiling and directs the investigation as serial homicides. Similarly, profiling of a single murder may indicate the offender had killed before or would repeat the crime in the future.

Primary Intent of the Murderer

In some cases, murder may be an ancillary action and not itself the primary intent of the offender. The killer's primary intent could be (1) criminal enterprise; (2) emotional, selfish, or cause-specific; or (3) sexual. The killer may be acting on his own or as part of a group.

When the primary intent is criminal enterprise, the killer may be involved in the business of crime as his livelihood. Sometimes murder becomes part of this business even though there is no personal malice toward the victim. The primary motive is money. In the 1950s, a young man placed a bomb in his mother's suitcase that was loaded aboard a commercial aircraft. The aircraft exploded, killing forty-four people. The young man's motive had been to collect money from the travel insurance he had taken out on his mother prior to the flight. Criminal enterprise killings involving a group include contract murders, gang murders, competition murders, and political murders.

When the primary intent involves emotional, selfish, or cause-specific reasons, the murderer may kill in self-defense or compassion (mercy killings where life-support systems are disconnected). Family disputes or violence may lie behind infanticide, matricide, patricide, and spouse and sibling killings. Paranoid reactions may also result in murder, as in the previously described Whitman case. The mentally disordered murderer may commit a symbolic crime or have a psychotic outburst. Assassinations, such as those committed by Sirhan Sirhan and Mark Chapman, also fall into the emotional intent category. Murders in this category involving groups are committed for a variety of reasons: religious (Jim Jones and the Jonestown, Guyana, case), cult (Charles Manson), and fanatical organizations such as the Ku Klux Klan and the Black Panther Party of the 1970s.

Finally, the murderer may have sexual motives for killing. Individuals may kill as a result of or to engage in sexual activity, dismemberment, mutilation, evisceration, or other activities that have sexual meaning only for the offender. Occasionally, two or more murderers commit these homicides together, as in the 1984–1985 case in Calaveras County, California, where Leonard Lake and Charles Ng are suspected of as many as twenty-five sex-torture slayings.

Victim Risk

The concept of the victim's risk is involved at several stages of the profiling process and provides information about the suspect in terms of how he or she operates. Risk is determined using such factors as age, occupation, lifestyle, physical stature, resistance ability, and location of the victim and is classified as high, moderate, or low. Killers seek high-risk victims at locations where people may be vulnerable, such as bus depots or isolated areas. Low-risk types include those whose occupations and daily lifestyles do not lead them to being targeted as victims. The information on victim risk helps to generate an image of the type of perpetrator being sought.

Offender Risk

Data on victim risk integrates with information on offender risk, or the risk the offender was taking to commit the crime. For example, abducting a victim at noon from a busy street is high risk. Thus, a low-risk victim snatched under high-risk circumstances generates ideas about the offender, such as personal stresses he is operating under, his beliefs that he will not be apprehended, the excitement he needs in the commission of the crime, or his emotional maturity.

Escalation

Information about escalation is derived from an analysis of facts and patterns from the prior decision process models. Investigative profilers are able to deduce the sequence of acts committed during the crime. From this deduction, they may be able to make determinations about the potential of the criminal not only to escalate his crimes (e.g., from peeping to fondling to assault to rape to murder) but also to repeat his crimes in serial fashion. One case example is David Berkowitz, the Son of Sam killer, who started his criminal acts with the nonfatal stabbing of a teenage girl and who escalated to the subsequent .44-caliber killings.

Time Factors

There are several time factors that need to be considered in generating a criminal profile. These factors include the length of time required (1) to kill the victim, (2) to commit additional acts with the body, and (3) to dispose of the body. The time of day or night that the crime was committed is also important, as it may provide information on the lifestyle and occupation of the suspect (and also relates to the offender risk factor). For example, the longer an offender stays with his victim, the more likely it is he will be apprehended at the crime scene. In the case of the New York murder of Kitty Genovese, the killer carried on his murderous assault to the point where many people heard or witnessed the crime, leading to his eventual prosecution. A killer who intends to spend time with his victim therefore must select a location to preclude observation or one with which he is familiar.

Location Factors

Information about location—where the victim was first approached, where the crime occurred, and if the crime and death scenes differ—provide yet additional data about the offender. For example, such information provides details about whether the murderer used a vehicle to transport the victim from the death scene or if the victim died at her point of abduction.

3. CRIME ASSESSMENT STAGE

The crime assessment stage in generating a criminal profile involves the reconstruction of the sequence of events and the behavior of both the offender and victim. Based on the various decisions of the previous stage, this reconstruction of how things happened, how people behaved, and how they planned and organized the encounter provides information about specific characteristics to be generated for the criminal profile. Assessments are made about the classification of the crime, its organized/disorganized aspects, the offender's selection of a victim, strategies used to control the victim, the sequence of crime, the staging (or not) of the crime, the offender's motivation for the crime, and crime scene dynamics.

The classification of the crime is determined through the decision process outlined in the first decision process model. The classification of a crime as organized or disorganized, first introduced as classification of Lust murder (Hazelwood and Douglas 1980), but since broadly expanded, includes factors such as victim selection, strategies to control the victim, and sequence of the crime. An organized murderer is one who appears to plan his murders, target his victims, display control at the crime scene, and act out a violent fantasy against the victim (sex, dismemberment, torture). For example, Ted Bundy's planning was noted through his successful abduction of young women from highly visible areas (e.g., beaches, campuses, a ski lodge). He selected victims who were young, attractive, and similar in appearance. His control of the victim was initially through clever manipulation and later physical force. These dynamics were important in the development of a desired fantasy victim.

In contrast, the disorganized murderer is less apt to plan his crime in detail, obtains victims by chance, and behaves haphazardly during the crime. For example, Herbert Mullin of Santa Cruz, California, who killed fourteen people of varying types (e.g., an elderly man, a young girl, a priest) over a four-month period, did not display any specific planning or targeting of victims; rather, the victims were people who happened to cross his path, and their killings were based on psychotic impulses as well as on fantasy.

The determination of whether the crime was staged (i.e., if the subject was truly careless or disorganized or if he made the crime appear that way to distract or mislead the police) helps direct the investigative profiler to the killer's motivation. In one case, a sixteen-year-old high school junior living in a small town failed to return home from school. Police, responding to the father's report of his missing daughter, began their investigation and located the victim's scattered clothing in a remote area outside the town. A crude map was also found at the scene, which seemingly implied a premeditated plan of kidnapping. The police followed the map to a location that indicated a body may have been disposed of in a nearby river. Written and telephoned extortion demands were sent to the father, a bank executive, for the sum of $80,000, indicating that a kidnap was the basis of the abduction. The demands warned police in detail not to use electronic monitoring devices during their investigative efforts.

Was this crime staged? The question was answered in two ways. The details in one aspect of the crime (scattered clothing and tire tracks) indicated that subject was purposely staging a crime, while the details in the other (extortion) led the profilers to speculate who the subject was, specifically that he had a law enforcement background and therefore had knowledge of police procedures concerning crimes of kidnapping, hiding the primary intent of sexual assault and possible murder. With this information, the investigative profilers recommended that communication continue between the suspect and the police, with the hypothesis that the behavior would escalate and the subject become bolder.

While further communications with the family were being monitored, profilers from the FBI's Behavioral Science Unit theorized that the subject of the case was a white man who was single, in his late twenties to early thirties, and unemployed and who had been employed as a law enforcement officer within the past year. He would be a macho outdoors-type person who drove a late model, well-maintained vehicle with a CB radio. The car would have the overall appearance of a police vehicle.

As the profile was developed, the FBI continued to monitor the extortion telephone calls made to the family by the subject. The investigation, based on the profile, narrowed to two local men, both of whom were former police officers. One suspect was eliminated, but the FBI became very interested in the other, since he fit the general profile previously developed. This individual was placed under surveillance. He turned out to be a single white man who was previously employed locally as a police officer. He was now unemployed and drove a car consistent with the FBI profile. He was observed making a call from a telephone booth, and after hanging up, he taped a note under the telephone. The call was traced to the residence of the victim's family. The caller had given instructions for the family to proceed to the phone booth the suspect had been observed in. "The instructions will be taped there," stated the caller.

The body of the victim was actually found a considerable distance from the "staged" crime scene, and the extortion calls were a diversion to intentionally lead the police investigation away from the sexually motivated crime of rape-murder. The subject never intended to collect the ransom money, but he felt that the diversion would throw the police off and take him from the focus of the rape-murder inquiry. The subject was subsequently arrested and convicted of this crime.

Motivation

Motivation is a difficult factor to judge because it requires dealing with the inner thoughts and behavior of the offender. Motivation is more easily determined in the organized offender who premeditates, plans, and has the ability to carry out a plan of action that is logical and complete. On the other hand, the disorganized offender carries out his crimes by motivations that frequently are derived from mental illnesses and accompanying distorted thinking (resulting from delusions and hallucinations). Drugs and alcohol, as well as panic and stress resulting from disruptions during the execution of the crime, are factors that must be considered in the overall assessment of the crime scene.

Crime Scene Dynamics

Crime scene dynamics are the numerous elements common to every crime scene that must be interpreted by investigating officers and are at times easily misunderstood. Examples include location of crime scene, cause of death, method of killing, positioning of body, excessive trauma, and location of wounds.

The investigative profiler reads the dynamics of a crime scene and interprets them based on his experience with similar cases where the outcome is known. Extensive research by the Behavioral Science Unit at the FBI Academy and in-depth interviews with incarcerated felons who have committed such crimes have provided a vast body of knowledge of common threads that link crime scene dynamics to specific criminal personality patterns. For example, a common error of some police investigators is to assess a particularly brutal lust-mutilation murder as the work of a sex fiend and to direct the investigation toward known sex offenders when such crimes are commonly perpetrated by youthful individuals with no criminal record.

4. CRIMINAL PROFILE STAGE

The fourth stage in generating a criminal profile deals with the type of person who committed the crime and that individual's behavioral organization with relation to the crime. Once this description is generated, the strategy of investigation can be formulated, as this strategy requires a basic understanding of how an individual will respond to a variety of investigative efforts.

Included in the criminal profile are background information (demographics), physical characteristics, habits, beliefs and values, preoffense behavior leading to the crime, and postoffense behavior. It may also include investigative recommendations for interrogating or interviewing, identifying, and apprehending the offender.

This fourth stage has an important means of validating the criminal profile—feedback no. 1. The profile must fit with the earlier reconstruction of the crime, with the evidence, and with the key decision process models. In addition, the investigative procedure developed from the recommendations must make sense in terms of the expected response patterns of the offender. If there is a lack of congruence, the investigative profilers review all available data. As Hercule Poirot observed, "To know is to have all of the evidence and facts fit into place."

5. INVESTIGATION STAGE

Once the congruence of the criminal profile is determined, a written report is provided to the requesting agency and added to its ongoing investigative efforts. The investigative recommendations generated in stage 4 are applied, and suspects matching the profile are evaluated. If identification, apprehension, and a confession result, the goal of the profile effort has been met. If new evidence is generated (e.g., by another murder) and/or there is no identification of a suspect, reevaluation occurs via feedback no. 2. The information is reexamined and the profile revalidated.

6. APPREHENSION STAGE

Once a suspect is apprehended, the agreement between the outcome and the various stages in the profile-generating-process are examined. When an apprehended suspect admits guilt, it is important to conduct a detailed interview to check the total profiling process for validity.

CASE EXAMPLE

A young woman's nude body was discovered at 3:00 p.m. on the roof landing of the apartment building where she lived. She had been badly beaten about the face and strangled with the strap of her purse. Her nipples had been cut off after death and placed on her chest. Scrawled in ink on the inside of her thigh vas, "You can't stop me." The words "Fuck you" were scrawled on her abdomen. A pendant in the form of a Jewish sign (Chai), which she usually wore as a good luck piece around her neck, was missing and presumed taken by the murderer. Her underpants had been pulled over her face; her nylons were removed and very loosely tied around her wrists and ankles near a railing. The murderer had placed symmetrically on either side of the victim's head the pierced earrings she had been wearing. An umbrella and ink pen had been forced into the vagina, and a hair comb was placed in her pubic hair. The woman's jaw and nose had been broken and her molars loosened. She suffered multiple face fractures caused by a blunt force. Cause of death was asphyxia by ligature (pocketbook strap) strangulation. There were postmortem bite marks on the victim's thighs, as well as contusions, hemorrhages, and lacerations to the body. The killer also defecated on the roof landing and covered it with the victim's clothing.

The following discussion of this case in the context of the six stages of the criminal-profile-generating process illustrates how this process works.

PROFILING INPUTS

In terms of *crime scene evidence*, everything the offender used at the crime scene belonged to the victim. Even the comb and the felt-tip pen used to write on her body came from her purse. The offender apparently did not plan this crime; he had no gun, ropes, or tape for the victim's mouth. He probably did not even plan to encounter her that morning at that location. The crime scene indicated a spontaneous event; in other words, the killer did not stalk or wait for the victim. The crime scene differs from the death scene. The initial abduction was on the stairwell; then the victim was taken to a more remote area.

Investigation of the *victim* revealed that the twenty-six-year-old, ninety-pound, four-foot-eleven white woman awoke around 6:30 a.m. She dressed, had a breakfast of coffee and juice, and left her apartment for work at a nearby day care center, where she was employed as a group teacher for handicapped children. She resided with her mother and father. When she would leave for work in the morning, she would take the elevator or walk down the stairs, depending on her mood. The victim was a quiet young woman who had a slight curvature of the spine (kyhoscoliosis).

The *forensic information* in the medical examiner's report was important in determining the extent of the wounds, as well as how the victim was assaulted and whether evidence of sexual assault was present or absent. No semen was noted in the vagina, but semen was found on the body. It appeared that the murderer stood directly over the victim and masturbated. There were visible bite marks on the victim's thighs and knee area. He cut off her nipples with a knife after she was dead and wrote on the body. Cause of death was strangulation, first manual, then ligature, with the strap of her purse. The fact that the murderer used a weapon of opportunity indicates that he did not prepare to commit this crime. He probably used his fist to render her unconscious, which may be the reason no one heard any screams. There were no deep stab wounds and the knife used to mutilate the victim's breast apparently was not big, probably a penknife that the offender normally carried. The killer used the victim's belts to tie her right arm and right leg, but he apparently untied them in order to position the body before he left.

The *preliminary police report* revealed that another resident of the apartment building, a white man, aged fifteen, discovered the victim's wallet in a stairwell between the third and fourth floors at approximately 8:20 a.m. He retained the wallet until he returned home from school for lunch that afternoon. At that time, he gave the wallet to his father, a white man, aged forty. The father went to the victim's apartment at 2:50 p.m. and gave the wallet to the victim's mother.

When the mother called the day-care center to inform her daughter about the wallet, she learned that her daughter had not appeared for work that morning.

The mother, the victim's sister, and a neighbor began a search of the building and discovered the body. The neighbor called the police. Police at the scene found no witnesses who saw the victim after she left her apartment that morning.

DECISION PROCESS

This crime's *style* is a single homicide, with the murderer's primary intent making it a sexually motivated *type* of crime. There was a degree of planning indicated by the organization and sophistication of the crime scene. The idea of murder had probably occupied the killer for a long period of time. The sexual fantasies may have started through the use and collecting of sadistic pornography depicting torture and violent sexual acts.

Victim risk assessment revealed that the victim was known to be very self-conscious about her physical handicap and size, and she was a plain-looking woman who did not date. She led a reclusive life and was not the type of victim that would or could fight an assailant or scream and yell. She would be easily dominated and controlled, particularly in view of her small stature.

Based upon the information on occupation and lifestyle, we have a low-risk victim living in an area that was at low risk for violent crimes. The apartment building was part of a twenty-three-building public housing project in which the racial mixture of residents was 50 percent black, 40 percent white, and 10 percent Hispanic. It was located in the confines of a major police precinct. There had been no other similar crimes reported in the victim's or nearby complexes.

The crime was considered very *high risk* for the offender. He committed the crime in broad daylight, and there was a possibility that other people who were up early might see him. There was no set pattern of the victim taking the stairway or the elevator. It appeared that the victim happened to cross the path of the offender.

There was no *escalation* factor present in this crime scene. The time for the crime was considerable. The amount of time the murderer spent with his victim increased his risk of being apprehended. All his activities with the victim removing her earrings, cutting off her nipples, masturbating over her—took a substantial amount of time.

The *location* of the crime suggested that the offender felt comfortable in the area. He had been here before, and he felt that no one would interrupt the murder.

CRIME ASSESSMENT

The crime scene indicated the murder was one event, not one of a series of events. It also appeared to be a first-time killing, and the subject was not a typical organized offender. There were elements of both disorganization and organization; the offender might fall into a mixed category.

A reconstruction of the crime/death scene provides an overall picture of the crime. To begin with, the victim was not necessarily stalked but instead confronted.

What was her reaction? Did she recognize her assailant, fight him off, or try to get away? The subject had to kill her to carry out his sexually violent fantasies. The murderer was on known territory and thus had a reason to be there at 6:30 in the morning: either he resided there or he was employed at this particular complex.

The killer's control of the victim was through the use of blunt force trauma, with the blow to her face the first indication of his intention. It is probable the victim was selected because she posed little or no threat to the offender. Because she didn't fight, run, or scream, it appears that she did not perceive her abductor as a threat. Either she knew him, had seen him before, or he looked nonthreatening (i.e., he was dressed as a janitor, a postman, or businessman) and therefore his presence in the apartment would not alarm his victim.

In the sequence of the crime, the killer first rendered the victim unconscious and possibly dead; he could easily pick her up because of her small size. He took her up to the roof landing and had time to manipulate her body while she was unconscious. He positioned the body, undressed her, acted out certain fantasies that led to masturbation. The killer took his time at the scene, and he probably knew that no one would come to the roof and disturb him in the early morning since he was familiar with the area and had been there many times in the past.

The crime scene was not staged. Sadistic ritualistic fantasy generated the sexual motivation for murder. The murderer displayed total domination of the victim. In addition, he placed the victim in a degrading posture, which reflected his lack of remorse about the killing.

The crime scene dynamics of the covering of the killer's feces and his positioning of the body are incongruent and need to be interpreted. First, as previously described, the crime was opportunistic. The crime scene portrayed the intricacies of a long-standing murderous fantasy. Once the killer had a victim, he had a set plan about killing and abusing the body. However, within the context of the crime, the profilers note a paradox: the covered feces. Defecation was not part of the ritual fantasy, and thus it was covered. The presence of the feces also supports the length of time taken for the crime, the control the murderer had over the victim (her unconscious state), and the knowledge he would not be interrupted.

The positioning of the victim suggested the offender was acting out something he had seen before, perhaps in a fantasy or in a sado-masochistic pornographic magazine. Because the victim was unconscious, the killer did not need to tie her hands. Yet he continued to tie her neck and strangle her. He positioned her earrings in a ritualistic manner, and he wrote on her body. This reflects some sort of imagery that he probably had repeated over and over in his mind. He took her necklace as a souvenir, perhaps to carry around in his pocket. The investigative profilers noted that the body was positioned in the form of the woman's missing Jewish symbol.

CRIMINAL PROFILE

Based on the information derived during the previous stages, a criminal profile of the murderer was generated. First, a physical description of the suspect stated that he would be a white man, between twenty-five and thirty-five, or the same general age as the victim, and of average appearance. The murderer would not look out of context in the area. He would be of average intelligence and would be a high school or college dropout. He would not have a military history and may be unemployed. His occupation would be blue-collar or skilled. Alcohol or drugs did not assume a major role, as the crime occurred in the early morning.

The suspect would have difficulty maintaining any kind of personal relationships with women. If he dated, he would date women younger than himself, as he would have to be able to dominate and control in the relationships.

He would be sexually inexperienced, sexually inadequate, and never married. He would have a pornography collection. The subject would have sadistic tendencies; the umbrella and the masturbation act are clearly acts of sexual substitution. The sexual acts showed controlled aggression, but rage or hatred of women was obviously present. The murderer was not reacting to rejection from women as much as to morbid curiosity.

In addressing the habits of the murderer, the profile revealed there would be a reason for the killer to be at the crime scene at 6:30 in the morning. He could be employed in the apartment complex, be in the complex on business, or reside in the complex.

Although the offender might have preferred his victim conscious, he had to render her unconscious because he did not want to get caught. He did not want the woman screaming for help.

The murderer's infliction of sexual, sadistic acts on an inanimate body suggests he was disorganized. He probably would be a very confused person, possibly with previous mental problems. If he had carried out such acts on a living victim, he would have a different type of personality. The fact that he inflicted acts on a dead or unconscious person indicated his inability to function with a live or conscious person.

The crime scene reflected that the killer felt justified in his actions and that he felt no remorse. He was not subtle. He left the victim in a provocative, humiliating position, exactly the way he wanted her to be found. He challenged the police in his message written on the victim; the messages also indicated the subject might well kill again.

INVESTIGATION

The crime received intense coverage by the local media because it was such an extraordinary homicide. The local police responded to a radio call of a homicide. They, in turn, notified the detective bureau, which notified the forensic crime scene unit, medical examiner's office, and the county district attorney's office. A task force was immediately assembled of twenty-six detectives and supervisors.

An intensive investigation resulted, which included speaking to, and interviewing, over two thousand people. Records checks of known sex offenders in the area proved fruitless. Handwriting samples were taken of possible suspects to compare with the writing on the body. Mental hospitals in the area were checked for people who might fit the profile of this type killer.

The FBI's Behavioral Science Unit was contacted to compile a profile. In the profile, the investigation recommendation included that the offender knew that the police sooner or later would contact him because he either worked or lived in the building. The killer would somehow inject himself into the investigation, and although he might appear cooperative to the extreme, he would really be seeking information. In addition, he might try to contact the victim's family.

APPREHENSION

The outcome of the investigation was apprehension of a suspect thirteen months following the discovery of the victim's body. After receiving the criminal profile, police reviewed their files of twenty-two suspects they had interviewed. One man stood out. This suspect's father lived down the hall in the same apartment building as the victim. Police originally had interviewed his father, who told them his son was a patient at the local psychiatric hospital. Police learned later that the son had been absent without permission from the hospital the day and evening prior to the murder.

They also learned he was an unemployed actor who lived alone; his mother had died of a stroke when he was nineteen years old (eleven years previous). He had had academic problems of repeating a grade and dropped out of school. He was a white, thirty-year-old, never-married man who was an only child. His father was a blue-collar worker who also was an ex–prize fighter. The suspect reportedly had his arm in a cast at the time of the crime. A search of his room revealed a pornography collection. He had never been in the military, had no girlfriends, and was described as being insecure with women. The man suffered from depression and was receiving psychiatric treatment and hospitalization. He had a history of repeated suicidal attempts (hanging/asphyxiation) both before and after the offense.

The suspect was tried, found guilty, and is serving a sentence from twenty-five years to life for this mutilation murder. He denies committing the murder and states he did not know the victim. Police proved that security was lax at the psychiatric hospital in which the suspect was confined and that he could literally come and go as he pleased. However, the most conclusive evidence against him at his trial were his teeth impressions. Three separate forensic dentists, prominent in their field, conducted independent tests, and all agreed that the suspect's teeth impressions matched the bite marks found on the victim's body.

CONCLUSION

Criminal personality profiling has proven to be a useful tool to law enforcement in solving violent, apparently motiveless crimes. The process has aided significantly in the solution of many cases over the past decade. It is believed that through the research efforts of personnel in the FBI's National Center for the Analysis of Violent Crime and professionals in other field, the profiling process will continue to be refined and be a viable investigative aid to law enforcement.

NOTE

1. Preparation of this manuscript was supported by an Office of Juvenile Justice and Delinquency Prevention grant (84JN-KOIO).The authors wish to acknowledge Allen G. Burgess, Cynthia J. Lent, and Marieanne L. Clark for contributions to this manuscript.

REFERENCES

Brussel, J. S. 1968. *Casebook of a Crime Psychiatrist*. New York: Grove.

CaseyOwens, M. 1994. The Anonymous Letter-Writer—A Psychological Profile? *Journal of Forensic Sciences* 29: 816–19.

Christie, A. 1963. *The Clocks*. New York: Pocket Books, pp. 227–28.

Geberth, V. J. 1981. Psychological Profiling. *Law and Order* (September): 46–49.

Hazelwood, R. R. 1983. The Behavior-Oriented Interview of Tape Victims: The Key to Profiling. *FBI Law Enforcement Bulletin* (September): 1–8.

Hazelwood, R. R., and J. E. Douglas. 1980. The Lust Murderer. *FBI Law Enforcement Bulletin* 49, no. 4 (April): 1–5.

Lunde, D. T. 1976. *Murder and Madness*. San Francisco: San Francisco Book Co.

Miron, M. S., and J. E. Douglas. 1979. Threat Analysis: The Psycholinguistic Approach. *FBI Law Enforcement Bulletin* (September): 5–9.

Palmer, S. 1960. *A Study of Murder*. New York: Thomas Crowell.

Reiser, M. 1982. Crime-Specific Psychological Consultation. *Police Chief* (March): 53–56.

Ressler, R. K., A. W. Burgess, J. E. Douglas, and R. L. Depue. 1985. Criminal Profiling Research on Homicide. In *Rape and Sexual Assault: A Research Handbook*, ed. Burgess. New York: Garland, pp. 343–49.

Rider, A. O. 1980. The Firesetter: A Psychological Profile, Part 1. *FBI Law Enforcement Bulletin* (June): 6–13.

Rizzo, N. D. 1982. Murder in Boston: Killers and Their Victims. *International Journal of Offender Therapy and Comparative Criminology* 26, no. 1: 36–42.

Rossi, D. 1982. Crime Scene Behavioral Analysis: Another Tool for the Law Enforcement Investigator. Official Proceedings of the 88th Annual IACP Conference. *Police Chief* (January): 152–55.

Vorpagel, R. E. 1982. Painting Psychological Profiles: Charlatanism, Charisma, or a New Science? Official Proceedings of the 88th Annual IACP Conference. *Police Chief* (January): 156–59.

OFFENDER PROFILES:
A MULTIDISCIPLINARY APPROACH

Robert K. Ressler, John E. Douglas, A. Nicholas Groth, and Ann Wolbert Burgess

In recent months, the FBI Law Enforcement Bulletin has featured several articles on the application of psychological profiles as an investigative technique in selected criminal cases. The use of psychological criminal analysis is the product of a pilot project initiated by the FBI in 1978. This initial project, aimed at formulating criminal offender profiles through investigative interviews with incarcerated felons, led to the development of an ongoing systematic study—the Criminal Personality Interview Program. This program is designed to identify the salient characteristics, motivations, attitudes, and behaviors of offenders involved in specific types of crime. Two members of the FBI Academy's Behavioral Science Unit, Special Agents Robert K. Ressler and John E. Douglas, and two internationally recognized authorities in the field of sexual assault, Dr. A. Nicholas Groth and Dr. Ann Wolbert Burgess, compose the research team for this project. Dr. Groth is director of the Sex Offender Program for the Connecticut Department of Correction and is a clinical psychologist who has worked extensively with convicted sexual offenders. Dr. Burgess is professor and director of nursing research at Boston University School of Nursing and is a clinical specialist in psychiatric mental health nursing who has worked extensively with victims of sexual assault. This chapter is a joint effort of members of this research team.

Published in a slightly different form in *FBI Law Enforcement Bulletin* 49, no. 10 (September 1980): 16–20.

The psychology of criminal behavior, its patterns, dynamics, and characteristics, is an inadequately addressed area of research. It is difficult to enlist the cooperation of an offender prior to trial, since open disclosure could serve to incriminate him. Following conviction, the offender's participation in a psychological evaluation is geared toward the desired outcome of his disposition hearing or pending appeals. After his incarceration, the offender generally becomes inaccessible to behavioral scientists. For the most part, attempts to research criminal behavior have been confined to individual case reporting, which is subject to an inability to differentiate the relevant from the irrelevant, and to a large-scale statistical analysis of offense data retrieved from police records, in which individual differences are treated as error. Therefore, it was believed that a systematic study of incarcerated offenders whose appeals had been exhausted, combined with a review of all relevant documents and pertinent case records, direct observations, and firsthand investigative-clinical interviews with the subject, might yield important insights into the psychological nature of criminal behavior.

The question remained as to whether incarcerated offenders would cooperate in such research. In order to determine the feasibility of the intended study, a pilot project was undertaken. Crimes in which the FBI either has primary jurisdiction or has traditionally assisted local agencies by providing technical assistance and special expertise, such as hostage/terrorism, skyjacking, extortion/kidnapping, assassination, and mass/multiple murder, were targeted for study. Guidelines were formulated in conjunction with the Legal Instruction Unit of the FBI Academy.

Eight convicted offenders were then approached and asked if they would be willing to be interviewed about their crimes. They were long-term incarcerated felons lodged in various state and federal penitentiaries and were selected for the gravity of their violent crimes. The results were very encouraging. Based on this response, plans were developed for an extended, ongoing systematic study of convicted offenders in order to better understand the patterns and dynamics of criminal behavior. Sexual homicide was selected as the initial area of primary focus and concentration because it is a lethal type of crime that attracts a great deal of public attention.

BACKGROUND OF FBI PROFILING

For the past few years, efforts at developing psychological profiles of suspects for individual cases of sexual assault/homicide have been undertaken by members of the Behavioral Science Unit.[1] These cases were referred to the unit by local police departments. From the available evidence and information, unit members developed a psychological composite of the suspect. The approach is one of brainstorming, intuition, and educated guesswork. The product was the result of years of accumulated investigative experience in the field and familiarity with a large number of cases. No formal data bank, however, has been developed against which new cases can systematically be compared. Also, there is little or no follow-up once an offender has been successfully apprehended and convicted. Consequently, there is very little subsequent input of information that would serve to sharpen and refine the existing body of knowledge.

Given the opportunity to interview identified offenders and realizing the need to develop a protocol to insure systematic retrieval of pertinent data, the Training Division engaged the services of Dr. A. Nicholas Groth and Dr. Ann Wolbert Burgess, two experts in the field of sexual assault who had been conducting specialized police schools on rape and child molestation for law enforcement agents at the FBI Academy. This professional affiliation provided a multidisciplinary approach to the study of the sex murderer, combining contributions from both law enforcement and the behavioral sciences.

From a review of the pertinent literature and from the direct, firsthand field experience and prior work of the researchers, this team proceeded to develop a data schedule for investigative inquiry and offender assessment.

This instrument provided not only guidelines for interviewing subjects but also a system of recording and coding relevant data to permit computer analysis and retrieval. This protocol (which continues to undergo revision and refinement) is divided into five sections: (1) physical characteristics of the offender, (2) background development, (3) offense data, (4) victim data, and (5) crime scene data. It encompasses the offender's physical description, medical/psychiatric history, early home life and upbringing, schooling, military service, occupation/vocational history, sexual development and marital history, recreational interests, criminal history, the characteristics of his offense, modus operandi, victim selection, and the scene of his crime.

Once the assessment schedule had been designed, it was administered to three groups of sexual offenders–sex murderers, rapists and child molesters, and sex offenders confined to a mental health facility. During the first year (1979) of the study, interviews with twenty-six men who were convicted of a sex-related homicide and were incarcerated in various institutions across the country were completed. The second group—rapists and child molesters incarcerated in a maximum security prison—consisted of approximately 125 adult male offenders who were administered the interview schedule. These subjects were equally divided between those who had sexually assaulted adults and those who had sexually assaulted children. Sex offenders committed to a security treatment (mental health) facility following conviction but prior to disposition composed the third group. Approximately a hundred men were interviewed, again equally divided between rapists and child molesters.

Computer programs were then written to process the data. It is anticipated that as this body of data accumulates, it will provide information about a number of issues pertaining to the sexual offender.

Interestingly, institution officials have been supportive of the research investigation efforts, and the offenders themselves have been very receptive to our solicitation for their help and participation in this study. Although a few have denied or minimized their culpability, the majority have provided information consistent with the known facts of the case.

What prompts convicted offenders to cooperate with law enforcement agents? A variety of reasons exist. For those troubled by what they have done, cooperation may be an effort to gain some perspective and understanding of their behavior or an effort to compensate and make some type of restitution. Others, especially if they feel forgotten or ignored, may respond to the fact that someone is paying attention and showing some interest in them. A selected number of multiple murderers appear to be fascinated with law enforcement, as evidenced by their attempts to become identified with the profession, that is, posing as law enforcement officers, holding positions such as security guards or auxiliary police, and such. These offenders welcome an opportunity to again associate themselves with investigative efforts. Some may expect that cooperation will result in favors or benefits; others may feel they have nothing to lose, since all their appeals have been exhausted and no realistic hope for parole or pardon exists. Finally, others may participate in the study because it provides an opportunity to dwell on and recapture the fantasies, memories, and accompanying feelings of the original offense. Whatever their reasons, noble or selfish, healthy or pathological, each in his own way contributes something toward understanding the variety and complexity of this category of crime.

STATISTICAL PROCEDURE

The reliability and the validity of the data retrieved from the study of these offenders will ultimately be tested by the accuracy with which predoctrines (offender profiles) derived from this data pool are fulfilled. It is from these data that various types of offender profiles are beginning to emerge. Although no two offenders are exactly alike, and there is a wide range of individual differences found among offenders who commit similar offenses, they also share some similarities or common traits. It will be both these important differences and the important similarities that serve to differentiate and identify different kinds or specific types of offenders within the same offense category.

GOALS AND PURPOSES OF PROGRAM

This criminal personality research program is designed to contribute to advances in the study of sexual homicide—a subject about which little dependable information is currently available—by establishing a national data bank from which reliable information can be retrieved. From the data derived from this research, offender profiles will be developed based on identifiable behaviors, traits, and characteristics. The profiles, in turn, will aid local law enforcement agencies in the investigation of the crime and the identification and apprehension of offenders. In addition, such profiles and related information will serve to improve interrogation techniques and interviewing skills and to identify those techniques which will be most productive with each type of offender.

Knowledge gleaned from this research will have important implications for crime prevention by identifying important biopsychosocial factors of an offender. It will assist by attempting to provide answers to such questions as:

1. What leads a person to become a sexual offender and what are the early warning signals?
2. What serves to encourage or to inhibit the commission of his offense?
3. What types of response or coping strategies by an intended victim are successful with what type of sexual offender in avoiding victimization?
4. What are the implications for his dangerousness, prognosis, disposition, and mode of treatment?

Current emphasis is on the rape-murderer, since the Training Division receives annually close to a hundred unsolved, sex-related homicides for review and analysis. This research program is envisioned as ultimately expanding to encompass a broader variety of felony crimes to include hostage taking and techniques to improve hostage negotiation. A further benefit will be the improvement of techniques of interviewing, interrogation, and informant targeting in criminal and espionage matters. The present study, which addresses sexual assault, is unique in that it represents the combined approaches of law enforcement/criminal justice and behavioral science/mental health professionals, as well as active participation and direct contribution from convicted felons, to combat this major type of serious crime.

NOTE

1. Richard L. Ault Jr. and James T. Reese, "A Psychological Assessment of Crime: Profiling," *FBI Law Enforcement Bulletin* 49, no. 3 (March 1980): 22–25.

SEXUAL HOMICIDE:

A MOTIVATIONAL MODEL

Ann W. Burgess, Carol R. Hartman, Robert K. Ressler,
John E. Douglas, and Arlene McCormack

The findings from this exploratory study are reported in terms of the descriptive background characteristics of thirty-six sexual murderers, their behaviors and experiences in connection with their developmental stages, and the central role of sadistic fantasy and critical cognitive structures that support the act of sexual murder. A five-phase motivational model is presented: (1) ineffective social environment, (2) formative events, (3) critical personal traits and cognitive mapping process, (4) attitude toward others and self, and (5) feedback filter.

For many years, motiveless murder has baffled law enforcement officials and mental health professionals (Satten, Menninger, Rosen, and Mayman 1960).[1] Motiveless killings, usually serial in nature (carried out by a single individual over a period of time), leave virtually no clues about the murderer's motive or identity. Although this kind of crime has existed throughout history (Lunde 1977), the number of such murders has never been as high (Ressler et al. 1985). According to the 1984 FBI Uniform Crime Report, 22.1 percent of murders committed in the reporting year had an unknown motive as analyzed by law enforcement. This figure takes on added meaning when it is compared to earlier reporting figures. In 1976, murders with an unknown motive represented 8.5 percent of all murders, 17.8 percent in 1981, and 22.1 percent in 1984, or an increase of 160 percent in an eight-year period.

Such seemingly motiveless murders were first covered extensively by the news media when New York City's "Son of Sam" killer, David Berkowitz, stalked victims, apparently chosen at random, and killed, them with a .44-caliber pistol.

Published in a slightly different form in *Journal of Interpersonal Violence* 1, no. 3 (September 1986): 251–72. Copyright © 1986 by Sage Publications, Inc. Reprinted by permission of Sage Publications, Inc.

Since then there has been considerable attention to these types of murders. People fear becoming the next random victim of these violent, often grisly crimes.

Sexual homicide results from one person killing another in the context of power, control, sexuality, and aggressive brutality. The psychiatric diagnosis of sexual sadism, sometimes applied to the victimizer, states that the essential feature of this deviant behavior (i.e., paraphilia) is the infliction of physical or psychological suffering on another person in order to achieve sexual excitement.

It has been difficult to gather dependable statistics on the number of sexual homicide victims for several reasons: (1) the victim is officially reported as a homicide statistic and not as a rape assault (Brownmiller 1975; MacDonald 1971); (2) there is a failure to recognize any underlying sexual dynamics in a seemingly "ordinary" murder (Cormier and Simons 1969; Revitch 1965); (3) those agencies that investigate, apprehend, and assess the murderer often fail to share their findings, curtailing the collective pool of knowledge on the subject (Ressler, Douglas, Groth, and Burgess 1980); and (4) conventional evidence of the crime's sexual nature may be absent.

When law enforcement officials cannot readily determine a motive for murder, they examine its behavioral aspects. In developing techniques for profiling murderers, FBI agents have found that they need to understand the thought patterns of murderers in order to make sense of crime scene evidence and victim information. Characteristics of evidence and victims can reveal much about the murderer's intensity of planning, preparation, and follow-through. From these observations, the agents begin to uncover the murderer's motivation, recognizing how dependent motivation is to the killer's dominant thinking patterns. In many instances, a hidden sexual motive emerges, a motive that has its origins in fantasy.

The role of fantasy in the motive and behavior of suspects is an important factor in violent crimes, especially sexual murders (Ressler et al. 1985). In the last twenty years, the role of sadistic fantasy has been explored in several studies (Brittain 1970; Reinhardt 1957; Revitch 1965, 1980; West, Roy, and Nicholas 1978), with MacCulloch and colleagues (1983) suggesting that sadistic acts and fantasy are linked and that fantasy drives the sadistic behavior. Current realization of cognitive structures, which help maintain behavior patterns (Beck 1976), combine with investigation of sadistic fantasies (Brittain 1970; MacCulloch, Snowden, Wood, and Mills 1983; Ressler et al. 1985), criminal reasoning (Yochelson and Samenow 1977; Samenow 1984), and criminal fantasy (Schlesinger and Kutash 1981), and serve as primary foundations for our conceptualization of a motivational model of sexual murder.

THE STUDY

Many people have speculated on various aspects of murder: epidemiological studies report on demographic data concerning victims and perpetrators (Constantino, Kuller, Perper, and Cypress 1977) and patterns of homicide (Rushforth, Ford, Hirsch, Rushforth, and Adelson 1977; Wolfgang 1958); murderers have been categorized in terms of motive (Revitch 1965), intent (Kahn 1971), number of victims (Frazier 1974), and type of victim (Cormier and Simons 1969). Our study of thirty-six sexual killers was not designed to examine motivation, yet our research yielded rich descriptive data about what moved these men to kill.

The basis for the Patterns of Homicide Crime Scene Project, from which this article is derived, has been reported elsewhere (Ressler, Burgess, Douglas, Hartman, and D'Agostino 1986). The project can be traced to the early 1970s, when agents of the FBI's Behavioral Science Unit (BSU) began, on an informal basis, to deduce certain offender characteristics by examining crime scene information. As a result, a preliminary framework for crime scene analysis and criminal profiling was formulated. Concurrent with the development of the criminal profiling project, a study was proposed to analyze crime scene patterns. Using case record review, direct observation, and firsthand investigative interviews, the study would examine convicted, incarcerated offenders.

This law enforcement study focused on analyzing crime scene evidence in order to identify the murderer. Data collection, which took place in various US prisons between 1979 and 1983, was performed by special agents of the FBI. The data set for each murderer consisted of the best available data from two types of sources: official records (psychiatric and criminal records, pretrial records, court transcripts, and/or prison records) and interviews with the offenders. The majority of offenders provided written consent to be interviewed. Interviews were all conducted in prisons with the cooperation of officials at the various correctional institutions.

Standard data collection forms were used. The forms not only provided guidelines for interviewing subjects but also established a system of recording and coding relevant data to permit computer analysis and retrieval. Information was requested about the offender and his background, about the offense, about the victim, and about the crime scene. Subjects were asked questions about childhood, adolescent, and adult behaviors or experiences that might be related to violence. In this article, we present a motivational model of sexual homicide based on (1) quantitative analysis of background data and (2) qualitative analysis of interview data from murderers.

This was an exploratory descriptive study of a small available sample of thirty-six sexual murderers. Because of the limitations of the study design, we present critical variables not for generalization purposes but as hypotheses for examination in subsequent research of sexual and "motiveless" murders. We have no data on a comparable control group, thus these findings should not be interpreted as showing a predictive role for certain childhood or adolescent experiences. Instead, we use the data in developing a motivational matrix for sexual murder.

FINDINGS

THE MURDERERS

The thirty-six men in the study began their lives with certain advantages. Most of them grew up in the 1940s and 1950s, a period when attitudes in the United States favored oldest, white male children; all subjects were male, the majority (thirty-three) were white, and many were eldest sons (four were only children, and four were adopted). They were of good intelligence, with 29 percent classified in the average range, 36 percent in the bright normal and superior range, and 15 percent in the very superior range. These attributes fostered in the offenders a certain sense of privilege and entitlement.

Initially, the majority of the men began life in two-parent homes. Half of the mothers were homemakers; three-quarters of the fathers earned stable salaries. Over 80 percent of the offenders described their family socioeconomic levels as average (self-sufficient) or better. Thus, mothers were in the home raising the children; fathers were earning stable incomes; poverty was not a factor in the financial status of families.

Although the families initially appeared to be functional with both parents present, problems were noted within the parents' backgrounds. Families had criminal (50.0%), psychiatric (53.3%), alcohol abuse (69.0%), drug abuse (33.3%), or sexual (46.2%) problems in their histories. It appears that parents of these men were often absorbed in their own problems. Thus, while being offered little guidance because of their parents' preoccupation with their troubles, the murderers as young boys were witness to these deviant role patterns of criminal behavior, substance abuse, and poor interpersonal relationships.

In 47 percent of cases, the father left the home before the subject was twelve; in 43 percent of the cases, at least one parent was absent at some time prior to the subject's reaching age eighteen. This loss of the father required many of the offenders to adjust to a new male caretaker during childhood and adolescent years.

Instability in the family residence was also noted in many cases (68%). In addition, 40 percent of the subjects lived outside the family home before age eighteen. Locations included foster homes, state homes, detention centers, and mental hospitals. The histories of frequent moving reduced the boys' opportunities to develop positive outside relationships that might have compensated for family instability.

Examination of performance behaviors of the subjects revealed that despite their intelligence and potential in many areas, performance in academics, employment, and military was often poor. Only one-third did average or better in school, with 68 percent receiving a fair to poor academic rating. The majority did not finish high school. Thus, although these men were intellectually bright, they did not perform to their abilities.

There was confirming evidence of abuse in the childhood histories of the thirty-six murderers. Physical abuse (13/31), psychological abuse (23/31), and sexual abuse (12/28) were noted. This reveals that many of the men experienced some type of childhood abuse. It is noteworthy that twenty-five of the thirty-six men had some type of psychiatric assessment or confinement as a child or adolescent.

BEHAVIORAL INDICATORS

Our analysis examined the results of a checklist of symptoms and behavioral experiences (see table 3.1). This checklist was derived from a standard list of sell-report indicators, used in research on a wide variety of psychosocial studies, and also included indicators of thinking patterns (daydreams) and behaviors derived from the FBI profilers' understanding of criminal behavior. However, readers should keep in mind that many of these behavioral symptoms have no consistent definitions or ways of measurement. For example, there is no method of measuring a pattern of lying or masturbation.

TABLE 3.1. Frequency of Reported Behavior Indicators in Childhood, Adolescence, and Adulthood for Sexual Murders

| | Frequency | | | | | |
| | Childhood | | Adolescence | | Adulthood | |
Behavior	n	(%)	n	(%)	n	(%)
Daydreaming	28	82	27	81	27	81
Compulsive masturbation	28	82	28	82	27	81
Isolation	28	71	26	77	26	73
Chronic lying	28	71	28	75	28	68
Enuresis	22	68	20	60	20	15
Rebellious	27	67	25	84	25	72
Nightmares	24	67	22	68	21	52
Destroying property	26	58	26	62	23	35
Fire setting	25	56	25	52	25	28
Stealing	27	56	27	81	25	56
Cruelty to children	28	54	28	64	27	44
Poor body image	27	52	27	63	26	62
Temper tantrums	27	48	26	50	25	44
Sleep problems	23	48	22	50	22	50
Assaultive to adults	25	38	25	84	28	86
Phobias	24	38	23	43	24	50
Running away	28	36	26	46	26	11
Cruelty to animals	28	36	26	46	25	36
Accident prone	24	29	22	32	22	27
Headaches	21	29	21	33	22	45
Destroying possessions	25	28	23	35	23	35
Eating problems	26	27	25	36	26	35
Convulsions	26	19	24	21	23	13
self-mutilation	26	19	24	21	25	32

NOTE: *n* = number of subjects with data

Childhood. An analysis of twenty-four checklist items indicates that over 50 percent of the murderers reported the following present in childhood: daydreaming (82%), masturbation (82%), isolation (71%), chronic lying (71%), enuresis (68%), rebelliousness (67%), nightmares (67%), destruction of property (58%), firesetting (56%), cruelty to children (54%), and poor body image (52%).

Adolescence. An analysis of twenty-four checklist items indicates that over 50 percent of murderers reported the following behaviors: assaultive to adults (84%), rebelliousness (84%), masturbation (82%), stealing (81%), daydreaming (81%), isolation (77%), chronic lying (75%), nightmares (68%), poor body image (63%), cruelty to children (64%), destroying of property (62%), enuresis (60%), and firesetting (52%).

Adulthood. An analysis of twenty-four checklist items indicates that over 50 percent of murderers reported that during adulthood, the following behaviors were present: assaultive to adults (86%), daydreaming (81%), masturbation (81%), isolation (73%), rebelliousness (72%), chronic lying (68%), poor body image (62%), stealing (56%), and nightmares (52%).

For descriptive purposes, we use the terms *internal behaviors* and *external behaviors*. Internal behaviors include thinking patterns and experiences within or unique to the individual; external behaviors are those overt actions that can be observed by others. The internal behaviors most consistently reported over the three developmental periods are daydreaming, compulsive masturbation, and isolation. The external behaviors most consistently reported include chronic lying, rebelliousness, stealing, cruelty to children, and assault on adults.

ROLE OF FANTASY

The central role of daydreaming and fantasy in the lives of the thirty-six murderers is critical to what motivated them to kill. Daydreaming has been defined as any cognitive activity representing a shift of attention away from a task (Singer 1966). A fantasy, as we define it, is an elaborate thought with great preoccupation, anchored with emotion and having origins in daydreams. A fantasy is generally experienced as thoughts, although the individual may be aware of images, feelings, and internal dialogue. Some people may be conscious only of thoughts, whereas others are conscious only of feelings. Fantasy is a normal way for adults as well as children to obtain and maintain control of an imagined situation.

However, the level of fantasy development may differ among people and is generally based on the individual's ability to identify certain thoughts as daydreams, to articulate their content, and retrospectively to recall this content. Singer (1966) observed that 96 percent of adults report that they daydream several times a day, and Beres (1961) noted that fantasy may either substitute or prepare for action. For various groups of people, fantasies may be sadistic (MacCulloch et al. 1983). It is not known how many people activate their sadistic fantasies and in what context this may occur, but Schlesinger and Revitch (1980) caution that once the fantasy builds to a point where inner stress is unbearable, the way for action is prepared.

Whereas psychological motives for violent behavior are usually conceptualized in the literature as having roots beginning with trauma, insult, and/or over-stimulation in early childhood, our thesis is different. We hypothesize that these men are motivated to murder by their way of thinking. Over time, their thinking patterns emerged from or were influenced by early life experiences. For example, a child abused by an adult caretaker begins to think about being hit every time an adult comes near him, dwelling on the hitting. He may imagine (fantasize) about someone coming to help him by beating up the adult. This thinking pattern may bring relief because someone has protected him in his fantasy. In addition, while being abused, the child may psychologically remove himself from the pain. He may pride himself on his control over pain in the face of abuse; for example, while being beaten he does not flinch or blink. This thinking pattern gives the child a sense of control, and, as a result, tension is relieved. The child can increase or decrease terror with different levels of arousal through fantasy. Development of this type of thinking pattern does not necessarily mean a child will grow up to be an abuser; our example illustrates the role of fantasy and its development.

In analyzing the data we obtained through interviews with the murderers, we attempted to link our quantifiable findings with indications from the murderers themselves of long-standing, aggressive thoughts and fantasies directed toward sexualized death. The findings suggest that these thought patterns were established early and existed in a context of social isolation.

Murderers were consciously aware of the central role of fantasy in their lives and of their preference for fantasy over reality. Even those men unaware of this reported that their thoughts became retaliatory or vengeful when they perceived themselves as being slighted, rejected, frustrated, or betrayed. Such thinking becomes an important component in the maintenance of sexually aggressive violent behavior.

The central role that fantasy plays in the thinking patterns of these men is noted in one of the subject's statements: "All my life I knew I was going to end up killing." It also was observed in the statement of a parent who, after her son was convicted of fetish robberies, feared the outcome of her son's moodiness and isolation would be "something really terrible and tragic."

EARLY FANTASY DEVELOPMENT

It is important to keep in mind that not all children respond to their environment with violent fantasies, and not all children who fantasize violence act out these fantasies. Nevertheless, from our interviews with the murderers in our study, the high degree of egocentricity in the murderer's negative, aggressive, sexualized fantasy and play is revealed.

As children, the murderers often thought of other children and family members as extensions of their inner worlds. The revealed intermittent awareness of the impact of their early childhood behavior on others. They were not influenced by the response of others to their behavior. It continued and repeated itself. They recounted tying up a smaller child and scaring him or destroying another child's toy. A man who eventually beheaded his victims did not associate that action with his early childhood activities that involved the systematic decapitation of his sister's dolls. He saw his actions as a response to his annoyance with his sister, not to his desire to dominate, bully, and hurt. Ritualistic play of tying up and scaring a younger child was not associated to one murderer's abuse as a child. His play was a reenactment. Murderers recounting violent and sadistic behavior as adolescents were more aware of the intentionality of their acts.

The interviews with the offenders are remarkable in the absence of any accounts of positive childhood fantasies. However, it is unclear whether such fantasies were actually nonexistent or whether early positive fantasies were lost in later negative perspectives and behaviors. The following example illustrates the pervasive nature of the child's negative daydreaming: "I felt guilty for having those thoughts [toward family] and submerged them and built up lots of hostility and then it got off into fantasy. . . . They should have noticed it at school, so excessive was my daydreaming that it was always in my report cards. . . . I was dreaming about wiping out the whole school."

EARLY SEXUALIZATION OF FANTASY

The childhood onset of sexual fetish interests was noted in the subjects. Several subjects described strong interest and attraction at approximately the age of five to high-heeled shoes, female underwear, and rope. The men were aware of the carryover of sexualized fantasies about these items into adolescence and adulthood. When the subjects began to murder, these items took on importance in ritualized aspects of their murders.

Evidence of childhood sexualized play in the lives of the murderers was also revealed by parents and caretakers. Some parents provided information about preschool sexual fantasies. In one case, a mother recalled finding her three-year-old son with one end of a string tied to his penis and the other end of the string shut in a bureau drawer, leaning backward to exert a pulling sensation on his penis. The boy's behavior suggested he had engaged in such activity earlier. It is most likely that this behavior was introduced initially by an older person; evidence suggests the boy's babysitter was responsible.

AGGRESSIVE COMPONENTS OF EARLY FANTASY

When murderers were asked to describe their early favorite play activities, some revealed a repetitive acting out of a core aggressive fantasy. These childhood fantasies were so dominant that they became persistent themes in play with other children or alone. In some cases, an original violation or assault was expressed. For example, one subject at age fifteen took younger boys into the bathroom of his residential facility and forced oral and anal sex on them, reenacting his own victimization at age ten but reversing his role from victim to victimizer. However, he did not consciously connect this behavior with his own earlier assaults. The assaultive rituals were his attempts at mastery and control over people and situations.

Another offender as an adolescent openly masturbated in his home, especially in front of his sisters, using their underwear in his masturbation rituals. He appeared oblivious to the inappropriate nature of his acts and was offended by his family's response, feeling that family members were rejecting, intolerant, and unfair. It is speculated that his behavior represented a hyperarousal state derived from one repressed memory from childhood.

Aggressive content in the form of death themes was also noted for those murderers who described their early fantasies. Death is an example of ultimate control. When directed toward oneself in childhood, it can be a counterreaction to overwhelming fear, and its dominance in thought and play reveals the child's troubled state of mind.

In one case, the twelve-year-old subject repeatedly played "gas chamber" with his sister. This game required his sister to tie him up in a chair, throw an imaginary switch, and when "gas" was introduced, the subject would grasp at his throat, drop to the floor, writhe convulsively, and "die." This game combined a sexual theme (compression of the carotid arteries for a sexual sensation) and death theme fantasy.

EARLY EXPRESSIONS OF SEXUAL AND AGGRESSIVE FANTASY

Early fantasies often give rise to behavior tryouts that are precursors to criminal behavior (MacCulloch 1983). These precursor behaviors have the capacity to move the child into pain-inflicting acts and to break through in subtle, as well as overt, ways. They may emerge as play-engagement behaviors with others (i.e., bullying younger children or putting pins in the rug for a sister to walk on) or actions involving only themselves (i.e., tying ropes around their necks or cutting parts of their bodies). Such behavior was noted in the reported cruelty to other children by the offenders as youths as well as in the offender's earliest encounters with law enforcement. Although such encounters are often dismissed as adolescent adjustment problems, they may be evidence of an escalation in aggressive acts toward others.

Especially illustrative of such escalation of fantasy expression is the previously cited example of the three-year-old boy who was observed by his mother with his penis tied to a bureau drawer. As a young adolescent, he was found by his parents in the bathtub practicing autoerotic asphyxia with his penis and neck tied to the cross-bar of the faucets. At age fourteen his parents took him to a psychiatrist after noticing rope burns on his neck. At age seventeen this same subject abducted a girl at knife-point, took her to a deserted area where he kept her all night, and released her in the morning. The adolescent was apprehended and then released; the charge on his record was "girl trouble." Of importance is the offender's shift in the object of aggression from himself to a woman. Not until late adolescence, when the offender began following women, confronting them with a knife, binding them, and fondling them was the offender sent to prison. After release from prison, his crimes escalated to the murder of three young women by asphyxia.

The early expressions of aggressive fantasies were often painful memories for the offenders to reveal and the ones, for various reasons, that were never discussed. They may have realized that they could have controlled their actions and that they were aware that they had crossed the line between fantasy and reality. In cases where the men were not apprehended for their early crimes, they learned they were not controlled by authority and that they could act violently and kill with impunity. Of the thirty-six, ten murdered as juveniles, thus realizing that they had the power over life.

MOTIVATIONAL MODEL OF SEXUAL HOMICIDE

To illustrate our hypothesis of the various factors that influenced the thirty-six sexual murderers to kill, we present a motivational model for understanding sexually oriented murder and sadistic violence. In addition to the data we collected, the interviews with the murderers serve as a basis for this model. The murderers' early development of an active, aggressive fantasy life (daydreams) combined with later sexual reinforcement (compulsive masturbation) and increasing detachment from social rules of conduct (social isolation) provide a framework that reinforces his subsequent violent behavior.

The model has five interacting components emphasizing interrelationships among (1) the murderer's ineffective social environment, (2) child and adolescent formative events, (3) patterned responses to these events, (4) resultant actions toward others, and (5) the killer's reactions, via a mental "feedback filter," to his murderous acts (see fig. 3.1).

(1) INEFFECTIVE SOCIAL ENVIRONMENT

It is often suggested by child and family theorists that the structure and quality of family and social interaction, especially in the way the child perceives family members and their interaction with him and with each other, are important factors in a child's development. For children growing up, the quality of their attach-

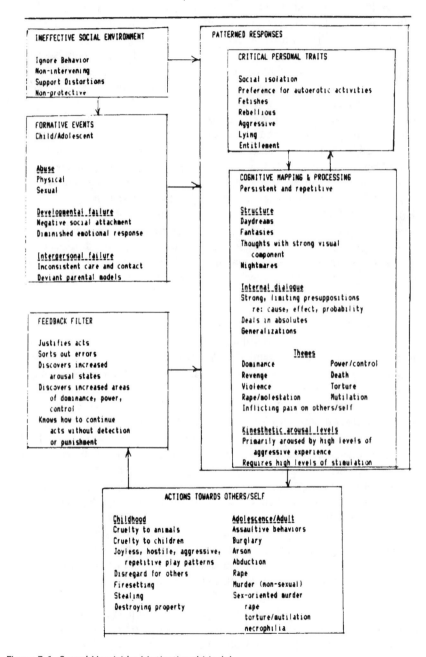

Figure 3.1. Sexual Homicide: Motivational Model.

ments to parents and to other members of the family is most important in how these children later as adults relate to and value other members of society. Essentially, these early life attachments (sometimes called "bonding") translate into a blueprint of how the child will perceive situations outside of the family. Thus, one of the primary functions of family life is to develop a child who has a positive bonding with his social environment.

In our population of murderers, this social bonding fails or becomes narrow and selective. Caretakers ignore, rationalize, or normalize various behaviors in the developing boy or, through their own problems (e.g., criminal behavior or substance abuse), support the child's developing distortions and projections ("I was framed"). People significant to the boy do not provide nurture and protection; rather, they impose adult expectations on the boy ("Boys should be strong and take care of themselves"). Adults are nonprotective and nonintervening on behalf of the boy. The boy may be punished for a specific antisocial act, but the social restriction does not register in an experiential and cognitive way; that is, the boy is reprimanded or brought to court, but he normalizes the behavior as, "All boys get into trouble." The ineffective social environment expands from caretakers to individuals in a community whose work brings them into contact with the young person (e.g., teachers, counselors, ministers, police).

(2) FORMATIVE EVENTS

There are three factors that contribute to the formative events component of out model. The first of these is trauma, in the form of physical or sexual abuse. The developing child encounters a variety of life events, some normative (e.g., illness, death) and others nonnormative. Those nonnormative events in the murderer sample include direct trauma (physical and/or sexual abuse) and indirect trauma (witnessed family violence). Within the context of the child's ineffective social environment, the child's distress caused by the trauma is neglected. The child is neither protected nor assisted in recovery from the abusive and overwhelming events; the external environment does not address the negative consequences of the events.

One assumption regarding early traumatic events is that the child's memories of frightening and upsetting life experiences shape the child's developing thought patterns. The type of thinking that emerges develops structured, patterned behaviors that, in turn, help generate daydreams and fantasies. The literature on children traumatized by sexual and physical abuse and by witnessing violence reports the occurrence of dreams, nightmares, and disturbing memories of the trauma (Burgess and Holmstrom 1974, 1979; Conte 1984; Pynoos and Eth 1985). Other studies have documented these children engaging in painful, repetitive acting-out of the traumas (Axline 1969; Gardner 1971; Terr 1979, 1981a, 1981b, 1983). Play of emotionally disturbed and troubled children often contains conflicted and obsessive themes, contrasting with the creative and flexible themes noted in nondisturbed children. We believe the traumatized child's play remains fixed on thoughts associated with the traumatic event and is held separate or encapsulated (Hartman and Burgess 1989) rather than integrated in play activities or in art expression through drawings (Wood, Burgess, and McCormack 1989). Successful resolution of traumatic events results in the child being able to talk about the event in the past tense and with equanimity. Unsuccessful resolution of the trauma underscores the victim's helplessness often with the emergence of aggressive fantasies aimed at achieving the dominance and control absent from reality (Burgess, Hartman, McCausland, and Powers 1984; MacCulloch et al. 1983; Pynoos and Eth 1985).

A second assumption regarding early traumatic events is that manifestations of the impact of distressing events, such as direct sexual and physical abuse, are influential in the child's social development (Burgess et al. 1984; Conte 1984; Pynoos and Eth 1985). Concurrent with the abusive event, the child may experience a sustained emotional/physiological arousal level.

When this sustained arousal level interacts with repetitive thoughts about the trauma, the child's perceptions and patterns of interpersonal relationships may be altered. For example, the child may show hyperaggressive behavior by striking out at parents or repeatedly assaulting a favorite pet.

The second factor contributing to the formative events component of our model is developmental failure. For some reason the child does not readily attach to his adult caretaker. This is the child who does not listen or respond to any limit setting and who often is described as aloof, cold, and uncaring. As a result of this negative social attachment (bonding), the caretaker has no influence initially over the child and later over the adolescent. In cases where the child has been psychologically deprived or neglected, he may feel a diminished emotional response.

Interpersonal failure, the third factor in this model component, is the failure of the caretaking adult to serve as a role model for the developing child. There are various reasons for this failure, including the caretaker being absent or serving as an inadequate role model (e.g., a parent with problems of substance abuse or an abusive parent). The child may experience a violent home environment where he sees aggression (drunken fights) associated with sexual behavior of adults.

(3) PATTERNED RESPONSES

The patterned responses component of the motivational model includes two subcategories: (1) critical personal traits and (2) cognitive mapping and processing. These subcategories interact with each other to generate fantasies.

Critical Personal Traits

In the normal growth and development of a child, positive personality traits of warmth, trust, and security help establish the child's relationships with others. These critical traits, in combination with an effective social environment, allow the child to develop competence and autonomy.

In the murderer group, there was a propensity for the thirty-six men to develop negative rather than positive personal traits. These negative personal traits interfere with the formation of social relationships and the development of an emotional capacity within the context of human encounters. Increased social isolation encourages a reliance on fantasy as a substitute for human encounter. In turn, individual personality development becomes dependent on the fantasy life and its dominant themes rather than on social interaction. Without human encounters and negotiations, there is failure to develop the corresponding social values, such as respect for others' lives and property.

The personal traits critical to the development of the murderers in our study include a sense of social isolation, preferences for autoerotic activities and fetishes, rebelliousness, aggression, chronic lying, and a sense of entitlement. The offenders' chronic lying underscores their lack of trust and commitment to a world of rules and negotiation. Rather, distrust and a sense of entitlement to whatever they can get dominate their perceptions. Their social isolation and aggression interact, restricting sexual development based on caring, pleasure, and companionship. Because they are so isolated, the men have little opportunity for interpersonal experiences that might modify their misconceptions about themselves and others. Their personal affective lives become dependent on fantasy for development. In turn, fantasy becomes the primary source of emotional arousal, and that emotion is a confused mixture of sex and aggression.

Cognitive Mapping and Processing

Cognitive mapping refers to the structure and development of thinking patterns that give both control and development to one's internal life (e.g., one's sense of self and beliefs about the world) and link the individual to the social environment (e.g., one's interpretation of others). The process of cognitive mapping generates the meaning of events for an individual and mediates sensory arousal patterns. In addition, it is a filtering system that allows for interpretation of new information (e.g., "I'm always being singled out"; "It's my life and I can live it my own way"). Cognitive mapping and processing are aimed at self-preservation and equilibrium through the reduction of the negative affects of helplessness, terror, and pervasive anxiety.

In the murderers, the mapping is repetitive and lacking socially enhancing cognitions, moving the individual to an antisocial position and view of the world. What emerges is a primary sense of entitlement to express oneself regardless of its impact on others. The thought and action are justified through the cognitive mapping of the murderer. The individual does not experience a positive impact with the social environment. This occurs because his fantasies and thinking patterns are a substitute for social relationships. They are designed to stimulate and reduce tension. A sense of self is developed and bolstered by the fantasies. The self-image is terrifying to imagined others and contributes to further social isolation. The process continues and becomes the primary source of energy for the psychological life of the individual. Imagined outcomes of control and dominance over others become a substitute for a sense of mastery of internal and external experience.

Parallel with the repetition of ideation of cognitive mapping is the neurohormonal influence on sensory arousal levels. The neurohormonal basis of the pleasure associated with aggressive fantasy activity is unknown. There is, however, substantial evidence that stressors elicit a central nervous system (CNS) opiod response in both animals (stress-induced analgesia) and human beings (van der Kolk, Greenberg, Boyd, and Krystal 1984). Elevated plasma levels of endogenous opiates have been documented in marathon runners (Colt, Wardlaw, and Frantz 1981), individuals who have undergone surgery (Cohen 1982), and patients who engage in self-mutilation (Coid 1983). This suggests that the source of the stressor may be external or internal. It also has been reported that removal of the stressor may be associated with opiate withdrawal-like symptoms: anxiety and irritability (Backland 1970; van der Kolk et al. 1984). In a recent analysis of the psychobiology of post-traumatic stress (PTS), van der Kolk et al. (1984) have suggested that the stress-approach behavior consistently displayed by individuals who suffer from PTS disorders may involve a conditioned CNS opiod response followed by withdrawal hyperreactivity. By analogy, compulsive-aggressive fantasy activity may also involve such a psychobiological mechanism. In this case, individuals reexpose themselves to traumatic situations through fantasy activity. The internally induced stressor elicits the opiod response, which brings relief and/or pleasure as well as avoidance of the noxious symptoms of opiate withdrawal.

Structures of cognitive mapping and processing include daydreams, nightmares, fantasies, and thoughts with strong visual components. There is internal dialogue of limiting beliefs regarding cause, effect, and probability. The subjects deal in absolutes and generalizations. The themes of their fantasies include dominance, revenge, violence, rape, molestation, power, control, torture, mutilation, inflicting pain on self/others, and death. High sensory arousal levels become the preferred state. The preoccupation with the aggressive themes, the detailed cognitive activity, and elevated kinesthetic arousal state eventually move the person into actions.

(4) ACTIONS TOWARD OTHERS

Childhood actions are based on the child's regard and caring for others as well as on self-respect and flexibility. In other words, behavior patterns reflect the private, internal world of the child.

Interviews with the murderers in our study revealed that their internal world is often preoccupied with troublesome, joyless thoughts of dominance over others. These thoughts are expressed through a wide range of actions toward others. In childhood, these include cruelty toward animals, abuse of other children, negative play patterns, disregard for others, firesetting, stealing, and destroying property. In adolescence and adulthood, the murderer's actions become more violent: assaultive behaviors, burglary, arson, abduction, rape, nonsexual murder, and finally sexual murder involving rape, torture, mutilation, and necrophilia.

The early expression of cruelty toward both animals and humans when not intervened and stopped, we believe, sets the stage for the future abusing behavior in two ways. First, the early violent acts are reinforced, as the murderers either are able to express rage without experiencing negative consequences or are impassive to any prohibitions against these actions. Second, impulsive and erratic behavior discourages friendships. The failure to make friends leads to isolation and interferes with the ability to resolve conflicts, to develop positive empathy, and to control impulses. Furthermore, there is no challenge to their beliefs that they were entitled to act the way they do. The men either as children or adolescents feel estranged from people. Although that does not mean that superficially they cannot relate to people, it does indicate that in terms of socially effective learning, they have major deficits. They are loners; they are self-preoccupied. Either by daydreaming or fantasies, they become absorbed in their own thoughts.

(5) FEEDBACK FILTER

Given the detailed and repetitive thinking patterns of these murderers, it is not surprising to learn that the murderer reacts to and evaluates his actions toward others and toward himself. These reactions and evaluations influence his future actions. We term this reacting the *feedback filter* because it both feeds back into the killer's patterned responses and filters his earlier actions into a continued way of thinking.

Through the feedback filter, the murderer's earlier actions are justified, errors are sorted out, and corrections are made to preserve and protect the internal fantasy world and to avoid restrictions from the external environment. The murderer experiences increased arousal states via fantasy variations on the violent actions. Feelings of dominance, power, and control are increased. The murderer develops increased knowledge of how to avoid punishment and detection. All this feeds back into the patterned responses and enhances the details of the fantasy life. For example, one of the murderers reported how he sat in prison ruminating on his fantasies regarding killing women and dismembering their bodies. As time went on, he became much more excited by his thoughts of disposing of the victims' bodies and tricking law enforcement agents. In this peculiar evolution of events, he now experienced himself as more involved in the social world.

MODEL SUMMARY

When adolescent and adult criminals are studied in terms of the contribution of past events to their criminality, emphasis previously has been on the event itself rather than on the subject's response and reaction to the event. In part, psychological models of motivation for sexual murder have focused on models of displacement of rage and frustration from primary caretakers in the lives of sexual murderers. Although these symbolic artifacts may operate, a more direct understanding of the potential for violence and criminal behavior resides in the fantasy life and basic cognitive operations of murderers. A context of justifying socially abhorrent acts provides support for the murderers' aggressive, violent fantasies. This structure, limited to its sensory arousal capacities, maintains and perpetuates the destructive acts.

Our motivational model suggests that traumatic and early damaging experiences to the murderers as children set into motion patterns of cognition. Although there may be initial attempts to work through the troublesome effects of the experience, attempts to do so become patterns for limiting choices such as aggression being the only method for dealing with conflict. In addition, a structure of thinking that motivates and sustains deviant behavior through developmental and interpersonal failure and through the alliance of distorted perceptions and affect begins to emerge. Of particular importance is the activation of aggression and its link with sexual expression. The lack of attachment to others gives a randomness to the sexual crimes; however, scrutiny of the thinking patterns of the offenders indicates that there is planning of the crimes whether they rely on chance encounters with any victim or whether they are planned to snare victims.

IMPLICATIONS

There are clinical implications from this study. Understanding the reinforcing quality of actions, be they in fantasy, play, or acting out behaviors, may lead to different notions regarding not only motivation but also behavior change. Exploratory efforts by clinicians are needed for methods to alter the structure of these fantasies. For example, the offender might be forced to relate to the victim position in the fantasy as a way to stimulate compassion for rather than violence to the victim.

This study raises concern about how to deal therapeutically with the notion of fantasy in the criminal population. We note that some levels of dwelling on fantasies has the capacity to escalate rather than diminish the power of the fantasy. Unless one alters the structure of the fantasy that moves toward the aggressive acts, the power can be increased.

This exploratory study suggests avenues for further research. Basic research in biological and psychosocial factors is necessary to explore the biochemical hormonal sensory levels associated with deviant fantasies of both youth and adults. We know that pessimistic cognitions are associated with lowered epinephrine levels in endogenous depression; what might research suggest regarding violent sexualized fantasies?

Basic research on the sensory arousal levels of people during fantasy might answer the question: Is there a basis of hormonal release addicting the person to violent fantasy and violent acts? And does the structure of fantasy differ between various groups of deviant offenders?

Research on a longitudinal basis of children's response to and recovery from sexual and physical/psychological abuse and research on the social context in which the child survives and recovers from abuse are important to any understanding of motivational factors. In this context, a control group of abused men who do not commit criminal acts is essential to identify the factors that help the victim recover and survive the abuse.

Our work and the research of others (Prentky et al. 1985) suggest that a typology of murderers is essential to investigate for a variety of reasons. First, any understanding of the typology may enhance law enforcement efforts both at persuading certain offenders to turn themselves in and at more narrowly focusing investigative efforts. Second, a classification system will give professionals working to curtail violent behavior a focus for intervention efforts that address the need to monitor, evaluate, and change salient personality characteristics. Measurements of these characteristics and methods of evaluating positive change are essential to prevent the tragic reality of released violent criminals repeating their crimes. Third, a classification system would facilitate dialogue between the various disciplines working with offenders and would encourage research into profiling of suspects from crime scene evidence, a technique currently in progress at the National Center for the Analysis of Violent Crime (Douglas, in preparation). Further, behavioral research efforts by law enforcement agencies are important to their development additional skill in reading the seemingly inert characteristics of crime scene evidence. Understanding the motivational and behavioral matrix of the offender increases law enforcement's utilization of the connection between patterns of thinking and behavior.

NOTE

1. Preparation of this article was supported by Department of Justice grants: Office of Juvenile Justice and Delinquency Prevention (#84-JN-KOIO) and National Institute of Justice (#82-CX-0065). We wish to acknowledge gratefully Allen G. Burgess, Marieanne L. Clark, and Mary Francis Jett for contributions to this article.

REFERENCES

Axline, V. M. 1969. *Play Therapy*. New York: Ballantine.
Baekeland, F. 1970. Exercise Deprivation: Sleep and Psychological Reactions. *Archives of General Psychiatry* 22: 365–69.

Beck, A. T. 1976. *Cognitive Therapy and the Emotional Disorders*. New York: International University Press.

Beres, D. 1961. Perception, Imagination and Reality. *International Journal of Psychoanalysis* 41: 327–34.

Brittain, R. P. 1970. The Sadistic Murderer. *Medical Science and the Law* 10: 198–207.

Brownmiller, S. 1975. *Against Our Will: Men, Women, and Rape*. New York: Simon and Schuster.

Burgess, A. W., C. R. Hartman, M. P. McCausland, and P. Powers. 1984. Response Patterns in Children and Adolescents Exploited through Sex Rings and Pornography. *American Journal of Psychiatry* 141, no. 5: 656–62.

Burgess, A. W., and L. L. Holmstrom. 1974. Rape Trauma Syndrome. *American Journal of Psychiatry* 131: 981–86.

———. 1979. *Rape: Crisis and Recovery*. Bowie, MD: Brady.

Cohen, M. R., D. Pickar, M. Dubois, and W. E. Bunney Jr. 1982. Stress-Induced Plasma Beta-Endorphin Immunoreactivity May Predict Postoperative Morphine Usage. *Psychiatric Research* 6, no. 1: 7–12.

Coid, J., B. Allohio, and L. H. Rees. 1983. Raised Plasma Metenkephalin in Patients Who Habitually Mutilate Themselves. *Lancet* (September 3): 545–46.

Colt, E. W. D., S. L. Wardlaw, and A. G. Frantz. 1981. The Effects of Running on Plasma Bendorphin. *Life Sciences* 28: 1637–40.

Constantino, J. P., L. H. Kuller, J. A. Perper, and R. H. Cypress. 1977. An Epidemiologic Study of Homicides in Allegheny County, Pennsylvania. *American Journal of Epidemiology* 106, no. 4: 314–24.

Conte, J. R. 1984. Progress in Treating the Sexual Abuse in Children. *Social Work*: 258–63.

Cormier, B. S., and Simons, S. P. 1969. The Problem of the Dangerous Sexual Offender. *Canadian Psychiatric Association Journal* 14: 329–34.

Douglas, J. E. *Profiling as an Investigative Technique*.

Eth, S., and R. Pynoos, 1984. Developmental Perspectives on Psychic Trauma in Childhood. In *Trauma and Its Wake*, ed. C. R. Figley. New York: Brunner/Mazel, pp. 36–52.

Frazier, S. H. 1974. Murder—Single and Multiple. *Aggression Research Publication ARNMD* 52: 304–12.

Gardner, R. A. 1971. *Therapeutic Communication with Children*. New York: Science House Books.

Hartman, C., and A. W. Burgess. 1989. Causes and Consequences of Sexual Assault. In *Child Maltreatment: Theory and Research on the Causes and Consequences of Child Abuse and Neglect*, ed. V. Carlson and D. Cicchetti. Cambridge: Cambridge University Press.

Kahn, M. W. 1971. Murderers Who Plead Insanity: A Descriptive Factor-Analytic Study of Personality, Social and History Variables. *Genetic Psychology Monographs* 84, no. 2: 275–360.

Lunde, D. T. 1976. *Murder and Madness*. San Francisco: San Francisco Book Co.

MacCulloch, M. G., P. R. Snowden, P. J. W. Wood, and H. E. Mills. 1983. Sadistic Fantasy, Sadistic Behaviour and Offending. *British Journal of Psychiatry* 143: 20–29.

MacDonald, J. M. 1971. *Rape Offenders and Their Victims*. Springfield, IL: Charles C. Thomas.

Prentky, R., M. Cohen, and T. Seghorn. 1985. Development of a Rational Taxonomy for the Classification of Sexual Offenders: Rapists. *Bulletin of the American Academy of Psychiatry and the Law* 13: 39–70.

Pynoos, R. S., and S. Eth. 1985. Children Traumatized by Witnessing Acts of Personal Violence: Homicide, Rape, or Suicidal Behavior. In *Post-Traumatic Stress Disorders in Children*, ed. Eth and Pynoos. Washington, DC: American Psychiatric Press, pp. 17–44.

Reinhardt, J. M. 1957. *Sex Perversions and Sex Crimes: A Psychocultural Examination of the Causes, Nature and Criminal Manifestations of Sex Perversions*. Springfield, IL: Charles C. Thomas.

Ressler, R. K., J. E. Douglas, A. N. Groth, and A. W. Burgess. 1980. Offender Profiling: A Multidisciplinary Approach. *FBI Law Enforcement Bulletin* 49, no. 10: 16–20.

Ressler, R. K., et al. 1985. Violent Crimes. *FBI Law Enforcement Bulletin* 54, no. 8 (August): 1–33.

Revitch, E. 1965. Sex Murder and the Potential Sex Murderer. *Diseases of the Nervous System* 26: 640–48.

———. 1980. Genocide and Unprovoked Attacks on Women. *Correctional and Social Psychiatry* 26: 6–11.

Rushforth, N. B., A. B. Ford, C. S. Hirsch, N. M. Rushforth, and L. Adelson. 1977. Violent Death in a Metropolitan County: Changing Patterns in Homicide 1958–74. *New England Journal of Medicine* 274, no. 1: 53–58.

Samenow, S. E. 1984. *Inside the Criminal Mind*. New York: Times Books.

Satten, J., K. Menninger, I. Rosen, and M. Mayman. 1960. Murder without Apparent Motive: A Study in Personality Disorganization. *American Journal of Psychiatry* 117: 48–53.

Schlesinger, L. B., and I. L. Kutash. 1981. The Criminal Fantasy Technique: A Comparison of Sex Offenders and Substance Abusers. *Journal of Clinical Psychology* 37, no. 1: 210–18.

Schlesinger, L. B., and E. Revitch. 1981. Stress, Violence and Crime. In *Handbook on Stress and Anxiety*, ed. I. L. Kutash and Schlesinger. San Francisco: Jossey-Bass.

Seghorn, T. K., R. J. Boucher, and R. A. Prentky. 1987. Childhood Sexual Abuse in the Lives of Sexually Aggressive Offenders. *American Academy of Child Adolescent Psychiatry* 26, no. 2 (March): 262–67.

Singer, J. L. 1966. *Daydreaming*. New York: Random House.

Terr, L. 1979. Children of Chowchilla: A Study of Psychic Trauma. *Psychoanalytic Study of the Child* 34: 547–623.

———. 1981a. Forbidden Games: Post-Traumatic Child's Play. *Journal of the American Academy of Child Psychiatry* 20: 741–60.

———. 1981b. Psychic Trauma in Children. *American Journal of Psychiatry* 138: 14–19.

———. 1983. Life Attitudes, Dreams and Psychic Trauma in a Group of "Normal" Children. *Journal of the American Academy of Child Psychiatry* 22: 221–30.

van der Kolk, B., M. Greenberg, H. Boyd, and J. Krystal. 1984. Inescapable Shock, Neurotransmitters, and Addition to Trauma: Toward a Psychobiology of Post-Traumatic Stress. *Biological Psychiatry* 20: 314–25.

West, D. J., C. Roy, and F. L. Nicholas. 1978. *Understanding Sexual Attacks*. London: Heinemann.

Wolfgang, M. E. 1958. *Patterns in Criminal Homicide*. Philadelphia: University of Pennsylvania.

Wood, J., A. W. Burgess, and A. McCormack. *Runaways and Their Drawings: Response Patterns Associated with Abuse*.

Yochelson, S., and S. Samenow. 1977. *The Criminal Personality*. New York: J. Aronson.

MURDERERS WHO RAPE
AND MUTILATE

Robert Ressler, Ann W. Burgess, Carol Hartman, John E. Douglas, and Arlene McCormack

In comparing sexual murderers with a history of sex abuse (n = 12) with murderers without such a history (n = 16), findings that approach a level of significance between early sexual abuse and sexual deviations include zoophilia (.06) and sexual sadism (.07), with the ultimate expression of the murderer's perversion being the mutilation of the victim. Murderers with sexual abuse histories report fantasizing about rape earlier than murderers without sexual abuse histories (.05) and report aversion to peer sex in adolescence and adulthood (.05). Significant differences in behavioral indicators comparing across developmental levels of childhood include cruelty to animals (.05), and differences approaching significance include isolation (.09), convulsions (.09), cruelty to children (.09), and assaultive to adults (.09). Significant differences in adolescence between murderers with child sexual abuse history versus nonhistory include running away (.01), sleep problems (.05), daydreams (.05), rebellious (.05), assaultive to adults (.05), and indicators approaching significance include temper tantrums (.09) and self-mutilation (.09).

The origins and significance of sexualized acts in the commission of a sexual crime have been implicit themes in the professional literature. Deviant sexual behaviors of offenders have been reported in terms of sexual dysfunction (Groth and Burgess 1977), sexual arousal (Abel 1982), sadistic fantasies (Brittain 1970; MacCulloch, Snowden, Wood, and Mills 1983), and childhood sexual abuse (Groth 1979; Seghorn, Boucher, and Prentky 1987).

In a report of a British study of sixteen male patients diagnosed with psychopathic disorders and hospitalized in a psychiatric facility, the crucial link between sadistic fantasy and behavior is discussed (MacCulloch et al. 1983). The authors raise the following question: If sadistic fantasy has a role in the genesis and maintenance of sadistic behavior, what factors lead some individuals to act out their fantasies? Although they state that they believe any answer would include multiple factors, the authors speculate that factors observed in their subpopulation of thirteen sadistic fantasizers include childhood abuse (being tied up and anal assault) and/or adolescent sexual experiences (MacCulloch et al. 1983).

The linking of childhood sexual abuse to subsequent problems and behavior is not a new idea. Freud in 1895 believed that hysterical symptoms of his female patients could be traced to an early traumatic experience and that the trauma was always related to the patient's sexual life. The trauma manifested itself when revived later, usually after puberty, as a memory. However, Freud later reversed his belief in 1905 and said that the sexual seductions his patients reported were not all reports of real events but fantasies created by the individual (Masson 1984). This reversal created a major shift in the priorities of psychological investigation. The external, realistic trauma was replaced in importance by infantile sexual wishes and fantasies.

In the past decade, clinicians (Herman 1981) and feminists (Rush 1980) have challenged this perspective and are now proposing that sexual abuse in childhood may have a common base in a wide range of social problems. The propositions are based on observations of the prevalence of early child sexual abuse found in populations of runaways (Janus, Scanlon, and Price 1984), juvenile delinquents (Garbarino and Plantz 1984), prostitutes (James and Meyerding 1977; Silbert and Pines 1981), psychiatric patients (Carmen, Ricker, and Mills 1984), substance abusers (Densen-Gerber 1975), and sex offenders (Groth 1979; Seghorn et al. 1987).

Although these studies have looked at various populations, none has examined sexual murderers. In an attempt to address the question raised by MacCulloch and colleagues about acting out sadistic fantasies, this article discusses results of an assessment of the relationship between sexual abuse in childhood or adolescence and sexual interests, activities, and deviations in convicted sexually oriented killers.

METHOD

Apprehension of a crime suspect is the job of law enforcement. In many crimes, this task is fairly straightforward when a motive (e.g., robbery, revenge) has been identified. However, in many crimes the motive is not readily apparent. FBI agents became involved in assisting local law enforcement agencies in their profiling of unsolved homicide cases in the early 1970s. These crimes, often referred to as "motiveless," were analyzed by the agents to include a sexual component.

The agents, sensitive to crime scene information, began their own efforts at classifying characteristics of the murderer by virtue of evidence found at the crime scene. From this evidence they devised a new typology that characterized crime scene patterns as being organized or disorganized. This typology inferred a motivational framework that included expectations, planning, and justification for the criminal action as well as "hunches" regarding postcrime behaviors. As a result, particular emphasis was placed on the thinking patterns dominating the murderer's actions indicating differences in acts committed against the victim and suggesting subcategories of motivational constructs.

The selection of subjects and methodology used to develop the organized/disorganized typology are reported elsewhere (Ressler et al. 1985). Briefly, FBI special agents collected data in various US prisons between 1979 and 1983. The data set for each murderer consisted of the best available data from two types of sources: official records and interviews with the offenders.

To qualify for the study, a murder had to be classified through crime scene observations and evidence as a sexual homicide. These observations included the following: victim attire or lack of attire; exposure of sexual parts of the victim's body, sexual positioning of victim's body, insertion of foreign objects into victim's body cavities, or evidence of sexual intercourse. Primary analysis was conducted on information about the crime scenes of thirty-six sexually oriented murderers.

Identifying murderers who had earlier been sexually abused was accomplished by using interview or official record information about whether the subject had been sexually abused as a child, adolescent, or adult. Information about symptoms and criminal behaviors was obtained in a similar manner. A "yes" response required confirmation through offender disclosure and background record; an answer recorded as "suspected" was based on the offender's recollection. For this aspect of the research, both answers were coded as "yes." We acknowledge the limitations of this variable, which could be either underreported due to memory loss over the years or incorrect because of offender error in memory reconstruction. In addition, the increased public attention to sexual victimization may have influenced offenders to give a positive response. It is important to keep in mind that all subjects in this study were convicted of sexually oriented murder. This report is based on our analysis of convicted, incarcerated, sexual murderers for whom there were data available on early sexual abuse in their life histories; on their sexual/aggressive interests, fantasies, and practices; and on their criminal behaviors. At the time of data collection, these men represented a group of sexually oriented murderers who were available for research purposes (that is, whose appeal process was complete) and who were also able to participate in the in-depth interview conducted by the agents. Murderers were excluded from the sample if they were acutely mentally disordered and unable to respond to interview questions (N = 2). They were selected for a project to investigate law enforcement profiling techniques (Ressler et al. 1985); in addition, they do not represent a random sample.

FINDINGS

When questioned about prior sexual abuse, twelve, or 43 percent, of those murderers responding (twenty-eight) indicated such abuse in childhood (age one to twelve); nine, or 32 percent, were abused in adolescence (age thirteen to eighteen); and ten, or 37 percent, as adults (over age eighteen).

Symptoms and behavior indicators. The comparison of sexual abuse in childhood and adolescence by symptoms and behaviors present in childhood, adolescence, and adulthood for murderers who had and who had not been sexually abused is presented in table 4.1. For the overwhelming majority of symptoms and behavioral indicators, the higher incidence is in the direction of those offenders who were sexually abused. Those sexually abused in childhood are significantly more likely than nonabused offenders to report the following symptoms in childhood: cruelty to animals, isolation, convulsions, cruelty to children, and assaultive to adults. In addition, those men sexually abused in childhood are more likely to report experiencing the following symptoms in adolescence: sleep problems, isolation, running away, self-mutilation, temper tantrums, rebelliousness, and assaultive to adults. In adulthood, differences are noted in the areas of poor body image, sleep problems, isolation, self-mutilation, and temper tantrums.

Those sexually abused in adolescence are more likely than nonabused offenders to report the following symptoms in adolescence: running away, fire setting, and cruelty to animals. In adulthood, differences for those sexually abused as an adolescent include the behavioral indicators of nightmares, daydreams, rebelliousness, and cruelty to children (see table 4.2)

Sexual issues. Our analysis of the total murderer sample found that over 50 percent of the murderers report concern with various sexual issues. These include sexual conflicts (69%), sexual incompetencies (69%), sexual inhibitions (61%), sexual ignorance (59%), and sexual dysfunction (56%). Regarding sexual activities, over 50 percent of all murderers report interests in pornography (81%), fetishism (stealing, wearing, or masturbating with women's undergarments; attraction to specific body parts, articles, or inanimate objects) (72%), and voyeurism (71%). A total of 39 percent report interests in bondage sex (S&M), and 25 percent indicate involvement in indecent exposure. Less than one-fourth disclose interest in sexual contact with animals (23%), obscene telephone calls (22%), rubbing against others (18%), cross-dressing (17%), prostitution (11%), and coprophilia (7%).

An analysis of the relationship between prior sexual abuse in childhood or adolescence and sexual issues shows that the sexually abused offenders are more likely to report sexual conflicts (92% versus 40%; p = .01), sexual dysfunction (69% versus 50%), and sexual incompetence (77% versus 60%). There is little or no difference in sexual ignorance between the two groups.

TABLE 4.1. Symptoms and Behaviors for Sexually and Nonsexually Abused Murders (in percentages)

Symptoms and Behaviors	Sexually Abused as a Child						Sexually Abused as an Adolescent			
	Symptoms as a Child		Symptoms as an Adolescent		Symptoms as an Adult		Symptoms as an Adolescent		Symptoms as an Adult	
	Sexually Abused	Not Sexually Abused	Sexually Abused	Not Sexually Abused	Sexually Abused	Not Sexually Abused	Sexually Abused	Not Sexually Abused	Sexually Abused	Not Sexually Abused
Enuresis	78	55	67	50	22	10	60	57	20	14
Poor body image	58	42	75	46	75	42*	56	63	56	60
Nightmares	78	50	78	55	67	45	80	60	100	40***
Eating problems	36	17	50	18	50	25	50	27	50	31
Sleep problems	60	27	70	27**	70	27**	67	40	67	40
Headaches	40	20	50	20	60	30	50	29	50	43
Accident prone	33	31	33	36	22	36	33	36	17	36
Convulsions	36	8*	30	15	28	8	14	25	14	13
Isolation	91	57*	100	62**	91	62*	88	75	75	75
Daydreams	91	71	91	71	91	71	100	71*	100	71*
Running away	36	36	73	23***	18	8	50	44		
Phobias	40	31	50	33	60	38	43	40	43	50
Chronic lying	73	64	73	71	64	64	88	65	75	59
Stealing	70	43	90	71	56	50	86	76	50	5
Destroying property	60	54	64	54	30	27	63	56	14	36
Self-mutilation	27	15	40	8*	54	17**	33	19	43	31
Temper tantrums	64	46	73	38*	70	31*	75	44	57	44
Rebellious	80	57	100	69**	90	62	100	75	100	63**
Cruelty to children	73	38*	67	62	50	25	75	59	63	25*
Fire setting	60	46	64	38	36	15	75	38*	38	19
Cruelty to animals	58	15**	58	31	40	29	67	31*	43	29
Assaultive to adults	50	17*	100	69**	90	79	100	75	100	76
Destructive to possessions	44	15	50	25	50	25	43	33	29	40
Compulsive masturbation	82	80	82	80	82	73	88	78	88	72

*P <.09; **P <.05; ***P <.01.

TABLE 4.2. Behaviors with Significant Differences between Sexually Abused and Non–Sexually Abused Murderers

Sexually Abused as a Child			Sexually Abused as an Adolescent	
Symptoms as a Child	Symptoms as an Adolescent	Symptoms as an Adult	Symptoms as an Adolescent	Symptoms as an Adult
Convulsions	Sleep problems	Poor body image	Running away	Nightmares
Isolation	Isolation	Isolation	Fire setting	Daydreams
Cruelty to children	Running away	Sleep problems	Cruelty to animals	Rebellious
Cruelty to animals	Self-mutilation	Self-mutilation		Cruelty to children
Assaultive to adults	Temper tantrums Rebellious Assaultive to adults	Temper tantrums		

An analysis of the relationship between sexual abuse in childhood and adolescence and participation in certain sexual activities indicates that the sexually abused murderers are more likely to engage in sexual contact with animals (40% versus 8%; p = .06), bondage sex (55% versus 23%), fetishism (83% versus 57%), obscene phone calls (36% versus 15%), indecent exposure (36% versus 21%), pornography (92% versus 79%), frottage (27% versus 15%), and cross-dressing (18% versus 7%). There is little difference or no difference noted in the area of voyeurism. Prostitution and coprophilia were dropped from this analysis due to an inadequate number of responses.

Rape fantasies. For nineteen of the thirty-six murderers who responded to a question about at what age they began to fantasize about rape, the ages range from five to twenty-five years old. The results of a test of mean age differences shows that sexually abused murderers (eleven) began to fantasize at an earlier age than did those not abused (eight), or ages 11.6 years versus 15.3 years (t = 1.99, p = 0.05).

First consensual sex. For nineteen murderers, the age of first significant, consensual sexual experience ranged from eleven to thirty-five years of age. The results of a test of mean age difference shows that sexually abused killers report an earlier age for this activity than do murderers not sexually abused (14.7 years versus 16.2 years). However, this difference was not statistically significant (t = 1.12, p = 0.14).

Aversion to sexual activity. It was clear to the interviewers that some of the murderers could not answer the question of age of consensual sex because they had never had such an experience. Thus in reply to the question about whether they experienced a marked aversion or inhibition to sexual activity with peers, the affirmative response of twenty-six offenders is not surprising.

Of these twenty-six, eleven were sexually abused as children and fifteen were not (see table 4.3). Results indicate that there is no difference in aversion to sexual activity in childhood for sexually versus nonsexually abused murderers (9% versus 7%). Murderers who were sexually abused in childhood are more likely than their nonabused counterparts to report aversion to sex in adolescence (73% versus 27%) and in adulthood (73% versus 33%; $p = 0.05$).

TABLE 4.3. Inhibition or Aversion to Sexual Activity of Sexually Abused and Nonabused Murderers (in percentages)

	Sexual Abuse			
	As a Child		As an Adolescent	
Aversion to Sexual Activity	Yes	No	Yes	No
	(11)	(15)	(8)	(18)
In childhood	9	7		
In adolescence	73	27	63	39
In adulthood	73	33	63	44

NOTE: n—numbers in parentheses.
*$p < 0.05$

Mutilation of murder victim. The results of assessing the relationship between sexual abuse in childhood and the mutilation of murder victims after death show a positive relationship (see table 4.4). Mutilation is defined as the deliberate cutting, usually after death, of the sexual areas of the body (breasts, genitals, abdomen). Sexually abused murderers are more likely to mutilate victims than are those offenders not sexually abused (67% versus 44%). We also see a positive relationship between adolescent sexual victimization and the mutilation of the murder victim (78% versus 42%; $p = .07$).

TABLE 4.4. Mutilation of Murder Victims and Sexual Victimization of Offender

	Mutilation of Victims		
Victimization	*Yes %*	*No %*	*N*
In childhood			
Yes	67	33	12
No	44	56	16
In adolescence			
Yes	78	22	9
No	42	58	19

*$p = 0.07$

DISCUSSION

SEXUAL INTERESTS AND BEHAVIORS

In our examination of sexual interests and behaviors, we find some association in our population between early sexual abuse and the development of sexual deviations or psychosexual disorders (DSM-III 1980). As described by the DSM-III (1980), the essential feature of psychosexual disorders is that unusual or bizarre imagery or acts are necessary for sexual excitement. In addition, the acts tend to be involuntarily repetitive and the imagery necessary for sexual arousal must be included in masturbatory fantasies. In the murderer sample, those sexually abused offenders were more likely to have the paraphilia of zoophilia and to begin to experience rape fantasies earlier than the nonabused group. The complexity and bizarreness of the offender's fantasy life needed to obtain and sustain emotional arousal suggest that the ultimate expression of his perversion is in the mutilation of the victim.

There are many significant differences of behavioral indicators comparing across developmental levels of childhood, adolescence, and adulthood for abused and nonabused murderers. We note the consistently reported behavior of isolation as an outcome of childhood sexual abuse with varied symptom clusters of sleep problems, nightmares, daydreams, poor body image, and convulsions; behaviors of self-mutilation, running away, temper tantrums, rebelliousness, fire setting, actions of cruelty to children and animals, and assault of adults. Some of the symptoms suggest internalized undisclosed sexual abuse (i.e., sleep problems, running away, self-mutilation, and poor body image), whereas other symptoms suggest externalized aggression.

Although it would not be expected to see differences between murderers who were sexually molested in childhood reporting a greater peer sex aversion than the nonmolested as a child, those molested in childhood do have more aversion of peer sex in adolescence, and those molested in adolescence also have a high report rate of aversion at this time. This finding suggests that there is a complex interaction between basic developmental issues of sexuality that interact with molestation at different times in the development of the child and are linked with avoidance of peer experiences in adolescence. It is speculated that this aversion not only jeopardizes the development of constructive and normative sexual and interpersonal experiences but also increases social isolation and fosters a reliance on fantasy for impulse development and discharge.

Hypersexuality or the sexualization of relationships is an important indicator of sexually abused children, and children can be expressive both verbally and behaviorally about sex. Often when this sexuality is expressed aggressively toward others, it reflects directly on the aggressive and exploitive nature of the initial abuse (Burgess et al. 1984). Sex, rather than linking these men (abused and nonabused) with their peers, somehow impedes the connection. One speculation is that the adult role of the abuser in the original childhood victimization is maintained in the repeated fantasy and thus the preferred sexual relationship is a child/adult pairing. In addition, relationships with younger children, peers, and adults are marked by aggression.

MURDER BEHAVIOR

One finding of our analysis of crime scene evidence approached a level of significance with sexual abuse. There was a striking difference in the style of sexual assaults on victims between sexually abused offenders and those offenders who did not report abuse. Those who were sexually abused in childhood tended to mutilate the body after killing, as contrasted with murderers who raped and then killed ($p = 0.07$). We speculate that undisclosed and unresolved early sexual abuse may be a contributing factor in the stimulation of bizarre, sexual, sadistic behavior characterized in a subclassification of mutilators.

Although we do not have systematic data collected on the intentions of the mutilations, some murderers volunteered information. One murderer said the mutilation was a way of disposing of the body, implying he had a pragmatic reason for the mutilation. However, the autopsy report revealed that in addition to cutting up the body, he also pulled out the victim's fingernails after death, something he claimed not to remember. This man went to prison for the first killing. When he was released, he knew he would kill again. He revealed that he sought the high level of emotional arousal not in the killing but in the successful dismemberment of his victims and the disposal of the parts without detection—an act that took thought and planning.

MacCulloch and colleagues (1983) observed in their sample of sex offenders with sadistic fantasies that from an early age, the men had difficulties in both social and sexual relationships. They suggest that this failure in social/sexual approach might be partly responsible for the development of a feeling of inadequacy and lack of assertiveness. This inability to control events in the real world moves the man into a fantasy world where he can control his inner world. This fantasy of control and dominance is bound to be repeated because of the relief it provides from a pervasive sense of failure. MacCulloch and colleagues (1983) suggest that when sexual arousal is involved in the sadistic fantasy, the further shaping and content of the fantasy may be viewed on a classical conditioning model; the strong tendency to progression of sadistic fantasies may then be understood in terms of habituation.

Eysenck (1968) argues the acting out of elements of the deviant fantasies is a relatively short step in those whose personalities predispose to repeated thinking or incubation. In these cases the fantasies would theoretically at least form part of a conditional stimulus class and possibly become a necessary condition for sexual arousal. Thus a conditioning model, writes MacCulloch and colleagues (1983), may explain not only the strength and permanence of sadistic fantasies in these abnormal personalities but their progression to nonsexual and sexual crimes. This model provides an explanation for what Reinhardt (1957) called the "forward thrust of sexual fantasies in sadistic murderers." Our last example of a mutilator murderer underscores the reality-orienting fantasy of successful disposal of the body as the cognitive set, driving repeated murders.

Although all murders in our study contained a sexual element, it was apparent that motives differed. Some victims were raped and then murdered; others were murdered and then sexually mutilated. Rapists who murder, according to Rada (1978), rarely report any sexual satisfaction from the murder nor perform sexual acts postmortem. In contrast, the sadistic murderer (Brittain 1970), sometimes called lust murderer (Hazelwood and Douglas 1980), kills prior to or simultaneously in carrying out a ritualized sadistic fantasy.

Evidence from this study suggests that the murderer with a sexual abuse history will first kill the victim to achieve control before he makes any sexual expression. The murderer may not necessarily have any orgastic experiences with the body but rather may masturbate on or beside the body. The release of tension may also occur through substitute action such as mutilation of the body or perhaps using, as noted with Brittain's study (1970), a phallus substitute.

Consistent with our study are others (Brittain 1970; MacCulloch et al. 1983) that underscore a feeling of relief and pseudonormal behavior following the murder. Many of the murderers recount going home and sleeping deeply after a murder. After several days, they would reflect on the murder in great detail.

IMPLICATIONS

The analysis of data specific to the variables of childhood sexual abuse and subsequent symptoms and criminal behaviors suggests that several variables (e.g., daydreams, isolation, cruelty to children and animals) play an important part in the subgroups (i.e., rape-murder and murder-mutilate) of sexual murderers. There is every indication that the motivation for murder is a complex developmental process that is based on needs for sexual dominance at the destructive expense of the victim. It appears from this exploratory study of convicted killers that there is an important difference in the symptom constellation among those with a history of sexual abuse and those without such a history. Although it is not clear whether there is a difference in psychological motivation for sexual murder, what is apparent is an early onset of specific behaviors that are noted in the subgroup of murderers who mutilate.

The association of the specific impact of sexual molestation in the lives of these offenders and subsequent mutilation of their victims requires further investigation. To speculate on a possible link between the adolescents who were sexually abused and those who mutilate the body suggests a premeditated pattern where acts of self-mutilation are then transferred and carried out on others.

Our exploratory study raises far more questions than it answers. Current understanding of disclosed childhood sexual abuse has focused on the initial treatment (Burgess et al. 1978; Conte 1984; Sgroi 1982), legal process (Buckley 1981), sequelae (Browne and Finkelhor 1984), and prevention efforts (Conte 1984; Swift 1977). Yet our understanding of undisclosed childhood sexual abuse and its long-term effects is limited in regard to gender differences and behavioral outcomes. It becomes even more imperative, given our findings on behavioral differences, that we not only learn how to detect cases of child sexual abuse early but also delve further into behavioral outcomes particularly in noncriminal abused adults.

For the men who repeat sexual murder, their internal processing and cognitive operations appear to sustain and perpetuate fantasies of sexually violent actions. As a result, clinicians are urged to take careful note of patients reporting sadistic as well as criminal fantasies and record a systematic history on the content, duration, progression, and affect triggered by the fantasy. For law enforcement, murder that appears to be motiveless—that is, the victim is a stranger and there is no profit to be gained from the death of the victim—suggests that the victim and offense must be seen as having symbolic meaning to the offender reflecting violent sadistic fantasies.

NOTE

1. Preparation of this article was supported by Department of Justice grants: Office of Juvenile Justice and Delinquency Prevention (#84-JN-AX-K010) and National Institute of Justice (#82-CX-0065). We wish to acknowledge gratefully Marieanne L. Clark for contributions to earlier drafts of this article.

REFERENCES

Beck, A. T. 1976. *Cognitive Therapy and the Emotional Disorders*. New York: International University Press.

Brittain, R. P. 1970. The Sadistic Murderer. *Medical Science and the Law* 10: 198–207.

Browne, A., and D. Finkelhor. 1984. The Impact of Child Sexual Abuse: A Review of the Research. Unpublished MS.

Buckley, J. 1981. *Child Sexual Abuse and the Law*. Washington, DC: National Legal Resource Center for Child Advocacy and Protection, American Bar Association.

Burgess, A. W., C. R. Hartman, M. P. McCausland, and P. Powers. 1984. Response Patterns in Children and Adolescents Exploited through Sex Rings and Pornography. *American Journal of Psychiatry* 141, no. 5: 656–62.

Burgess, A. W., C. R. Hartman, R. K. Ressler, J. E. Douglas, and A. McCormack. 1986. Sexual Homicide: A Motivational Model. *Journal of Interpersonal Violence* 1, no. 3 (September 1986): 251–72.

Carmen, E. H., P. P. Rieker, and T. Mills. 1984. Victims of Violence and Psychiatric Illness. *American Journal of Psychiatry* 141, no. 3: 378–83.

Conte, J. R. 1984. Progress in Treating the Sexual Abuse in Children. *Social Work*: 258–63.

Densen-Gerber, J., and J. Benward. 1976. *Incest as a Causative Factor in Antisocial Behavior*. New York: Odyssey Institute.

Eysenck, H. J. 1968. A Theory of the Incubation of Anxiety/Fear Response. *Behaviour Research and Therapy* 6: 309–21.

Freud, S. 1895. *Totem and Taboo*. New York: New Republic Edition.

Garbarino, J., and M. C. Plantz. 1984. *Child Maltreatment and Juvenile Delinquency: What Are the Links?* Pennsylvania State University, unpublished MS.

Groth, A. N. 1979. Sexual Trauma Is the Life Histories of Rapists and Child Molesters. *Victimology* 4, no. 1: 10–16.

Groth, A. N., and A. W. Burgess. 1977. Sexual Dysfunction during Rape. *New England Journal of Medicine* 14: 764–66.

Hazelwood, R. R., and J. E. Douglas. 1980. The Lust Murderer. *FBI Law Enforcement Bulletin* 49, no. 4 (April): 1–5.

Herman, J. 1982. *Father-Daughter Incest*. Cambridge, MA: Harvard University Press.

James, J., and J. Meyerding. 1977. Early Sexual Experience and Prostitution. *American Journal of Psychiatry* 134, no. 12: 1381–85.

Janus, M. D., B. Scanlon, and V. Price. 1984. Youth Prostitution. In *Child Pornography and Sex Rings*. Lexington, MA: Lexington Books.

MacCulloch, M. G., P. R. Snowden, P. J. W. Wood, and H. E. Mills. 1983. Sadistic Fantasy, Sadistic Behaviour and Offending. *British Journal of Psychiatry* 143: 20–29.

Masson, J. M. 1984. *The Assault on Truth: Freud's Suppression of the Seduction Theory*. New York: Farrar, Straus, and Giroux.

Rada, R. T. 1978. Psychological Factors in Rapist Behavior. In *Clinical Aspects of the Rapist*. New York: Grune and Stratton, pp. 51–52.

Reinhardt, J. M. 1957. *Sex Perversions and Sex Crimes: A Psychocultural Examination of the Causes, Nature and Criminal Manifestations of Sex Perversions*. Springfield, IL: Charles C. Thomas.

Ressler, R. K., et al. 1985. Violent Crimes. *FBI Law Enforcement Bulletin* 54, no. 8 (August): 1–33.

Ressler, R. K., A. W. Burgess, J. E. Douglas, C. R. Hartman, and R. B. D'Agostino. 1986. Sexual Killers and Their Victims: Identifying Patterns through Crime Scene Analysis. *Journal of Interpersonal Violence* 1, no. 3: 288–308.

Revitch, E. 1965. Sex Murder and the Potential Sex Murderer. *Diseases of the Nervous System* 26: 640–48.

Rush, F. 1980. The Best-Kept Secret. Englewood Cliffs, NJ: Prentice-Hall.

Samenow, S. E. 1984. *Inside the Criminal Mind*. New York: Times Books.

Seghorn, T. K., R. J. Boucher, and R. A. Prentky. 1987. Childhood Sexual Abuse in the Lives of Sexually Aggressive Offenders. *American Academy of Child Adolescent Psychiatry* 26, no. 2 (March): 262–67.

Sgroi, S. M. 1982. *Handbook of Clinical Intervention in Child Sexual Abuse*. Lexington, MA: Lexington Books.

Silbert, M. H., and A. M. Pines. 1981. Sexual Child Abuse as an Antecedent to Prostitution. *Child Abuse and Neglect* 5: 407–11.

Swift, C. 1977. Sexual Victimization of Children: An Urban Mental Health Center Survey. *Victimology* 2, no. 2: 322–26.

THE MEN WHO MURDERED

Robert K. Ressler et al.

Statistics from the FBI's Uniform Crime Reports document the alarming number of victims of sexually violent crimes. One of the disturbing patterns inherent in these statistics is that of the serial or repetitive criminal. Law enforcement officials have questioned whether a small percentage of criminals may be responsible for a large number of crimes, that is, a core group of habitual serious and violent offenders. This has been documented in one study on juvenile delinquents,[1] and other studies have reported similar results,[2] with average estimates of from 6 to 8 percent of delinquents composing the core of the delinquency problem.

To address this problem, law enforcement is studying techniques to aid in apprehending serial offenders. These techniques require an in-depth knowledge of the criminal personality, an area that, until recently, was researched primarily by forensic clinicians who interviewed criminals from a psychological framework or by criminologists who studied crime trends and statistics. Missing from the data base were critical aspects relevant to law enforcement investigation. Researchers have now begun to study the criminal from law enforcement perspectives, with a shift in focus to the investigative process of crime scene inquiry and victimology.

Published in a slightly different form in *FBI Law Enforcement Bulletin* 54, no. 8 (August 1985): 2–6.

Our research is the first study of sexual homicide and crime scene patterns from a law enforcement perspective. It includes an initial appraisal of a profiling process and interviews of incarcerated murderers conducted by FBI special agents. The interviews contain specific questions answered from compiled sources plus lengthy, open-ended interviews with the murderers themselves. A subsample of thirty-six sexual murderers was selected for analysis to develop further information for profiling these murders. Here, we present what we learned about these thirty-six men. It is important to recognize that we are making general statements about these offenders. Not all statements are true for all offenders, although they may be true for most of the thirty-six men or for most of the offenders from whom we obtained data. Responses were not available from all offenders for all questions.

BACKGROUND CHARACTERISTICS

Although their birth years ranged from 1904 to 1958, most of the thirty-six offenders (all male) grew up in the 1940s and 1950s. They were predominantly white and were usually eldest sons (first or second born), which gave them a distinct advantage, given the dominant-male attitudes in the country at that time.

Most of these men, as adults, had pleasant general appearances, suggesting that as boys they were not unattractive. Their heights and weights were within the norms, and few had distinguishing handicaps or physical defects to set them apart in a group of boys or men. The majority of the men were of average or above-average intelligence, with one-third having superior intelligence.

The majority initially began life in two-parent homes, and half of the mothers were homemakers. Although the majority of fathers worked at unskilled jobs, they were steadily employed; only five men reported the family living at substandard economic levels.

Thus, poverty was not a significant factor in the socioeconomic status of families; mothers were in the home; fathers were earning stable incomes; the subjects were intelligent, white, eldest sons. With such positive personal characteristics and social factors, the question is: What went wrong? Is there any evidence of what may have turned these men into sexually oriented murderers?

FAMILY BACKGROUND

It is often argued that the structure and quality of family interaction is an important factor in the development of a child, especially in the way the child perceives the family members and their interaction with him and with each other. For children growing up, the quality of their attachments to parents and other members of the family is important in how these children become adults and relate to, and value, other members of society. Essentially, these early life attachments (sometimes called bonding) translate into a map of how the child will perceive situations outside of the family. Because of this, we were especially interested in specific factors within family relationships that best show the offenders' levels of attachment to people.

The family histories of these men revealed that multiple problems existed in the family structure. Half of the offenders' families had members with criminal histories; over half of the families had psychiatric problems. This suggests insufficient contact between some family members and the offender as a child, as well as the possibility of inadequate patterns of relating. Nearly 70 percent of the families had histories of alcohol abuse; one-third of the families had histories of drug abuse, and sexual problems among family members were either present or suspected in almost half of the reported cases. Thus, it is unlikely that most of the offenders experienced a good quality of life or positive interactions with family members.

When examining the patterns described by the murderers regarding their own families, one is impressed by the high degree of instability in homelife and by the poor quality of attachment among family members. Only one-third of the men reported growing up in one location. The majority (seventeen) said they experienced occasional instability, and six reported chronic instability or frequent moving. Over 40 percent of the men lived outside the family home before age eighteen in places such as foster homes, state homes, detention centers, or mental hospitals. Twenty-five of the men for whom data were available had histories of early psychiatric difficulties, thereby minimizing their opportunity to establish positive relationships within the family. In addition, the families had minimal attachment to a community, reducing the child's opportunities to develop positive, stable relationships outside the family that might compensate for family instability.

As stated earlier, both parents were present in over half (twenty) of the cases, with the father being absent in ten cases, the mother being absent in three cases, and both parents being absent in two cases. However, of importance is that in seventeen cases, the biological father left home before the boy reached twelve years of age. This absence was due to a variety of reasons, including separation and divorce. It is not surprising, then, that the dominant parent of the offender during the rearing phase of his life was the mother (for twenty-one cases). Only nine offenders said the father was the dominant parent, and two said both parents shared the parenting roles.

Perhaps the most interesting fact revealed was that most offenders said they did not have a satisfactory relationship with their father, and their relationship with their mother was highly ambivalent in emotional quality. Sixteen of the men reported cold or uncaring relationships with their mothers, and twenty-six reported such relationships with their fathers.

Twenty of the offenders had no older brothers, and seventeen had no older sisters. In terms of having a strong role model during formative years, these men lacked an older sibling who might make up for parental deficiencies. Instead, they had to compete with younger siblings in an emotionally deficient environment.

Compounding the offenders' limited opportunities for positive attachments were their perceptions of parental discipline. Frequently, the men reported discipline as unfair, hostile, inconsistent, and abusive. These men believed they were not dealt with fairly by adults throughout their formative years.

This quote from a serial murderer illustrates these beliefs:

> See, if I had my way, you guys would never have grown up or become FBI agents. I wanted the whole world to kick off when I was about nine or ten. I didn't want my family to break up; I loved them both. There was a lot of fighting and that had me crying watching it at night. They divorced. I've got two sisters, and my mother treated me like a third daughter, telling me what a rotten father I have. I'm supposed to be identifying with my dad and I never did. I got an older sister that beats up on me a lot—five years older. I got a younger sister that lies on both of us and gets us punished. I had the instinct to feel like I'm getting a rotten deal.

The data have suggested that most of the thirty-six murderers, while growing up, had weak attachments to family members. They felt uninvolved with their fathers, ambivalent toward their mothers, and little attachment to younger siblings. The parents were preoccupied with their own problems of substance abuse, criminality, or aberrant sexual behavior and were often arguing. It appears that while parents offered little guidance, they were role models for deviant patterns.

INDIVIDUAL DEVELOPMENT

When looking at individual development of the offenders, two factors stand out—the dominance of a fantasy life and a history of personal abuse.

Many of the murderers were able to describe the importance of a fantasy life in their early development. These fantasies were primarily violent and sadistic in nature. Twenty offenders had rape fantasies before age eighteen, and seven of these men acted out these fantasies within a year of becoming consciously aware of them.

There was evidence of abuse in the childhood histories of these men. Physical abuse (13/31), psychological abuse (23/31), and childhood sexual abuse (12/31) were noted.

When the offenders were asked to rank their sexual interests, the highest ranking activity was pornography (81 percent), followed by compulsive masturbation (79 percent), fetishism (72 percent), and voyeurism (71 percent). It is interesting to note the seemingly solitary pattern of these sexual expressions.

It appears that the childhood physical and sexual abuse experienced by these offenders was manifested in their preference for fantasy life. In addition, when questioned about the murders themselves and their preparations for the murders, the men identified the importance of fantasy to the rapes and murders. After the first murder, the men found themselves deeply preoccupied and sometimes stimulated by their memories of the act, all of which contributed to fantasies for subsequent murders.

One begins to understand how an early pattern used to cope with an unsatisfactory family life might turn a child away from reality and into his own private world of violence where the child can exert control. The control of the fantasy becomes crucial first to the child and later to the man. These are not fantasies of escape to something better, as one often sees in children recovering from sexual assaults and abusive treatment. These men did not overcompensate for the stimulation and aggression by idyllic thinking or creative interests. Rather, their energies were funneled into fantasies of aggression and mastery over other people, suggesting a projected repetition of their own abuse and identification with the aggressor. As one murderer stated, "Nobody bothered to find out what my problem was and nobody knew about the fantasy world."

PERFORMANCE

Examination of performance behavior of these murderers revealed another paradox. Despite intelligence and potential in many areas, performance in academics, employment, sexual relationships, and military service was often poor. In all of these areas, performance did not match potential. Although these men had the intelligence to perform well in school, academic failure was seen in their having to repeat elementary grades. The majority did not finish high school. In addition, school failure was frequently mentioned by the men, suggesting that they related this early failure to their sense of inadequacy.

The men also had the intelligence needed to perform skilled jobs; however, most offenders had poor work histories in unskilled jobs, and only 20 percent had ever held steady jobs.

About half of the offenders entered the military. Only four of the fourteen who were in military service received honorable discharges, and one of the four had a criminal history in the service. Two men received general discharges, three were dishonorably discharged, three had undesirable discharges, and two received medical discharges.

The sexual performance of the offenders was generally at an autoerotic (solo sexual activity) level. Although twenty men were able to state an age of first consenting sex to orgasm, they did not report an extensive, peer-related sexual history. The ages of first consenting sexual experience ranged from eleven to twenty-five. Of the sixteen who did not report an age, it was clear to the interviewers that many never experienced consenting "normal" sex. There was an obvious preference for autoerotic activity.

The interviews with the offenders revealed many expressions of low self-esteem prior to the murders. Many offenders felt a sense of failure beginning at a young age. Again, we can speculate on the importance of fantasy life. It appears that what compensates for poor performance is the fantasy, in which the variables can be controlled.

RESULTANT ATTITUDES AND BELIEFS

In reviewing background characteristics for the offenders as a group, a pattern emerges as we look at issues critical to sexual homicide. Although the personal strengths of the murderers (high intelligence, good appearance, average socioeconomic family status, oldest son or first/second born) are usually positive attributes for success, something occurs that causes a negative outcome for these men. From the perceived quality of family structure and function, the history of abuse, the dominance of fantasy, the preference for solo sex, and the performance failure of these men, the data suggest the emergence of certain attitudes.

DEVALUATION OF PEOPLE

The men in the study experienced low social attachment, felt detached from family members as well as from peers, and did not experience the bonding through which people develop sensitivity toward other people. The murderers frequently described themselves as loners or as feeling different from others their age. The resultant attitudes include beliefs that do not consider or are insensitive to the needs of others. Essentially, the offenders do not value relationships they are self-centered.

WORLD VIEWED AS UNJUST

The men perceived discipline in the home, school failures, and other inadequate performance as part of an unjust and unfair world. Their resultant belief is that other people are responsible for their fates.

AUTHORITY AND LIFE VIEWED AS INCONSISTENT

These men view authority and life as inconsistent, unpredictable, and unstable. As a result, the offenders do not value or trust authority.

OBSESSION WITH DOMINANCE THROUGH AGGRESSION

The intense desire to be strong, powerful, and in control becomes an obsession to dominate through aggression. This desire results from the way the offenders responded to the abuse in their families. It was subsequently manifested in their fantasies and later in their acts.

AUTOEROTIC PREFERENCE

The men reported few attachments to persons outside of the family. Rather, they admitted to an autoerotic preference (masturbation) that combined with fantasies of aggression and the realities of the abuse they were concurrently experiencing. Their visual interests (pornography, fetishism, and voyeurism) reinforced the sex and aggression.

FANTASY IS REALITY

The offenders' active participation in the social world is limited, and their efforts at performing and fitting in are frustrated. Their need for a sense of adequacy and mastery of life is noted in their development of private worlds where fantasy and delusions predominate. This retreat triggers the thoughts that dictate criminal behavior.

DEVIANT BEHAVIORS

The data suggest that the deviant behaviors of rape, mutilation, torture, and murder have some roots in both the offenders' background characteristics and their attitudes and beliefs (see fig. 5.1). The deviant behavior identified at the crime scene provides some clues for understanding the type of criminal personality responsible for the crime.

Figure 5.1. General Characteristics, Resultant Attitudes and Beliefs, and Deviant Behaviors of 36 Sexual Murderers

BACKGROUND CHARACTERISTICS		
Family Background	**Individual Development**	**Performance**
Detachment	Dominance of fantasy	School failure
Criminality	History of personal abuse	Sporadic work record
Substance abuse		Unskilled employment
Psychiatric problems		Poor military record
Sexual problems		Solo sex
Inconsistent discipline		

RESULTANT ATTITUDES AND BELIEFS	DEVIANT BEHAVIORS
Devaluation of victim and society	Rape
World viewed as unjust	Mutilation
Authority/life viewed as inconsistent	Torture
Autoerotic preference	Murder
Obsession with dominance through aggression	
Fantasy as reality	

RAPE

Rape is sexually deviant behavior that exhibits absolute disregard for the worth and value of an individual. Rape fantasies range from having power and control over a victim to more violent sadistic fantasies. Those who rape before killing are seeking to dominate others, regardless of the consequences; those who sexually assault after death (necrophilia) need the absence of life to have total domination without fear of resistance and/or rejection. In both cases, there is a high amount of sexual dysfunction, most frequently ejaculatory failure. This inadequacy is projected onto the victim and may play a part in the escalation to murder.

MUTILATION AND TORTURE

The act of mutilation may be predicated on a primary fantasy (sadism) or on a secondary fantasy (e.g., disposing of the body). A mutilation fantasy includes symbolic patterns to the cuttings and markings on a body or the amputation of the sexual parts of the body. This is in contrast to the practical aspect of dissecting a body for disposal or transportation purposes.

Torturing a victim is part of a sadistic fantasy. Such fantasies include some type of stimulus enhancing an autoerotic condition and include slicing, cutting, burning, pulling out hairs or body parts, and biting.

MURDER

Murder is the ultimate expression of dominance. The offender's aggression is self-generated from his own fantasies, not from any societal model of strength or power. His idea of mastering other people emerges through his violence and aggression. For these murderers, sexual interest is linked with violence and exploitation rather than gentleness or pleasure. Murder fantasies range from conscious deliberate planning to a spontaneous outburst of rage. Although the offender's fantasy life develops his predatory activities, the first actualizing of the fantasy makes them real. Acting out the fantasy links the fantasy with reality, and the fantasy becomes reality. The offender believes he can now control reality.

CONCLUSION

What, then, can we glean from an analysis of background information and interviews with thirty-six sexual murderers? Although any speculations are general in nature and will not apply to every sexual killer, our sample indicates that child/adolescent energies were funneled into fantasies rather than into goal-directed learning behavior. Excessive involvement in solo sex, noted through the frequency of masturbation and the preference for visual isolated sexual experiences, such as fetishes and voyeurism, may have a link with the offender's dominant fantasy world. A high interest in pornography detracts from engaging in reality and relationships and further reinforces the fantasy. Excitement lies within the offender, not in his relationships with other people.

The roots of the murderer's actions appear to stem from their background experiences. The combination of low social attachment, physical, emotional, and/or sexual abuse, and a dominance of a violent, sexualized fantasy life sets into motion the attitudes and beliefs that trigger the deviant behavior of rape, mutilation, torture, and murder. One of the major relationship deficiencies for these murderers is in their interaction with men, perhaps stemming from the absent, cold, and unavailable father.

An understanding of some of the dynamics behind sexually deviant behavior provides law enforcement officials some insight into the suspects they are trying to identify and apprehend.

NOTES

1. M. E. Wolfgang, R. M. Figlio, and T. Sellin, *Delinquency in a Birth Cohort* (Chicago: University of Chicago Press, 1972).

2. R. M. Figlio and P. E. Tracy, "Chronic Recidivism in the 1968 Birth Cohort," unpublished MS, Washington, DC, NIJJDP, 1983; D. M. Hamparian, R. Schuster, S. Dinitz, and J. P. Conrad, *The Violent Few* (Lexington, MA: D.C. Health, 1978); L. W. Shannon, "A Longitudinal Study of Delinquency and Crime," in *Quantitative Studies in Criminology*, ed. C. Wellford (Beverly Hills: Sage Publications, 1978).

THE SPLIT REALITY OF MURDER

Robert K. Ressler and Ann W. Burgess

Murder is very real. It's not something you see in a movie. You have to do all the practical things of surviving.

—Serial murderer convicted of killing ten people

Murder is, indeed, very real. Yet to many serial killers, their fantasies of murder are as real as their acts of murder. To them, their existence is split into two realities: the social reality of the "normal" world where people do not murder and the psychological vitality of the fantasy that is the impetus for the killer to commit his heinous crime. It is a split reality because the fantasy life is such a preoccupation. It becomes an additional reality, distinguishable from the "other" reality of the day-to-day social world.

Interviews with thirty-six convicted sexual murderers have provided insights into their attitudes, beliefs, and justifications for their crimes. In order to interpret the murderer's sense of what is important, this chapter presents thoughts and beliefs articulated by the murderers themselves. First, we discuss the structure of conscious motives for murder, the killer's longstanding fantasy of violence and murder. Second, we look at what happens when the fantasy of murder is played out through its various phases. By presenting our interpretation of the fantasy's importance to the serial killer, we hope to suggest perspectives for law enforcement on the investigation of sexual homicide.

Published in a slightly different form in *FBI Law Enforcement Bulletin* 54, no. 8 (August 1985).

MOTIVE AND FANTASY

How does the motive for a murder evolve, and what triggers the murderer to act? Many murders puzzle law enforcement because they appear to lack the "usual" motives, such as robbery or revenge. Motives, however, need to be determined, since understanding the motive is critical to the subsequent apprehension of a suspect.

The thirty-six murderers in our study, replying to this fundamental question of what triggered their first murders, revealed that as a group, they were aware of their long-standing involvement and preference for a very active fantasy life and they were devoted to violent sexual fantasies. Most of these fantasies, prior to the first murder, focused on killing, while fantasies that evolved after the first murder often focused on perfecting various phases of the murder. The following illustrates an early fantasy of one of the serial murderers that developed following the move of his bedroom to a windowless basement room. This fantasy seemed to introduce him in a more conscious way to a fantasy life, which occupied much of his life: "I was eight years old, having nightmares, that's when I went off into the morbid fantasy and that's when the death trip started. The devil was sharing my bedroom with me, he was living in the furnace. The furnace was there battling away in the corner with an eerie glow in the middle of the night."

This man later in the interview described a conscious awareness of his motive to kill: "I knew long before I started killing that I was going to be killing, that it was going to end up like that. The fantasies were too strong. They were going on for too long and were too elaborate."

Following the first murder, the fantasy becomes reality that requires a change in the structure of the fantasy in order to repeat the crime. The same murderer tells of this fantasy development: "It was almost like a black comedy of errors, the first killings, two people, it was terrible because I made three fatal errors in the first twenty-four hours. I should have been busted . . . I saw how loose I was and I tightened it up and when it happened again and again I got tighter and tighter and there weren't any more slips."

Motivation operates on many levels. We are referring here to the conscious or preconscious awareness of the murderers, the structure of their fantasies, and the resultant act of murder. We use the term *preconscious* since many of the interviews with the murderers reveal this level. The man would state he remembered having vague thoughts or was able to remember some parts of his thinking but did not have this awareness clearly structured in his mind. This response in subjects led to our belief that much of the motive and intent in the form of fantasies are vague and loosely formulated until the murderers actually kill. With the reality of the murder, the fantasy feeds off itself and becomes more structured. As more murders are committed, the phases of the murders become more organized.

Although we discuss the "first" murder, many offenders reported a history of sadistic behavior toward animals, such as killing, maiming, and threatening small animals (cats, birds, fish). In one case, the murderer, as a young boy, had acquired the nickname "Doc," apparently from his fondness for slitting open the stomachs of cats and observing how far they could run before they died.

One murderer connected his murderous acts to dismembering his sister's doll heads. "I used to do my sister's dolls that way when I was a kid . . . just yanked the head off her Barbie dolls." Although this offender was able to note the connection to his early violent fantasies, many offenders were not able to make this link.

We are not discussing any motives based on childhood experiences. Instead, we are referring to a level of motivation that later in the life of the offender serves as a basis for or triggers the murder.

It is at this later level of motivation that the offender's fantasy life reflects itself in his social behavior—the line between fantasy and reality blurs. The offender may become isolated or socially aloof rather than acting on the fantasy. This social isolation perhaps helps in inhibiting his desire to act on sadistic behavior and threatening the fantasy. What these thirty-six men revealed in terms of their first murder was that something happened externally to them that moved them to act out this fantasy.

The key person in the fantasy—the one doing the killing, maiming, or tor-turing—is the perpetrator himself. Sometimes, perpetrators fantasize self-victim-ization, such as ordering their own evisceration, but most victimize others in their fantasies. Their actions are mentally rehearsed and are accompanied by emotion. The fantasy life is varied and has many dynamics that are idiosyncratic to the murderer.

A variety of factors can trigger the offender to act on his fantasy, including certain interactions between the murderer and the victim. The following case illustrates the murderer's recall of the triggering event of the victim trying to escape but not of the murder:

> *Subject:* We were upstairs and I was taking my clothes off. That's when she started back downstairs. As a matter of fact, that's the only time I hit her. I caught her at the stairs.

> *Agent:* What happened?

> *Subject:* She wanted to know why I hit her. I just told her to be quiet. She was complaining about what time she would get home and she said her parents would worry. She consented to sex . . . then I remembered nothing else except waking up and her dead in the bed.

Some murderers were aware of their fantasy to rape and their motive to kill. The fantasy of one juvenile who was caught after his first rape depicted total con-trol over women. He was infuriated at the female judge who sentenced him to a residential facility, and he continued to rape when on leave from the facility. The rape fantasy escalated to include murder when there was a threat to this power and control, that is, his detection. One rape victim was killed because she showed some assertiveness by running away, even though she had said she wouldn't tell. The murderer revealed his fantasy for total control when he said, "When I think she is going to tell, I know I have to kill her." He raped and murdered four more victims.

Some of the murderers in our study did not report fantasies in a conscious way. Instead, they often described states of dysphoria, such as they were not feeling well, they were depressed, or they had been drinking. These descriptions often revealed an underlying stress that may have been based in their fantasy. The following is an example:

> *Subject:* It was the same as with the other one. I had been drinking at the bar. I don't even remember leaving. I don't know what made me kill her. I don't even know why I raped her. I had a good-looking wife at home. I saw her get into her car and I walked up and got in the car with her, yelled at her, took her down there where I raped her. I kept telling her I didn't want to hurt her but I just started choking her.

We suspect that these offenders were preoccupied with a kind of internal dialog that sustained anger, discontent, irritability, or depression. Drinking or drugs are attempts at moderating the internal stress, yet the fantasy continues. These offenders are unaware of how much internal dialog they experience. For example, when chastized by a teacher or boss, these offenders talk to themselves about it—"If I ever got that son of a bitch I'd rip him apart; I'd smash him up." One offender, after performing poorly in the service and being intimidated by his sergeant, went AWOL on a drinking binge. While out on the street, he beat a drunk to death after the man grabbed at him. The offender felt justified in his actions and was unaware of the intensity of his rage or the impact of his blows. He then beat to death a second man. Finally, he abducted a female acquaintance. When he awoke the next morning, her dead body was beside him with a broomstick impaled in her vagina with such force that it had penetrated her lungs. Although he believes he killed her, he has no recollection of the incident. He even helped the police look for her.

Most people are aware of their fantasy life in terms of making pictures and carrying on dialogue. When people report hearing voices, it is most often a hallucination. It is often described as either a voice from the outside or as someone transmitting thoughts into their mind. Something is in their heads of which they are consciously aware, but they believe it is in the control of someone else and that they are the passive victim.

The fantasy of the serial murderer is a separate, distinct reality. It is vibrant and vital, distinguishable from the "other" reality of the social world. The offender believes he can move from one reality to the other, that ideas generated in fantasy are viable. No fantasy thought is ever seen as abnormal. For example, one murderer's fantasy involved an exceptionally good sexual experience, and when the woman's behavior did not match the fantasy, he became enraged and killed her.

Fantasies provide a sense of control to the offender. For the serial murderer, they become obsessions. Efforts are made to improve the fantasy's weak areas, and once this is accomplished, the offender moves to gain access to a victim. The symbolic figure in the fantasy is replaced with a real person in reality.

PHASES OF A MURDER

The fantasy underlying a sexually oriented murder drives the offender's actions through various phases of that murder. The act of murder has at least four major phases, including 1) antecedent behavior, which includes the motives and planning or thinking about the murder; 2) the murder itself, including gaining access to the victim and carrying out the crime; 3) disposal of the body; and 4) post-crime behavior, including reaction to the discovery of the body.

PHASE 1: ANTECEDENT BEHAVIOR

Murder is a behavioral act. Motivations for this behavior include a conscious fantasy, plan, directive, or reason to kill or a triggering environmental cue that activates an unconscious fantasy for murder. Murderers who operate primarily on a conscious motivational level usually remember their thoughts prior to the murder. One of the murderers in our study described his entangled fantasy and perversions and said, "I had a compulsion during the day and hoped it would settle down—hoped I could wipe it out drinking." It did not settle down, and he acted out the fantasy and murdered after leaving the bar.

Murderers who are triggered into action by an environmental cue often state that they cannot remember their precrime behavior, although they can recall how they murdered. They state they found themselves in a compromising situation, and they reacted with explosive rage. ("She was screaming and I strangled her.") These killers usually described a spontaneous murder. The vagueness of the crime continued with subsequent murders; however, the men are aware that they will kill again.

PHASE 2: COMMITTING THE MURDER

Selecting a victim begins the acting-out level for the murderer with a conscious fantasy. The offender may have a list of criteria for choosing a victim, and many murderers are known to seek out the right victim. A delay before killing the victim often implies conscious planning and rehearsing of the fantasy. In these cases, the murderer often held an elaborate fantasy, laced with violence, aggression, torture, and sexuality, which also included the fate of the victim.

The history and circumstances of the victim are often important to the offender's fantasy. The victim may be symbolic of someone in the offender's history, as in one case where all the young women killed were symbolic of the offender's sister for whom he harbored great jealousy. Certain actions of the victim may also trigger the fantasy. One murderer, who selected his victims through hitchhiking, said, "She was playing up the role, the big beautiful smile and getting in the car, which was kind of tragic, but she had advertised to get blown away."

For the murderer without a conscious fantasy, a certain person or situation may, for example, cue in a strong belief of an unjust world. The offender feels unfairly treated, and this sets into motion the justification to kill. As one murderer said, "I couldn't perform sometimes. Somebody made fun of me and I blew my stack."

Killing the victim moves the offender to another level of the fantasy. At this point, the reality of murder comes into play. The victim may not die the way the offender planned. The offender might have to use more violence, he may feel more frightened than anticipated, or he might be startled by the fact he feels excited. Some murderers are exhilarated that they broke the rules, that they killed. Some will kill again, while others will, in horror over what they did, turn themselves in to the police.

During this phase, murderers are also confronted with the reality of a dead body. There is no such thing as killing with impunity—there is always some response. Some murderers respond by covering the body, washing the wounds, or otherwise caring for the body, a response that exhibits remorse or concern for the victim. Some murderers hide or bury the body, raising some questions about their motives. One reason for hiding or burying the body is to keep the secret and maintain control. Other murderers openly display the corpse in a public area, hoping the display will shock and offend society.

Some murderers need to believe that they will not show any concern for the victim. The actual murder goes beyond their fantasies of that killing. One murderer described his heightened excitement when driving his car with the dead bodies in the trunk. There is confirmation and reinforcement of the fantasy and pleasure or triumph in the power of the kill. These killers may torture and then kill or kill and then mutilate the body.

The power of the fantasy during the murder is illustrated by one fetish burglar. He killed his victims only when he was interrupted, but not because he was afraid of being identified. He was acting out an intense fantasy, and the unexpected interruption made him furious. He acted on this rage and felt justified in the murder.

PHASE 3: DISPOSING OF THE BODY

After committing the murder, the offender must decide what to do with the body. If this confrontation with reality has not been anticipated, the murderer may give himself up to the authorities. As one murderer said, "It blew my mind killing those people. I wasn't ready for that. The fantasies were there, but I couldn't handle the death trip and dead bodies. I freaked out and gave myself up."

It is unclear why some murderers just leave the body, while others use elaborate methods of disposing of the body. One offender who described his internal dialogue as he confronted the body of his first murder victim said, "I got a dead body on my hands. People see me come in here. How am I going to pack this out? Am I gonna put it in a double bag or sheet and carry it out of here? I figured the smaller the better. I chopped it up . . . stuffed some in the refrigerator . . . dumped guts in vacant lots . . . throwing pieces here and there whatever came out of the bag first . . . I was scared."

In a second case, the murderer described a planned dismembering of the body after killing the victim in a car. He then carried the body in a bag, up two flights of stairs to the apartment he shared with his mother, passing two persons coming down the stairs. He said, "it took meticulous work . . . about four hours . . . dismembering it, getting rid of the blood, the gore, completely cleaning the bathroom."

Some murderers became involved with the body through sexually sadistic acts. This may be part of the old fantasy or development of a new one. While the offender who "freaked out" and gave himself up was in prison, he spent an enormous amount of psychic energy rehearsing and mastering the body disposal phase. After his release, he murdered eight more women. He stated, "I got rid of that icky feeling of messing with the dead. Only one guy that gets more casual around a body than me . . . a mortician or a pathologist. But some of my fantasies were so bizarre that it would turn the stomach of a pathologist."

PHASE 4: POSTCRIME BEHAVIOR

During this phase, the murderer's fantasy becomes reality, providing a sense of purpose for the offender. The authorities are looking for him so he now focuses his energies on not getting caught and perhaps even into improving his methods for the next murder.

An important aspect of the postcrime behavior is the discovery of the body. This discovery is sometimes included in the fantasy, and the murderer may try to maintain his level of excitement. He may telephone or write to the police, or he may be in a crowd at the scene when the body is discovered. The murderer may even confess to the crime in order to accompany police to the location of the body.

The importance of postcrime events to the overall fantasy is illustrated by one case in which the offender worked as a hospital ambulance driver. He kidnapped his victims from the parking lot of a restaurant and took them to another location, where he raped and murdered them. He then anonymously telephoned the police to report seeing a body, returned to the hospital to receive the ambulance call, and then drove the ambulance with the body back to the hospital. In essence, he orchestrated a scene that he had rehearsed numerous times in his mind.

CONCLUSION

Sexual homicide is an act of control, dominance, and performance that is representative of an underlying fantasy embedded with violence, sexuality, and death. Yet for some killers, one act of murder fulfills their fantasy, while others feel compelled to continue killing.

Some murderers, while in prison, attempt to determine how they failed in the murder in order to be successful the next time. Their need to repeat the act of murder is connected with their sense of control.

Other murderers live in fear of repeating the crime; their compulsion to kill is bewildering to them. They don't want to get caught, yet at the same time they are hoping they will be caught. Several murderers wrote "stop me" statements in notes to police or on the wall at the murder scene, while others turned themselves in to police. Yet the fantasies continued. One killer stated, "It is a development . . . getting tired of a certain level of fantasy and then going even farther and even more bizarre. Year after year [the development continued] and finally it got off in such deep ends that I'm still not exposed to the worst of the fantasies that I have."

Interviews with sexual murderers provided information about their fantasies, which, in turn, provide us with a partial answer to murders that appear to be motiveless. These crimes are committed, in part, as a result of the acting out of a psychological fantasy. These fantasies are extremely violent and range from rape to mutilation or torture and murder. Fantasies are an important part of the offender's basic personality and move beyond normal sexual, consenting, pleasure-based daydreams to aggressive, sadistic, and destructive thoughts. These fantasies become so vivid that they provide the impetus for the offender to act them out with victims of opportunity.

It is important for law enforcement officers to be aware of the existence of these fantasies and of the types of individuals who have them. While the crime, and therefore the fantasy, may appear to be bizarre to law enforcement, it is essential to realize that these fantasies play an important part in the offender's basic personality. Therefore, as law enforcement officers become sensitive to this phenomenon and seek out clues that imply the presence of fantasy, they will aid in profiling and apprehending the offender.

CLASSIFYING SEXUAL HOMICIDE CRIME SCENES:

INTERRATER RELIABILITY

Robert K. Ressler and Ann W. Burgess

The unsolved homicide presents a major challenge to law enforcement officers. These unsolved cases, which often include a sex-related component, usually have no apparent motive. The victim has been sexually abused, and the nature of the killing indicates behavior patterns that reflect sexual deviation, specific character traits, and perhaps even psychopathology. Also referred to as lust murders, these murders often include severe beating and multiple stabbing of the victim, body mutilation (such as removal of sexual organs), and sexualized positioning of the body after death.[1]

The FBI's Behavioral Science Unit (BSU) has been involved since 1972 in assisting city, county, and state law enforcement agencies in their investigations of unsolved murders by preparing profiles of the unidentified offenders after extensive examination of the crime scene data, victim characteristics, and autopsy reports. This profile may include the perpetrator's age, race, sex, socioeconomic and marital status, intellectual and educational level, occupation, lifestyle characteristics, arrest history, location of residence in relation to the scene, and certain character traits.

The agents responsible for preparing the offender profiles have found it useful to classify the type of crime and the organizational structure of the crime

Published in a slightly different form in *FBI Law Enforcement Bulletin* 54, no. 8 (August 1985): 12–17.

scene. The crime is classified as sex-related, nonsexual, or unknown. Evidence of a sexual component anywhere within the crime scene justifies the sex-related classification. The organizational structure of the crime scene is determined by evidence of the amount of planning and premeditation by the offender, as well as of the offender's control over the victim. For example, a weapon taken to a crime scene and carried away suggests planning, as contrasted with a weapon used and left at the crime scene, suggesting opportunity and spontaneity.

In sex-related crimes, the structure of the crime scene provides insight into the offender's patterns of behavior. For example, a well-organized crime scene indicates an offender with a conscious plan of action after the murder to avoid detection and apprehension.

Currently, the BSU is systematically studying their profiling procedures through scientific and statistical analyses. Because of the importance of correctly classifying the crime and the crime scene, we needed to establish the reproducibility of these classifications. This section reports our investigation of the agents' ability to reproduce independently each other's classifications. This ability to replicate decisions is called interrater reliability.

STUDY DESIGN

Six BSU special agents with varying levels of experience in profiling participated in the reliability investigation. Data from sixty-four murder scenes, covering a variety of circumstances both sexual and nonsexual, were selected for the study. For each crime scene selected, one of the participating agents was thoroughly familiar with the case. This agent presented a short description of the crime scene and showed crime scene photos.

The presentation was restricted solely to information immediately available at the crime scene; no information from laboratory tests or later investigation was divulged. This restriction allowed the other agents to focus on immediate data. Other details of the investigation, if discussed by the presenter, might have influenced the agents in forming their opinions. Therefore, we decided to have the agents make judgments based on minimal unbiased data. We theorized that if there was good agreement among the presenter and the other agents, then the agreement would become even better if more detailed information was available. Thus, the most stringent test of interrater reliability would be based on the minimal data presentation.

After the presentation, the agents were allowed to ask questions about the crime scene data in order to remove any misunderstandings generated from the presentation. The combined presentation and question-and-answer period took about ten minutes. The following is an example:

Case A: This case involves an elderly couple found shot to death in their rural farmhouse. The woman was shot with a .410-gauge shotgun in the back of the head, apparently as she was typing a letter. She died immediately. When the elderly gentleman came home, he also was shot with a .410-gauge shotgun by a person who lay in wait. Neither body was moved or molested. There was no indication of any manipulation of the bodies after the initial gunshot, and nothing was taken from the home. There was no sign of forced entry and no evidence of defense wounds or escape attempts. Apparently, the victims were totally surprised. Because of these facts, it was difficult to establish a motive.

Question: Were there any fingerprints or footprints found?
Answer: There were fingerprints and footprints found at the scene, but they were not necessarily foreign to the people who had normal access to the house. There were no suspicious fingerprints, footprints, etc.
Question: Did the weapon belong at the scene?
Answer: The weapon was not found at the scene.

At this point, the agents were asked to make a determination of both the type of crime and the structure of the crime scene.

DATA ANALYSIS

TYPE OF CRIME

After a presentation similar to the above, each agent was asked to classify independently the crime. Although the presenter had additional information available to him, he also classified the crime solely on the basis of what he believed the crime scene information indicated. The breakdown of the sixty-four murders by type, as given by the presenters, is listed in figure 7.1.

Figure 7.1. Homicide Classification by Presenters

Type	Number	Percent
Sexual	46	71.9
Nonsexual	8	12.5
Unknown	10	15.6
Total	64	100.0

Sexual Homicide

There are various observations and evidence that point to a crime being classified as sex-related, including the body's attire or lack of clothing; exposure of the victim's sexual parts (such as breasts or genitals); sexual positioning of the body; sexual injury; evidence of sexual activity on, in, or near the body; and evidence of substitute sexual activity or sadistic fantasy. Case B is an example of a sexual homicide.

> *Case B:* A female was found behind a group of trees about 100 yards from a main road of a major city. Her clothes had been carefully removed, a stick has been inserted into her vagina, her breasts had been amputated, and her head had been beaten so severely that her face was obliterated. A bloody rock was lying to the right of the head. Evidence of sperm was found on the victim's dress and body. Her pantyhose had been removed carefully, and her clothing was not torn.

Nonsexual Homicide

Cases judged nonsexual in nature have no evidence supporting a sexual component. Case C illustrates this type of murder.

> *Case C:* A priest was found dead in a confessional booth. The investigation indicated that he was probably talking to someone on the other side of the booth who came around, opened the door, and stabbed him. There were multiple stab wounds in the victim's chest area, and the murder weapon was not left at the scene.

Unknown Homicide

When it is not obvious whether a crime is sex-related, the homicide is classified as unknown. For example, a skeleton buried or abandoned may not provide useful evidence, and a partially decomposed body may give confused indications, especially if the body has been mauled by an animal.

STRUCTURE OF THE CRIME SCENE

After the classification of crime type, each agent was asked to classify independently the structure of the crime scene as organized, disorganized, mixed, or unknown. The presenter also classified the crime scenes based on what he believed the scene alone indicated. The distribution of the sixty-four murder scenes, as given by the presenters, is shown in figure 7.2.

Figure 7.2. Crime Scene Classification by Presenters

Crime Scene Type	Number	Percent
Organized	31	48.4
Disorganized	21	32.8
Mixed	9	14.1
Unknown	3	4.7
Total	64	100.0

Organized Crime Scene

The organized crime scene indicates planning and premeditation on the part of the offender. For example, the crime may be committed in a secluded or isolated area selected by the murderer, or the victim may be killed in one location and transported to another.

> *Case D:* This case involved a series of homicides in which the victims, who were found in rivers, had automotive parts tied to their bodies. The female victims were all grossly mutilated (removal of breasts and feet, pelvic damage). The victims had been reported as missing during the course of a day; one never returned after shopping. There were indications that they had been kept for several days before being thrown into the river. The murderer would have needed a car to transport them from where they were last seen alive to where their bodies were discovered.

Disorganized Crime Scene

The disorganized crime scene indicates spontaneity and a more frenzied assault. The scene itself is most likely the location of encounter.

> *Case E:* A 16-year-old girl was last seen leaving to ride her horse in a favorite riding area. Police were notified when she was several hours late in returning home. A search team found the girl's body one-half mile from the farm where she lived. Her body was face up, spread-eagled, jeans and underpants pulled down to the ankles, a hooded sweatshirt draped across the left breast, her bra was pulled below both breasts, and another item of clothing was draped across her neck. A 10-inch vertical cut was present at the base of her neck; another cut was just below her right jaw. Blunt-force wounds were present on her head. It was determined at the crime scene that she had been raped, but probably after death.

Mixed Crime Scene

The mixed crime scene has signs of both organization and disorganization. There may be two or more offenders involved in the homicide, or the offender may begin the crime in an organized manner before his planning deteriorates as unanticipated events occur. Inconsistencies are noted in the behavior of the offender. Although the organized or disorganized classifications fit many cases, not all crime scenes fit into one of these categories. In addition, crime scenes may display varying degrees of organization and disorganization. It is in these instances that the mixed category is useful.

> *Case F:* A 21-year-old woman's body, partially hidden from view, was found at a garbage dump. The body had stab wounds in the vagina and groin, and the

victim's throat had been slashed. In addition, her nipples had been amputated and her face severely beaten. Her hair had been cut and was found hanging from a nearby tree branch. Test results indicated the victim had been sexually assaulted and murdered shortly after leaving her job. Investigation revealed two brothers were involved in the murder, one of whom the victim was living with at the time of her death.

Unknown Crime Scenes

The unknown scene pertains to those cases that cannot be classified based on immediate crime scene data. For example, a decomposed, buried body probably would not provide enough information upon which a classification could be based.

RESULTS

TYPE OF CRIME

Not all participating agents were available to classify each of the sixty-four homicide types (sexual, nonsexual, or unknown). In total, the six agents made 285 classifications, sixty-four of which were made by the agent presenting the case. Thus, there were 221 classifications that could be used for comparison with the presenter's classifications. Of these, 180 classifications (81.4 percent) agreed with the presenter's classification.

Of the six agents, one agent made fifty-seven (89 percent) of the presentations. Because the percentage of his presentations was so large, comparing his classifications with the presenter's would not be informative. The agreement rate for the other five agents and the number of cases they classified are shown in figure 7.3. Given the minimal amount of information supplied by the presenter, these agreement rates are high.

Figure 7.3. Agreement of Agents' Homicide Type Classifications with Presenter's Classification

Agent	Cases Classified	Case Agreed	Percent Agreement
1	62	48	77.4
2	40	35	87.5
3	55	45	81.8
4	30	23	76.7
5	27	25	92.6

When the classifications of each agent were compared with those of any other agent, the agreement rate ranged from 77 percent to 100 percent. Again, these are high agreement rates.

STRUCTURE OF CRIME SCENE

There were 220 classifications of the structure of the crime scene (organized, disorganized, mixed, unknown) that could be used for comparison with the presenter's classification. Of these, 163 (74.1 percent) agreed with the presenter (see fig. 7.4.)

Figure 7.4. Agreement of Agents' Crime Scene Classifications with Presenter's Classification

Agent	Cases Classified	Cases Agreed	Percent Agreement
1	62	48	77.4
2	40	28	70.0
3	55	42	76.4
4	29	15	51.7
5	27	23	85.2

The agreement rate between any two agents ranged from 45 percent to 89 percent. The agreement rates of agents with the presenter and with each other varied substantially. This appears due mainly to variation in experience and involvement with the process of classifying crime scenes. The agreement rates among the three agents routinely involved with this process ranged from 62 percent to 80 percent. Given the minimal data supplied by the presenter, these agreement rates must be considered good. However, classification in any field is a skill learned and reinforced by continuous involvement. In the medical field, for example, the diagnosis of a patient's medical condition is similarly learned and reinforced through continuous involvement.

The interrater reliability study evaluated the agreement of agents in classifying homicide by the type of crime and by the structure of the crime scene. In particular, the classification of crime scenes as organized has proven to be useful in profiling offenders in unsolved and motiveless murders.

This study demonstrated that there is reliability in the classification of crime types and scenes by BSU agents. Given only minimal information about the crime, agreements of agents with respect to crime types was high (at least 77 percent). Agreement of agents with respect to classifying the crime scene, while not as high as the crime-type agreement, appeared to be related to agent experience and involvement in the classification process. For experienced and active agents, who were given only minimal information about the crime scene, agreement rates ranged from 62 percent to 80 percent. More information would certainly have improved the agreement rates.

NOTE

1. Robert A. Hazelwood and John Douglas, "The Lust Murderer," *FBI Law Enforcement Bulletin* (April 1980): 6.

CRIME SCENE AND PROFILE CHARACTERISTICS OF ORGANIZED AND DISORGANIZED MURDERERS

When requested by a law enforcement agency to assist in a violent crime investigation, the agents at the Behavioral Science Unit (BSU) of the FBI Academy provide a behaviorally based suspect profile. Using information received from law enforcement about the crime and crime scene, the agents have developed a technique for classifying murderers into one of two categories—organized or disorganized, a classification method evolving from years of experience and knowledge. In the service of advancing the art of profiling, the agents were anxious to know if this classification system could be scientifically tested. This article describes the research study and statistical tests performed by a health services research staff on data collected.

OBJECTIVES OF THE STUDY

Thirty-six convicted sexual murderers were interviewed by FBI agents for a study on sexual homicide crime scenes and patterns of criminal behavior. These study subjects represented twenty-five serial murderers (the murder of separate victims, with time breaks between victims ranging from two days to weeks or

Published in a slightly different form in *FBI Law Enforcement Bulletin* 54, no. 8 (August 1985): 18–25.

months) and eleven sexual murderers who had committed a single homicide, double homicide, or spree murder.

The major objectives of this study were to test, using statistical inferential procedures, whether there are significant behavioral differences at the crime scenes between crimes committed by organized and disorganized murderers and to identify variables that may be useful in profiling organized and disorganized murderers. In order for the study to achieve its objectives, the agents first had to classify the thirty-six murderers into the organized or disorganized group, the breakdown being twenty-four organized murderers and twelve disorganized murderers.

RESULTS OF ANALYSES

The study determined that there were significant differences in the crime scenes of organized and disorganized offenders and that certain background differences were also found between them. There were four aspects of the crime where differences between organized and disorganized murderers were analyzed: (1) the murderer's action during the offense, (2) victim characteristics, (3) use of vehicles in the crime, and (4) types of evidence left at the crime scene. Table 8.1 provides the profile characteristics that achieved levels of significance between the organized and disorganized murderers, while table 8.2 shows the crime scene characteristics for the two groups.

Table 8.1. Profile Characteristics of Organized and Disorganized Murders

ORGANIZED	DISORGANIZED
Average to above-average intelligence	Below-average intelligence
Socially competent	Socially inadequate
Skilled work preferred	Unskilled work
Sexually competent	Sexually incompetent
High birth order status	Low birth order status
Father's work stable	Father's work unstable
Inconsistent childhood discipline	Harsh discipline as a child
Controlled mood during crime	Anxious mood during crime
Use of alcohol with crime	Minimal use of alcohol
Precipitating situational stress	Minimal situational stress
Living with partner	Living alone
Mobility with car in good condition	Lives/works near crime scene
Follows crime in news media	Minimal interest in news media
May change jobs or leave town	Significant behavior change (drug/alcohol abuse, religiosity, etc.)

Table 8.2. Crime Scene Differences between
Organized and Disorganized Murderers

ORGANIZED	DISORGANIZED
Planned offense	Spontaneous offense
Victim a targeted stranger	Victim/location known
Personalizes victim	Depersonalizes victim
Controlled conversation	Minimal conversation
Crime scene reflects overall control	Crime scene random and sloppy
Demands submissive victim	Sudden violence to victim
Restraints used	Minimal use of restraints
Aggressive acts prior to death	Sexual acts after death
Body hidden	Body left in view
Weapon/evidence absent	Evidence/weapon often present
Transports victim or body	Body left at death scene

ORGANIZED OFFENDER: PROFILE CHARACTERISTICS

Organized offenders have a high birth order, often being the first-born son in a family. The father's work history is generally stable, and parental discipline is perceived as inconsistent.

Although the organized offender has an average or better than average IQ, he often works at occupations below his abilities, yet prefers a skilled occupation. His work history is also sporadic.

Precipitating situational stress, such as problems with finances, marriages, employment, and relationships with women, is often present prior to the murder. The organized offender is socially adept and is usually living with a partner.

The organized offender may report an angry frame of mind at the time of the murder or state he was depressed. However, while committing the crime, he admits being calm and relaxed. Alcohol may have been consumed prior to the crime.

The organized offender is likely to have a car that is in good condition. Evidence of continued fantasy is present in terms of taking remembrances of the victim or crime scene. Newspaper clippings of the crimes are often found during searches of the subject's residence, indicating the offender followed the criminal investigation in the newspaper.

CRIME SCENE

The initial observation at the crime scene of an organized offender is that some semblance of order existed prior, during, and after the offense. This scene of methodical organization suggests a carefully planned crime that is aimed at deterring detection.

Although the crime may be planned, the victim is frequently a stranger and is targeted because he or she is in a particular location staked out by the offender. In this sense, the victim becomes a victim of opportunity. Victims of serial murderers have been noted to share common characteristics. The offender often has a preference for a particular type of victim and thus may spend considerable time searching for the "right" victim. As one offender said: "I'm a night person. Plenty of times that I went out looking, but never came across nothing and just went back home. I'd sit waiting, and as I was waiting, I was reliving all the others."

Common characteristics of victims selected by an individual murderer may include age, appearance, occupation, hairstyle, or lifestyle. Targeted victims in this sample included adolescent male youths, hitchhiking college coeds, nurses, women frequenting bars, women sitting in automobiles with male companions, and solitary women driving two-door cars.

The organized offender is socially adept and may engage in conversation or a pseudorelationship with the victim as a prelude to the attack. Offenders may use impersonation as a method to gain access to a victim. The offender's demeanor is not usually suspicious. He may be average or above average in appearance, height, and weight; he may be dressed in a business suit, uniform, or neat, casual attire. In the organized style of attack, aimed at gaining the confidence of the victim, there is first the effort to use verbal means to capture the victim rather than physical force. The organized offender frequently uses his or the victim's vehicle in the offense.

Rape, as well as murder, may be the planned crime. Murder is always a possibility following rape; the assailant threatens the victim's life and brandishes a weapon. Sexual control is continued past conversation to demands for specific types of reactions (fear, passivity) during the sexual assault. When the victim's behavior stops being passive and compliant, aggression may be increased by the offender.

Control over the victim is also noted in the use of restraints, such as a rope, chain, tape, belt, clothing, chemical, handcuffs, gag, and blindfold. The way weapons are used may suggest a sadistic element in the offender's plan. The killing is eroticized, as in torture where death comes in a slow, deliberate manner. The power over another person's life is seen in one example in which a murderer described tightening and loosening the rope around the victim's neck as he watched the victim slip in and out of a conscious state.

Fantasy and ritual dominate with the organized offender; obsessive-compulsive traits surface in the behavior and/or crime scene patterns. The offender often brings a weapon with him to the crime, taking it with him upon departure. He carefully avoids leaving evidence behind and often moves the body from the death scene.

While sexual acts are part of the fantasy planning of the crime, murder may not be a conscious motive until there is a triggering cue. This is illustrated by one murderer's following statement: "I had thought about killing her . . . saying what am I going to do when this is over. Am I going to let her go so she can call the cops and get me busted again? So when she took off running—that decided it in my mind that killing her was what I was going to do."

CASE EXAMPLE OF AN ORGANIZED OFFENDER

The following case involves the rapes and murders of five women by one juvenile offender.

Victim 1: A woman in her late twenties was found about 150 yards into a wooded culvert area outside her apartment. Her car was found in the parking lot.

Re-creating the scene, police speculated that the victim was approached after she parked her car. It was known she arrived home late at night from work. She was found in a stream after being assaulted, drowned, and strangled. Her head had been held under water while she was being strangled. There was no evidence of severe beating to the body; although some defense wounds were present, mutilation did not occur.

The only item taken from the victim was a ring of little value. The victim was found partially clothed. Her shoes, found further down the trail, suggested the location of the sexual assault. Footprints were present at this site; tire tracks were not. The victim lived in a high-rise building with many apartments, parking lots, and cars.

Victim 2: A woman in her mid-twenties was found fully dressed in a wooded area less than a quarter mile from the location of the first victim. She was not near water. She had been stabbed to death repeatedly in the chest. Although there was evidence of sexual assault, there was no overkill to the body, no mutilation. Again, the victim was coming home late at night. Apparently she parked her car and was abducted prior to reaching her apartment.

Victim 3: This victim was similar in physical appearance, age, and manner killed to the second victim. There was evidence of sexual assault; underclothing in disarray suggested she was re-dressed after death. A stocking was missing, although her shoes were on.

Victim 4: Several months later, a similar crime occurred in the same general vicinity. A black woman, in her early thirties, was found dead. She usually worked late and arrived home between 2:00 and 3:00 a.m. Her car was also parked where she would have entered the apartment building. Although discovered further away than the other victims, she was still not more than a half mile from where she lived. There was evidence of sexual assault, and she too had been strangled and drowned. The method and location were similar to the first crime scene and was consistent with the work schedule of the victim.

Victim 5: The fifth victim, a woman in her mid-twenties, was last seen at a party at 1:30 or 2:30 a.m. She left the party with several people and was later found dead in the same wooded culvert area as previous victims. She was found stabbed several times in the chest and had been partially buried in the culvert. There was evidence of sexual assault.

Considering the dynamics and pattern of the aforementioned case, the following crime scene assessment and subsequent criminal personality profiling would be possible.

The offender selects victims who are returning home during the late evening or early morning hours. The assaults generally take place near the victims' homes as they are walking from their parked cars. The offender is watching the parking areas for single women returning during these times. He takes the victims from the apartment complex to wooded areas close by for the assaults. He chooses the time and place of assault. Since no scream or resistance is evident, one must assume the assailant carries a weapon and instructs the victims to accompany him to the secluded area. This indicates a persuasive, articulate person who convinces them no harm will come to them if they "do as he instructs." He would be manipulative and have a history of antisocial traits and behavior. He is youthful and aggressive, probably macho.

Since he uses the same MO in each assault, one must assume he knows the territory well, both the traveled built-up areas and the surrounding woods. He probably lives in the area, is youthful, and has grown up and played in the woods as a child. He is a long-term resident.

Medical examination and crime scene assessment show rape prior to death, and death is sudden with minimal mutilation, again indicating the well-planned crime by the organized antisocial criminal. The victims are "sized up" prior to the approach, and the killer knows they will not resist if he promises release after rape. He has raped before the killing started, but some life trauma has triggered the taking of the life of victim 1. The offender has had past problems with law enforcement, and once he has killed, he feels he must continue to kill to avoid victims testifying against him. He does not value the life of a victim over the chance that she may identify him to the police.

In summary, the assailant in the five homicides is an organized, antisocial personality. He is a youthful white man, has good intelligence, is articulate and manipulative. He fits into the community and has lived there for many years. He lives in proximity to all victims. He precipitates his crimes with alcohol and/or drugs, possibly is first born in his family, and is sexually competent. He probably has a girlfriend yet had a recent problem with her prior to the first killing. Considering his age, he would live with a single parent and would have no car since he selects victims on foot, sometimes using their cars in the assault. He probably would follow the media reports of the crime and may be in a crowd of onlookers when the police locate the bodies.

The police investigation in this case of multiple rape-murder led to a seventeen-year-old white male living very close to all victims who lived within a one-mile radius in a large city suburb. He was bright, yet a marginal achiever in school, lived with his mother, and did not own a car. He was known as a macho ladies' man and a "con artist" among his peers. He used beer and marijuana to precipitate his offense and selected victims in an area he grew up in. He had a girlfriend he called "his fiancée" who jilted him shortly before the first murder, when she went away to college. He followed the crime in the paper and on one occasion watched the police investigator from his window. He had a lengthy juvenile record, including sexual assault and rape.

DISORGANIZED OFFENDER: PROFILE CHARACTERISTICS

The disorganized offender is likely to be of below-average intelligence or of low birth status in the family. Also, harsh parental discipline is sometimes reported. The father's work history is unstable, and the disorganized offender seems to mirror this pattern with his own inconsistent and poor work history. Typically, this offender is preoccupied with recurring obsessional and/or primitive thoughts and is in a confused and distressed frame of mind at the time of the crime.

The disorganized offender is socially inadequate. Often, he has never married, lives alone or with a parental figure, and lives in proximity to the crime scene. This offender is fearful of people and may have developed a well-defined delusional system. He acts impulsively under stress, finding a victim usually within his own geographic area.

The disorganized offender is also sexually incompetent, often never having achieved any level of sexual intimacy with a peer. Although the offenders in this sample claimed to be heterosexual, there is a clear suggestion that the disorganized offender is ignorant of sex and often may have sexual aversions.

CRIME SCENE

The overall imprint of the disorganized crime scene is that the crime is committed suddenly and with no set plan of action for deterring detection. The crime scene shows great disarray. There is a spontaneous, symbolic, unplanned quality to the crime scene. The victim may be known to the offender, but age and sex of the victim do not necessarily matter.

If the offender is selecting a victim by randomly knocking on doors in a neighborhood, the first person to open a door becomes the victim. The offender kills instantly to have control; he cannot risk that the victim will get the upper hand.

The offender uses a blitz style of attack for confronting the victim, who is caught completely off guard. He either approaches the victim from behind, unexpectedly overpowering her, or he kills suddenly, as with a gun. The attack is a violent surprise, occurring spontaneously and in a location where the victim is going about his or her usual activities.

The offender depersonalizes the victim, targeting specific areas of the body for extreme brutality. Overkill or excessive assault to the face often is an attempt to dehumanize the victim. Such facial destruction may indicate knowledge of the victim or that the victim resembles or represents a person who has caused the offender psychological distress. The offender may wear a mask or gloves, use a blindfold on the victim, or cover the victim's face as he attacks. There is minimal verbal interaction except for orders and threats. Restraints are not necessary, as the victim is killed quickly.

Any sexually sadistic acts, often in the form of mutilation, are usually performed after death. Offenders have attempted a variety of sexual acts, including ejaculating into an open stab wound in the victim's abdomen. Evidence of urination, defecation, and masturbation has been found on the victim's clothing and in the home. Mutilation to the face, genitals, and breast; disembowelment; amputation; and vampirism may also be noted on the body.

Disorganized offenders might keep the dead body. One murderer killed two women and kept their body parts in his home for eight years. He made masks from their heads and drums and seat covers from their skins. Earlier, he had exhumed the bodies of eight elderly women from their graves and performed similar mutilative acts.

The death scene and crime scene are usually the same in murders committed by the disorganized offender, with the victim being left in the position in which she or he was killed. If the offender has mutilated the body, it may be positioned in a special way that has significance to the offender.

No attempt is made to conceal the body. Fingerprints and footprints may be found, and the police have a great deal of evidence to use in their investigation. Usually, the murder weapon is one obtained at the scene and is left there, providing investigators with evidence.

CASE EXAMPLE OF A DISORGANIZED OFFENDER

Murder 1: A husband returning from work at 6:00 p.m. discovered his wife's body in the bedroom of their home. An autopsy revealed she had been murdered sometime in the morning after being confronted by the assailant as she went to empty the garbage outside. The victim was shot in the head four times and thereafter disemboweled with a knife obtained in her home. Other than slash wounds to breasts and mutilation to internal reproductive organs, no evidence of sexual assault or molestation was found. The victim was first slashed in the abdomen, and the assailant pulled her intestines out of the body cavity. The victim had what was later determined to be animal feces in her mouth. Garbage was strewn about the house. A yogurt cup was found, and indications were that the murderer used the cup to collect blood from the victim, which he then drank.

Crime 2: On the same date, a house burglary occurred within one-quarter mile of the victim's residence. Garbage was strewn throughout the home. Evidence indicated the burglar urinated on female clothing and also defecated in the house. No one was home at the time.

Crime 3: Two days later, the carcass of a dog was found in the same neighborhood. The dog had been shot in the head, and the bullet was determined to have come from the gun used in the first murder. The dog was disemboweled.

Murder 2: Four days after the first slaying, a woman, waiting for a male friend to pick her up for a day's outing with her neighbor, noticed the man's car had pulled into her neighbor's driveway. She telephoned to say she would be right over; however, receiving no answer, she looked out her window again to note the man's car was now gone. Becoming suspicious, she went over to the house and discovered the bodies of her male friend, her female neighbor, and the neighbor's child. A twenty-two-month-old infant was missing from the home; however, a bullet hole was found in the pillow of the child's crib, along with what appeared to be brain and skull matter. This was also found in the half-filled bathtub, indicating the child had been killed and the body washed and removed from the scene. The female victim had been severely slashed and mutilated. She had been murdered in the bedroom where she had been disemboweled from breast bone to pelvic area. Internal organs, including spleen, kidneys, and reproductive organs, had been removed and mutilated. No attack was noted to external genitals. The murderer had attempted to remove an eye and also had inserted a knife into the anal canal, cutting the victim severely in this area. Definite fingerprints with blood were found on the abdomen, shoulders, and legs of this victim. In addition, a ring of blood was found on the floor, indicating a bucket-type container was used to collect blood.

The following information was extracted from a profile developed by the BSU:

Suspect description: White male aged 25–27; thin, undernourished appearance; single, living alone in a location within 1 mile of the abandoned station wagon owned by one of the victims. Residence will be extremely slovenly and unkempt, and evidence of the crimes will be found at the residence. Suspect will have a history of mental illness and use of drugs. Suspect will be an unemployed loner who does not associate with either males or females and will probably spend a great deal of time in his own residence. If he resides with anyone, it will be with his parents. However, this is unlikely. Subject will have no prior military history; will be a high school or college dropout; probably suffers from one or more forms of paranoid psychosis.

The police narrowed their search to a one-mile radius of the stolen vehicle, seeking a man of the suspect's description. A twenty-seven-year-old white man, five-foot-eleven and weighing 149 pounds, was located in an apartment complex within the same block as the abandoned car. The man was in possession of a gun that matched the murder weapon in the slayings. Also found in the apartment were numerous body parts thought to be animal and possibly human. The man had previously been diagnosed as a paranoid schizophrenic and had been committed to a mental facility after he was found sucking blood from a dead bird. After he had been released, he was found in the desert bloodstained and wearing a loincloth. He told police he was sacrificing to flying saucers. He was released by police; however, later a child's body was found in the same vicinity. Evidence was found in his apartment indicating his obsession with blood, mutilation, and possible cannibalism of humans and animals.

CONCLUSION

In summary, this research study of differences between organized and disorganized sexual murderers with regard to profile characteristics and crime scene indicators provides an important foundation for the investigative technique of criminal profiling. By achieving the two study objectives, we have established that variables do exist that may be useful in a criminal profile and that do differentiate between organized and disorganized sexual murderers. It is important to be aware of the limitations of this study. We do not mean to imply that all unsolved cases can be profiled successfully. We wish to emphasize that this study was exploratory and indicates that we have identified significant variables in crime scene analysis.

A second important step can now be taken—that is, performing test profiles using previously identified variables and comparing results with cases that have already been profiled by BSU agents. These test profiles would be the second phase for advancing the scientific study of the profiling process. Further refinement of profile characteristics and deductive reasoning used by "experts" will provide an advancement in the state of the art in building an "expert knowledge-based system" for law enforcement. Expert knowledge-based systems are a subset of the field of artificial intelligence and are derived by using knowledge and reasoning patterns of experts to create computer programs that emulate these experts. These systems are easy to use, require minimal training, and have English-language interface with the users. Expert systems, currently used in many fields, are continually being adapted as more knowledge is gained through their use and application. As in these other applications, expert systems will never replace skilled law enforcement representatives but are a tool that is continually being updated by the knowledge gained through use.

INTERVIEWING TECHNIQUES FOR HOMICIDE INVESTIGATIONS

This section discusses techniques that have been used in the interviews of persons who have already been convicted. Law enforcement officers should seek appropriate legal advice before using these techniques in attempts to obtain judicially admissible confessions.

One goal of the study of sexual homicide crime scenes and criminal behavior patterns was to explore how murderers commit their crimes. An in-depth analysis of interviews with convicted murderers allowed us to retrieve first-hand information about their patterns of values and beliefs, patterns of information storage, levels of recall on the crimes, and admission of responsibility for the murders.

This article presents our experiences in interviewing convicted serial sexual murderers with the hope of adding to law enforcement's knowledge of interviewing techniques. Although our interviews were conducted with murderers already convicted and incarcerated, we believe our observations provide insight for interviewing suspects in order to identify a killer.

Published in a slightly different form in *FBI Law Enforcement Bulletin* 54, no. 8 (August 1985).

TERMS OF THE INTERVIEW

Before beginning any interview, the interviewer needs to be thoroughly familiar with any pertinent existing information, including crime scene photographs, records, and files. This information can be used not only to draw conclusions but also to establish a focused interest in the offender. By showing interest, respect is conveyed to the suspect, an initial objective in establishing rapport. Although it is often difficult in cases of violent and brutal crimes, this show of respect often allows the interviewer to get to the point of the interview more quickly since less time will be spent by the subject in evaluating the interviewer.

To be successful, the interviewer needs to convince the subject that the interview can be beneficial for him or her. In our study, some offenders admitted their crimes. In these situations they found value in the interview, believing they were contributing to increased understanding or to clarity other people's conclusions about them. Offenders who would not admit to their crimes cooperated in order to point out why it was impossible for them to have committed the crimes. Other offenders consented to the interviews in order to "teach" police how the crimes were committed and motivated. Those who refused interviews had reasons ranging from advice of an attorney to their own psychotic states.

THE COMMUNICATION LINK

Rapport was the key communication link in our interviews. Once established and recognized, it allowed the interviewer to lead the interview and to reestablish communication when it broke down. Rapport was frequently gained when the investigator mirrored, below the level of conscious awareness, the subject's spoken and unspoken behavior. This included matching the words of the subject, adopting aspects of his posture, and speaking in a similar tone and rate of speech.

ELICITING INFORMATION

Once communication had been initiated and rapport established, the questioning began. In our study, the what/where/when sequencing and descriptions of places where the crime events occurred were sought first. Next, the interviewing agents asked questions about how the victim was chosen. Finally, questions about thoughts, feelings, and images were posed.

Questions were generally organized around four phases of the murder: (1) the precrime phase, (2) the murder event, (3) the disposal of the body, and (4) the postcrime phase.

Precrime Phase. Conscious motive for the murder was often elicited by asking what triggered the murder. Those murderers with conscious intent were able to describe this in detail. Those without conscious motive would usually say they could not remember why they killed, but they were able to describe their feelings prior to the murder. Reconstructing the scene prior to the murder helped interviewing agents determine the cues that moved the offender's murder fantasy into action. For example, offenders were asked to describe their day prior to the murder and their thoughts and feelings before encountering the victim.

The Murder Event. Memory recall of details specific to the murders varied among the offenders interviewed. Those murderers who deliberately planned the murder through a fantasy generally continued to remember details about certain aspects of the murder. During one interview, the agents remarked that the subject seemed to have almost total recall. The subject corrected the agents: "Actually, that's overblown because I really don't (remember everything). I have shabby memory on things I don't want to remember, and things that are shocking or very vivid, I don't forget. I trip on those for years."

What the subject avoids or refuses to talk about provides information on areas where strong emotions may exist. (In one case, the murderer began the interview by stating he would not discuss his family.) The interviewer should concentrate on important aspects of the event, such as how the suspect gained access to the victim; conversation and behavior involving the victim; transporting the victim from one location to another; what the murderer did sexually before, during, and after the victim's death; methods of torture; behaviors after the victim's death (such as mutilation or amputation); and thoughts and feeling during these acts.

Disposal of the Body. Our interviews with the murderers made clear the importance of a fantasy in disposing the victim's body. Once the act was committed, the murderer had to decide what to do with the body. At this phase, the murderer may first consciously realize the reality of his act. Our questions concentrated on what was done with the body, how the offender left the scene, what (if anything) was taken from the body or the crime scene, and what thoughts and feelings did the murderer experience during these various acts.

Postcrime Phase. A series of behaviors occur after a murder. We asked each offender what he did right after the murder (did he wash or change clothes, go out with friends, go to sleep, or eat); how he thought and felt about it; whether he dreamed about it; whether he returned to the crime scene, attended the funeral, read about the murder in the newspaper; or talked to police. We were careful to include questions about the recovery of the body (did the offender assist police in the recovery, was he present when the body was recovered, and was his confession necessary for police to find the body).

SPECIFIC TECHNIQUES

Because of the importance of fantasy to sexual homicide, information about a subject's fantasy can be valuable. However, people with a long-standing fantasy life may not talk about it easily. Often a low-key approach is successful in encouraging the discussion of the fantasy. A fantasy is an elaborate thought with great preoccupation and emotion. The person keeps going back to the thoughts. The subject may only be aware of images, feelings, and internal dialogue at certain heightened times.

One of the indications of the presence of a fantasy is the great amount of detail provided by a subject, details that provide the best information on how the subject operates. For many of the murderers we interviewed, their detailed planning was their statement of superiority, control, and cleverness. The fantasy usually provided a sense of power and control, as well as emotional stimulation. In some instances, the fantasy appeared to protect them from becoming totally disorganized or psychotic. We discovered this, through interviews, in their reports of becoming enraged when victims interrupted their plans. These murderers were very sensitive to being called crazy or maniacal, as they associated those characteristics with carrying out acts in ways that are stupid, foolish, and not in control.

The importance of terminology used in the interview was illustrated in one case:

Agent: Do you think your fantasy life was out of control?

Subject: I'm going to have to change your terminology, not because I'm banting words, but my fantasy world, no I don't think it was out of control, I think my world of realism was out of control. My perception of the real world was distorted.

This exchange illustrated how the murderer felt in control of his fantasy and out of control in the real world.

In contrast to murderers who consciously plan a crime through fantasy, our interviews revealed that some murderers acted more in response to external cues. Such people may not be able to relate why a particular act happened. These murderers were concerned with particular acts at certain times; suddenly, they lost control. It is possible to talk about the existence of the fantasies without eliciting details of them and to obtain information about the serial murderer's blockage of certain memories:

Agent: Did you have any unusual fantasies preoccupying you to any period of time or that you felt you were over-involved in?

Subject: Well, I can't say if I have or I don't. There are a lot of aspects of this crime I can't give an answer, cause I put up a mental block. I don't want to think of it. It makes me do bad time. I'm doing a long time and I just block it clear out.

The murderer confirms the likelihood that the fantasies are there; however, additional techniques, such as hypnosis or therapy, would be needed to access the information.

CONTINUUM OF ADMISSION

The offender generally took one of three positions regarding guilt—admitting the crime, admitting lack of total recall, and not admitting the crime. In our study, the majority of murderers admitted their crimes. Some of the murderers turned themselves in to the police; others admitted to the crime when they were apprehended. Still others admitted guilt when confronted with evidence. As one murderer told the interviewing agents, "The police unwrapped the broomhandle and that did it." Several of the murderers interviewed were unable to remember actually committing the murder but agreed the evidence incriminated them.

One group of murderers interviewed did not admit to their crimes even after their convictions for the murders. When confronted with such individuals, the interviewer should attempt to determine if the individual is lying (which implies conscious intent) or if the individual is denying (which implies subconscious intent).

To the offender, lying to an investigator provides a form of control. It may detour the investigator and waste valuable time, as in situations in which incorrect names and addresses are given.

One way investigators identify lies is on the basis of the amount of detail a subject provides. Fantasy worlds or delusions are usually very detailed. However, when a subject tries to feign psychosis or delusion, his story usually appears inconsistent and lacking in detail. Investigators detecting this type of defense and bringing it to the offender's attention may be successful. In one case, the murderer claimed to have committed the murders because of instructions from a centuries-old dog. The agents refused to accept this ploy. They pointed out good-naturedly that the murders had been carefully planned and executed, which was a lot to expect from a dog. The murderer finally accepted the "credit" for the crimes and discussed them in detail with the interviewers. Even when suspecting that a subject is lying or denying, the interviewer should try to maintain an atmosphere of mutual respect.

There are reasons why a suspect might deny a crime. The denial might serve to protect the subject from legal action as well as from the psychological impact of admitting such a crime. One murderer interviewed denied any actual knowledge of committing the crime. He stated that he was coerced, forced to confess to the crimes, and possibly drugged before entering a plea of guilty. In the interview with the agents, he had an elaborate answer for each piece of evidence presented. He said friends had given him the hundred pairs of high-heeled shoes in his closet. He argued that photographs found in his possession were not his because he would not be such a sloppy photographer. He presented extreme detail for each piece of evidence brought against him to "prove" why he could not have been the murderer.

There also may be cases where the murderer justifies in his own mind the issue of admitting or denying guilt. The following statement from a serial murderer illustrates this position:

> *Agent:* Could the police have done anything for you in order to get a confession?
>
> *Subject:* Well, at first I didn't admit my guilt. I wouldn't admit to anybody. But I didn't really deny either.

We found that when someone outright denied they had murdered or had anything to do with the crime, the use of an imaginary third person was helpful. The agents would go through the details of the crime and ask the subject why he thought this third person would commit such an act. This technique projected responsibility or guilt away from the subject and onto someone else. Note this strategy in the following interview by the agents with a murderer:

> *Agent:* Suppose we do it this way. Let's just divorce you from that situation. I'm sure you've thought about it a lot. Suppose it wasn't you involved and it was someone else. What, in your mind, would be the reasons for someone doing something like that?
>
> *Subject:* I'd say she either said or did something extremely wrong.
>
> *Agent:* Like what, for instance?
>
> *Subject:* Well, it could have been that his (sexual) performance was inadequate. She might have thought it was. Or he might have thought it was and she said something about it.

This conversation illustrates that the murderer was able to provide a reason (sexual inadequacy) for the crime being committed and suggests that the intent to kill was triggered into action through an internal dialogue process within the offender.

Often someone who denies justifies his or her actions by blaming someone else. In our study, for example, a murderer justified his killing by describing the victim as a "tramp." One reason a murderer may not be able to admit the crime is that admission would destroy his premise of justification.

Obtaining information from suspects is a critical technique for law enforcement. Well-developed skills in interviewing can provide important information, which can be linked with crime scene data. Through the use of various interviewing techniques, the investigation can receive maximum benefit from the interview process. Interview techniques discussed in this article have given members of the FBI's Behavioral Science Unit new insight for tapping into the fantasy systems of these criminals and for effectively dealing with their defenses.

CRIME PROBLEMS

THE LUST MURDERER

Robert R. Hazelwood and John E. Douglas

O n August 29, 1975, the nude, mutilated body of a twenty-five-year-old mother of two was found near Columbia, SC. Both breasts had been removed, the reproductive system had been displaced, numerous cut and stab wounds were evidenced by the body, and there was indication of anthropophagy.[1]

This was the scene of a lust murder, one of the most heinous crimes committed by man. While not a common occurrence, it is one that frightens and arouses the public as does no other crime.

Of primary concern are those factors that differentiate the lust murder from the more common sadistic homicide, physical evidence present at the scene that may assist in determining the responsible individual(s), and possible personality characteristics of the murderer. It is not the authors' contention that the material presented is applicable to all such crimes or their perpetrators but rather that the majority of the crimes and offenders involved will exhibit the characteristics set forth. The data presented here have not been quantified but are based upon the authors' examination of case reports, interviews with investigative personnel, and a careful review of the literature. Minor variations of the terms used may occur, depending on the source of reference.

It is the authors' contention that the lust murder is unique and is distinguished

Published in a slightly different form in *FBI Law Enforcement Bulletin* (April 1980): 18–22.

from the sadistic homicide by the involvement of a mutilating attack or displacement of the breasts, rectum, or genitals. Further, while there are always exceptions, basically two types of individuals commit the lust murder. These individuals will be labeled as the organized nonsocial and the disorganized asocial personalities.

THE ORGANIZED NONSOCIAL

The organized nonsocial (nonsocial) lust murderer exhibits complete indifference to the interests and welfare of society and displays an irresponsible and self-centered attitude. While disliking people in general, he does not avoid them. Instead, he is capable of displaying an amiable facade for as long as it takes to manipulate people toward his own personal goal. He is a methodical and cunning individual, as demonstrated in the perpetration of his crime. He is fully cognizant of the criminality of his act and its impact on society, and it is for this reason that he commits the crime. He generally lives some distance from the crime scene and will cruise, seeking a victim. Dr. Robert P. Brittain, author of "The Sadistic Murderer," has stated, "They (sadistic murderers) are excited by cruelty, whether in books or in films, in fact or fantasy."[2]

THE DISORGANIZED ASOCIAL

The disorganized asocial (asocial) lust murderer exhibits primary characteristics of societal aversion. This individual prefers his own company to that of others and would be typified as a loner. He experiences difficulty in negotiating interpersonal relationships and consequently feels rejected and lonely. He lacks the cunning of the nonsocial type and commits the crime in a more frenzied and less methodical manner. The crime is likely to be committed in proximity to his residence or place of employment, where he feels secure and more at ease.

THE CRIME

The lust murder is premeditated in the obsessive fantasies of the perpetrator. Yet the killer may act on the "spur-of-the-moment" when the opportunity presents itself. That is to say, the murderer has precisely planned the crime in his fantasies but has not consciously decided to act out those fantasies until the moment of the crime. Consequently, the victim is typically unknown to the killer, a fact borne out by the cases studied by the authors.

The location of the victim's body may be indicative of the type of murderer involved. Typically, the asocial type leaves the body at the scene of death, and while the location is not open to the casual observer, there has been no attempt to conceal the body. Conversely, the nonsocial type commits the crime in a secluded or isolated location and may later transport it to an area where it is likely to be found. While there may be no conscious intent to be arrested, the nonsocial type wants the excitement derived from the publicity about the body's discovery and its impact on the victim's community.

The lust murder is committed in a brutally sadistic manner. While the victim may be either male or female, the crime is predominantly heterosexual and intraracial in nature. The victim's body exhibits gross mutilation and/or displacement of the breasts, rectum, or genitals and may have been subjected to excessive stabbing or slashing with a sharp instrument. The victim's death typically occurs shortly following abduction or attack, and the mutilation that takes place follows death. Dr. J. Paul de River notes in his book, *Crime and the Sexual Psychopath*: "The lust murderer, usually, after killing his victim, tortures, cuts, maims or slashes the victim in the regions on or about the genitalia, rectum, breast in the female, and about the neck, throat and buttocks, as usually these parts contain strong sexual significance to him, and serve as sexual stimulus."[3]

If, however, there is physical or medical evidence indicating the victim was subjected to torture or mutilation prior to death, this factor indicates that the perpetrator was the nonsocial rather than the asocial type.

Seldom will the lust murderer use a firearm to kill, for he experiences too little psychosexual gratification with such an impersonal weapon. Most frequently, death results from strangulation, blunt force, or the use of a pointed, sharp instrument. The asocial type is more prone to use a weapon of opportunity and may leave it at the scene, while the nonsocial type may carry the murder weapon with him and take it when departing the scene. Therefore, the murderer's choice of weapon and its proximity to the scene can be greatly significant to the investigation.

Dr. de River comments that the instrument itself may be symbolic to the murderer and he may place it in a position near the victim. This is a form of pride and exhibitionistic behavior and can be sexually gratifying to him.[4]

The investigator may find that the victim has been bitten on the breasts, buttocks, neck, abdomen, thighs, or genitals, as these body areas have sexual associations. Limb or breast amputation, or in some instances total dissection, may have taken place. Dissection of the victim's body, when committed by the nonsocial type, may be an attempt to hinder the identification of the victim. The asocial individual approaches his victim in much the same way as an inquisitive child with a new toy. He involves himself in an exploratory examination of the sexually significant parts of the body in an attempt to determine how they function and appear beneath the surface.

Occasionally, it will be noted that the murderer has smeared the victim's blood on himself, the victim, or the surface on which the body rests. This activity is more frequently associated with the asocial type and relates to the uncontrollable frenzy of the attack.

Penis penetration of the victim is not to be expected from the asocial individual but is predominantly associated with the nonsocial type, even to the extent of "necrophilia."[5] These activities on the nonsocial's part reflect his desire to outrage society and call attention to his total disdain for societal acceptance. The asocial type more commonly inserts foreign objects into the body orifices in a probing and curiosity-motivated, yet brutal, manner. Evidence of ejaculation may be found on or near the victim or her clothing.

Frequently, the murderer will take a "souvenir," normally an object or article of clothing belonging to the victim, but occasionally it may be a more personal reminder of the encounter—a finger, a lock of hair, or a part of the body with sexual association. The souvenir is taken to enable the murderer to relive the scene in later fantasies. The killer here is acting out his fantasy, and complete possession of the victim is part of that fantasy. As previously mentioned, the perpetrator may commit an anthropophagic act, and such an act is indicative of asocial involvement.

Finally, the scene itself will exhibit much less physical evidence when the murderer is the nonsocial type. As stated, the individual categorized as the nonsocial type is very cunning and more methodical than the asocial type, who commits a more frenzied assault. It is interesting to note, however, that both types may be compelled to return to the scene, albeit for different reasons. While the asocial type may return to engage in further mutilation or to relive the experience, the nonsocial type returns to determine if the body has been discovered and to check on the progress of the investigation. Instances have occurred when the nonsocial type changed the body's location to insure its discovery.

Of interest is the almost obsessive desire of the nonsocial type to assess the police investigation, even to the extent of frequenting police "hangouts" to eavesdrop on discussions of unsolved crimes, or in some manner, inserting himself into the investigation. In one case, the murderer returned to the scene after it had been examined by police laboratory technicians and deposited articles of clothing worn by the victim on the day she died. In both of two other cases, the killer visited the cemetery site of the victim and left articles belonging to the victim on her grave. It is as though he were involved in a "game" with the authorities. Such actions appear to further his "will to power" or desire to control.[6]

PORTRAIT OF THE LUST MURDERER

What set of circumstances create the individual who becomes the lust murderer? The authors do not possess the expertise to explain the multiple and complex casual factors associated with the psychological development of the individual who commits such a heinous crime. But it is generally accepted that the foundation of the personality is formed within the first few years of life. While extreme stress, frequent narcotic use, or alcohol abuse can cause personality disorganization in later life, it is the early years that are critical to the personality structure and development.

Seldom does the lust murderer come from an environment of love and understanding. It is more likely that he was an abused or neglected child who experienced a great deal of conflict in his early life and was unable to develop and use adequate coping devices (i.e., defense mechanisms). Had he been able to do so, he would have withstood the stresses placed on him and developed normally in early childhood. It must be emphasized that many individuals are raised in environments not conducive to healthy psychological development, yet they become productive citizens. These stresses, frustrations, and subsequent anxieties, along with the inability to cope with them, may lead the individual to withdraw from the society, which he perceives as hostile and threatening.

Through this internalization process, he becomes secluded and isolated from others and may eventually select suicide as an alternative to a life of loneliness and frustration. The authors have designated this reaction to life as disorganized asocial. This type possesses a poor self-image and secretly rejects the society that he feels rejects him. Family and associates would describe him a nice, quiet person who keeps to himself but who never quite realized his potential. During adolescence, he may have engaged in voyeuristic activities or the theft of feminine clothing. Such activities serve as a substitute for his inability to approach women sexually in a mature and confident manner.

The individual designated by the authors as the organized nonsocial type harbors similar feelings of hostility but elects not to withdraw and internalize his hostility. Rather, he overtly expresses it through aggressive and seemingly senseless acts against society. Typically, he begins to demonstrate his hostility as he passes through puberty and into adolescence. He would be described as a troublemaker and a manipulator of people, concerned only for himself. He experiences difficulties with family, friends, and "authority figures" through antisocial acts that may include homicide. Thomas Strentz and Conrad Hassel, in the June 1978 issue of *Journal of Police Science and Administration*, wrote of a youth who had first murdered at the age of fifteen and was committed to a mental institution. After his release, he murdered and dismembered eight women.[7] It is the nonsocial's aim to get even with society and inflict pain and punishment upon others.

THE ROLE OF FANTASY

As noted, the lust murder is premeditated in obsessive fantasies experienced by both the asocial and nonsocial murderers. Fantasy provides them an avenue of escape from a world of hate and rejection. Dr. James J. Reinhardt in his book *Sex Perversions and Sex Crimes* has written:

> A study of these cases almost invariably reveals a long struggle against what Reik calls the "forward thrust." By fantasy the murderer attempts to wall himself in against the fatal act, while at the same time gratifying the compulsive psychic demands in the development and use of fantasy. These sadistic [fan-

tasies] seem always to have preceded the brutal act of lust murder. These fantasies take all sorts of grotesque and cruel forms. The pervert, on this level of degeneracy, may resort to pornographic pictures, grotesque and cruel literary episodes, out of which he weaves fantasies. On these, his imagination dwells until he loses all contact with reality, only to find himself suddenly impelled to carry his fantasies into the world of actuality. This is done, apparently, by drawing human objects into the fantasy.[8]

James Russell Odom, tried and convicted with James Clayton Lawson for the brutal lust murder described at the beginning of this article, stated that while he and Lawson were at a mental institution, they would express their fantasies about women: "(Odom) raping them and Lawson mutilating them . . . we had fantasized so much that at times I didn't know what was real."[9]

If he acts out the fantasy (commits the crime), his goal will be to destroy the victim and thereby become the sole possessor. James Lawson (mentioned above) is quoted as saying: "Then I cut her throat so she would not scream . . . at this time I wanted to cut her body so she would not look like a person and destroy her so she would not exist. I began to cut on her body. I remember cutting her breasts off. After this, all I remember is that I kept cutting on her body."[10]

The victim may represent something he desires sexually but is unable to approach. Lawson speaks again, "I did not rape the girl. I only wanted to destroy her."[11]

Rarely encountered is the asocial type who is capable of normal heterosexual relationships. He may desire such relationships, but he also fears them. Dr. Reinhardt, on an interview with a famous lust murderer, wrote: "he at first denied ever attempting any sex play with girls. Two days later with one of his rare shows of emotion he said, looking much ashamed, that twice, later correcting himself to eight times, he had touched girls 'on the breasts' and then pressed 'on the leg.' Always having done this, he would immediately burst into tears and 'be upset and unable to sleep.'"[12]

THE PSYCHOLOGICAL PROFILE

A psychological profile is an educated attempt to provide investigative agencies with specific information as to the type of individual who committed a certain crime. It must be clearly stated at the outset that what can be done in this area is limited, and prescribed investigative procedures should not be suspended, altered, or replaced by receipt of a profile. Rather, the material provided should be considered and employed as another investigative tool. The process is an art and not a science, and while it may be applicable to many types of investigations, its use is restricted primarily to crimes of violence or potential violence.

When prepared by the FBI, the profile may include the perpetrator's age, race, sex, socioeconomic and marital status, educational level, arrest history, location of residence in relation to the scene, and certain personality traits.

A profile is based on characteristic patterns or factors of uniqueness that distinguish certain individuals from the general population. In the case of lust murder, clues to those factors of uniqueness are found on the victim's body and at the scene and would include the amount and location of mutilation involved, type of weapon used, cause of death, and the position of the body. The profiler is searching for clues that indicate the probable personality configuration of the responsible individual.

In preparing the profile, it is preferable to have access to the scene prior to its disturbance. In most instances, this is impossible. In lieu of being at the scene, the profiler must be provided investigative reports, autopsy protocols, detailed photographs of the body, scene, and surrounding area, as well as a map depicting the victim's last known location in relation to its present location and any known information pertaining to the victim and her activities.

There are violent crimes in which there is an absence of uniqueness; therefore, it is not possible to provide a profile. However, this is not likely to occur in the case of a lust murder.

SUMMARY

While not a common occurrence, the lust murder frightens and arouses the public as does no other crime. The lust murder involves the death and subsequent mutilating attack of the breasts, rectum, and genital areas of the victim. The crime is typically heterosexual and intraracial in nature and is committed by one of two types of individuals: The disorganized asocial personality or the organized nonsocial personality.

The organized nonsocial type feels rejection by and hatred for the society in which he lives. His hostile feelings are manifested overtly, and the lust murder is the final expression of the hatred he feels. The disorganized asocial type also feels rejection and hatred for his world, but he withdraws and internalizes his feelings, living within a world of fantasy until he acts out that fantasy with his victim.

While commonalities exist in the commission of the lust murder, there are certain factors that may indicate the personality type involved. These factors include the location of the body, evidence of torture or mutilation having occurred prior to death, smearing of the victim's blood, evidence of penis penetration or anthropophagy, and the availability of physical evidence at the scene.

The crime is premeditated in the obsessive fantasies experienced by both the asocial and the nonsocial types, yet it is a crime of opportunity, one in which the victim is not usually known to the murderer.

The use of psychological profiling in such crimes may be of assistance in determining the personality type involved. It is a search for clues indicating the probable personality configuration of the responsible individual(s). It is a useful tool, but it must not alter, suspend, or replace prescribed investigative procedures.

NOTES

1. Anthropophagy: Consuming the victim's flesh or blood.

2. Robert P. Brittain, "The Sadistic Murderer," *Medical Science and the Law* 4 (1970): 202.

3. J. Paul de River, *Crime and the Sexual Psychopath* (Springfield, IL: Charles C. Thomas, 1950), p. 40.

4. J. Paul de River, *The Sexual Criminal* (Springfield, IL: Charles C. Thomas, 1950), p. 233.

5. Necrophilia: A desire for relations with the dead.

6. Calvin S. Hall and Lindsey Gardner, *Theories of Personality*, 2nd ed. (New York: John Wiley & Sons, 1970).

7. Thomas Strentz and Conrad V. Hassel, "The Sociopath—A Criminal Enigma," *Journal of Police Science and Administration* (June 1978).

8. James J. Reinhardt, *Sex Perversions and Sex Crimes* (Springfield, IL: Charles C. Thomas, 1957), pp. 208–209.

9. Statement of Odom as reported by the *Record*, April 7, 1976, p. 1A.

10. Statement made to South Carolina law enforcement authorities by James Clayton Lawson on September 3, 1975.

11. Ibid.

12. Reinhardt, *Sex Perversions and Sex Crimes*, pp. 221–22.

RAPE AND RAPE-MURDER

ONE OFFENDER AND TWELVE VICTIMS

Robert K. Ressler, Ann W. Burgess, and John E. Douglas

This study analyzes data pertaining to twelve rapes and rape-murders committed by one male adolescent offender over a four-year period. All offenses except the first were committed while the offender was under psychiatric and probationary supervision. The use or relinquishment of violence by the offender was found to be dependent on subtle interpersonal factors. The authors stress the importance of the use of crime scene data and interviews of patients who have committed sex crimes, the role of psychological profiles in apprehension of suspects, and the contribution of law enforcement as a data resource.

Rape-murder, a crime of increasing concern in our society, results from one person killing another in the context of power, sexuality, and brutality. Although the literature is replete with reports on the murderer, it is relatively silent on the victim. This omission from the clinical literature significantly impedes our understanding of the possible variables in a rape assault and handicaps our progress in victimology. To contribute to the study of rape-murder, we report on twelve rapes committed by a male teenager over a four-year period in which five of his victims were murdered following the rape.

Published in a slightly different form in "Rape and Rape-Murder: One Offender and Twelve Victims," *American Journal of Psychiatry* 140 (January 1983): 36–40. Copyright © 1983 by the *American Journal of Psychiatry*. Reprinted with permission from the American Psychiatric Association.

PROFILE OF THE OFFENDER

The offender, born twenty-four years ago in the Midwest, was the youngest of three children and had an older adopted brother and natural sister. It is reported that he was an Rh baby and required a complete blood transfusion at birth. He has reportedly suffered no major health problems. The parents separated and divorced when he was age seven, and both parents remarried shortly thereafter. He continued to live with his mother even though her second marriage dissolved when he was twelve. He completed age-level work until his senior year in high school, when he was involuntarily withdrawn from school due to excessive absenteeism and lack of progress.

He was of average intelligence and had aspired to attend college. He was athletically inclined and played league baseball. He was outgoing, often attended social events, and had a close circle of friends, both male and female. He saw himself as a leader, not a follower.

The offender's antisocial behavior was first recorded when he was age nine, when he and three other boys were caught by the school principal writing cusswords on the sidewalk. The boys were required to wash the sidewalk until the words were removed. His criminal record started when he was age twelve with assaultive and disruptive behavior involving breaking into an apartment and stealing property valued at $100. At age thirteen he was charged with driving without an operator's license; at age fourteen he was charged with burglary and rape and committed two minor acts of petty larceny as well as stealing a car. He readily admitted using alcohol and drugs of all types from his early teen years. He worked sporadically throughout his high school years as part of a program whereby he attended school in the morning and worked in the afternoon.

The offender was sent out of state to a psychiatric residential facility following the first felony of rape and burglary at age fourteen. During his eighteen-month stay, he received individual insight-oriented psychotherapy, and the discharge recommendation was that he live at home, attend public school, and continue psychotherapy on a weekly outpatient basis, with his mother actively involved in his treatment. Three weeks after returning home from the residential facility, he was charged with attempted armed robbery—an act intended to be rape. It took one year for him to come before a judge for sentencing on this charge, and in that time he had committed the first rape and murder but had not yet been charged for that offense. The disposition on the attempted armed robbery was probation and outpatient psychotherapy; he had served eight months when he was apprehended for the five murders. His psychiatric diagnoses according to DSM-II have included adolescent adjustment reaction, character disorder without psychosis, and multiple personality. At the time of his arrest for the murders the young man was nineteen years old, weighed sixty-five kilograms, and was one hundred seventy centimeters tall call. He was given five life sentences for the five rape-murders. After two years of incarceration, he admitted to six additional rapes for which he was never charged.

PROFILE OF THE VICTIMS

All of the twelve victims were female, and they represented different ethnic groups. They ranged in age from seventeen to thirty-four years and were older than the offender by one to fifteen years. Several victims were taller and heavier than the offender. Nine of them were total strangers to him; he knew three by sight. Two of the nine women who were strangers to him recognized him after his capture. Most of the victims were of middle-income status, and the majority lived in the apartment complex where the offender lived with his mother. All of the victims except one high school student were employed full-time and worked in such positions as teachers, postal supervisors, store buyers, airline stewardesses, and administrative assistants. Some of them also had part-time jobs and/or were continuing their college education. Most of the victims were not married; several were divorced. Two were known to have children. Five of the women were raped and murdered; five were raped only by the offender; and two were gang raped. One escaped from the offender before he could commit a sex crime. Most of the victims were approached at knife point as they entered the elevator in their apartment building. All rape murder victims were abducted from the same location, killed in different areas, and found fully clothed. The time spent in locating their bodies ranged from one day to six weeks.

DATA COLLECTION

Data were collected in two ways: through interviews with the offender and completion of an interview guide and through the use of police reports, court evaluation records, photographs of crime scene investigations, and medical examiners' reports. An obvious limitation to the interviews was having to rely on the offender's memory and reconstruction of the crimes. This bias was countered with documentation from prison and court records. On the other hand, the offender's admission of six additional rapes adds to the data not available through official channels. Another methodological drawback was that the information on what victims said and did came from the offender.

FINDINGS

The analysis of the data suggests that the offender's criminal behavior changed in two major ways: The sexual aggression escalated from rape to rape and murder, and the offenses increased in frequency over time (see table 11.1). Of special note are the facts that 1) all rape and murder offenses except the first were committed while he was under psychiatric supervision and on probation, 2) the six rapes that were not charged to him were also committed while he was under psychiatric supervision and on probation, and 3) the five homicides were not linked to one offender and did not appear to include rape until he was apprehended and described the offenses.

Table 11.1 Escalation of the Criminal Behavior of an Adolescent Boy

Boy's Age Years:	Offense	Victim's Age	Disposition
12	Petty larceny		Probation
12	Disrupting school		Probation
13	Driving without an operator's license		Case continued until his 18th birthday
14	Burglary and rape	25	Sent to state psychiatric center
14	Petty larceny		Sent to state psychiatric center
14	Breaking and entering		Sent to state psychiatric center
16	Rape	25	Never charged
16	Rape	25	Never charged
16	Burglary and rape (codefendant)	17	Never charged
16	Rape (codefendant)	25	Never charged
17	Attempted armed robbery	22	Probation and outpatient therapy
18	Rape	25	Never charged
18	Rape and murder	24	Life imprisonment
19	Rape and murder	22	Life imprisonment
19	Rape and murder	34	Life imprisonment
19	Rape	25	Never charged
19	Rape and murder	27	Life imprisonment
19	Rape and murder	24	Life imprisonment

RAPE AND INTENDED RAPE:
THE FIRST SEVEN OFFENSES

The first rape with which the offender was charged was when he was fourteen and occurred in the apartment next to where he lived with his mother. He had returned home from a party and had gone to bed but woke up fantasizing about the twenty-five-year-old divorced neighbor woman who often employed him for small errands. He got up, went outside wearing a ski mask, scaled the apartment wall like a "cat burglar," and entered the woman's third-floor apartment through the balcony door. He raped the woman several times, left through the front door, returned to his own apartment, and went to sleep. He was apprehended three weeks later and was eventually convicted on the basis of evidence found in the apartment, that is, fingerprints and clothing, rather than the victim's identification of him. A woman judge sentenced him to an out-of-state psychiatric residential facility.

The second rape (the first one with which he was never charged) occurred when he was sixteen and home from the residential facility for Christmas vacation. The evening before he returned to the facility, he approached a woman in the elevator in the apartment complex and at knife point took her to another location and raped her. The second rape with which he was never charged, third in the sequence, occurred three months later when he approached a woman in the parking lot of a local school he attended while at the residential facility. He forced the woman at knife point to drive to her apartment, where he raped her. The third and fourth rapes with which he was never charged included codefendants. While on a weekend pass, the offender and two other patients from the residential facility stole a car, traveled out of state, broke into a house, and stole two guns and money, and each raped a seventeen-year-old girl who was in the house. The offender returned home; however, his mother immediately sent him back to the residential facility, and he was counseled on his runaway behavior. Three months later he and another patient went to a local swimming pool. They broke into the women's locker room and raped a young woman, covering her head with a towel.

The sixth rape (the fifth for which he was never charged) occurred before the first rape-murder he committed and involved a woman he had seen in his own apartment building. He obtained an air pistol, captured her in the apartment elevator, took her to a storage room, and, covering her face with her jacket, raped her twice.

An attempted armed robbery (an act intended to be rape) occurred three weeks after his release from the residential treatment facility. He targeted a woman entering the elevator of the apartment complex, donned a ski mask, and held a knife to her. She was successful in escaping.

> She broke . . . pushed me out of the way and started going to the front of the elevator, pushed the button to open the door and started to run and she stumbled.

I'd started to run after her and stumbled over her and at that point the knife fell and she was on the ground hollering and I was on the ground next to her, scared to death. My mind went blank. I ran out of the building. [He was subsequently arrested.]

RAPE AND MURDER: THE LAST SIX OFFENSES

The offender selected the last six victims at random as he watched cars drive into the apartment complex where he lived. Once he targeted a victim, he would walk behind her, follow her into the apartment elevator, pull his knife, and tell her it was a holdup. Then they would leave the building, either for the victim's car or for an area near the apartment complex. In one case the pattern was reversed. The offender was hitchhiking and was given a ride by a woman who was going to a party in his apartment complex. She let him off at his building; he watched her park her car and then ran across the complex, entered the elevator with her, and captured her there. All abductions and murders occurred within his own territory. Thus, known territory was a distinct advantage for him. ("Going somewhere that I didn't know or where the cops patrolled might get me caught. I knew what time the cops came by in the morning because I'd be sitting there.") Indeed, he was right. One of the reasons he was not caught until after the fifth murder was that the police were looking for strangers—especially suspicious strangers—not a teenager living in the area.

The offender's use of either verbal or physical strategies to assert control over the victim depended on the victim's initial response. The victim who was compliant when he showed a weapon received no additional threats or orders. Victims who screamed received verbal threats and those who refused to cooperate were physically struck.

INTERACTION BETWEEN OFFENDER AND VICTIM

Reconstruction of the victims' talk and actions as viewed from the offender's perspective revealed that conversation and behavior served to either neutralize or escalate his affective state.

Murder victim 1, rape victim 7. The woman's talk ("She asked which way I wanted it") raised the offender's suspicion of her lifestyle. After the rape and while both were dressing, he had not decided on his next action. The woman's sudden attempt to escape triggered in him feelings of anger and frustration that resulted in increased aggression. He stated: "She took off running down the ravine. That's when I grabbed her. I had her in an armlock. She was bigger than me. I started choking her . . . she stumbled . . . we rolled down the hill and into the water. I banged her head against the side of a rock and held her head under water. Death was determined to be from strangulation. ·

Murder victim 2, rape victim 8. The woman's talk consisted of many questions ("She wanted to know why I wanted to do this; why I picked her; didn't I have a girlfriend; what was my problem; what I was going to do"), which served to annoy him. The woman, talking while driving the car, suddenly stepped on the accelerator and attempted to counter his control by threatening to drive the car into a tree. He turned off the ignition and put his foot on the brake, and the car slid sideways. The car stopped, and the woman got out and ran across the road screaming for help. He said: "I go into the woods after her. I see her run from behind a tree and that's when I go after her. From then on I knew I had to kill her. She trips over a log and that's when I catch up with her and I just start stabbing her." The victim was stabbed fourteen times in the chest.

Murder victim 3, rape victim 9. The offender claimed he had not decided whether he would kill this woman. He would not let her talk ("The more I got to know about the women the softer I got"). He ordered her to be quiet and turn on the radio. He described his thinking as follows:

> I was thinking . . . I've killed two. I might as well kill this one, too. . . . Something in me was wanting to kill. . . . I tied her up with her stockings and I started to walk away . . . then I heard her through the woods kind of rolling around and making muffled sounds. And I turned back and said, "No, I have to kill her. I've got to do this to preserve and protect myself."

The woman died from twenty-one stab wounds to the left side of the thorax and upper abdomen.

Rape victim 10. The offender had decided to kill this woman, but her talking saved her life ("She told me her father was dying of cancer"). Her talk evidently neutralized his aggression due to his identification with the situation ("I thought of my own brother who had cancer. I couldn't kill her. She had it bad already"). He threw her car keys out of the window and ran off into the woods.

Murder victim 4, rape victim 11. The offender had decided to kill this woman. Her resistance and attempt to escape triggered his violence.

> She scratched me across the face. I got mad; she started to run. I got up from falling down and chased her. She ran into a tree. I caught her. We wrestled, rolled over the embankment into the water. I landed with my face in the water. . . . That's where the idea to drown her came. . . . She was fighting and she was strong but I put her head under the water and just sat there with my hands on her neck.

The cause of death was drowning.

Murder victim 5, rape victim 12. This woman's talk led the offender to realize that she knew him. This knowledge escalated his fear of being apprehended and, in turn, led him to confess the four previous murders. The decision to kill was made quickly. "We were walking along, through the culverts, underneath the highway. That's when I pulled out the knife and without even saying anything, I stabbed her ... maybe fifty to a hundred times." He buried the victim's body in a shallow grave.

BEHAVIOR FOLLOWING THE MURDERS

Following each murder, the offender would usually take an item of jewelry from the woman's body for a souvenir, go back to the woman's car and search through her purse for money, drive her car for an extended period of time, park the car several blocks from his apartment, return to his apartment and go to bed, and watch television and newspapers for reports about the discovery of the body.

DISCUSSION

PSYCHODYNAMICS OF RAPE-MURDER

Some reports have suggested that rapists rarely murder[1] but that when they do, the motives are social rather than personal; that is, they murder to silence the victim and prevent detection.[2] This motive differs from lust murder, whereby sexuality and aggression fuse into a single psychological experience known as sadism.[3] Rada argued, and we agree, that rapists are capable of murder but for different reasons than the lust murderer.[4] One reason, Rada suggested, is that in some rapists there appears to be a progressive increase in aggressive fantasies about women that over time may eventually lead to murder.

The case we have reported suggests that for some rapists there is a progression in the offender's intent or decision making toward killing. With the first three murders the offender made the decision to kill the women during the period he interacted with them, but in the last two murders, he decided ahead of time to kill them. This case also suggests an additional dimension to motive in rape-murder. The modern view of rape regards it as an act of violence expressing power as one motive.[5] We suggest that the psychological motive of power expands for the rapist-murderer from a need for power over one person ("It was a real turn-on to realize the victims weren't reporting or identifying me") to a need for power over a collective group ("I'm too slick for them") that included the police, judges, psychiatrists, and psychologists.

This case illustrates the influence of an individual's affective state when combined with various degrees of intent to commit murder. A review of the offender's last six offenses suggests that two affective states may influence the decision to kill: escalating the anger motive in the rapist may trigger aggressive behavior aimed at establishing dominance and authority, and stimulating fear and decreasing the power motive in the rapist may trigger aggressive behavior aimed at self-preservation.

INTERVIEWING PATIENTS CHARGED WITH CRIMES

The fact that the offender was under psychiatric supervision when he committed most of his criminal acts suggests that close attention be paid to psychiatric interviewing techniques. We offer the following two suggestions.

1. When interviewing a patient who has been charged with crimes, one should pay careful attention to the deviant behavior and focus on all dimensions of the interactional aspects of the crime. If possible, and if it is within agency policy, one should gather supplementary data regarding the crime scene, the victim's statements, police interviews, and official reports and talk with staff who have worked with the patient. These corroborating data will lend a perspective other than the patient's for assessment of and challenge to the patient. The interviewer should maintain a high index of suspicion when the patient denies committing or refuses to calk about the crime or deviant behavior and should consider the possibility that he or she is concealing other secretive and dangerous behavior. A parallel can be drawn between the dynamics of sex and secrecy and incest and treatment.[6]

2. Rape and attempted rape behavior should be viewed as serious and chronic and thus repetitive. The interviewer should not assume that a patient with a history of sexual assault has committed it only the number of times for which he or she is charged. When the patient has been under stress and especially at times when he or she has been charged with other criminal acts (e.g., breaking and entering, stealing cars, larceny), the interviewer should inquire about concurrent assaultive behavior or rape fantasies. Our findings support those from Groth and associates' study of convicted sex offenders recommended for treatment. Those authors reported that each offender had committed an average of five sexual assaults for which he was never apprehended.[7]

PSYCHOLOGICAL PROFILES

The fact that a psychiatrist wrote a psychological profile of the offender we have described suggests the need for further work in this area. The psychological profile is a critical technique in police work on unsolved crimes. In a comparison of the profile with the data obtained from the offender, two points can be made. First, no one speculated that the murder victims had been raped. The fact that they all were found fully clothed and without clinical evidence of sexual intercourse made the cases seem not sexually related. The offender admitted raping the victims several times. The possibility that he had a sexual dysfunction—retarded ejaculation—was never considered.[8] Second, the profile report speculated that because he targeted women and used their underwear to bind them, he felt hostility toward his mother. Interview data suggested another authority figure in his life: "That woman judge sent me to a diagnostic center. That's what started me off resenting authority. . . . Nobody could tell me what to do or when to do it or how to do it."

CONCLUSIONS

Gaps do exist in fully understanding a criminal act in general, and a sexual homicide in particular, because each of the various professionals and disciplines involved work with only one part of the picture. Cooperation through sharing information and collaborating on cases is often not practiced in the work setting. We undertook this study to address this gap in the transfer and sharing of criminal data. Frazier encouraged the research step of developing descriptive patterns of murder as human action, with the caution to avoid simple, reductionistic conclusions about the causes of murder.[9] We agree with this position and encourage studies across disciplines.

NOTES

1. J. Selkin, "Rape." *Psychology Today* (January 1975): 70–72, 74, 76.

2. E. Podolsky, "Sexual Violence," *Medical Digest* 34 (1966): 60–63.

3. A. N. Groth with H. J. Birnbaum, *Men Who Rape* (New York, Plenum Press, 1979), p. 44.

4. R. T. Rada, "Psychological Factors in Rapist Behavior," in *Clinical Aspects of the Rapist*, ed. Rada (New York, Grune and Stratton, 1978).

5. A. N. Groth, A. W. Burgess, and L. L. Holmstrom, "Rape: Power, Anger, and Sexuality," *American Journal of Psychiatry* 134 (1977): 1239–43.

6. A. W. Burgess and L. L. Holmstrom, "Sexual Trauma of Children and Adolescents: Pressure, Sex and Secrecy," *Nursing Clinics of North America* 10 (1975): 551–63.

7. A. N. Groth, R. Longo, and B. McFadin, "Undetected Recidivism among Rapists and Child Molesters," *Crime and Delinquency* 28 (1982): 450–58.

8. A. N. Groth and A. W. Burgess, "Sexual Dysfunction during Rape," *New England Journal of Medicine* 297 (1977): 764–66.

9. S. H. Frazier, "Murder—Single and Multiple," *Aggression* 52 (1974): 304–12.

part 2:

CONTEMPORARY ARTICLES ON CRIMINAL PROFILING

HOW TO INTERVIEW A CANNIBAL

Robert K. Ressler

By all accounts, Bob has had more impact on criminology, crime theorizing, and writing than any other single figure. Before Ressler, the FBI knew surprisingly little about the psychology of the dangerous criminal. In terms of the serial murderer, the FBI knew nothing. Now, after a thirty-year FBI career and his development of the Violent Criminal Apprehension Program, he has become a legend, thanks in part to his two best-selling books, Whoever Fights Monsters *and* I Have Lived in the Monster —Inside the Minds of the World's Most Notorious Serial Killers. *In both books, Ressler provides readers with insights into the criminal mind and telling behind-the-scenes anecdotes. His interviews with forty of the nation's worst serial killers have provided the world with revealing personal glimpses. The one that follows not only is shocking but also lays out the art of interviewing in a forensic way.*

When Bob arrived at the Behavioral Sciences Unit (BSU) at the FBI Academy in Quantico, Virginia, in 1974, he apprenticed in profiling under Howard Teten and Pat Mullany, a two-man team already renowned among law enforcement agencies for their combined expertise in solving unsolvable homicides. Known among the BSU staff as "Mutt and Jeff" and "Fric and Frac," the two mentored Ressler in the fledgling art and science of profiling. Teten received his guidance from famed New York psychiatrist Dr. James A. Brussel, who had astounded the country in 1956 with

Published in a slightly different form as "How to Interview a Cannibal," in *Whoever Fights Monsters* by Robert K. Ressler and Tom Shachtman (New York: St. Martin's Press, 1992); "Interview with a Cannibal: Jeffrey Dahmer," in *I Have Lived in the Monster* by Robert K. Ressler (New York: St. Martin's Press, 1997), chap. 6. Copyright © 1992, 1997 by Robert K. Ressler. Reprinted by permission of St. Martin's Press.

an amazingly accurate profile of the Mad Bomber of New York City. Mullany, a former Christian brother, had been profiling since 1972.

In brief, Bob received his BS from Michigan State University in 1962. In 1968, he received his MS from the same university. He served in the US Army between 1957 and 1959, then again between 1962 and 1970. He joined the Federal Bureau of Investigation in 1970 and served until 1990, at which time he retired. Since then, he has served as the director of the Forensic Behavioral Services, a Virginia-based organization dedicated to consulting the area of violent criminal behavior, criminal personality profiling and crime scene assessment. He has written more than twenty professional articles as well as four books, including Justice Is Served *and* The Crime Classification Manual.

In the following pages, allow me to lead you into the mind of the rarest of rare of all serial criminals—the one who kills then cannibalizes his victims. Thus far in human history, as far as we know, there has been no greater, indeed deeper, abyss than the murderous mind of Jeffrey Dahmer. This young man tortured, killed, and ate the body parts of at least sixteen boys. He acted not out of any particular motive, such as anger, revenge, or driving need, but from a source no one can understand. For this compendium, I offer my insights about interviewing serial murderers in order to assist the reader in gaining some perception about the mind of a monster and its thought processes. We must never forget that in America, and throughout the world, there are many Jeffrey Dahmers walking among us.

For this book, I have divided my contribution into two sections: "Understanding Organized and Disorganized Crime," excerpted from chapter 6 of my *Whoever Fights Monsters* (1992), and "Interview with a Cannibal: Jeffrey Dahmer," from *I have Lived in the Monster* (1997).

UNDERSTANDING ORGANIZED AND DISORGANIZED CRIME

To most people, when confronted by evidence of violent criminality, the behavior may seem an enigma, even a unique occurrence. Very few of us are used to grisly murders, mutilations, bodies thrown into ravines—and the majority who are ignorant of such matters includes most local police, who seldom encounter crimes of this sort. Even outrageous, unspeakable criminal behavior is not unique and not incomprehensible, however. These sort of murders have occurred before, and, when properly analyzed, can be understood well enough so that we can even break them down into somewhat predictable patterns. By the late 1970s, the Behavioral Sciences Unit had accumulated a large amount of experience in assessing these sort of crimes. The usual police officer might never have seen an act of disembowelment or cannibalism during his career, but because so many police departments sent us their unusual cases for analysis, we were used to looking at such crime scenes and could get past the average person's disgust at them and discern what the evidence revealed about the probable perpetrator.

Amassing this knowledge was one thing. Communicating it to our audience—those police officers who sought our help in tracking down violent criminals—was another. To characterize the types of offenders for police and other local law enforcement people, we needed to have a terminology that was not based in psychiatric jargon. It wouldn't do much good to say to a police officer that he was looking for a psychotic personality if that police officer had no training in psychology; we needed to speak to the police in terms that they could understand and that would assist them in their searches for killers, rapists, and other violent criminals. Instead of saying that a crime scene showed evidence of a psychopathic personality, we began to tell the police officer that such a particular crime scene was "organized," and so was the likely offender, while another and its perpetrator might be "disorganized," when mental disorder was present.

The organized versus disorganized distinction became the great divide, a fundamental way of separating two quite different types of personalities who commit multiple murders. As with most distinctions, this one is almost too simple and too perfect a dichotomy to describe every single case. Some crime scenes, and some murderers, display organized as well as disorganized characteristics, and we call those "mixed." For instance, Ed Kemper was a highly organized killer, but his mutilation of bodies after death was more typical of a disorganized one. In the following pages, I'll paint the principal characteristics of both classic organized and classic disorganized offenders. Please remember that if I say that a particular attribute is characteristic of an organized offender, it is not so 100 percent of the time but is something that is *generally* applicable. For instance, I say that the organized offender hides the bodies of his victims; in our research interviews, and in analysis of crime scenes, we found this to be true more than three-quarters of the time. That's enough to make the generalization hold up pretty well, but not enough to make it an absolute condition for our characterization. All the "rules" of profiling are like that. Though the distinction between organized and disorganized itself is very apparent once recognized, the list of attributes that go along with each of the categories has grown over the years, as we have learned more details about these murderers, and it continues to be enlarged.

When trying to figure out whether the crime has been perpetrated by an organized or disorganized offender, we look at crime-scene photographs, and, if possible, we examine information from or about the victim. For instance, we try to assess whether or not this particular victim meant a low risk for the criminal. It would be a low risk if the victim was frail or weak. Where did the victim become a victim? When Monte Rissell abducted a prostitute from a deserted parking lot in the early morning hours, he chose a victim who might not be missed for some time. Knowledge that the perpetrator would deliberately choose such a victim can be important in trying to apprehend him.

We ordinarily divide the crime into four phases. The first is the precrime stage, which takes into account the "antecedent behavior" of the offender. Often, this is the last stage about which we finally obtain knowledge, though it is the first in temporal sequence. The second phase is the actual commission of the crime; in this stage, we place victim selection as well as the criminal acts themselves, which may include far more than murder—abduction, torture, rape, as well as the killing. The third phase is the disposal of the body; whereas some murderers do not display any concern about having the victim found, others go to great lengths to avoid its discovery. The fourth and final phase is postcrime behavior, which in some cases can be quite important, as some offenders attempt to inject themselves into the investigation of the murder or otherwise keep in touch with the crime in order to continue the fantasy that started it.

The major attribute of the organized offender is his planning of the crime. Organized crimes are premeditated, not spur of the moment. The planning derives from the offender's fantasies, which, as I've shown in earlier chapters, have usually been growing in strength for years before he erupts into overt antisocial behavior. John Joubert had his crimes in mind for years before the opportunity for a slashing murder presented itself and he crossed the line into action. Rissell, too, had had violent fantasies for years before a likely victim showed up in that parking lot after the night when, in his mind, he had been spurned by his former girlfriend.

Most victims of organized offenders are targeted strangers; that is, the offender stakes out or patrols an area, hunting someone who fits a certain type of victim that he has in mind. Age, appearance, occupation, hairstyle, and lifestyle may be elements in the choice; David Berkowitz looked for women who were alone or sitting with men in parked cars.

The organized offender often uses a ruse or con to gain control over his victim. This is a man who has good verbal skills and a high degree of intelligence, enough to lure the victim into a vulnerable area. Control is of the essence for the organized offender, and law enforcement personnel learn to look for control as an element in every facet of the crime. An organized offender might offer a prostitute a fifty-dollar bill, give a hitchhiker a ride, assist a disabled motorist, tell a child that he's taking him to his mother. Since the crime has been planned, the offender has devoted time to figuring out how to obtain victims and may have perfected the ruse. John Gacy promised money to young men in a homosexual transient district in Chicago if they would come home and perform sex acts with him. Ted Bundy used his charm, but also the aura of authority that some police paraphernalia gave him, to lure young women into his car. With the organized killer, the victims are personalized; the offender has enough verbal and other interchange with the victims to recognize them as individuals prior to killing them.

The disorganized killer doesn't choose victims logically and so often takes a victim at high risk to himself, one not selected because he or she can be easily controlled; sometimes this lack of choice produces a victim who will fight back hard enough so that later the body reveals defensive wounds. Moreover, the disorganized killer has no idea of, or interest in, the personalities of his victims. He does not want to know who they are and many times takes steps to obliterate their personalities by quickly knocking them unconscious or covering their faces or otherwise disfiguring them.

Therefore, the major attribute of the organized killer is planning, which in this sense of the word means that the killer's logic is displayed in every aspect of the crime that is capable of being planned. The disorganized offender's actions are usually devoid of normal logic; until he is caught and tells us his version of the crimes, chances are that no one can follow the twisted reasoning he uses to pick his victims or to commit his crimes.

During the criminal act, the organized offender adapts his behavior to the exigencies of the situation. After Ed Kemper shot two young women on a college campus, he had the presence of mind to drive past security officers at the gate with the two dying women in his car, without alarming the officers. Though admittedly in a state of anxiety, Kemper was not on a hysterical shooting spree. He was able to adapt his behavior to the danger of getting past the checkpoint. Other murderers, less organized, might have panicked and attempted to drive through the gates at high speed, thereby attracting attention, but Kemper behaved as if he had nothing to hide and was "successful" in getting away with his crime that night. Adaptability and mobility are signs of the organized killer. Moreover, organized killers learn as they go on from crime to crime; they get better at what they do, and this shows in their degree of organization. If the police have a series of five homicides that demonstrate the same MO, we advise looking most closely at the earliest one, for it will most likely have "gone down" closest to the place where the killer lived or worked or hung out. As he becomes more experienced, the killer will move the bodies farther and farther away from the places where he abducts his victims. Often that first crime is not thoroughly planned, but succeeding ones will display greater forethought. When we see more planning in a later crime than in an early one, we know we're after an organized killer.

This leap forward in criminal expertise is an important clue to the nature of the offender. In the previous chapter, I've detailed how evidence of improved criminal behavior helped refine a profile that led to the capture of John Joubert. Another offender who improved his crimes, and steadily escalated them in violence, was Monte Rissell. Only after he was caught and convicted for a series of rape-murders did he confess that he had committed a half-dozen rapes earlier in his teenage years, rapes for which he was never caught. He began by attacking victims in the apartment complex in which he and his mother lived; later on, while at a youth facility, he forced a woman whom he abducted in a parking lot to drive to her residence, where the rape took place. Still later, he drove a car out of state to find a victim. Each time, he made it less and less likely that he would be identified as the rapist. It was only when he reversed this pattern that he was actually caught: Rissell's last six crimes, of which five were murders, again occurred in or near the apartment complex where he lived. Even in that last series of murders, there was some escalation: With his first three murder victims, he made the decision to kill them during the rapes; with the last two, he had consciously decided to kill them even before the actual abductions.

Further evidence of planning that sometimes becomes available to police investigators lies in the organized offender's use of restraints—handcuffs, ropes, and the like. Many murderers take what we call "rape kits" along when they hunt victims, so that they will not have any difficulty restraining those whom they wish to assault. The presence of a rape kit also allows the offender to have a submissive victim, something essential to his fantasies. We once assisted in the investigation of a bizarre sexual murder on a Bronx rooftop: We noticed that the murderer had not brought anything with him to immobilize the victim; he had taken his tools for that task from her own clothing and handbag. The absence of a rape kit helped us profile a killer who was not organized.

Was there a vehicle used? To whom did it belong? Someone as disorganized as Richard Trenton Chase, I had told the police when his murders were still unsolved, would most likely have walked to the scene; I was certain of this because I had decided that the killer displayed all the signs of a disorganized offender, one too mentally ill to drive a vehicle while at the same time controlling his victims. As the reader will recall, the part of the profile that really helped the police a good deal was my insistence that the killer would reside within a locus of a half mile from the site of his latest victims. Like Chase, the disorganized killer walks to the scene or takes public transportation, whereas the organized offender drives his own car or sometimes takes the victim's car. If the disorganized offender owns a car, it will often appear unkempt and in poor condition, as will his dwelling. The organized offender's car will be in proper condition.

Taking one's own car, or a victim's car, is part of a conscious attempt to obliterate evidence of the crime. Similarly, too, the organized offender brings his own weapon to the crime and takes it away once he is finished. He knows that there are fingerprints on the weapon, or that ballistic evidence may connect him to the murder, and so he takes it away from the scene. He may wipe away fingerprints from the entire scene of the crime, wash away blood, and do many other things to prevent identification either of the victim or of himself. The longer a victim remains unidentified, of course, the greater the likelihood that the crime will not be traced back to its perpetrator. Usually the police find the victims of an organized killer to be nude; without clothing, they are less easily identified. It may seem a very large step from wiping away fingerprints on a knife to decapitating a body and burying the head in a different place from the torso, but all these actions are in the service of preventing identification of the victim and of the killer.

The disorganized killer may pick up a steak knife in the victim's home, plunge it into her chest, and leave it sticking there. Such a disorganized mind does not care about fingerprints or other evidence. If police find a body rather readily, that is a clue that the crime has been done by a disorganized offender.

Organized ones transport the bodies from the place that the victims were killed and then hide the bodies, sometimes quite well. Many of Ted Bundy's victims were never found. Bob Berdella, a Kansas City, Missouri, killer who, like John Gacy, abducted, tortured, and killed young boys, cut up their bodies into small pieces and fed them to the dogs in his yard; many that were so treated could never be identified.

A different dynamic seems to have been at work in the instance of the Hillside Strangler, who was later identified as two men. The victims were found, and the killers later turned out to have been quite organized offenders. Their desire seems to have been an egotistical one—to flaunt the bodies in front of the police rather than to conceal them in an effort to prevent tracing the killers through identification of the victim.

An organized offender may sometimes stage a crime scene or death scene in order to confuse the authorities. Such staging takes a fair amount of planning and bespeaks a mind that is working along logical and rational lines. No disorganized offender is capable of staging a crime scene, although the very chaos of some crime scenes later attributed to disorganized offenders may at first give rise to various contradictory theories of what has happened at the site.

When law enforcement personnel look at a crime scene, they should be able to discern from the evidence, or lack of it, whether the crime was committed by an organized or disorganized perpetrator. A disorganized crime scene displays the confusion of the killer's mind and has spontaneous and symbolic qualities that are commensurate with his delusions. If the victim is found, as is often the case, he or she will likely have horrendous wounds. Sometimes the depersonalization of the victim by the attacker manifests itself in an attempt to obliterate the victim's face or in mutilation after death. Often the death scene and the crime scene are the same for the disorganized offender; he does not possess the mental clarity of mind to move the body or conceal it.

The organized offender often takes personal items belonging to his victims as trophies or to deny the police the possibility of identifying the victim. Wallets, jewelry, class rings, articles of clothing, photograph albums—all of these, once belonging to victims, have been found in the dwelling places of organized killers after their arrests. Usually, these are not items of intrinsic value, such as expensive jewelry, but, rather, items that are used to recall the victim. These trophies are taken for incorporation in the offender's postcrime fantasies and as acknowledgment of his accomplishments. Just as the hunter looks at the head of the bear mounted on the wall and takes satisfaction in having killed it, so the organized murderer looks at a necklace hanging in his closet and keeps alive the excitement of his crime. Many take photographs of their crimes for the same purpose. Sometimes trophies of the crime, such as jewelry, are given to the killer's wife or girlfriend or mother, so that when she wears it, only the killer knows its significance. John Crutchley was convicted only of kidnapping and rape, but I believed his actions to be extremely similar to those of an organized serial killer: He had dozens of necklaces hanging on a nail in his closet. Though Monte Rissell stole money from the purses of his rape and murder victims, he also took jewelry from them and kept it in his apartment. He further extended his fantasy involvement with the victims by driving their cars for hours after he had killed them.

The disorganized murderer doesn't take trophies; rather, in his confused mental state, he may remove a body part, a lock of hair, an article of clothing, and take it with him as a souvenir whose value cannot be discerned.

As I have said earlier, all these crimes are sexual in nature, even when there is no completed sexual act with the victim. Truly organized killers generally complete a sexual act with a living victim, taking full advantage of the situation to rape and torture before murdering someone. Even if they are impotent in ordinary circumstances, while they are punching, slashing, strangling, and whatever, they are able to have sex, and they do. The disorganized killer often does not complete the sex act, or, if he does, completes it only with a dead or entirely inanimate victim. The disorganized killer kills quickly, with a blitz style of attack. The organized offender seeks to increase his erotic interest through keeping the victim alive and performing perverted and destructive acts on the victim. Power over the victim's life is what this type of offender seeks. John Gacy brought his victims near death several times before the actual murders, so that he could enjoy their suffering while he raped them. During rapes, the organized offender demands that the victim display submissive behavior and act fearful and/or passive. If a victim fights back, the organized offender's aggressive behavior usually becomes heightened, sometimes so much that a man who had originally planned only on raping a victim escalates his violence into murder when the victim resists.

In stages three and four, the organized offender takes steps to hide the bodies of his victims, or otherwise attempts to conceal their identity, and then keeps track of the investigation. He does so in order to elongate the time period in which his fantasy seems to be in control of events. In one particularly egregious case of postcrime fantasy, the killer was a hospital ambulance driver. He would kidnap his victims from the parking lot of a restaurant and transport them elsewhere for rape and murder. Unlike many organized offenders, he would leave the bodies in locations that were only partially concealed and then would call the police and report seeing a body. As the police rushed to the location of that body, the offender rushed back to the hospital so that when the call from the police came to the hospital for an ambulance to be dispatched, he would be in a position to answer that call. He derived especial satisfaction from driving the ambulance to the dump site, retrieving the body that he himself had killed and transporting it back to the hospital.

Organized and disorganized killers have very different personalities. The ways in which those personalities develop, and the behavioral consequences of those developmental patterns, are often important to unraveling a crime.

The disorganized offender grows up in a household where the father's work is often unstable, where childhood discipline is harsh, and where the family is subject to serious strain brought on by alcohol, mental illness, and the like. By contrast, our interviewing of murderers found that the organized killer's childhood was characterized by a father who had steady and stable work but where the discipline was inconsistent, often leaving the offender with a feeling that he was entitled to everything.

The disorganized offender grows up to internalize hurt, anger, and fear. While normal people also internalize these emotions to some degree—that's necessary in order to live together in a society—the disorganized offender goes far beyond the norm in his internalization. He is unable to let off steam and lacks the verbal and physical skills for expressing these emotions in the proper arenas. He can't be easily counseled because he can't tell the counselor very much about the emotional turmoil inside him.

Part of the reason for unexpressed anger within the disorganized offenders is that they are not normally handsome people. They don't appear attractive, as measured by others, and they have a very poor self-image. They may have physical ailments or disabilities that make them different, and they are not comfortable being different. Rather than accepting their disabilities, they believe themselves to be inadequate, and they act in an inadequate manner, thus reinforcing their hurt, anger, and isolation. Disorganized offenders tend to withdraw from society almost completely, to become loners. Whereas many organized killers tend to be reasonably attractive, outgoing, and gregarious, the disorganized ones are incapable of relating to other people at all. Therefore, the disorganized offender will most likely not be living with a member of the opposite sex and probably not even with a roommate. If they live with anyone else, chances are it will be a parent, probably a single parent at that. No one else will be able to stomach their strange ways, so the disorganized offender is alone, possibly a recluse. Such offenders actively reject the society that has rejected them.

Commensurate with these disorganized offenders' poor self-image is that they are underachievers. In general, they are less intelligent than the organized offenders, but most are not seriously deficient. However, they never live up to their potential, either in school or in the workplace. If they work at all, it will be at a menial job, and they are habitually disruptive because of their inability to get along with other people. They also accept that they underachieve. When the killer of the young woman on that Bronx rooftop was questioned by the police, he said he was an unemployed actor. That was wishful thinking. Actually, he was an unemployed stagehand—certainly by his own lights an underachiever in the theatrical profession.

By contrast, the organized offender, rather than internalizing hurt, anger, and fear, externalizes them. This is the boy who "acts out" in school, who does aggressive and sometimes senseless acts. In years past, the public has believed that all murderers have been disruptive and outwardly violent in their childhoods, but that stereotype is applicable only to the organized offender. The disorganized boy is quiet in school, maybe too quiet; often, when he is caught for a heinous crime, teachers and fellow students from his childhood hardly remember him. And when his neighbors are interviewed, they characterize him as a nice boy, never any trouble, who kept to himself and was docile and polite. On the other side of the coin, the organized offender is recalled by everyone from his childhood as the bully, the class clown, the kid who made people notice him. As opposed to being loners, organized offenders are gregarious and they like crowds. These are the guys who pick fights in bars, who drive cars irresponsibly, and who are described throughout life as troublemakers. They may land jobs that are above menial labor and commensurate with their intelligence and then act out in such a way as to provoke a confrontation that will result in their being fired. Such stresses often lead to their first murders. A former Ohio police officer in the midst of job troubles, difficulties with the law, and woman troubles abducted a young woman and, almost by accident, murdered her. With disorganized killers, this important factor, the precrime situational stress, is often absent; their crimes are triggered by their mental illness, not by events in the outside world that affect them.

Instead of feeling inferior to people, organized killers feel superior to nearly everyone. Gacy, Bundy, and Kemper all belittled the police who were too stupid to catch them and the psychiatrists who were too inept to understand them. They overcompensate, often believing themselves to be the smartest, most successful people to have come down the pike, even when they are only moderately so and not particularly distinguished except by the monstrousness of their crimes. After the crime, they often follow the progress (or nonprogress) of the investigation in the news media; the disorganized offender takes little or no interest in the crime after it has been committed.

There is another area in which the organized offenders seem to be successful: in the sack. Often, they have had multiple sex partners. As good con artists with excellent verbal skills, they are often able to persuade women (or men, in some cases) to have sex with them. They may be superficially attractive and good amateur psychologists. However, they are unable to sustain normal, long-term relationships. Their lives are characterized by having many partners, none of whom stick with them for very long. A disembowelment killer in Oregon had many affairs with women, none very deep or of long duration. Ted Bundy's main squeeze before his incarceration said that he was an unexciting sex partner. Most if not all of the organized killers have tremendous anger toward women, often expressed in the belief that a certain female is not "woman enough" to "turn him on." The ranks of organized offenders contain many rapists who beat up women, they reported, because the women did not stimulate them to orgasm.

Organized offenders are angry at their girlfriends, at themselves, at their families, and at society in general. They feel that they've been mistreated during their entire lives and that everything is stacked against them. If they're so smart and clever, why haven't they made a million dollars or—as Charlie Manson wanted—had a career as a rock star? They all believe that society has conspired to keep them down. Manson felt that had he not been in jail during his early life, his songs would have been very popular. Manson's rhetoric led his followers to believe they were stimulating class warfare by their murders. Ed Kemper believed he was taking victims from the rich and the middle class and in so doing striking a blow for the working stiffs. John Gacy thought he was ridding the world of no-account punks and "little queers. " In their murders, these men strike back not only at the individual victims but at society as a whole.

Organized and disorganized: two types of killers. Which are the more prevalent and dangerous? That's hard to answer, but perhaps we can approach an answer by means of our research and some educated guesses about modern society. Our research into murderers is acknowledged to be the most broad-based yet completed. In it, we judged two-thirds of the murderers to be in the organized category, as opposed to one-third in the disorganized; perhaps those ratios carry through in the overall population of killers, only some of whom are behind bars, as our interviewees were.

My guess is that there has always been a certain unchanging fraction of disorganized killers in society, from the earliest days until the present—men who are quite deranged and who now and again go on killing sprees that stop only when they are caught or killed. We can't do much about the disorganized murderers; there'll probably always be one or two among us. It is my sincere belief, however, that the number and percentage of organized killers are growing. As our society grows more mobile, and as the availability of weapons of mass destruction increases, the ability of the antisocial personality to realize his rapacious and murderous fantasies grows apace.

INTERVIEW WITH A CANNIBAL: JEFFREY DAHMER

PART 1

In January of 1991, about six months after I retired from the FBI, I was invited to give a course in criminal profiling and child sexual exploitation in Milwaukee, under the aegis of the University of Wisconsin and in conjunction with my former colleague Ken Lanning. This was a routine assignment for us, and I gave little thought to its consequences even after I learned from newspaper headlines about Jeffrey Dahmer's arrest in Milwaukee in the summer of 1991. Dahmer was accused of committing seventeen murders in that area and around his childhood home in Bath, Ohio. But I was certainly gratified to receive, in August, a letter from a Milwaukee detective who had attended my January course and who was actively involved in the Dahmer investigation: "I can't tell you enough how helpful the information you presented was in the recent events here in Milwaukee," he wrote. "Knowing what to look for has been of great assistance to both me and to the other investigators involved [in the Dahmer case] as well."

Later on, my involvement with the Dahmer case became more direct and personal. In the fall, I was contacted by both the defense and by a policeman who passed my vita on to the prosecution. My friend Park Dietz was going to appear for the prosecution, but in this instance my opinion differed from his and I agreed to consult for the defense. Although I did not feel that Dahmer was legally or medically innocent of his crimes, I did believe there were extenuating circumstances that made for grist for the insanity issue. In my view, Dahmer was neither a classic "organized" nor a classic "disorganized" offender; while an organized killer would be legally sane, and a disorganized one would be clearly insane under law, Dahmer was both and neither—a "mixed" offender—which made it possible that a court could find him to have been insane during some of the later murders.

It was unlikely that I would ever get to testify in this case because of the presence of expert psychiatrists on both sides. However, my view was different from that of even the most expert psychiatrists in that I specialize in the criminal aspects of behavior, not the deviant aspects of it. The idea of "Ressler for the defense" raised eyebrows. Milwaukee County district attorney E. Michael McCann, for the prosecution, vigorously opposed my potential testimony. He said in court that my former colleagues in the Behavioral Science Unit even objected to such testimony. The rumor circulated that I had sought to participate in this case. That was not true. As I have explained before, in my work after leaving the FBI I have never asked to be an expert witness in any particular case, but I have frequently been called out of the blue and asked to do so. This rumor, begun by my former colleagues in the BSU, followed me and was even brought up in a murder case in Texas in an attempt to keep me from testifying for the defense in that case. Professional jealousies last long and are hard to stamp out.

And as for testifying for the defense anywhere, I hold to the belief that an expert has only one opinion and must be prepared to give it and not to change it, no matter which side calls the expert to testify. In the Dahmer case, my position was neither for nor against Dahmer's innocence. I could not appear in support of his actions or behaviors, nor did I condone in any way his killing of seventeen human beings— but I did believe that my expertise could contribute to an understanding of the man and his crimes that would provide the necessary basis for a fair adjudication of the case. And so I agreed to work with Dahmer's attorney, Gerald P. Boyle.

I did so because of the plea that Gerry Boyle wanted Dahmer to make. On January 13, 1992, Boyle announced to the press and the court that Dahmer, who had originally pleaded "not guilty by reason of insanity" to the charges, would change his plea to "guilty but insane." The guilty-but-insane plea is permitted under Wisconsin law, though not under the laws of many other states. What it meant was that regardless of the outcome of the actual trial, Dahmer would spend the rest of his life in some sort of secure facility. If the defense won the case, that facility would be a mental hospital; if it lost, the facility would be a prison "This case," Boyle told the press, "is about [Dahmer's] mental condition."

Trying to evaluate that mental condition, I was scheduled to begin a two-day-long interview with Dahmer a week after the announcement. In preparation for that interview, I toured Dahmer's apartment, accompanied by officers of the Milwaukee Police Department, and reviewed the evidence. I studied what was then known of the man and his crimes, in order to be able to evaluate Dahmer for Boyle within the larger context of serial killers and the patterns to which they most frequently adhere.

The child of a middle-class upbringing in a small town in Ohio, Dahmer was only eighteen when he killed his first human being near his home in Bath, in 1978. Eight years went by before the urges moved him to kill again, but then the killings escalated: one in 1986, two in 1988, one in 1989, four in 1990, and eight in 1991. Finally, a young black man named Tracy Edwards escaped from Dahmer and flagged down a Milwaukee police car to help him take off the handcuffs with which Dahmer had restrained him.

In Dahmer's apartment, after his arrest, police found body parts, photographs of the victims, and many other grisly souvenirs of his murders of young men, including evidence of cannibalism and torture. Investigation showed that the police had had several chances to get Dahmer earlier, before the last handful of murders had occurred. For instance, in 1988 a young Laotian boy had escaped from his apartment, where Dahmer had lured him with the promise of money for posing for photographs and then had attempted to drug him into insensibility. Dahmer, who had previously been convicted for alcohol-related offenses, was convicted here of a sex offense that was a second-degree felony. Permitted to remain out on bail pending his sentencing, he committed another murder. When he was sentenced, it was to a year of part-days in prison and attendance at alcoholism classes, rather than to a full-time lockup. At that moment, there were many reports of young men missing from the area in which Dahmer had taken the Laotian boy, and enough pieces of evidence to specifically tie Dahmer directly to three of those missing men. But the connections to Dahmer were not made by law enforcement. (Had the authorities made good use of the FBI's VICAP crime analysis system at that time, that connection might well have been more glaringly apparent, and Dahmer might have been prevented from killing more young men.)

When Dahmer applied for early parole from his part-time prison, even his father, one of his staunchest defenders, wrote to the court objecting to Jeffrey's release before completion of a treatment program, but Dahmer was set free anyway. He then went on an ever-accelerating killing spree. The authorities had at least two more opportunities to catch up with him. On July 8, 1990, the screams of a potential victim were loud enough to force Dahmer to let the boy go, and the incident was reported to the police, along with a description of an assailant named Jeff and the address of the apartment—but no real investigation was made. And in late May of 1991, another opportunity occurred in connection with Dahmer's abduction from a mall of another Laotian boy, who happened to be the younger brother of the child who had escaped him three years earlier. This boy, too, escaped after being sexually assaulted and ran naked through the streets, where a crowd gathered and gave him assistance until the police arrived. Dahmer came to the scene some moments later. Incredibly, the police and fire units that responded to an emergency call gave in to Dahmer, who told them that the boy was his lover and was just very drunk. The cops even went back with the Laotian boy to Dahmer's apartment, where Dahmer showed them the boy's identification and one of the pictures he had taken of the boy before drugging him. The police ignored the stench in the apartment and left Dahmer with his victim; within minutes after the police had left his premises, he strangled the boy.

When finally arrested for murder in the summer of 1991, Dahmer initially tried to deny his crimes, but the mountain of evidence—a drum containing body parts, dried and lacquered skulls, hundreds of photos of victims, and so on—quickly changed his mind, and he gave fairly detailed confessions to the murders. He confessed not only to killing the young men but also to such awful practices as copulation with the corpses, cannibalism, and prolonged torture as a prelude to the murders. Dahmer tortured some of his victims by drilling holes in their skulls and pouring acid directly on their brains.

Imagine, if you will, a voice that is resonant and low, apparently laconic, relaxed and articulate, but with palpable overlays of enormous tension and attempts to control what it is that he is saying. It was a voice and a manner diametrically opposed to that of John Wayne Gacy. With Dahmer, the words are squeezed out, one or two at a time, or, at most, phrase by phrase. To encourage him to go on, I would murmur "mmm-hmm" after each phrase, but for ease of reading I have eliminated these in the transcript. Dahmer wanted to give the appearance of cooperation, and to impress me with the idea that he was looking back on what he had done with some objectivity, as though it had been another and very different person who had committed the murders.

Please keep in mind that it was not my task to get Dahmer to admit his crimes—he had already confessed—but rather to try and gain some insight into his reasons for the crimes, and into his state of mind at the time they were committed. At the outset of our conversation, I tried to impress on Dahmer that he was in a unique position to provide information that would be helpful in preventing the future crimes of others, and that would be of prime assistance in helping attorney Boyle prepare to properly defend him in court. With the preliminaries over, we started right in on his earliest memories of violence.

RESSLER: This goes back to Bath, Ohio, with your first human offense, of taking a life. Prior to that time . . . ?
DAHMER: There was nothing.
RESSLER: No assaults, anything like that?
DAHMER: No. Violence against me. I was attacked for no reason.
RESSLER: Give me a short rundown on that.

DAHMER: I was up visiting a friend's, and was walking back home in the evening, and saw these three seniors in high school approaching. I just had a feeling that something was going to happen, and sure enough, one of them just took out a billy club and whacked me on the back of the neck. For no reason. Didn't say anything, just hit somebody. And I ran.

RESSLER: I imagine that was pretty frightening to you.

DAHMER: Yeah.

RESSLER: Did that stick in your mind for a long time?

DAHMER: Not until . . . yeah, it did, for about a year.

RESSLER: So this was the first time that you were involved in any kind of violence, and you were the recipient. Let's go back and discuss your family, the breakup of your family. It's hurtful to a lot of people, to people that have done what you have done, and that becomes an element in your life, as well. So let me ask you: Was there ever a sexual assault against you by any member of your family at any time?

DAHMER: No.

RESSLER: Inside or outside of the family?

DAHMER: No.

RESSLER: So that was not a factor in your case. Now, I've read about your interest along the lines of dissecting animals and things of that nature. When did that start?

DAHMER: About fifteen or sixteen. It was off and on.

RESSLER: That was after you had been hit by those guys, right?

DAHMER: Er—yes.

RESSLER: Did it start with a biology class in school?

DAHMER: I think it did. We had to do—we were dissecting a baby pig.

RESSLER: And how would you describe your fascination with, uh, dismemberment [Dahmer chortles], with the animals, y'know?

DAHMER: It just was . . . well, one of them was a large dog found by along the side of the road, and I was going to strip the flesh off, bleach the bones, and reconstruct it, and sell it. But I never got that far with it. I don't know what started me on this; it's a strange thing to be interested in.

RESSLER: Yeah, it is.

DAHMER: It is.

Some interviewers might try to be objective when dealing with a person in this situation, thinking that by doing something else—either showing agreement with him or revulsion at his acts—they would stop the flow of his conversation. My technique is different. When something is strange, and it feels appropriate in the moment to say so, I express that overt judgment. In this instance, I think, it helped Dahmer to feel as though I, too, was looking back with amazement on the odd things that he had somehow been involved in and from which he now wanted to distance himself.

RESSLER: Now about the dog, there was something about a head on a stick out behind your house?

DAHMER: That was just done as a prank. I found a dog and cut it open just to see what the insides looked like, and for some reason I thought it would be a fun prank to stick the head on a stake and set it out in the woods. And brought one of my friends back to look at it and said I'd stumbled upon that in the woods. Just for shock value.

RESSLER: Uh-huh. And how old were you then?

DAHMER: Probably . . . sixteen.

RESSLER: What year was that?

DAHMER: Around late seventies.

RESSLER: That's interesting.

At that time, I was at the FBI Academy in Quantico but retained ties to the Cleveland area, where I had worked as an agent for several years. Cops in Ohio forwarded a set of photographs to me, which depicted dismembered and beheaded animals on sticks, in a circle, situated in a wooded area. They wanted to know whether this reflected cult or Satanic activity and asked if I could provide any clues as to the sort of personalities that might be involved in such activity. There wasn't enough information for me to really come up with anything at that time. I thought it was adolescents messing around. During my interview with Dahmer, though, I became unnerved by the idea that I might have had a glimpse into the developing mind of someone who would later become one of the nation's worst serial killers—and I hadn't known it. Even if I had called attention to the possibility that the perpetrator of the dog-head circle was someone who might later become a full-fledged danger to society, nothing would have happened because the perpetrator was just a juvenile, and his crimes had not yet become fully developed. During the interview, I asked Dahmer whether he had really been involved in this doghead circle, and he denied it had any significance.

DAHMER: I wasn't into any occult then; it was just a prank.

RESSLER: So you weren't involved in any sort of thing with a group of these heads?

DAHMER: No. Where was it located?

RESSLER: Somewhere south of Cleveland.

Now we were ready to head into the more serious territory, that of the murders themselves. Note, in the following section, how Dahmer applies magical thinking to the story of how he came upon his victim—as though events conspired to just sort of make it happen. This kind of thinking tries to absolve the thinker from responsibility for his actions. He has a scenario in his mind, a pickup of a hitchhiker, and when it begins to happen in real life, he feels he is swept up in it and has to complete the final parts of it.

RESSLER: You're about eighteen years old when this first murder takes place? Just kinda give me a rundown on that. This guy was a hitchhiker, right?

DAHMER: I had been having, for a couple of years before that, fantasies of meeting a good-looking hitchhiker, and [dramatic pause] sexually enjoying him.

RESSLER: Did that come from any movie or book or anything like that?

DAHMER: It didn't; it just came from within.

RESSLER: From within.

DAHMER: And that just happened to be the week when no one was home—Mom was off with David, and they had put up at a motel about five miles away; and I had the car, above five o'clock at night; and I was driving back home, after drinking; and I wasn't looking for anyone—but, about a mile away from the house, there he was! Hitchhiking along the road. He wasn't wearing a shirt. He was attractive; I was attracted to him. I stopped the— passed him and stopped the car and thought, "Well, should I pick him up or not?" And I asked him if he wanted to go back and smoke some pot, and he said, "Oh, yeah." And we went into my bedroom, had some beer, and from the time I spent with him I could tell he wasn't gay. I, uh, didn't know how else to keep him there other than to get the barbell and to hit him, over the head, which I did, then strangled him with the same barbell.

RESSLER: Okay, stop right there. You said that the fantasies—you had the fantasies for several years? That would go back to—first stage—when?

DAHMER: Sixteen.

RESSLER: Do you have any idea at all, in your recollection, of what would start bringing this type of fantasy to mind, of actually taking somebody physically by force or—was killing involved, too? Taking a life?

DAHMER: Uh, yeah. It all—it all revolved around having complete control. Why or where it came from, I don't know.

RESSLER: Did you feel inadequate in relationships with people, like you didn't, couldn't have relationships that would endure?

DAHMER: In the township where I was at, homosexuality was the ultimate taboo. It was never discussed, never. I had desires to be with someone, but never met anyone that was gay, that I know of, so that was sexually frustrating.

RESSLER: Okay. You say that the guy was going to leave, and you didn't particularly want him to leave, and that hitting him was a way of delaying him. You took the barbell and what, rendered him unconscious? And what transpired after that?

DAHMER: Then I took the barbell and strangled him.

RESSLER: And after that? Had there been sexual activity before then?

DAHMER: No. I was very frightened at what I had done. Paced the house for a while. Ends up I did masturbate.

RESSLER: Were you sexually aroused by the event? By having him there?

DAHMER: By the captivity.

Dahmer keeps trying to shock me with his homosexuality and his perverse sexual gratification, but I am not going to allow that to happen. On the other hand, I do want him to know that I am following his reasoning and understand it.

RESSLER: Now he's unconscious, or he's dead, and you have him, and you know he's not going anywhere, and that was a turn-on?
DAHMER: Right. So later that night I take the body to the crawl space. And I'm down there and I can't get any sleep that night, so I go back up to the house. The next day, I have to figure out a way to dispose of the evidence. Buy a knife, a hunting knife. Go back the next night, slit the belly open, and masturbate again.
RESSLER: So you were aroused at just the physique?
DAHMER: The internal organs.
RESSLER: The internal organs? The act of evisceration? You were aroused by the cutting open of the body?
DAHMER: Yeah. And then I cut the arm off. Cut each piece. Bagged each piece. Triple-bagged it in large plastic trash bags. Put them in the back of the car. Then I'm driving to drop the evidence off a ravine, ten miles from my house. Did that at three o'clock in the morning. Halfway there, I'm at a deserted country road, and I get pulled over by the police. For driving left of center. Guy calls a backup. Squad. Two of 'em there. They do the drunk test, I pass that. Shine the flashlight on the backseat, see the bags, ask me what it is. I tell 'em it's garbage that I hadn't gotten around to dropping off at the landfill. And they believe it, even though there's a smell. So they give me a ticket for driving left of center—and I go back home.

A peripheral note: I recalled this description by Dahmer of bagging the body in regard to a case in Japan, where body parts were discovered in separate trash bags in Tokyo's Inokashira public park. There, the disposal seemed unique and worthy of great comment and wonder. But such a method had been used by Dahmer and by several other serial killers in the United States. What seems highly unusual to one observer is often not unusual at all—just something about which most laymen have little knowledge.

RESSLER: Were you nervous when they stopped you?
DAHMER: That's an understatement.
RESSLER: Well, they apparently didn't perceive your nervousness, though, to the point of pursuing the bags, or anything like that. They just got into a routine.
DAHMER: Yeah.
RESSLER: And then you did what with the bags?
DAHMER: Put them back, under the crawl space. Took the head, washed it off, put it on the bathroom floor, masturbated and all that, then put the head back down with the rest of the bags. Next morning—we had a large buried

drainage pipe, about ten feet long—put the bags in there, smash the front of it down, and leave it there for about two and a half years.

RESSLER: When did you come back for it?

DAHMER: After the army, after working for about a year in Miami. When the rest of the family was away, while they were at work, I opened up the drainage pipe, took the bones, smashed them into small pieces, scattered them in the underbrush.

RESSLER: Why did you smash the bones?

DAHMER: To make a final end of it. The necklace he was wearing, and the bracelets on him—I drove about five miles away, and threw them over a bridge into a river.

RESSLER: You didn't keep anything from that event?

DAHMER: No. Burned the clothes.

RESSLER: Okay. I don't want to go through every one of them, but there are some that I want to zero in on because I have questions.

In the following section, Dahmer speaks not only about his next homicide but about his particular sexual orientation. Hearing what he said, I was reminded of the British serial killer Dennis Nilsen, whose relations to his male victims also took the same kind of turn—a refusal of penetration and the use of the victim's body as a sexual object rather than as that of a consensual sexual partner, an action that indicated a far less normal sexual orientation than conventional homosexuality. Nilsen said in a Central Television interview that for him the most exciting part of the sex-and-murder pattern was the moment when he lifted the dead victim and saw the dangling limbs, which represented Nilsen's power and control over the victim and the victim's passivity.

RESSLER: The very next homicide, that would occur when?

DAHMER: Nineteen eighty-six. I invited one guy I had met in front of a gay bar back to the Ambassador Hotel, just for a night of thrills and sex. And I was already using the pills on people.

RESSLER: What type of drugs were you using?

DAHMER: [A prescribed sleeping medication], sleeping pills.

RESSLER: How did you get into that?

DAHMER: I'd been going to the bath club for a while, and a lot of the people I met wanted anal sex, and I wasn't interested in that, and I wanted to find a way to spend the night with them, enjoy them, without having to perform that, and because I worked third.

RESSLER: And so it becomes a matter of control?

DAHMER: Yeah. And because I worked third shift, I went to the doctor, told him I had trouble sleeping during the day. He prescribed that, and I started using it.

RESSLER: Is that why you asked for the prescription? To get a sleeping potion?

DAHMER: Mmm-hmm.

RESSLER: And then you began to experiment with it in the bathhouse, by passing it on to people?

DAHMER: Mmm-hmm. Using about five pills.

RESSLER: What'd you—put it in a drink or something? And how'd you find it affected them?

DAHMER: Usually rendered them unconscious, for about four hours.

RESSLER: What was the normal dosage?

DAHMER: One.

RESSLER: So you're jacking it up five times, going for a quick effect?

DAHMER: Mmm-hmm.

RESSLER: How long did it usually take for them to go out?

DAHMER: A half hour.

RESSLER: So you'd have to entertain them for a half hour until they'd conk out. My understanding is you got into some difficulty at the bathhouse?

DAHMER: They complained about me, used the excuse that I was an alcoholic [to have Dahmer excluded from membership].

RESSLER: Was it your conscious design to learn how to use these drugs?

DAHMER: Right. And to have control over people without hurting them.

RESSLER: Did you have thoughts at that time of getting somebody back to your house?

DAHMER: Not at all! That's why I started using the mannequin. Did you know about that? I wanted to find a way to satisfy myself without hurting anyone.

RESSLER: So the mannequin was a substitute, then?

DAHMER: Right. It started gradually, going to the bookstores, drinking again, and it was just an escalation.

RESSLER: Were you trying to stay away from that stuff?

DAHMER: Yeah. For about two years. In about '83, I started going to church with my gramma. I wanted to straighten my life out. Went to church, read the Bible, tried to push out any sexual thoughts at all, and I was doing pretty well for about two years. Then one night I was sitting in a local library, reading a book, minding my own business, and this young guy comes up and throws a note in my lap and quickly walks away. It says, "Come down to the lower level bathroom and I'll give you a blow job." And I thought—"This was ridiculous, it would take more than that to"—and I laughed it off, didn't think much of it. But sure enough, after about two months, I started, the compulsion, the drive. Increased sexual desires. I started drinking again. Going to the bookstores. At that time I was pretty much on top of the urges, but I wanted to find a way to satisfy without hurting anyone. So I joined the bath club, went to the gay bars, and tried to satisfy with the mannequin. And there was the graveyard incident. I read the obituaries about an eighteen-year-old who had died. I went to the funeral home, viewed the body; he was attractive.* When he was buried, I got a shovel and wheelbarrow, was going to take the body back home. About midnight I went up to the graveyard, but the ground was frozen, and so I abandoned that idea.

RESSLER: What got you into the idea of getting a corpse?

DAHMER: The mannequin deal didn't satisfy. Didn't work. So I started going to the bath club. Worked, for a while. Then when I was kicked out of the bath club, I started hanging around the bars.

RESSLER: Did you find it was pretty easy to get people out of the bars to go with you? Pretty routine: end of the night, you pair up with someone?

DAHMER: Right. And he was a nice-looking guy. Asked him back to the hotel room. We drank, I was drinking this 151 proof rum, rum and Coke. Made him the drink. He fell asleep, and I continued drinking that, and I must've blanked out because I remember nothing before waking up in the morning. He was on his back, his head was over the edge of the bed, and my forearms were bruised, and he had broken ribs and everything. Apparently I'd beaten him to death.

RESSLER: You have no recall of having done that?

DAHMER: I don't recall doing that and I had no *intention* of doing that. I remember looking for the empty bottle of 151. *That* was missing. Out the window, or something: I didn't even know what happened to that.

RESSLER: So that was a blank-out?

DAHMER: A *total* blank-out.

Belief that they do not have a memory of the moment of killing is common among multiple murderers, although often the opposite is true—they cannot forget the moment of murder, get gratification from the act, and want to repeat it. Conventional psychiatric explanations of stress and trauma concur with this notion, that a dissociative state is induced at the moment of greatest tension, and this causes a blackout. Note that the situation is very similar to that of murders by John Gacy, but while Gacy told me that he had no idea of how a dead body got into his room or house, Dahmer, who couldn't remember the murder in the hotel room, nonetheless believed he had committed it.

RESSLER: So you wake up in the morning, and he's dead. And what do you do from there?

DAHMER: Extremely horrified. I had no intention of doing anything. So I hit upon this idea that—I had to do something with the body. Put him in the closet. Go down to the Grand Mall, buy a large suitcase, with wheels on the bottom. Put him in that. Get the room for another night. Sitting around horrified, wondering what the hell I'm going to do. Then the next night, that following

---

*Dahmer told me later, when the tape was not rolling, that at the funeral home he had become so excited that he had gone into the bathroom and masturbated.

night about one o'clock in the morning, I check out, get a taxi, have the guy help me put the bag in the back, ride to Gramma's. I take the suitcase, put it in the fruit cellar, and leave it there for about a week.

RESSLER: And it didn't produce any smells, or—?

DAHMER: No, because it was November. Cold. And it was during Thanksgiving week, I couldn't do anything with it because relatives were coming.

RESSLER: Why did you feel compelled to take the body with you? Why not just leave it in the room?

DAHMER: Because the room was in my name.

RESSLER: Now what if [the room] was in his name, would you have just left the body?

DAHMER: Definitely.

RESSLER: Okay, so you keep the body down there for about a week. What's your next step?

DAHMER: When my Gramma goes to church for a couple hours, I go down and get it; take a knife, slit the belly open, masturbate; then deflesh the body and put the flesh into bags; triple-bag the flesh, wrap the skeleton up in an old bedsheet, smash it up with a sledgehammer; wrap it up and throw it all out in the trash on Monday morning. Except the skull. Kept the skull.

RESSLER: How long did you keep that?

DAHMER: About a week. Because I put it in undiluted bleach. That cleaned it, but it made it too brittle, so I threw it out.

RESSLER: Weren't you concerned with putting these things in the garbage? The garbage men could have found out—caused problems, right there?

DAHMER: Didn't know how else to do it. That's why I triple-bagged it. After that, my moral compass was so out of whack, and the desire, the compulsion, was so strong, that I just continued with that mode.

RESSLER: Did Gramma ever get any wind of anything unusual going on?

DAHMER: Just some bad smells that she complained of.

RESSLER: Now, at one point you leave Gramma's. Why did you do that?

DAHMER: Well, I just thought that after spending eight years with her, by that time, I felt it was time to get my own place, where I wouldn't be so restricted. I continued the month's rent, did the yard work, shoveling snow, and she made me meals, so when I got my own place, it worked out nicely. We helped out each other.

RESSLER: And the first place you got was—?

DAHMER: Twenty-fourth Street. And that's when I took that picture of [the first Laotian victim]. I never intended to hurt him.

RESSLER: This was a young guy, wasn't he? How old was he?

DAHMER: Thirteen, fourteen. I thought he was older. You know, Asian guy can be twenty-one, and still look like he's a young kid.

RESSLER: Yeah, they can. What prompted that?

DAHMER: It was Sunday morning. Walking along the street. Wanted some sexual

activity. Saw him. An attractive guy. Offered him fifty dollars for some pictures. He agreed. I took two pictures, gave him the drink, and thought he was
out. He got away, and the police came.

RESSLER: So that backfired on you? You were arrested and all. That's a matter of
history.

DAHMER: Mmm-hmm. We went back, the detective and I, to the apartment. They
did a search. They never did find that skull I had, in a lower chest of drawers
in the hallway. But they did find everything else.

RESSLER: How did they miss that?

DAHMER: It was under clothes and all. So they missed the bags back in Ohio, and
now, missed the skull.

RESSLER: Sloppy police work. If they'd found that, it would've changed things
considerably, huh?

DAHMER: Yeah. And getting out of the hotel room like I did. Not too usual. Luck.

In the following interchanges, note how Dahmer deliberately misconstrues
what I am speaking about. I am saying that the willingness of gay men to take up
with strangers is a dangerous practice for them—but he perceives all mention of
danger as talk about danger to himself, not to others.

RESSLER: The majority of your victims came from the gay bars, gay districts.
What do you think of their willingness to take up with strangers? Would you
not consider this to be dangerous behavior?

DAHMER: I had thought of that, but the compulsion overrode everything.

RESSLER: It seems that you had worked out a pretty good scheme for getting
people to go with you. Pretty predictably, if you would go out in the evening
and you had this on your mind, you pretty well knew you'd score?

DAHMER: Right.

RESSLER: But sometimes it didn't work. Why?

DAHMER: Well, sometimes—very seldom—I'd get very drunk, and come back with
someone who wasn't as attractive as I'd thought they were, and I'd have a hang-
over in the morning and they'd leave. Other times I wouldn't have them killed,
but I just don't want to be with them. That happened three or four times. Other
nights, I didn't want anyone, and I'd just go back and watch a video, read.

RESSLER: You didn't have that many videos, did you?

DAHMER: I must've spent thousands of dollars, over the years, on pornographic videos.

RESSLER: But the police didn't find very much in the way of a collection?

DAHMER: As the years went on, I'd winnow out the tapes and magazines that
didn't really appeal to me, my tastes. Aside from the porno films, the Jedi
films [Star Wars trilogy], the figure of the Emperor, he had total control, fit
in perfectly with my fantasies. I felt, by that time, so completely corrupt that
I identified completely with him. I suppose a lot of people like to have complete control; it's a fantasy a lot of people have.

RESSLER: This concept of dominance and control. Would you say that it escalated, from the second victim on up to the last?

DAHMER: Mmm-hmm.

RESSLER: And you start perfecting your technique of getting people back to the house and—?

DAHMER: It became the drive and focus of my life, the only thing that gave me satisfaction.

RESSLER: You mentioned that you had dabbled in the occult. Was this an attempt to tap more power?

DAHMER: Yeah, but not serious. Made some drawings. I used to visit occult bookstores, get materials, but I never used any rituals with the victims. I probably would have, six months later, if I hadn't been arrested.

RESSLER: I have a copy of one drawing you made. Now, this is pretty much fantasy, huh?

DAHMER: It would've been real, another six months.

Dahmer wanted to construct what he called variously a "power center" or a "temple," composed of a long table on which he would place six skulls. Two complete skeletons would flank the table, one at either end, supported by a stand or suspended from the ceiling. A large lamp would come from behind the center of the table and extend six blue globes of light over the skulls. Statues of chimeras would complete the scene. My purpose was to build an environment from which Dahmer could tap into another level of awareness or being, in order to attain success in love and finance.

RESSLER: You wanted to buy the equipment, all that stuff?

DAHMER: Well, I already had the lanterns, skeletons.

RESSLER: Did you ever think you could tap any power beyond—?

DAHMER: I was never sure. I had no experience doing it, but . . .

RESSLER: The maintaining of the skeletons, the skulls, the hair, the body parts—tell me, what was behind that?

DAHMER: The maintaining of the skulls was a way to feel that I had saved at least something of their essence, that I wasn't a total waste in killing them. The skeletons I was going to use for the temple, but that was never the motivation in killing them, that was an afterthought.

RESSLER: Why would you think that a deceased part would maintain control, maintain a relationship? Because they're rather inanimate, and—?

DAHMER: It didn't. But I was fixated on this aspect of it.

RESSLER: It seems that you always had a problem with people leaving you.

DAHMER: They were all one-night stands; they made it clear that they had to be back to work. And I didn't want them to go.

RESSLER: Was that realistic? Did you ever think of instead of the violent ends of these things, of latching on to somebody with a mutual interest, and doing it on a permanent basis? A marriage of sorts?

DAHMER: I couldn't do that. Once I was at the apartment, I was already deep into a mode of doing things and I never met anyone that I felt I could trust in that kind of relationship.

RESSLER: So the fact that you were into this type of behavior—you couldn't share that with anyone?

DAHMER: No.

RESSLER: How about discarding it? Starting fresh, with a partner?

DAHMER: I was thinking about doing that very thing, the night of my arrest. I had everything ready to put acid on.

RESSLER: Is that why you bought those four boxes of acid?

DAHMER: Never used it. Sixteen gallons.

RESSLER: That's why: to dispose of everything, shut everything down?

DAHMER: I didn't know. I knew I had to move out of the apartment, and I was debating whether I should keep the skulls or just abandon everything.

RESSLER: Did you have any feeling of loss with the thought of getting rid of this stuff?

DAHMER: A great deal. That's why I was so torn over should I do it or not.

RESSLER: On the other side of the coin: had you met somebody whom you enjoyed, was compatible with you, and who would consensually set up living arrangements, and you could have gotten rid of all the stuff, could you have done that? Even after, say, the tenth, twelfth, fourteenth victim?

DAHMER: The person would have bad to be totally compliant, willing to do whatever I wanted, and there just aren't many people like that.

RESSLER: That's true.

DAHMER: And if I had met, like, one of the guys that did a striptease act, maybe, but it's awfully hard to find somebody like that.

RESSLER: So you're saying to me that you would have preferred that, but it wasn't possible to find somebody who would agree to that type of arrangement?

DAHMER: I didn't have much time to go looking. I was working six days a week, I had time restrictions, and I wanted something right away.

At this point in the conversation, rather than continue discussing how he might have pursued a more conventional homosexual relationship, Dahmer chose to tell me that on one occasion when he made a pickup, it was *he* who had been drugged, so drunk that he found himself tied up and with a wax candle stuck in his anus. Too drunk to remember what his assailant looked like, he did remember feeling like a victim, although he claimed that neither the abduction nor the sense of being a victim had any effect on his later crimes. I ended this digression by returning to the main issue, his deadly techniques. I asked him about attempting to turn people into zombies by drilling holes into his victims' heads—with a power drill—and injecting mild acid into their brain cavities by means of a turkey baster. His intent was to kill the intellect of the victim and to keep their bodies alive and compliant. This action seemed to me the ultimate expression of Dahmer's inability to relate in any normal way to another human being. Interestingly, Park Dietz and I had consulted to the plaintiff—a victim's family—in a civil case against Berdella, which came to trial in 1991–92. In that case, the murderer had also attempted to turn his victims into what he called "sex toys." Berdella had injected animal tranquilizers that he had obtained from veterinary medicine supply houses.

RESSLER: When the zombie thing didn't work with the first guy, did you try it again?

DAHMER: I figure I'd try it again, and double-dosed him, and that proved to be fatal. There was no strangling involved in those. Then I tried [to inject] boiling water. Later he woke up, felt groggy. I gave him more pills, went back to sleep. Did it the next night, left him there during the days.

RESSLER: Did you leave him tied up, or—?

DAHMER: No, just lying there. Then he died that night.

RESSLER: Expired. How about [name of another victim]?

DAHMER: Gave him the first injection while drugged, went for a beer, came back and—

RESSLER: Was this before or after the police got there?

DAHMER: Before. The first injection was before. He left the apartment. They brought him back, thought he was drunk, I gave him the second injection, and that turned out to be fatal.

RESSLER: Was that immediate, or—?

DAHMER: Immediate.

RESSLER: Now, the last victim—

DAHMER: He was the brother of the one that [I'd photographed]. I was just walking in the mall, ran into him, didn't know him from Adam—how many are the chances of that happening? Astronomical.

RESSLER: Yeah. Lots of the cards in alignment, for some unknown reason. That last one is important; let's go through it from A to Z. You encountered him where? In the mall? Did you go to the mall often, for contacts?

DAHMER: No, just to drink beer and eat pizza. I was on my way out of the mall, he was on his way in, I offered him fifty dollars, took two pictures of him while we were there, gave him the drink, did the drilling.

RESSLER: How deep did you go with the drilling?

DAHMER: Just through the bone. Injected him, he was sleeping; went for a quick beer across the street before the bar closed; and I was walking back and saw him sitting on the sidewalk, and somebody had called the police. I had to think quickly, and told 'em that he was a friend that had gotten drunk, and they believed me. Halfway up a dark alley, at two in the morning, with police coming one way and fire trucks coming the other. Couldn't go anywhere. They ask me for ID, I show 'em ID; they try to talk with him, he answers in his native tongue. There's no blood showing, they checked him out and figured he was real drunk. They told me to take him back; he was not wanting to go back and one officer grabbed him on one arm, the other officer grabbed him on the other arm, and they walked him up to the apartment.

RESSLER: Did they examine him, look for wounds?

DAHMER: Not really. He had had just a slight scrape. They laid him on the sofa, looked around the apartment. They didn't go into my bedroom. If they had, they would've seen the body of [a previous victim], still lying in there. They saw the two pictures that I'd taken earlier, lying on the dining room table. One of 'em said to the other, "See, he's telling the truth." And they left.

Here we have the evidence of a classic tragedy unfolding. When the police walked away, Dahmer then killed his victim—and after that, he killed several more before he was apprehended. A little bit of training and education in criminal personality profiling and crime scene assessment would have gone a long way toward making sure that police did not make the sort of classic mistake that permitted Dahmer to kill this young man. However, while I do fault the police for not understanding the situation with the "drunk" young victim, and for doing only a cursory examination of Dahmer's apartment, a search that missed all the evidence that was only inches away, it is important to realize that in this situation Dahmer was very persuasive, intelligent enough to be able to convince the police that nothing beyond the ordinary was happening at his residence or in his relationship to the young man. Many serial killers are persuasive charmers. After several hours on the first day, we decided to continue the interview in a second session, the next day. The remainder of our interchanges is the subject of the following chapter.

PART 2

In our second session, I tried to probe more specifically for information about the relationship of his fantasies to the process of killing. Many serial killers, for instance, keep trophies or souvenirs of their victims, Dahmer had done this to a point far beyond that reached by other killers. As we began, I noted to Dahmer that he had many posed pictures of slim-waisted male models on his apartment walls, and told him that I assumed these were men he did not know, who were, in essence, fantasy mates for him. He agreed with my characterization. I then asked him whether the noses in his photographs of the victims replicated some of those on the walls.

DAHMER: That was just to accentuate their physiques.

RESSLER: Before and after death, right?

DAHMER: Right.

RESSLER: Now, what did that mean to you?

DAHMER: It was just a way to exercise control and to make them look the way I wanted them.

RESSLER: Keeping these photos then was important to you as well.

DAHMER: I'd use them to masturbate.

RESSLER: And you had a lot of 'em. And you didn't hide them, they were lying out on a table, and—?

DAHMER: I did before; but by that time [of the arrest] I was getting so sloppy that . . .

RESSLER: Where would you hide them before?

DAHMER: I had a small box that one of my alarms came in, and I'd put them in there.

RESSLER: But eventually you had them out, lying around? And the police saw them?

DAHMER: No, they were in a drawer.

RESSLER: I notice you also kept drivers' licenses. Why did you hang on to them?

DAHMER: Well, the number of victims was increasing, and I just hadn't gotten around to disposing of the stuff.

RESSLER: And you almost had assembled an entire skeleton?

DAHMER: Yeah. But the glue didn't work, and I was going to put the parts together with tin, but I didn't get around to it.

RESSLER: But that was the plan, huh? Part of that power thing?

DAHMER: Right.

Many a serial murderer develops a sense that he cannot be caught, especially if the authorities have missed all the clues he has inadvertently or sometimes even intentionally left behind. This feeling intensifies when, as Dahmer did, he appears to have momentarily triumphed over the authorities. He develops an attitude of personal omnipotence: he has committed the ultimate crime and gotten away with it, and the evidence seems to show him that he can continue to do so. This attitude is critical to his success and to his downfall. It keeps him going for a long time, but eventually it makes him become careless; that is the point at which he is usually caught.

RESSLER: To go back to the boy in the apartment, after the police left, did you not think you were going to have some trouble?

DAHMER: I didn't think so, no.

RESSLER: Did you think it was over? Didn't you think it was dangerous, they might come back, and now you'd have the kid in the apartment? Have to get him out of there real quick?

DAHMER: He was already . . . damaged, so I decided to kill him and take my chances.

RESSLER: And how soon did you dismember and get rid of the body?
DAHMER: The next day.
RESSLER: How long did that take?
DAHMER: About two hours.
RESSLER: Is that all?
DAHMER: I'd become good at it. Always a messy job. Worked quickly.
RESSLER: Always in a bathtub?
DAHMER: Right.
RESSLER: And you got rid of it. Did a lot go down the toilet? And you never
    clogged it?
DAHMER: No, I never did clog it.

Dahmer's perverse pride of workmanship and matter-of-fact recital of such grisly details are enough to make anyone's stomach turn—but it was only by staying with him through these matters that I could hope to get him talking enough to allow me to gain more insight into his personality and strange deeds. I knew enough to speak of dismembering people in bathtubs because I'd studied killers such as Nilsen and Berdella, who had used such techniques to facilitate their crimes. Sometimes, in these cases, medical examiners will marvel at the precision with which the killer has done a dismemberment and recommend that investigators look for a perpetrator who would be a medical doctor or a butcher. They are generally wrong in their recommendations, having missed an important psychological point. When a killer removes himself from the horror of his crime and the humanity of his victims, he is able to dismember without the emotional baggage that a normal person would carry with him to the process of, say, cutting off a person's arm. When we cut off a chicken's leg in the process of preparing our dinner, we don't think of the human ramifications of the act. So serial killers who have reached the point of dehumanizing their victims can dismember them in that same disinterested way.

I asked Dahmer whether he had ever read anything about other serial killers such as Gacy. He said he had not learned about Gacy until he, Dahmer, had already killed several people. I was not sure whether or not he was lying because killers often read about the crimes of other killers, taking from these both satisfaction that other people have acted in this manner and sometimes learning techniques as well.

Note how when I ask him whether he has tortured his victims, he purposely declines to acknowledge that pouring acid on a brain would be considered torture by most normal thinking human beings.

RESSLER: Were any of these kids tortured?
DAHMER: Never. Never.
RESSLER: It was always the eliminating of their consciousness through drugs and
    eventually death—?

DAHMER: I wanted to make it as painless as possible.

RESSLER: When did most of the sexual activities occur?

DAHMER: After drugging.

RESSLER: Do you think it was realistic, to keep them in that state?

DAHMER: Not drugged, no. That's why I started drilling. 'Cause drugging was not working.

RESSLER: Did you have any problem with hurting? When they were conscious and hurting, was that a problem?

DAHMER: That's why I couldn't go through with it with [name of victim].

RESSLER: With the hammer?

DAHMER: With the mallet . . .

RESSLER: Did you hit him hard?

DAHMER: Yeah. I hit him hard.

RESSLER: But it didn't render him unconscious?

DAHMER: No. And he ended up calling the police. But they didn't believe him. And he was a couple miles from my place before I carried him back. No. I just talked him down. I had the knife with me, but I couldn't bring myself to use it.

At this point in the conversation, Dahmer almost suddenly escalates into an explanation of his cannibalism.

RESSLER: Did you ever do any biting?

DAHMER: Uh, yeah. With the first one on Twenty-sixth Street.

RESSLER: Could you tell me about that?

DAHMER: Well, after he was dead I did bite the neck.

RESSLER: Just once?

DAHMER: Hard.

RESSLER: Did you ever repeat that? And what was behind that, the motivation?

DAHMER: Uh, perverse sexual practice.

RESSLER: And did you repeat that?

DAHMER: No.

RESSLER: Just the one time?

DAHMER: Uh-huh. Except for the eating.

RESSLER: And what was behind that?

DAHMER: Just the feeling of making him part of me.

RESSLER: Where did that come from? Did you read about it somewhere?

DAHMER: No. It was internal. Oh, I may have read about cannibalism somewhere, but it didn't—It was just another step, escalation.

RESSLER: What victim did that start with?

DAHMER: M. He was after [the Laotian]. I think the third one at the apartment.

RESSLER: That would make it Number Seven or so.

DAHMER: I guess.

RESSLER: How did this come about?

DAHMER: During dismemberment. Saved the heart. The biceps. Decided to put—cut 'em into small pieces, washed 'em off, put it in clear plastic freezer bags, and put 'em into my storage freezer, just as an escalation, trying something new to satisfy. And I would cook it, and then look at the picture and masturbate.

RESSLER: Afterwards? Did that have any sort of positive effect, that ritual?

DAHMER: Mmm-hmm. It made it feel like they were more of a part of me. Sexually stimulating.

RESSLER: Okay. When you put the heart aside, and that stuff—did you repeat that with any others?

DAHMER: Just . . . the last guy. Saved the heart and biceps.

RESSLER: Did you eat the heart later?

DAHMER: No. Arrested.

RESSLER: But there was a sexuality attached to that?

DAHMER: Right.

Sometimes it is best to start a discussion of difficult matters with just an initial foray and then to digress to other subjects before returning to the main one. Dahmer had something in particular he wanted the world to know, and I encouraged him to talk about it.

RESSLER: So you never had any interest in children? Your preference was what?

DAHMER: Fully adult males.

RESSLER: About your own age?

DAHMER: Mmm-hmm.

RESSLER: White, black, and brown.

DAHMER: That's the thing. Everybody thinks it's racial, but they were all different. The first one was white, the second one was American Indian, third was Hispanic, the fourth was mulatto. The only reason I picked blacks was because there were a lot of 'em in the gay bars, and I always ran into a lot of 'em.

RESSLER: The area you canvassed was within walking distance of your house? And that area is predominantly black?

DAHMER: Black and Hispanic. If I could've struck up a conversation with a white, very good-looking type of guy, I would've taken them back [to the apartment]. But I never did. Seven of them were black, of the seventeen.

RESSLER: So it really was an area thing, not—?

DAHMER: Yeah. I hope that can get cleared up.

RESSLER: Have you been hassled in the jail about that, black guys hassle you?

DAHMER: Yeah. They think it's . . . a racial thing.

We went on to discuss his elaborate security system, his system of locking up evidence such as photographs in boxes, his careful wrapping of body parts in freezer bags. He was concerned with the apartment being broken into and his trophies discovered. Yet there were several occasions on which people had come into the apartment and seen what could be incriminating evidence.

DAHMER: Yeah, [the building manager] came in, opened the freezer, saw the meat. But it was packed and I told him it was store-bought. And then one time another guy got murdered in his apartment, and the detective questioned me about that, came into the apartment.

RESSLER: They actually came into the apartment? Talked to you about that? As a witness?

DAHMER: Right. And I thought he was questioning me as though it was something that I had done. But he didn't see anything.

RESSLER: How about with the apartment manager? Wasn't there something in the refrigerator?

DAHMER: Not at that time, although with M—— I hadn't finished the dismembering because I had to go to work, and half his body was still in the bathtub. There was a smell. The manager called the police, middle of the night, while I was at work. They kicked down the door, the apartment door, two doors down from my apartment, thinking someone had died in that.

RESSLER: I'm getting the impression that a lot of people look at things and don't know what they're seeing, like with the trash bags in the back of the car. And the police were not well enough trained. Like with the [second] Laotian boy, if the police had been trained to be a little more observant, that one would have been over, right then, wouldn't it?

DAHMER: Probably.

RESSLER: What if, that particular night, [the police] had indicated that, well, "We have to look into your bedroom"—would you have allowed them to look in?

DAHMER: I wouldn't have had any choice.

RESSLER: What would you have done if they had asked for your consent? "I'd like to take a look through the house. Mind if I look through the house?"

DAHMER: I would have made up some story that I had—uh—pictures back there that I'd feel embarrassed to let him see and try to bluff my way out.

RESSLER: So you wouldn't deny him or refuse him, just try to convince him not to go back there?

DAHMER: Try to convince him.

RESSLER: Where did you get that degree of calm? In situations like that, people start trembling, and—?

DAHMER: I was, the first time that they came . . . uh, I don't know.

RESSLER: You seemed to remain fairly calm, outside, with the Laotian kid; you were fairly cool and collected.

DAHMER: It was such an overwhelming situation that I don't know where I got the sense of calm, I don't know!

RESSLER: Did you feel like it could be over right then?

DAHMER: Oh, yeah, I was pretty sure about that, the way the cops were acting.

RESSLER: But your only alternative was to run like hell, and that wouldn't have been—?

DAHMER: Not too smart. And I couldn't do that.

RESSLER: When the apartment manager came in, several occasions, did he not? The smell? How did that go?

DAHMER: I'd either blame it on the freezer or the fish tank.

RESSLER: The fish tank? Was that plausible?

DAHMER: I didn't think it was, but he seemed to believe it.

When Dahmer opened a closet and the manager smelled the contents of a thirty-gallon plastic trash barrel filled with the acid solution in which Dahmer has been dissolving bones, the manager almost passed out. Dahmer told the manager that was where he put the bad water from the fish tank, and the man believed him. Shortly thereafter, Dahmer threw out the trash barrel, with its contents, and obtained a huge blue oil drum.

RESSLER: What was in that?

DAHMER: The headless torsos.

RESSLER: Now, what was the idea, was this blue tank kind of a holding tank, for processing them later?

DAHMER: For the acid. To work on the torsos.

RESSLER: Were you going to dispose of those torsos, or make skeletons of them?

DAHMER: They were to be disposed of.

RESSLER: Were you going to keep parts, or bones?

DAHMER: No. Everything that went in there was to be disposed of.

RESSLER: For disposal. Okay. Why did you keep souvenirs of certain ones, and not others?

DAHMER: Well, early on, I saved things because I hadn't done the acid technique. Later on, I saved all the skulls, except two. I tried to dry them out in the oven, but the temperature setting was too high and they just flaked.

RESSLER: What do you mean, flake?

DAHMER: After an hour at 120 degrees, I heard this popping noise. Opened the door, and the bones were all in flakes because the moisture inside came out too quickly. So those were ruined. The others, I kept. And there were two complete skeletons.

RESSLER: What was the idea of the lights?

DAHMER: Those were blue globe lights. I turned the top light off so you'd have an eerie, dark feeling to the setting—just for the effect.

RESSLER: That would've been some sight!

DAHMER: Like in the Jedi movies.

RESSLER: This spray-painting of skulls. What was behind that?

DAHMER: To give them a more uniform look. After a matter of weeks, some of them wouldn't be as white as others, and it was just an artificial look, something like for a commercial.

RESSLER: I saw pictures, and they almost did look like a commercial venture. Did you stand those out at all? Have them out?

DAHMER: Long ago. One time I brought a guy back from Chicago, he saw them, thought they were store bought.

RESSLER: Was he concerned about 'em?

DAHMER: He asked me was I into the occult, and I said no, I just bought 'em through the decades.

RESSLER: And he accepted that? He was the only one who ever saw 'em?

DAHMER: Mmm-hmm. A nice-looking guy. Bragging about how he won the leatherman contest in Chicago.

RESSLER: Keeping everything in the apartment—bones, skulls, body parts, the heads—weren't you concerned that somebody would get into the apartment?

DAHMER: I was. That's why I went to great lengths with the security system.

RESSLER: Some of the people, the bottom of the feet were chopped away. What was behind that?

DAHMER: That was simply to give the acid more surface area to disintegrate the flesh, because the bottom of the feet are usually pretty tough.

Dahmer was somewhat amazed that I asked about this and that I seemed to understand his need to do this in order to efficiently dispose of the bodies. He suggested that I would have made a good serial murderer. I responded that I'd been around murderers a long time, and we shared a laugh. I then tried to use the apparent camaraderie to press on to obtain information on practices that Dahmer had not discussed with others. For instance, drawing on my knowledge of the progressions in other murderers, I postulated that Dahmer might have tried to drink blood from his victims. He admitted that he had tried it, out of "curiosity," but hadn't liked the experience nor found it stimulating—and his criterion for continuing any practice, I knew, was finding that it excited him.

We went on to discuss two instances that did not end in homicide. In the first, a young man survived "the drink" at Gramma's, and Dahmer let him go, but the man later needed hospitalization and reported the incident to the police, who did not follow up very well. Here is the verbatim story of the second.

RESSLER: How about this kid that you whacked with a hammer?

DAHMER: He left in a rage, said he was going to call the police. Came back, fifteen minutes later, knocked on my outside door. Let him in. Said he needed money for the phone or the taxi or something. Thought that was incredible. That he came back—d'you believe that?

RESSLER: Instead of going to the police or—?

DAHMER: I was afraid of letting him go again, so we scuffled on the living room floor for about five minutes. We were both worn out. I talked him down. We sat in the bedroom until seven in the morning. I tried to calm him down; he said he wasn't going to call the police anymore. We both walked up to Twenty-sixth and Wisconsin, I called him a taxi, and that was the last I saw of him.

RESSLER: Pretty amazing that he didn't report it.

DAHMER: He did, but he gave them some wild story that I had conked him, and they didn't believe him.

Frequently, a murderer will try to assign blame for his deeds on drinking or drugs. While intoxicants can certainly relieve people of inhibitions, they are almost never the "cause" of murderous actions. However, questions about drugs and alcohol often enable a murderer to speak more readily about the deadly deeds.

RESSLER: Booze has really been a problem in your life, hasn't it?

DAHMER: It has. That was my way of handling the home life. The divorce. And the hits. I drank to blot out the memory. It worked for a while. And it worked even better in the army.

RESSLER: Were you always drinking when victims were picked up?

DAHMER: Mmm-hmm.

RESSLER: But not to the point of losing it? Because you say you like to control your environment. If you drink too much, you'd lose control.

DAHMER: Right. I stuck to beer.

RESSLER: When you went out to meet someone, did you start drinking before then?

DAHMER: Yeah. Beer. And then throughout the evening I'd drink.

RESSLER: And then coming back, and, say, before the actual killing?

DAHMER: I always had beer in the freezer.

RESSLER: And afterwards?

DAHMER: Mm-hmm. Right.

RESSLER: When you were cutting the bodies up? Still drinking?

DAHMER: Still drinking.

RESSLER: So you were keeping yourself in a kind of, in a semi—?

DAHMER: Lubricated state.

RESSLER: Did you feel like that was necessary?

DAHMER: It seemed to make it easier.

RESSLER: Did you receive gratification from the actual cutting?

DAHMER: At first I did, but it got to be routine.

RESSLER: And the sexual activity after death?

DAHMER: Pleasurable.

RESSLER: How about doing the cutting up?

DAHMER: It wasn't as pleasurable as having them whole.

I asked whether he knew what he was doing was wrong, for instance, with the first victim, the hitchhiker. He agreed that he had known it was wrong, which partially explained why nearly eight years elapsed between that first victim and the second. The murder had been "reality," even though it had meshed with the fantasy, and, Dahmer said, it had "scared the hell out of me." He noted that this murder had come just a few months after the breakup of his family, about which he had been very "depressed."

RESSLER: Did you always, right up to the last, know that this was definitely wrong?

DAHMER: Oh, yeah.

RESSLER: Did you ever reach a point where you said to yourself, "This is absolutely crazy"?

DAHMER: Getting out of control? Yeah. At the point where I started doing the drilling. That was the twelfth, or something like that.

RESSLER: At that point you knew you were—?

DAHMER: Getting to be too much.

RESSLER: Losing it?

DAHMER: Yeah.

RESSLER: But did you say to yourself, "I'm not going to do this again"?

DAHMER: No, I wanted to try to use it to get that zombie technique.

RESSLER: Why do you think dominance, control, power over others was so important to you? To the average person, those are important factors, but not to carry it to the extent that you have.

DAHMER: If I'd had normal interests and hobbies, like sports or something like that, if I hadn't been so obsessed with doing what I was doing, it probably wouldn't have been as important. But why I had that, I don't know. [*Long pause*] It would make life more attractive, or fulfilling.

RESSLER: Okay. But it's power and control—out of control, y'know what I mean? D'you realize today that that was not realistic?

DAHMER: Now I do.

RESSLER: Did you ever reach a point of self-doubt, where you said that "what I'm trying to attain, I'm never going to attain"? "Just spinning my wheels, here"?

DAHMER: It seemed like that, after the drilling technique started. But before that, no.

RESSLER: Did you feel that, when the drilling started, you were going to be caught?

DAHMER: No. I thought I could avoid detection. It was after losing the job that my dominos started to fall.

RESSLER: That was not much before your arrest?

DAHMER: Maybe a month.

RESSLER: Why did you lose your job?

DAHMER: Because I called in one night—I had that black weightlifter with me. I thought I had one more day of sick leave, but I didn't. So I decided to spend the night with him, thought I'd still have a job in the morning. But that did it.

We had an extended discussion about his having called in sick. I pursued this point because it was my belief that the dates of Dahmer's sick leaves should have been coordinated with missing persons reports in order to determine if there were other possible victims whose murders he had not confessed. Also, I pursued it because of my belief that employer records of patterns of sick leave (and ordinary vacation leave) of suspects ought to be consulted in all instances where a rash of murders or rapes has afflicted a community.

We returned to the main subject: Dahmer's practices with the dead bodies. He had tried to keep facial masks, following some instructions in a taxidermy magazine, but the result "turned a bit moldy," so he threw it out. He had the fantasy of putting together a complete skeleton, varnishing the bones, putting in hooks and eyes to permit the bones to be linked to one another. I pointed out that he could have bought such a skeleton at a medical school supply store, but he said that if he'd done that, the result "wouldn't be a remembrance—it would have been a stranger." He was interested in the skeletons, the skulls, and other parts as elements in the "power center" he fantasized about making. What, I asked, was the purpose of this power center?

DAHMER: I would've tried to develop some sort of incantation or ritual, to tap into power, spiritual power.
RESSLER: At this point, what do you think of the whole idea?
DAHMER: Ridiculous. That's become obvious.
RESSLER: So you would have placed yourself in the chair, focused on the scene, and then what—meditate?
DAHMER: Right. At that time, I thought that sort of thing might be possible, but I didn't know.
RESSLER: What's the thing about the yellow contact lenses?
DAHMER: The two central characters in both of those films [*Return of the Jedi* and *Exorcist III*] had glass tints to their eyes that exuded power. And that was part of the fantasy.
RESSLER: You actually wore these [contact lenses], did you not, sometimes?
DAHMER: Only in the bars.
RESSLER: Did people comment on it?
DAHMER: They noticed it. Said the eyes were nice-looking. I didn't get a sense of power from wearing them, but it fit in with my fantasy.

We discussed what I characterized as certain "careless mistakes" that he had made—going out for a beer when the Laotian boy was asleep, which allowed the boy to get out to the street. Dahmer admitted that this was a mistake, and so were such things as allowing bloodstains to remain on the wall in his apartment. That had come, he said, from a "quick puncture to an artery" of one man, before the victim was dead: the artery had spurted more than he had thought it would. This had also resulted in stains on the rug. Dahmer contended that he was "so deep into it" that none of these things really bothered him. He had had the rug cleaned several times, and told the cleaner that the red stain was colored food dye from part of his work—a lie that the cleaner did not question.

I moved on to victim selection. The people Dahmer picked up from malls or on the street were not always gay. He said that hadn't mattered because he had been looking for physique, and in any case, the sexual activities that he performed were not consensual and took place while the victim was unconscious or dead. He said that one of every three he approached in a mall would agree to come back to his place and be photographed, while in the gay bars the proportion was two out of three. With one of the latter, Dahmer mixed up the cups of "the drink," drank it himself, and later woke up to find the partner gone and that he had made off with three hundred dollars of Dahmer's money.

I proceeded to go through the entire list of the murders to find clues to his state of mind at the time of each. The key event seemed to me to have been what happened in the Ambassador Hotel murder in 1986. I asked him what was going on in his life at that moment in time.

DAHMER: By then I had given up trying to resist the desires, but I was just meeting people, bringing 'em back, and taking the [prescribed sleeping medication]. Just having a night of sex with them. There was no violence in my thoughts at all.

RESSLER: This was at your grandmother's?

DAHMER: Yes, I was living at Gramma's.

RESSLER: So you'd tried to resist for a while, but you did give in to it?

DAHMER: Yeah. So I'm just going to the bars, bookstores, the bath club.

RESSLER: But this particular time, you wake up and the guy is dead. From that time to January '88, there's a couple of years' spread, but from January '88 to March '88, there's only a two months' spread. After the Ambassador one, did you find that pleasurable—

DAHMER: No.

RESSLER: —or frightening?

DAHMER: Frightening.

RESSLER: For what reason?

DAHMER: It was totally unplanned; it was a total surprise to me that it had happened.

RESSLER: Then the one in January '88, the first one. Was there a plan involved before you went out and did that one?

DAHMER: No. I hadn't been planning on meeting anyone, but he just happened to be there at the bus stop. And I didn't even bother going to the bars that night. I was planning on going to the bars and doing some drinking . . .

RESSLER: So you didn't go out with a plan of finding someone and bringing them back?

DAHMER: The plan was just drinking. And going home. They had a striptease act.

RESSLER: And him coming back to Gramma's with you, what was that—just chain of events?

DAHMER: Yeah. We got undressed. Just laid around. Body rubs. Masturbated. And I—uh—found him attractive enough that I wanted to keep him. So I just made him the drink, and that was that.

Note again how in the mind of the killer the event seems at least partially precipitated by the actions of the victim that the death is at least partially the fault of the victim. My next series of questions was designed to learn whether a particular murder had been planned or spontaneous. We went through them in temporal sequence. The next one was March of 1988.

RESSLER: Where did you encounter him?

DAHMER: Couple bars. I had been drinking all night, and I was on my way out, and he was standing in the doorway, and that's when I saw him and made the offer.

RESSLER: And then back to Grandmother's, and the drugging, and all?

DAHMER: Same scenario, mm-hmm.

RESSLER: When you were bringing him back to Gramma's, did you think how it was going to end up?

DAHMER: Mm-hmm.

RESSLER: At that point, you know what's—?

DAHMER: At that point, there's no doubt—the scenario . . . mm-hmm.

RESSLER: So then a year goes by. We're talking March of '89. At that point, when you go out, are you looking for somebody?

DAHMER: I was. Yeah. I was. It was at the end of the night. Bar closing. I was on my way out. He starts up a conversation with me, which was . . . unusual. And I ask him if he wants to go back, and we do—and it's the same, after that.

RESSLER: You were planning to do this?

DAHMER: Yeah. Yeah. I was looking for someone to come back with.

RESSLER: Did you know homicide was going to occur?

DAHMER: When I met him, I did. Not before. Like I said, I was on my way out, and he made a pass at me.

The next murder occurred fourteen to fifteen months later. What, I asked, were the circumstances of that one?

DAHMER: Met him in front of a bar. He was a male hustler, very good looking. Offered him money, we went back, and—same scenario.

We entered upon a period of discussing names, dates, locations, circumstances, with Dahmer answering "Right" or "Mm-hmm" or "That was Milwaukee" to my questions. It was chilling to hear him respond with such offhandedness, as though we were checking off items on a laundry list to see whether everything had come back from the cleaners. For instance, on one murder, Dahmer condensed the acts of premeditation, hunting, and murder to the following terse statement: "I was going out to look for someone, but didn't know if I'd meet anyone; and I did, and then I planned it." Dahmer knew precisely where and under what circumstances he met his victims and had not forgotten their names or descriptions. The most important psychological point was that he described as "planned" those murders where he went trawling for a victim and "spontaneous" as those where he more or less accidentally met someone, although he made his pickups in places where such arrangements are often done and therefore had a reasonable expectation that a pickup might occur.

RESSLER: When you went to Chicago, did you go there to meet someone?
DAHMER: Yeah.
RESSLER: Did you think it would result in homicide?
DAHMER: Yeah, probably.

I asked about the role of fantasy in his preparation for murder. For serial killers, the problem is that reality—the actual killing of a victim—never lives up to their best fantasies. The fantasy is always better and is continually being refined and perfected so that it stays one step ahead of the killings. I asked Dahmer whether, in the midst of the series of murders, he had fantasized greatly about what was to happen before he went out to hunt for a victim.

DAHMER: Just . . . using pictures of past victims. The videotapes, the pornography videotapes, the magazines. I didn't have any elaborate fantasies before I went out.
RESSLER: But there was a continuation [of the fantasy by] using these things, the skulls, things of that nature?
DAHMER: Right.
RESSLER: Was there a point at which the pictures and parts weren't cutting it, and there was a desire to go out and do it again? Was that a conscious thing, that you were desiring to—?
DAHMER: Yeah. It was. The pictures weren't as fulfilling as actually having someone there.
RESSLER: So the pictures and pornography were just something that you could [use to] fill in the gaps between—
DAHMER: Right.
RESSLER: Between events.
DAHMER: Right.
RESSLER: What were your feelings during viewing the bodies and dismemberment?

DAHMER: Viewing the pictures wasn't as good as having them there, but it gave me a feeling of satisfaction that at least I had something to remember them by.

RESSLER: Toward the end, when things are starting to pile up, did the burdens outweigh the satisfactions?

DAHMER: Toward the end, yeah. With . . . [name of victim].

RESSLER: Were you getting tired of the routine?

DAHMER: That's why I was using the drum.

I asked him again about his sexual preferences—if all things had been equal, what sort of person he would have wanted as a sexual partner.

DAHMER: I would have liked to have, like on the videotape, a well-developed white guy, compliant to my wishes. I would have preferred to have him alive and permanently staying with me.

RESSLER: Would he be out working, out in the world, or just there for you?

DAHMER: Just there for me.

Less preferable, but still desirable, Dahmer said in answer to other questions, was to put someone in the "zombie state." Going down the scale, he then said he would have preferred "what I'd been doing," hunting men in bars and bringing them back for murder. Down further on the scale of desirability, though, he said there was "nothing." Not ordinary homosexual sex, not heterosexual sex, but just no partners. Or, perhaps, pornography.

RESSLER: Beyond that?

DAHMER: Celibacy.

RESSLER: Without mental anguish or harassment contributing to that—?

DAHMER: Celibacy, no sexual activity at all.

RESSLER: No urges, no compulsion.

DAHMER: Right. Which was the state I was trying to get myself in during those two years when I was going to church with Gramma.

RESSLER: So you were consciously trying to attain that, knowing it would keep you out of trouble?

DAHMER: Right, right.

RESSLER: When these killings were going on, did you feel in any way like they were justified, like you had a right to do what you were doing?

DAHMER: I always tried to not get to know the person too well. Made it seem like it was an inanimate object. Depersonalized them. But I always knew it was not the right thing to do. I had feelings of guilt.

RESSLER: Did you ever think that the other person had done something wrong, and you were justified in—?

DAHMER: No. That's what Palermo, the state psychologist, thought I was doing it to rid the world of evil people, and no, I never felt that way.

RESSLER: None of this deep psychological stuff, eh? It's not always that way. Maybe Palermo's read my book.

We shared a laugh, and the sessions were over. Dahmer agreed to meet with me for future interviews and research once the trial was over. He seemed to have enjoyed my company. I told him to take care of himself and that he smoked too much. He replied that perhaps he would get cancer and die of it, and that would solve everybody's problem of what do with him.

It was clear to me from the interview that Dahmer would have to be incarcerated for the remainder of his life but that the more appropriate setting for holding him away from society would be a mental hospital and not a prison. He was mentally ill, though at times he appeared to be sane and rationalized his behavior.

Our society does not seem to recognize gradients in mental illness—when someone is crazy, we expect that person to be wild-eyed, drooling at the mouth, and never in control of his faculties. But there are insane people who can frequently appear to be functioning, sane human beings, even though deep down, at a fundamental level, they are beyond sanity: Dahmer, in my view, was one of those people.

My sessions with Dahmer served, along with those of psychiatrists, as a basis for his defense, though through legal maneuvering and horse trading I was not called to take the stand during the trial itself.

During the proceedings, Milwaukee County district attorney E. Michael McCann argued that Dahmer had been sane during his killings because, ghoulish though his actions were, he knew what he was doing at all times, and he knew right from wrong and even went to great lengths to conceal the murders because, McCann charged, Dahmer had known they were wrong. Among the expert witnesses appearing for the prosecution was Dr. Park Dietz, who described Dahmer as sane because of the amount of premeditation that went into his choosing and pursuing victims and the amount of control he exhibited in fooling the police, disposing of the bodies, and so on.

Gerry Boyle for the defense argued that though Dahmer was aware of what he was doing, and knew right from wrong, he was unable to conform his actions to what he knew was right. Boyle went beyond this generalization on insanity to contend that Dahmer suffered specifically from necrophilia and thus was legally not responsible for his actions and should be committed to an institution for the mentally ill. However, the tactic of saying specifically that Dahmer suffered from necrophilia backfired because the prosecution was able to point out that Dahmer had had sex with some victims while they were still alive and had used a condom. The prosecution was also able to focus on the issue of control, saying that Dahmer had controlled his impulses well enough so that he only killed when and where he wanted to. The law of Wisconsin is fairly explicit in holding that when someone is in control of his actions, he is to be considered sane.

The jury full of laymen essentially agreed that a crazy person must act in a crazy manner most of the time or else not be considered truly crazy. Therefore, they judged Dahmer to have been legally sane at the time of his crimes. With such a judgment already made, the jury then had to find Dahmer guilty of fifteen murders, and he was sent to prison for fifteen life terms, an estimated 936 years. There is no death penalty in Wisconsin.

He remained in prison for several years, during which, according to attorney Boyle, he refused to accept special protection and insisted on being out in the general population. At the end of November 1994, he was murdered by a black inmate—as he had feared he might be. In a prison bathroom, Dahmer was bludgeoned to death by Christopher J. Scarver, who was also serving a life sentence for murder. Scarver had been convicted even after telling people that a family of voices told him that he was the Son of God and which people he could trust and not trust.

Many people felt that Dahmer's violent death was a fitting end to him, while others, including some editorial writers, were annoyed that Scarver had cheated the public out of its right to have Dahmer suffer for many more years for the crimes he had committed.

In my opinion, neither Dahmer nor Scarver should ever have been in a prison, but both should have been permanent residents of a mental institution.

The real problem is that people like Dahmer present a dilemma for society, which has not evolved proper ways to deal with them. Focusing on notions of right and wrong does not begin to approach the complex reality of what Dahmer did. In the 1970s, when I asked serial killer Edmund Kemper whether his personality and problems were covered in DSM-II, Kemper thought his problem would not be covered until the DSM was in its sixth or seventh edition—which would not be published until well into the next century.

SEXUAL FATALITIES

Robert R. Hazelwood, P. E. Dietz, and Ann W. Burgess

Roy Hazelwood served not only eleven years in the US Army, attaining the rank of major, but also twenty-two years in the FBI, sixteen in the Behavioral Science Unit at the FBI Academy. He holds a BS in sociology and an MS in counseling and guidance, and he performed a one-year fellowship in forensic medicine.

Today, Roy is a consultant on violent crime in both criminal and civil cases. In addition to being retained by United Nations as a consultant on the Bosnian war crimes, he has lectured in all fifty states, in numerous European countries, and throughout Canada and the Caribbean. Roy has conducted and published research on autoerotic fatalities, serial rape, juvenile sexual offenders, sexual sadism, and the wives and girlfriends of sexual sadists. He has testified as an expert witness in both criminal and civil trials, and his testimony has been accepted in city county, state, and federal courts. Roy has also testified before committees of the US Senate and the US House and before a presidential commission.

Hazelwood has published more than forty articles in peer-reviewed journals and has coauthored five books. He has also contributed chapters to five books and currently serves on the editorial review boards of four professional journals. He is currently an affiliate professor of administration of justice at

Published in a slightly different form as "Sexual Fatalities: Behavioral Reconstruction in Equivocal Cases," *Journal of Forensic Science* 27, no. 4 (October 1982): 763–73. Copyright © 1982 by the *Journal of Forensic Science*. Reprinted by permission.

George Mason University, and he has previously served as an adjunct faculty member of the University of Virginia, a member of the associated faculty with the University of Pennsylvania and the technical faculty of the Southern Police Institute, and a faculty member of the FBI Academy and the US Army Military Police School.

Roy has received awards and/or certificates from more than sixty organizations representing the academic, mental health, and law enforcement communities. His academic awards include Distinguished Alumni from Sam Houston University. He was twice awarded the prestigious Thomas Jefferson Award for research from the University of Virginia. Today, he is frequently interviewed by the media and has appeared on numerous television programs, including New Detectives *(Discovery),* American Justice *(A&E),* NBC's Dateline, FBI Profilers *(The Learning Channel), and the Law Enforcement Training Network.*

During the late 1970s, it became apparent to me as part of my work in the Behavioral Science Unit at the FBI Academy that research studies were urgently needed in the exploding phenomenon known to us profilers as autoerotic, or sexual, fatalities. Spanning a broad range, such deaths occur as a result of or in association with sexual activity, including deaths from natural causes during intercourse or masturbation, autoerotic asphyxia deaths, and lust murder. In most cases, homicide investigators can ascertain with a high degree of certainty who did what to whom and why thorough ordinary investigative techniques. But in a few cases, the manner of death—suicide, murder, or accidental—is more elusive.

In March 1982, Ann Burgess, a professor in the School of Nursing at Boston University; P. E. Dietz, an associate professor of law at the University of Virginia; several colleagues; and I published an article in the *Journal of Forensic Science* titled "Sexual Fatalities: Behavioral Reconstruction in Equivocal Cases" in which we attempted to provide postmortem behavioral analysis and reconstruction aid in what happened in three sexual deaths that showed ambiguous or conflicting evidence of manner of deaths. Our focus, of course, was on the partners and their intents. Needless to say, such equivocal cases could never be resolved with 100 percent certainty. However, the three of us felt that our behavioral analyses and reconstructions enhanced by years of experience with related cases that we assisted in solving was sound as we investigated the death scenes and relevant settings and interviewed the survivors.

Between 1977 and 1982, 160 cases of autoerotic fatalities were submitted to the Behavioral Science Unit by agencies throughout the United States and Canada. Of these deaths, one hundred fifty occurred accidentally, but ten remained equivocal after a thorough investigation and analysis. They included accidental sexual deaths attributable to the use of ligatures compressing the neck, airway obstruction, various form of electrical stimulation, injurious agents causing extreme chest compression, and chemicals or gases. We were solicited by investigative agencies for opinions on the manner of death or the possibility of second-party involvement. Although provided with considerable well-documented reports that included innumerable photographs, autopsy findings, and information about the victim's history, we nonetheless spoke with families and associates of the victims, investigating officers, medical examiners, and other researchers.

In any investigation of a sexual fatality, the initial question one asks is whether the deceased was alone in committing suicide or dying accidentally. Was another person present? If so, was the death intended? These two questions involve complex issues of fact, behavior, and intent and cannot always be answered. We were not going to render our opinions in such cases without detailed information about both the scene and the victim's history.

Following are five cases of sexual fatalities: two as to whether a sexual fatality was an accident or a suicide (cases 1 and 2) and three (cases 3, 4, and 5) in which the evidence suggested the presence of another person who may have murdered. For each, allow me to present the facts. Think critically about what is known and develop a rationale for your opinion. Then read our behavioral analysis and reconstruction.

ACCIDENT OR SUICIDE?

CASE 1

A thirty-three-year-old man was discovered dead in an unfinished room on the second floor of a warehouse where he was employed as a security guard at night. He was in an upright position with his feet on the floor. A rope, attached to a wall behind him, passed over a beam approximately six feet (two meters) above him and ended in a hangman's noose, which encircled his neck. He was nude except for a black leather belt around his waist and a pair of handcuffs that passed through the belt and secured his wrists in front. A handcuff key was found in his right hand, and his left hand held his penis. Around his left ankle was a shipping tag secured by wire, and on the tag was the notation "77-0130 5/11/77." About the circumference of his penis was a surgical-like incision, which accommodated a washer. Beneath the victim, two cinderblocks rested on newspapers spread on the floor. Feces and ejaculate were on the newspapers. A cigarette butt of the type smoked by the victim was located 1.5 feet (0.45 meters) in front of him. Against a wall, to the rear of the victim and neatly stacked, were a pair of men's trousers, a shirt, and a pair of ankle boots. His service revolver and holster were also in the room. The large room was otherwise empty, with barren cinderblock walls. The victim's automobile was parked outside the warehouse; its interior was in disarray and contained several empty cans, snack cartons, and wrappers and several magazines, including *Forum* and *Oui*.

He had made a career as a peace officer and worked in this capacity during the day. Five days after discovery of the body, a box containing his badge, credentials, undershorts, and uniform was found behind some boxes on the floor below the death scene.

He had lived in a one-bedroom efficiency apartment, a search of which revealed bondage magazines. Although not unkempt, the apartment was not tidy—for example, there were dirty dishes in the sink.

The victim sometimes stayed with his wife of ten years, from whom he had been separated for six months. On the evening preceding his death, he had visited his wife and made arrangements to take their son (with whom he enjoyed a very close relationship) to the zoo the next day. According to his wife, he had appeared to be in normal spirits during the visit. His wife was the beneficiary of his life insurance policy.

In the hours preceding his death, he had called a female acquaintance at 1:30 a.m. and again at 4:30 a.m., requesting that she visit him at the warehouse, but she had refused.

At the time of his death, he was experiencing financial difficulties, working at a second job, and said to have been occupationally dissatisfied. His coworkers described him as having changed from a relatively outgoing individual to one who seemed depressed and overworked. (He worked an excessive amount of overtime to obtain additional salary.) On at least two occasions during the week preceding his death, he had made suicidal statements, such as "I ought to put a .38 in my mouth," and "I can understand why someone would kill themselves."

His wife said that approximately two years previously, he had begun practicing sexual bondage at home and had requested that she tie him up and whip him and that she allow him to reciprocate. She said that she had declined to participate.

In this case, the death scene had many features commonly found in autoerotic fatalities: secluded location, incomplete suspension, bondage, the use of a hangman's noose, nudity, and the presence of ejaculate. When further investigation uncovered the victim's history, however, the manner of death became uncertain because indicators of suicide were also present.

The victim had experienced some of the stressors and exhibited some of the behaviors commonly found among persons with suicidal intent. He was experiencing marital, financial, and occupational problems; his coworkers described him as being overworked and depressed; he had been rejected by his female acquaintance on two occasions on the very morning of his death; his possessions had been neatly placed at the scene; and he had made two suicidal statements in the week preceding his death. These are highly suggestive that the victim intended to end his life.

We believe, however, that the victim did not intend to die on this occasion but died accidentally during autoerotic activity. This opinion was derived through several considerations.

The victim's interest and involvement in sexual bondage and sado-masochistic activities are well documented by his wife's verification of his interest in bondage and flagellation for at least two years before his death. Bondage materials were found in his apartment, and at the time of his death, he was handcuffed and held the key in his right hand. Handcuffs are a common bondage device, and the key serves as a self-release mechanism. The washer fixed around his penis is a masochistic feature. At the time of death, he was totally nude except for the belt and was holding his penis in his left hand. While nudity is consistent with autoerotic fatalities, it is most unusual in suicide. The black leather belt suggests a leather fetish symbolic bondage.

Had the victim intended to take his life by hanging, it would not have been necessary to fashion so exotic a ligature as a hangman's noose; a simple loop would have sufficed. Having previously stated, "I ought to put a .38 in my mouth," he might have used his .38 revolver, which was found in the room where he died. It is probable that he kept the weapon in proximity in the event someone entered the building. Had he intended to die by hanging, he would have had no need for this weapon. He had affixed a tag to his ankle. While it may be argued that the numerals "0130" represent the time (in military hours) of the first call to his friend, there are thirteen wraps in a hangman's noose and the middle digits in the notation are also thirteen. In our opinion, the tag was a prop used by the victim in his ritualistic fantasy. In our opinion, if the victim had intended to die, he would not have hidden his uniform and identification but would have placed them where they could readily be found.

Typically, a person with suicidal intent makes plans for death but not plans for the future. In this instance, the victim visited his son on the evening preceding his death and arranged to take him to the zoo the following day. The victim's automobile and residence were extremely cluttered and contained sexual materials and bondage paraphernalia. It is unlikely that an individual would intend for such materials to be found.

Despite his separation, he had made no changes in the beneficiary of his life insurance policy. Considering the close father-son relationship, it seems likely that if he had planned to die, he would have taken steps to ensure that his preadolescent son would be financially secure.

Our reconstruction of the death scenario is that the victim was acting out an execution fantasy when he accidentally died. (Such a fantasy is not uncommon and is documented in several cases in our study.) This is evidenced by the hangman's noose, the secured wrists, the "body tag" on the ankle, and the cigarette butt immediately in front of him, representing the "last smoke."

CASE 2

A twenty-seven-year-old white man was living in a common-law situation with a woman two years his junior. They had lived together for three years. On the day of his death, she left him alone in their home while she went shopping. Upon her return, she went to the kitchen to put away her purchases and found a handwritten note on the kitchen table:

> Sharon, the obvious solution to the problem finds me hanging in the bathroom. But it won't be so awful cause in my own kinky way I'll have enjoyed the method of my demise (as will be evident by the unusual attire). Loved you. Sorry, Bill.

Upon reading the note, the woman at first thought it to be a joke and went to the bathroom. When she attempted to open the door, she found it blocked by the victim's body. After forcing the door open, she found him partially suspended by a ligature around his neck. He was clad in a pink sweater, pantyhose, panties, a brassiere, and high-heeled boots, all of which belonged to her.

She denied any knowledge of his desire to cross-dress and reported that she had never had any reason to suspect transvestism. She reported that they had had a normal sexual relationship for three years, during which he had never suggested sexual bondage or asphyxiation.

The paper on which the note was written had deep and worn creases, suggesting that it had been repeatedly folded, opened, and refolded.

The facts that the victim acted alone, was not totally suspended, and was cross-dressed indicated that his death was an autoerotic fatality. In labeling his own behavior "kinky," he indicated his awareness of the deviant nature of this sexual activity. In stating that he would enjoy the hanging, he reveals that he previously had similar experiences and found them pleasurable. These facts create a strong presumption that his death was accidental.

This presumption is overcome by the fact that the content of his note clearly implies suicidal intent. The investigating authorities properly ruled this death as a suicide. Nonetheless, the fact that the note appeared to have been repeatedly folded creates a question as to whether he may have used this note repeatedly as a "prop" for a suicide fantasy or as a farewell to his lover in the event he should die during a self-hanging episode. In any event, his note indicates that he was aware that his self-hanging created a substantial risk of death.

A QUESTION OF MURDER

CASE 3

A twenty-two-year-old single woman was discovered dead by her sister, who had been staying with the victim temporarily. The sister had been away for two days and returned on a Sunday evening at 9:00 to discover a note on the front door requesting that she be as quiet as possible, as a man was sleeping on the kitchen floor. She went directly to her bedroom and did not discover the victim until the following morning.

The deceased was found in an arched position with an electrical cord that passed over a doorknob and wrapped around her ankles and was attached to her neck via a slipknot. Her abdomen, thighs, and forearms rested on the floor, and her feet were pulled back toward her head. The right side of her head was against the door's edge, and her hair was entangled in the slipknot. She was clothed only in a blouse that she normally wore for sleeping. Commercial lubrication cream was found in the victim's vagina, and a battery-operated vibrator was found 4 feet (1.2 meters) from her body. The only trauma exhibited was a 1.5-inch (4-centimeter) contusion above and behind her right ear. The scene was not disturbed, and there was no sign of a struggle. On her bed were a series of drafted letters she had written in response to an advertisement seeking a possible sexual liaison.

Autopsy revealed no evidence of recent intercourse, and no alcohol or other drugs were detected in the body. The cause of death was determined to be asphyxia resulting from laryngeal compression.

The victim had been in excellent physical condition, had made plans for a canoe trip on the day following her death, and had recently been in good spirits. She was sexually active but was reportedly disappointed in her sexual relationships, as she had difficulty attaining orgasm. She used contraceptive cream and a diaphragm to prevent pregnancy, and these items were located in her car. Although her sister found the note at 9:00 p.m. Sunday, a neighbor reported seeing the note early that morning.

The victim's position illustrates features found in a number of autoerotic asphyxias, including interconnection of the neck with the limbs and the arching and binding of the body. Her state of undress and the presence of lubrication cream and a battery-operated vibrator indicate sexual activity.

A critical element in the resolution of this case was the fact that examination of the slipknot (self-rescue mechanism) revealed that the victim's hair was entangled in it and would have precluded its release. This observation, coupled with the contusion above the right ear and the fact that her head was adjacent to the door's edge, suggests that the victim attempted to disengage the ligature by pulling the slipknot. Not being able to do so, she thrashed about, striking her head on the edge of the door, thereby causing the contusion. The autopsy surgeon reported that the contusion would have been insufficient to render her unconscious and that it is not likely that victim could have been forced into such a position without being unconscious or leaving evidence of a defensive struggle. The question of the note on the door was never resolved. Its presence since early Sunday morning suggests that a male visitor had been there on Saturday evening. The victim's draft letter to a man, whom she had not yet met, further suggest that she was alone at the time of her death, as it is unlikely that she would have had such letters on her bed had she been entertaining a male friend there. The death was officially ruled accidental, and the matter was closed.

CASE 4

A thirty-year-old single woman was found dead in her locked apartment. She was nude and lying supine on a blanket on the bedroom floor. A pillow was beneath her buttocks, elevating them. Her legs were slightly spread, and her arms were by her sides. A blouse was lodged in her mouth and covered her face. Next to the body was a dental plate belonging to the victim. Near her left foot were and empty beer can, an ashtray, and a drinking glass. Neither the body nor the scene exhibited signs of a struggle. The victim's clothes and purse (containing her keys) were on her bed. A vibrator and leather bondage materials were found in her closet. The door was locked with a spring bolt. The autopsy indicated that she had died of suffocation.

While the body condition was consistent with either masturbation or sexual activity with a partner, the victim's sexual paraphernalia were found in her closet, not near her body. The leather bondage items in the closet suggest previous sexual bondage activity. Although we are familiar with several confirmed auto-erotic fatalities involving mechanical airway obstruction, none involves the insertion of a gag to such a depth in the oropharynx. Consultation with forensic pathologists confirmed our suspicions that it would be next to impossible for one to asphyxiate oneself in such a manner. Although the door was locked and the victim's keys were in her purse, the lock was spring-activated and would have locked upon closing. The victim's willing participation is suggested but not proved by the absence of defense injuries, signs of a struggle, or alcohol or drugs in her body. In sexual acts involving bondage or manual restraint between con-senting partners, one partner depends on the other for release, thereby allowing that person wide latitude in the act. We concluded that the death occurred during sexual activity that included use of the gag and at least one other person. It is not possible to determine whether the other person(s) intended to kill the victim. Thus, in our opinion, the manner of death was homicide, but we are unable to determine whether this was murder or manslaughter.

CASE 5

A sixty-five-year-old single man was found dead in his one-bedroom apartment while his stereo blasted hard rock music.

His abdomen was in contact with the floor next to the bed, and his arms were pulled onto the bed behind him. His wrists were tied with a short length of rope. A black leather belt tied to a telephone cord extended from his wrists to the bed headboard. The belt was too small to have been worn by the victim, and three additional belts of various sizes were also found the room. The telephone had been pulled from the wall.

The victim's feet were tied to the footboard by another piece of rope. He wore only and undershirt and an athletic supporter. A jacket covered his head, which was lying on a dresser drawer. Beneath the jacket, two knit shirts were wrapped around his head, and a white T-shirt, which had been used as a gag, was tied tightly around his head.

Resting on an air conditioner above the victim's headboard was *Penthouse* magazine, opened to a page depicting two women fondling one another. The room had been ransacked, and some personal items (such as his watch and some clothes) were missing, though expensive stereo equipment and over $600 in cash were found in the room. He had a collection of tapes of classical music, and his friends confirmed that he preferred such music.

He had been seeking information on homosexuality. And examination of a homosexual pornographic magazine found in his bedroom revealed his fingerprints on the corona of a penis pictured in the magazine as well as several smudged prints on other penes in the book.

He had a history of heart disease, and his death was attributed to airway obstruction and coronary thrombosis. During the autopsy, the victim's anus was found to be tunneled, a condition commonly present in individuals who repeatedly act as the receptive partner in anal intercourse. As noted by the medical examiner, however, this is also common in other individuals of the victim's age.

The question in this instance was whether the deceased had been murdered or had died while engaging in sexual bondage activities, either alone or with another person. The complexity and tightness of the binding were such as to have precluded his being able to tie them himself. That the telephone cord had been torn from the wall strongly suggests the presence of a second person, as it is unlikely that an individual would disable his own telephone to obtain bondage materials. The T-shirt used to gag the victim was tied so tightly that it caused the victim's lower jaw to recede far behind the upper jaw. These observations, coupled with the fact that his radio was tuned to a hard rock station, though he preferred classical music, leave little doubt that a second party was present when he died. The question remains as to whether he had been murdered.

As mentioned, the room had been ransacked, but valuables were left undisturbed. Drawers were pulled out, tables overturned, and the scene littered with clothing. Even though the victim was bound and gagged, two shirts and a jacket had been placed over his head unnecessarily.

In our opinion, the victim had brought a person to his room for the purpose of engaging in sexual bondage activities. He was lying supine on the bed, allowing himself to be bound the wrists and ankles with the small lengths of rope and to be gagged with the T-shirt. He suffered a heart attack, and his partner, thinking him dead, panicked and attempted to make it appear to be a robbery by ransacking the apartment. The dresser drawer beneath the victim's head indicates the room had been ransacked while he was still on the bed. Frightened, remorseful, and unable to look at the victim's face, his partner wrapped the shirts around the victim's head. After the unidentified person left the room, the victim began struggling against his bonds and rolled off the bed.

After arriving at this conclusion, one of us (Hazelwood) provided the requesting agency with a criminal personality profile of the unidentified sexual partner:

> The offender is a Hispanic male between the ages of 19 and 25 years. He is a high school dropout and is either unemployed or employed in a menial job requiring little or not contact with the public. It is believed that the subject was associated with the victim in some capacity. While having little education, he has average or better social intelligence. He frequents adult book stores, purchasing heterosexually oriented bondage literature. At the time of the offense, he resided alone or with his family and lived within walking distance of the scene. He from an upper lower socioeconomic environment and has either moved or joined the military since the death. He would be described by friends and family as a quiet, passive type of person who is an "underachiever." It is possible that he has a history of juvenile offenses. He is single and his social life is restricted to a few male friends.

The police later developed a suspect who was a twenty-year-old Hispanic man who had resided with his family within three blocks of the death scene. He knew the victim and had joined the military shortly after the victim's death. The young man had gone AWOL and had sent a letter to his commanding officer advising that he was contemplating suicide and had been depressed for the "last three months." The letter was written in April. The victim had died in January. Although we believe the victim's death was unintended and that this is a case of manslaughter, we cannot be certain that it was not murder.

DISCUSSION

Suicidal sexual fatalities are extremely rare. To our knowledge, the only unequivocal autoerotic suicide case that has been published is case B in R. E. Litman and C. Swearingen's paper, in which the authors emphasize depression, orientation toward death, and suicidal thoughts among bondage practitioners.[1] In our series of sexual fatalities, there is only one unequivocal suicide, and that case involved a partner who assisted the man's suicide at his direction.

We believe there should be strong presumption that the manner of death in an autoerotic fatality is accident. This view contrasts sharply with that of O. Richardson and H. S. Breyfole, who in 1946 wrote that mere proof of hanging should overcome the legal presumption against suicide, should eliminate the need for proof of motive, and should "cast the burden of going forward with evidence upon the party claiming that death was accidental."[2] In our view, if a hanging is accompanied by clear indications of sexual activity (not merely the presence of ejaculate), it should be presumed accidental in the absence of evidence to the contrary. This is not to say that the decedent was unaware of the risk, for there is a substantial body of opinion and some very suggestive evidence that men who engage in autoerotic asphyxia are indeed aware of a risk to their lives. The question, not answerable, is whether their knowledge of the risk should be viewed as similar to that of motorcyclists who ride without helmets, skydivers, those who habitually inject heroin, or those who play Russian Roulette.

Cases 1 and 2 illustrate many of the factors that must be taken into account in considering whether an autoerotic fatality might be a suicide. A suicide note in the handwriting of the decedent, left where it would certainly be found, is the best single indicator that an autoerotic fatality was suicidal. Yet even when this is present, as in case 2, one must consider whether the note is prop for suicide fantasy that has been enacted repeatedly.

As illustrated by cases 3 and 4, behavioral reconstruction is complicated considerably when there is suggestive but inconclusive evidence of the presence of second party. Case 3 apparently did not involve a second party, despite preliminary indications to the contrary. Cases 4 and 5 probably represent an unusual group of sexual manslaughter cases.

A. Usher mentions an English case in which a prostitute was suffocated with a pillow by a client who subsequently said that he frequently used suffocation as foreplay.[3] A woman he had picked up shortly before the prostitute's death confirmed this, saying he had almost suffocated her.[4] Usher refers to the death as a murder but does not indicate how manslaughter was ruled out. Case 4 may be analogous to the one Usher mentions, though the victim's possession of bondage equipment and the indications that she was a willing participant weight the evidence toward unintended death.

One of the earliest documented fatalities from sexual asphyxia, that of the musician Kotzwarra in London in 1791, involved a second person. Kotzwarra had persuaded Susanna Hill, a prostitute, to hang him for his sexual pleasure and instructed her to cut him down after five minutes. When she did so, he was dead. She was tried for murder, but the court regarded the event as an accidental manslaughter.[5] We think it likely that case 5 is analogous to the case of Kotzwarra and Susanna Hill in two respects: (1) the decedent probably requested bondage and asphyxia for his sexual pleasure, and (2) it is unlikely that either decedent or his partner intended his death.

The possibility remains, however, that case 4, case 5, or both were, in fact, murders in the course of sexual activity. In addition to the reasons for thinking otherwise that are set forth in the case analyses, it should be noted that asphyxia, while a frequent mechanism in sexual murders, is far more often accomplished in murders through manual or ligature strangulation or through suffocation with an external object, such as a pillow, than through the use of gag materials.

A novelist with forensic science experience, P. D. James, has written a fictional account of a murder camouflaged as an autoerotic fatality and subsequently altered to appear like a suicide.[6] A colleague has tc us of one case in which a murder is believed to have been committed by a police officer who attempted to conceal it as an autoerotic fatality but neglected to arrange an escape mechanism. The case reported by R. K. Wright and J. Davis, in which two prostitutes left an intoxicated client tied up after robbing him, resembled an autoerotic asphyxia in a few respects but did not appear to have been intentionally camouflaged.[7]

CONCLUSIONS

In the United States, sexual murders outnumber autoerotic fatalities, which, in turn, outnumber cases of sexual manslaughter. Even for the most experienced medical examiners and law enforcement investigators, a small number of these deaths remain equivocal after all efforts at resolution. In the above examples, we have attempted to illustrate the importance of careful investigation (a subject we have developed at greater length elsewhere[8]) and detailed behavioral analysis and reconstruction in resolving equivocal sexual fatalities. The practical importance of these distinctions lies in the response of family members and friends to sexual fatalities, in the life insurance benefits that may be awarded according to whether the death was an accident or a suicide, and in the potential prosecution of living persons in possible homicides.[9]

We are familiar with several fatalities during sexual bondage between partners in which information subsequently obtained form the partner made it possible to determine with reasonable certainty that the death constituted murder, manslaughter, or suicide. In the absence of such an informant, however, the intent of the deceased or of a missing partner can only be inferred from their behavior. Postmortem behavioral analysis requires not only historical information about the victim elicited through interviews with third parties, such as knowledge of the physical evidence from the scene and elsewhere, including those locations where the victim's personal possessions are kept.

The sexual fatality caseload of a jurisdiction is likely to be considerably lower than the caseload of vehicular, gunshot, poisoning, drowning, and other deaths. For this reason, most investigators, regardless of discipline, do not have the opportunity to acquire experience with more than a few dozen sexual fatality cases in the course of their careers. Yet even where the best-equipped laboratories and interdisciplinary teams are available, final determination of the intent of the participants remains a matter of judgment. Whether the legal authority to render such judgment rests with a law enforcement officer, a medical examiner, a coroner, a coroner's jury, or a court, a small proportion of sexual fatalities involve misleading or ambiguous clues. For these equivocal cases, we recommend consultation with specialists who have experience in both sexual fatalities and postmortem behavioral analysis.[10] In such cases, consultation is most useful when sought early in the investigation so that investigative leads can be pursued before evidence is altered or destroyed and before memories become lost, blurred, or otherwise inaccessible.

NOTES

1. R. E. Litman and C. Swearingen, "Bondage and Suicide," *Archives of General Psychiatry* 27, no. 1 (July 1972): 80–85.

2. O. Richardson and H. S. Breyfogle, "Medicolegal Problems in Distinguishing Accident from Suicide," *Annals of Internal Medicine* 25, no. 1 (July 1946): 22–65.

3. A. Usher, "Sexual Violence," *Forensic Science* 5 (1975): 243–55.

4. Ibid.

5. M. Hirschfeld, *Sexual Anolmalies: The Origins, Nature, and Treatment of Sexual Disorders* (New York: Emerson Books, 1948), pp. 374–77.

6. P. D. James, *An Unsuitable Job for a Woman* (New York: Charles Scribner's Sons, 1972).

7. R. K. Wright and J. Davis, "Homicidal Hanging Masquerading as Sexual Asphyxia," *Journal of Forensic Sciences* 21, no. 2 (April 1976): 387–89.

8. R. R. Hazelwood, P. E. Dietz, and A. W. Burgess, "The Investigation of Auto-erotic Fatalities," *Journal of Police Science and Administration* 9, no. 4 (December 1981): 404–11.

9. C. E. Curvey, "Effect of the Manner of Death in Medicolegal Cases on Insurance Settlements Involving Double Indemnity," *Journal of Forensic Sciences* 19, no. 2 (April 1974): 390–97.

10. R. R. Hazelwood, P. E. Dietz, and A. W. Burgess, *Autoerotic Fatalities* (Lexington, MA: Lexington Books, 1983).

USING A FORENSIC
LINGUISTIC APPROACH
TO TRACK THE UNABOMBER

James R. Fitzgerald

The writer's language is to some degree the product of his own action; he is both the historian and the agent of his own language.

—Paul De Man

The Unabom investigation began on May 25, 1978, at the University of Illinois in Chicago. On that date, in the parking lot of the university, the first of sixteen bombing incidents occurred. A police officer was injured. The last bombing incident attributed to the Unabomber occurred seventeen years later in April of 1995, in Sacramento, California. A forestry lobbyist was killed in that incident. It would still be almost an entire year, numerous pseudonymous letters later (including one in which an airliner departing Los Angeles International Airport was threatened to be destroyed), and the virtually forced publication by a major American newspaper of a thirty-five-thousand-word manifesto before an individual named Theodore J. Kaczynski was finally arrested. Before it was over, the Unabomber's actions killed three people, injured dozens more (some critically), and almost destroyed an airliner mid-flight with one of his destructive devices.

What happened between 1978 and 1996 was, at the time, the largest and most expensive criminal investigation ever undertaken by the Federal Bureau of Investigation (FBI). It encompassed a time frame of almost eighteen years, a

Written for this anthology.

total complement of several hundred federal and local law enforcement officers and support employees, and an estimated $50 million in investigative costs. It also incorporated one of the most extensive and comprehensive text analysis projects in the history of the United States's criminal justice system.

What is not clearly known to many is that it was not fingerprints or DNA that helped identify this elusive serial bomber. Nor was it an informant, an eyewitness account, explosive residue, or serial numbers off the various parts of the sixteen bombs that the Unabomber assembled and used against his victims. What eventually led FBI investigators to a small cabin on a hillside in Lincoln, Montana, and to the subsequent arrest of Kaczynski, were the writings of the bomber himself.

Fourteen separate documents were written by the person who eventually came to be called the Unabomber by the FBI. In early 1996, once Kaczynski was identified as a viable suspect in the case, his brother and mother turned over another 178 of his documents to the FBI. This article describes the forensic linguistic methods used by the FBI in examining the nearly two hundred Unabomber/Kaczynski documents associated with this investigation. I will also illustrate how these documents became arguably the strongest evidence in establishing the probable cause to search the Montana cabin of Kaczynski, arresting him, and assuring his conviction in federal court.

Before exploring the linguistic aspects undertaken, the overall context of this case is provided with information on the bombings, the role of victimology, and the early stages of the investigation. I then shift to a personal, insider account of the latter stage of the investigation as the written documents became central to the case and led to the arrest and ultimate conviction of this serial bomber.

THE BOMBINGS

As with many serial bombers, the Unabomber's explosive devices became more deadly with time. (The acronym "UNABOM" was developed in the early stage of the investigation. It is the result of the identities and/or associations of the early bombing victims, that is, universities and airline bombings = UNABOM.) Many of his early devices were crudely designed, and they lacked the sophistication to either detonate properly or, if they did, lacked the firepower to kill the intended target. All his bombs were designed to kill people, not destroy buildings or the like. However, as the bombings continued over the years, his devices not only were more powerful but also became increasingly more lethal in design, as they were also wrapped in nails, tacks, and other metal objects in an attempt to ensure his victims would be killed. This is indicative of an elevated level of anger, rage, and frustration at his victims and at society, something that the FBI profilers, that is, experts in criminal behavior and the requisite offender personality characteristics, were very much aware of at the time. It was correctly opined that this person would not stop bombing until he was apprehended or until he died.

The offender also wanted to make sure that investigators knew that they were his bombs when they were discovered. Practically all of the bombs had the initials *FC* scribed on one of their metallic parts. The Unabomber would claim in a later letter that this stood for Freedom Club.

The Unabomber both mailed and physically placed his bombs at locations in his attempts to kill his targets. While many of his early bombs were placed at certain locations to be moved or picked up by a victim, his latter attacks, post-1987, were all mailed. The mailed bombs were typically packages wrapped in brown paper and heavily stamped. The devices were designed to explode in the face of the person opening the package. However, in two separate incidents, five years apart, the Unabomber used a one-page, typewritten letter to entice the recipient to open the bomb-laden package. Both times it worked.

In the fourth bombing in 1980, a letter was received via the mail by the then–president of United Airlines at his Chicago-area home. It was addressed to him personally. The letter encouraged him to read a book that he would receive in the very near future. The referenced book, *Ice Brothers*, written by Sloan Wilson, eventually did arrive. Upon the victim opening the package, and then opening the front cover, the bombing device contained within the hollowed-out book exploded. He was seriously injured.

In 1985, a package was mailed to a University of Michigan professor in Ann Arbor. His secretary opened the envelope fastened to the package and pulled out a one-page, typewritten letter. The letter encouraged the recipient to open the attached package. The package purportedly contained "(an) initial version of (my) dissertation relating to the topic of the history of science." The package was opened, a bomb exploded, and the female victim was seriously wounded as a result.

These two letters, composed five years apart by the Unabomber, provided the first non-bomb-related insight into the mind of this offender. They came to be known as the ruse letters, designed to trick the victim into opening the forthcoming or attached packages. The envelopes reflected bogus return addresses, and the letter writer used two separate pseudonyms as signatories. They provided for investigators an early glimpse into the language ability, at least as it pertained to writing and composition skills, of this serial bomber. However, further glimpses would have to wait. The Unabomber would not send his next letter to anyone for another eight years.

VICTIMOLOGY

Victimology, in behavioral analysis parlance, is described as the totality of personal information available about a particular victim in a particular crime and how those factors may have contributed to him or her becoming a victim of said crime. Factors include gender, age, family situation, personality traits, employment, security consciousness, and so forth. Victimology played a large role in the investigation of the UNABOM case. However, until the arrest of the Unabomber, and a search of his cabin, it was never clear how or why he was choosing his victims.

As mentioned above, the earliest victims of the Unabomber included university professors and airline executives, airline facilities, and an airliner itself. By the mid-1980s, and into the mid-1990s, his target selection expanded to include commercial computer stores, a geneticist, researchers, an advertising executive, and a pro-lumber company lobbyist.

In the latter stages of the UNABOM investigation, the FBI launched an intensive campaign in an attempt to determine a nexus, or a list of commonalities, among the victims. An extensive questionnaire was assembled that delved into virtually every aspect of the victims—personal, academic, professional, and spiritual lives. It was sent to every surviving victim and to close family members and professional colleagues of the deceased victims.

The findings were, at best, inconclusive. While there were some obvious similarities in professions among the victims and the intended victims, all white males, the common elements essentially ended there. There were no other clearly defined commonalities among the victims. Whatever rationale and means used by the Unabomber to choose his intended victims were still unknown to the investigators.

However, the one item of potential evidentiary value uncovered by the use of this questionnaire was that virtually all of the victims were listed in *Who's Who in America* (WWA). This popular reference book, found at the time in most public and academic libraries, was apparently used by the Unabomber to ascertain specific home and business addresses for his victims. This was determined because of minor variations of the actual names and addresses of several of the victims and the name and address information as it is listed in WWA. These variations on the bombing packages of these victims, which were actually the result of the Unabomber using older editions of WWA, led investigators to believe that the Unabomber had access to one or more versions of this book. He was using it not necessarily to choose his victims but once having chosen them for whatever reason to attain their mailing locations.

Based on this information, FBI agents proceeded to practically every library in the United States and asked librarians questions about their copies of WWA and what persons may have been requesting it, using it, copying it, and so forth. While some potential leads resulted from this particular strategy, the investigation continued with no viable suspect having been identified.

THE INVESTIGATION

After a seven-year hiatus between 1987 and 1993, the Unabomber started bombing again. This ended the speculation that he was dead. It was later learned that he halted his bombing because he perceived he was almost identified and/or arrested in Salt Lake City in 1987. This is when he was observed by an eyewitness, and the famous composite sketch of the hooded man, wearing sunglasses, was released by the FBI.

One of the Unabomber's next victims was a Yale University professor who lost part of his hand to a bomb in June of 1993. Then, for reasons still not entirely clear, the Unabomber began writing letters in 1993. This time they were not ruse letters but letters attempting to explain his ideology. He sent these initial letters to the *New York Times* (NYT).

It was clear in 1993 that the Unabomber was now back in business. The initial investigation, begun in 1978, had been undertaken by several different federal law enforcement agencies, working mostly independent of each other. These agencies included the FBI, the United States Postal Inspection Service (USPIS), and the Bureau of Alcohol, Tobacco and Firearms (ATF). However, upon the reemergence of the Unabomber in 1993, the United States Department of Justice ordered the formation of the UNABOM Task Force (UTF). It was to be established in San Francisco, California. The FBI was designated as the lead agency. This task force also incorporated the USPIS and the ATF.

During the first year of the UTF, all the appropriate investigative areas were covered. These included a detailed forensic reexamination of all the bomb components, reinterviews of all living victims and witnesses, a fresh look at all the leads previously covered in the case, proactive media releases, and a publicized reward of $1 million. Also, the design and implementation of a computer software program was undertaken in which all associated names, universities, data bases, leads, and such could be maintained for investigative purposes. Perhaps the first "linguistic"-based aspect of the Unabom case occurred during this time frame. It became known as the "Nathan R" investigation.

As with all the letters sent by the Unabomber, one of the early letters sent to the NYT was forwarded to the FBI laboratory for the usual forensic examination. Upon conducting the various investigations at the lab, it was determined that this particular letter contained indented writing. Indented writing is generally invisible to the naked eye, and it is usually the result of someone writing on a separate piece of paper on top of the one in question. On this particular document, the indented writing read, "Call Nathan R 7:00 PM."

The FBI launched an all-out campaign to learn the identity of "Nathan R." Numerous public data bases were reviewed in an attempt to learn the whereabouts of every adult in the United States with the first name Nathan and a last name beginning with the letter R. Hundreds of Nathan Rs were identified and interviewed nationwide. They were all asked the same series of questions. The interviews related to whether they knew anyone whom they may suspect of wanting to injure or kill people by means of mailed or placed explosive devices and who may have called them (that is, one of the Nathan Rs) around a certain date on or about 7:00 PM. None of these leads provided any information of value.

Next, the FBI began looking for adult men with the first name Nathan and the middle initial R. This, too, led to hundreds of interviews, ultimately all of them fruitless. When this particular aspect of the investigation was made public, other potential leads developed, but again none contained anything of evidentiary value. There was even a Midwestern radio talk show host, whose name happened to be Nathan something—or—other, who claimed it was his radio program that the Unabomber was supposed to call one night. He even made direct broadcast appeals to the Unabomber to call his show again. While this particular radio personality may have benefited from a temporary ratings boost during this time, it did not benefit the FBI in its attempt to identify the Unabomber.

Finally, in what could best be described as an anticlimatic ending to this aspect of the UNABOM investigation, the Nathan R lead was discontinued. It was determined, upon conducting several reinterviews at the NYT, that the newspaper employee who first came into possession of this particular letter was the one who wrote a short note to himself to call his friend. This note was written on a piece of paper on his desk that happened to be placed on top of the newly received UNABOM letter, thus resulting in the indented writing on the examined document. It was the NYT employee who had a friend named "Nathan R" whom he was supposed to call early one evening. The name had absolutely no connection to the mysterious bomber. This represented another lead, among many at the time, destined to go nowhere.

Two more fatal bombings attributed to the Unabomber occurred in late 1994 and early 1995, respectively. And, as he foretold in his early 1995 letters, on June 24 of that year, the manifesto was received, via the mail, by the NYT and three other recipients. While the aforementioned traditional methods of investigation continued, it was realized shortly thereafter that a wealth of evidence was now in possession of the investigators. This evidence was in the form of the extensive and detailed writings of a bomber who had avoided identification and eluded investigators for so many years.

The UTF management in San Francisco felt that they needed assistance in this particular aspect of the investigation. They contacted what is presently known as the Behavioral Analysis Unit (BAU) at the FBI Academy, in Quantico, Virginia, and requested a criminal profiler to be temporarily assigned to the UTF. The initial request was for the BAU member to stay in San Francisco for thirty days. Instead, it turned into a fourteen-month assignment over the next two years.

Prior to leaving Quantico in early July of 1995, I was brought up to date on the UNABOM investigation, discussed various pending issues related to it, and was given a collection of documents to read. Soon, I was en route to San Francisco and the UTF. Even before landing at San Francisco International Airport on the way to the UTF, I decided that I would concentrate on the cumulated writings of the Unabomber in order to attempt to learn all I could about him. I felt that while the early letters would be important, his recently received manifesto would represent the strongest reflection of his present-day persona. This was his pride and joy, something on which he had obviously expended a lot of time and effort. Before long, I knew that thirty-five-thousand-word document better than anyone, with the possible exception of the individual who wrote it.

THE DOCUMENTS

A. THE U-DOCS

As of mid-1995, there were a total of fourteen Unabom documents (U-Docs). This number would not change. The first document (U-1), dated June 3, 1980, was one of the ruse letters described above. The last U-Doc was the manifesto (U-14), titled "An Industrial Society and Its Future" by "FC." (The same initials also chiseled onto parts of his bombs.) It was received by the NYT and others on June 24, 1995. Its theme was effectively summed up in its very first sentence: "The industrial revolution and its consequences have been a disaster for the human race." The rest of the tome consisted of the Unabomber providing numerous examples of how this perceived condition came about, why it persists, and what should be done about it.

The other twelve documents consisted of an additional ruse letter (also described above) and other documents that fell into the categories of ideological letters and brokering letters. The former documents consisted of letters in which the Unabomber attempted to explain his philosophical rationale as to why he felt justified in carrying out his bombing campaign. This philosophy centered upon the evils of modern society and how it has evolved into a maddening technological quagmire. His expressed solution involved society's return to a simpler, agrarian society, whereupon everyone would live in tribes of no more than thirty to forty people. The latter documents consisted of letters in which the Unabomber was attempting to broker a deal for the publication of his manifesto.

The brokering, or deal, the Unabomber requested was as follows: If the NYT, or the *Washington Post* (WP), agreed to publish his manifesto in full and within a certain time frame, he would cease and desist from bombing-to-kill in the future. However, even if published, he did maintain the right to bomb for purposes of sabotage.

The NYT had great difficulties in resolving this issue. Should it refuse to accede to the demands of a terrorist? Or should it publish the manifesto, as was requested by the FBI in an attempt to stop the bombing and perhaps identify this person? This matter would not be resolved until several months later.

The Unabomber could not resist at this time in also displaying his marketing skills. Document U-8 was received by the *San Francisco Chronicle* shortly before the NYT and others received the manifesto. In this very short communication, the Unabomber claimed that he would blow up an airliner out of Los Angeles International Airport (LAX). For the next several days, LAX was at a greatly heightened security level, with long lines of passengers at check-in counters and flights consistently several hours behind schedule. However, in the letter that accompanied the manifesto to the NYT, received several days later, the Unabomber explained that he wanted to play one last prank on the American public, since it had such a short memory. There was no bomb at LAX. However, he apparently knew that the publicity this threat generated would provide much more attention to him and his manifesto.

The recipients of these brokering U-Docs were as interesting as they were varied. The primary recipient of these letters was the NYT. It was the Unabomber's newspaper of record and where he wanted his manifesto published, although he stated that the WP would suffice, if necessary. The letters to the NYT included a nine-digit secret number. The Unabomber included this, much like *FC* on his bombs, to assure that any document sent by him could be authenticated as being from him alone, not from a copycat. Also receiving ideological U-Docs at or about the same time were three individual researchers (one a former bombing victim) and the *San Francisco Chronicle*. In addition to the NYT, the manifesto was received by the WP, *Penthouse*, *Scientific American*, and a University of California at Berkeley sociology professor.

All the U-Docs were typewritten. The typewriter used throughout all the letters was a 1930s vintage SmithCorona. The fifty-six-page manifesto was received by the recipients in the form of carbon copies. From 1993 on, all the U-Docs were postmarked from northern California, mostly from the San Francisco Bay area. There was one mailed from Sacramento, California—hence the reason why San Francisco was chosen as the location of the UTF.

B. INITIAL ANALYSIS

In July of 1995, on my arrival to the FBI's San Francisco division and after initial introductions to the UTF management, I informed them of my desire to spend the first several weeks doing little but familiarizing myself with the writings of the Unabomber. They agreed. I wanted to see photographs of each letter, including the front and back of each envelope, just to make sure that the photocopies I was working with accurately reflected the documented itself. Also, I wanted to know everything about the victims and/or recipients of each bomb and each letter.

I was about to embark upon an investigative journey involving the review of almost forty thousand words on almost seventy pages, each containing text expressed in single-spaced typewritten format, all written pseudonymously by FC (or the same person using some other bogus name as in the ruse letters), and who also happened to send or place explosive devices with these documents. In view of this, I decided to pay very close attention to my own analytical protocol and methodology. I was aware that someday I might be asked to defend, in a court of law, exactly what was done in relation to these documents.

In conducting a text analysis of this scope, it is important to have several sets of the same documents. Of course, the original version of any document related to a criminal case should be sent to the appropriate laboratory for microscopic examination for such things as indented writings, fingerprints, hairs and fibers, and DNA. It should then be maintained with all of the proper chain-of-custody rules. Ideally, the copies (photographs if available) should be kept in separate binders, all marked accordingly for retrieval purposes. One set should be the pristine set, that is, a set that is not marked at all and left exactly as is. This set is reserved for making additional copies to show one or more communications to someone else for an objective opinion about a particular linguistic finding and not biasing them with previously made markings or highlighting. This unmarked set also serves as the set to simply pick up and read from time to time in an attempt to find other topic-, format-, or style-related issues that may have been previously missed. Another set of documents is the working set, designed for marking, highlighting, tabbing, and such.

Simple color-coded highlighting in text analysis was found to be valuable in the review of these documents. For example, one color was used for orthographical or grammatical mistakes, of which there were very few, if any, in these documents.

The prescriptive spelling and grammar rules of the approximate time frame of when an author writes is paramount in an analysis such as that conducted in the UNABOM investigation, in which the writings eventually spanned several decades. While these rules are fundamentally static, there have been recognized changes over the years in the United States. In view of this, several books were obtained in an attempt to best gauge what was acceptable or unacceptable in these writings, during the time frame in which they were written. Among those books were the 1982 edition of *The Handbook of Good English* by Edward D. Johnson, the 1979 edition of *Webster's New Collegiate Dictionary*, and the 1996 edition of *The American Heritage Dictionary of the English Language*.

Another color highlighter was used for sometimes difficult or confusing orthographical or grammatical usage in which the author was, in fact, correct. Common mistakes observed in anonymous text at the Behavioral Analysis Unit include the misuse of to, too, two; there, their, they're; its, it's; and your, you're. Proper usage of such forms is arguably reflective of at least an above-average command of the English language. Yet another color highlighter was used for unusual words or phrases (admittedly a subjective judgment) and one more color highlighter for what may be apparent biographical features, whether or not the author intended them to be.

In addition, a reliable numbering system should be set up for reference purposes for any set of examined documents. On first arriving at the UTF, I learned that the documents were simply referred to by their postmark dates. I would hear, "Take a look at the April 20th letter to Dr. Gelerntner." This seemed unwieldy and ineffective. In an effort to streamline the document categorization system, I came up with a simple alphanumeric system to designate one document from the other. By chronological order of the postmarks, the documents were numbered one through fourteen. A *U* (for UNABOM) was used as an alpha-designator because it was optimistically assumed that someday there would be other documents that could then be compared to them; the new ones would naturally be assigned another alpha designator. *IQ* for "questioned documents" and *K* for "known documents" are commonly used for these purposes. However, at the UTF, there were no *K* documents at that time. And it was felt that using *U* to describe the documents composed and sent by the Unabomber would make it easier for everyone to remember.

Creating a glossary/index for the manifesto proved very beneficial to the UTF. Oftentimes, discussions would take place among investigators in which a certain phrase or topic was referred to in U-14, and it was not easily located because of the sheer size of the document. So even though the UTF had the Zy-Index word search software program, by which words or phrases could be accessed easily, I still felt it a worthwhile exercise for me to go through the manifesto page by page, paragraph by paragraph, and assemble my own glossary/index. It took the better part of a solid week, but I managed to create a fifteen-page alphabetically and chronologically based product, respectively, that I could distribute to all the investigators involved in the case, some of whom were not completely comfortable using a computer software program such as Zy-Index. It was also an excellent method to get to know the manifesto even better. This type of product also went a long way in establishing an early positive liaison between the newly arrived team member (me) and the rest of the investigative team.

Four weeks in a row, I studied the manifesto and the other, earlier letters, day and night. I wanted to familiarize myself with them from cover to cover. The thirty-five-thousand words of the manifesto did not make for easy consumption. The writing style was what could be best described as dry and humorless. Unless the reader was very much interested in the ongoing mantra concerning the evils of technology and all the other listed societal maladies, it was relatively boring reading. Some mornings I would start reading at the middle of the manifesto, just so my mind would be fresh when I reached the end of it. This forced reading proved invaluable. I eventually realized that the Unabomber's writings enlightened me to so much more than just his rambling philosophies. They also told me a great deal about the author himself.

Some early observations regarding the Unabomber's writings include:

1. He was an experienced writer, with an excellent knowledge and command of the English language. There were virtually no mistakes in his writings.
2. The format of the manifesto was like that of an academic thesis from the 1950s or 1960s. There was a title page/cover and then a correction page.

Then, in the body of the paper, he numbered each paragraph, reaching a total of 232 paragraphs, which was then followed by thirty-six notes, much like endnotes. He also included a diagram of his so-called Power Process. (This concept is vaguely described by FC as being biologically based within all humans and composed of four "elements." They are goal, effort, attainment of goal, and autonomy.) The paper also included footnotes and bibliographical references.

3. He used British variants for his spelling of two words, *analyse* and *licence*. He used alternate variants in the spelling of two words, *wilfully* and *instalment*. He did not deviate in the spellings of these words throughout the U-Docs.

4. There was an ongoing theory formulated at the UTF, which was never substantiated, that he had a fascination with the concept of wood. The return addresses on the envelopes as well as the victims themselves almost always reflected a wood-themed issue. These included a victim with the actual last name of Wood, another victim living in Ann Arbor, and other fictitious names and streets in the return address incorporating wood themes. His last victim was a forestry lobbyist. When this issue was publicized in the media, the Unabomber disputed it in one of his subsequent letters to the NYT. He even addressed this notion in a sarcastic sense in the bogus return address of one of his later letters in which it read, "Frederick Benjamin Isaac Wood, 9th and Pennsylvania Aves." Of course, the first three letters of each name, followed by the last name, read "FBI Wood," and "9th and Pennsylvania Aves." is the address of FBI Headquarters in Washington, DC.

5. In spite of his otherwise vitriolic rhetoric about modern-day American society and all its negative trappings, there was only one business entity mentioned by name in the manifesto: the Sylvan Learning Center, a company geared toward the tutoring of children in various academic subjects. Coincidence or not, he used another wood reference in Sylvan. His reflected view of this company was mixed, yet nonetheless, a rather unusual example by him of that which is allegedly wrong with modern society. Surprisingly, following the theme of his manifesto, there was no mention of IBM, Microsoft, General Motors, or any airlines or aircraft companies.

6. The writer dated himself somewhat by using the words *Negro, broad,* and *chick,* the latter two used to describe women.

7. He underlined particular words and phrases throughout the manifesto. These were obviously important to him and he wanted to emphasize them.

8. Some of the distinctive, less commonly observed words and phrases (admittedly, a subjective judgment) used by the Unabomber included: *chimerical, coreligionist, delimited, anomie,* and *middle-class vacuity.*

There was one other phrase, *cool-headed logicians*, which I did not necessarily take particular note of at the time. However, several months later, someone else did, and it changed the course of the investigation.

9. Content-wise, the following themes were mentioned most commonly in the U-Docs:
   a) Society—254 times
   b) Power—234 times
   c) Technology—198 times
   d) Freedom, autonomy, and/or liberty—125 times
   e) Psychology—55 times

It was during one of my trips back to Quantico in the summer of 1995 that I had my first personal contact with a forensic linguist. Through a colleague of mine at the FBI, I was invited to the home of Dr. Roger Shuy, who at the time was teaching at Georgetown University. He had recently been given a copy of the manifesto (it had not yet been published in full in the media) and had volunteered his time to provide some insight into the linguistic characteristics of these thirty-five-thousand-words of the Unabomber. During the course of that enlightening afternoon, I provided Shuy with other pertinent facts regarding the investigation to date. His report arrived at the UTF later that autumn, and his observations relating to the writings were notable. Contact was maintained with Shuy throughout the next several months of the investigation. His positive influence on the UNABOM investigation from a forensic linguistic perspective was greatly appreciated.

C. TEXTUAL INFLUENCES ON THE UNABOMBER'S WRITINGS

Obviously, in any forensic linguistic-based investigation and/or text analysis, knowing what a writer is reading, or at least culturally exposed to, is important in attempting to ascertain his identity and/or learn more about him. The Unabomber directly referenced five publications in the manifesto. They are:

1. *The Ancient Engineers* by L. Sprague DeCamp
2. *The True Believer* by Eric Hoffer
3. *Violence in America: Historical and Comparative Perspectives* by Roger Lane
4. *Chinese Political Thought in the 20th Century* by Chester C. Tan
5. *Scientific American*, numerous articles.

I made sure that I became familiar with each book or magazine article referenced by the Unabomber. This helped me better understand how the author's ideas, or personal philosophies, were shaped. It also revealed which ideas may have been original or which ones may have been borrowed from elsewhere. It was not long before the UTF realized that the Unabomber's stated ideas were not all that original. Many of his ideas were based on the writings of Jacques Ellul and his 1964 book, *The Technological Society*, and on the beliefs of the Luddites, who protested the advent of the Industrial Revolution in England in the early nineteenth century.

When FC provided a quote from a particular book, it then was researched by specific page numbers. It was then easy to determine which edition or printing of a book he was using. (Editions of some books differ in their pagination.) This would assist in determining the time frame that he used or even purchased these books. If they were mostly sold at certain universities at a certain time, it could help localize the Unabomber's early days.

It is also important to take note of what a writer is *not* referencing in this type of analysis. This can provide telltale biographical information about an anonymous or pseudonymous author. In the case of the Unabomber, he did not mention any specific movies, television shows, news or radio programs, weekly news magazines, or at that time the relatively new (at least for the general public) Internet. It was believed that the Unabomber either had minimal exposure to these media sources, or if he had exposure, he refused to be influenced by them, at least in his writings. Later, it was learned that he was living in a cabin with no electricity; therefore, no television (and possibly radio) was available to him. This would also preclude him from having Internet access, but then again, with the way he railed against technology, he most likely would not have used it anyway.

After a month or so of reading and rereading the manifesto, I came upon what I thought at the time was a significant find. As mentioned earlier, the text in this document was written virtually mistake free. However, I finally found an apparent mistake. It was relatively minor, and something that I had skipped over a number of times initially, but I felt it to be a mistake nonetheless. In paragraph 185, the Unabomber writes: "As for the negative consequences of eliminating industrial society well, you can't eat your cake and have it too."

In the United States, when choosing to use this relatively popular proverb, most people say or write, "You can't have your cake and eat it too." While not a mistake in spelling, grammar, or punctuation, it was very interesting that in spite of how careful this writer was in crafting his manifesto, he made what seemed to be a simple mistake. Perhaps it was in his haste or just carelessness, but for whatever reason, he transposed the two verbs in this well-known proverb.

Finally, I found him to be linguistically "wrong" about something. This man, who had successfully sent bombs to people over the last seventeen-plus years without ever leaving a substantive clue, who wrote in almost perfect English, and who had challenged the most famous newspaper in the world to defy him, had made a mistake. I could finally articulate to those around me a specific linguistic find of some probative value. While there was no other corpus to compare it to,

I felt that at some point this phrase, and the way the Unabomber wrote it, might provide additional clues about him. I would later find out I was right, but for the wrong reason.

After four and a half months at the UTF, and the eventual publication of the manifesto by the WP in September of 1995, my supervisor at the FBI Academy in Quantico requested my return from San Francisco. After all, my full-time assignment was with the Behavioral Analysis Unit. With the investigation ongoing, but with no one suspect in view, and my analysis of the textual material essentially complete, in early December of 1995, I returned to Virginia.

I maintained telephonic contact with my UTF associates over the next couple of months. They were all working hard on various investigative issues, but there was still no one viable UNABOM suspect. That all changed in late February of 1996.

D. THE T-DOCS

On February 23, 1996, I was in my office at the FBI Academy, performing the duties that I expected when I first arrived there ten months earlier. However, on that Friday afternoon, I received a telephone call from my colleagues at the UTF. They told me very little information other than that they had a document that they wanted me to review. They asked me to look at it and based on my knowledge of the manifesto to advise them of any similarities. The only information I was provided was that it was written in the early 1970s.

The document that I received via a fax machine was twenty-three pages long, typewritten, and double-spaced. There was no cover page and no title, nor was it signed by anyone. I sat down and began to read.

It should be noted that during my time in San Francisco, and even once or twice after I left, I was asked by my UTF colleagues to review a letter, an article, even books, in an attempt to determine any similarities between those documents and the manifesto. I undertook those assignments with an open mind, usually to be disappointed several paragraphs, several pages, or several chapters into the project. The disappointment was the result of the fact that the authors were clearly not the same.

However, the document that was faxed to me that cold winter afternoon in 1996 seemed uncannily familiar. It was like I had read it before, yet I knew that I had not. The very first sentence read, "In these pages it is argued that continued scientific and technical progress will inevitably result in the extinction of individual liberty." After reading the document once, twice, and a third time, and marking and highlighting numerous portions feverishly, I realized that the ideas expressed here were virtually identical to those in the manifesto. Issues such as technology, society, power, liberty, and their associative "evils" were replete throughout. At twenty-three pages, it could easily have been an early outline for the manifesto.

After my third reading, I immediately called the UTF. I spoke with Terry Turchie, who was the assistant special agent in charge (ASAC) and the operational supervisor of the UTF. I had numerous questions for him. He answered them by advising me that several days earlier a Washington, DC, attorney had called the UTF, advising that his client thought that his brother might possibly be the Unabomber. The attorney was authorized to forward to the FBI a copy of a document of which he was in possession—the same one that was faxed to me. The attorney and his as-of-now unnamed client wanted the FBI to look at this document, compare it to the writings of the Unabomber, and decide if it was worth pursuing. I emphatically told ASAC Turchie that based on my analysis of this document, and my knowledge of the manifesto, and barring any sophisticated forgery attempt, "You've got your man!"

I was adamantly convinced of the common authorship after reading this document. The varied but related topic selection, the forcefulness of opinion and position, the similarity in phrasing and wording, and even the chronological order in which the issues were presented all pointed to a writing style very much like that present in the manifesto. Naturally, we would need more writings and/or evidence than this to establish the probable cause necessary for an arrest, but this was an excellent place to start. ASAC Turchie was very happy to hear my opinion, and he immediately requested that I return to San Francisco to resume my UNABOM-related duties. So, once again, I was en route to the UTF—this time, with a specific suspect in mind.

As it turns out, the aforementioned document was the first Ted Document (T-Doc) to be received. It was written by Ted Kaczynski in 1971 and apparently mailed (without a bomb) to one or more unidentified US politicians. The brother, shortly thereafter identified as David Kaczynski, thought that it best represented the writing style as well as the philosophy of Ted, and he decided that this document was the one to initially give the FBI for analysis.

Since the mother and brother of Ted Kaczynski were now cooperating with the FBI, they began the process of providing to the UTF every letter, document, report, sketch, and so forth, that their Ted ever wrote, composed, or drew. Fortunately, they saved practically everything he ever sent to them or that somehow wound up in their possession. They confirmed for us that their Ted was very intelligent, well educated, and a recluse, as he was living by himself in a remote cabin on a hillside in Lincoln, Montana.

Upon later reading a transcript of an interview with David, I learned how he began suspecting that his own brother may be the Unabomber. It started with a request by David's wife, Linda, asking him to read the manifesto on the Internet.

She then urged him to compare the writings of the brother-in-law that she had never met but had heard plenty about to the manifesto. He approached the tasking skeptically. He simply did not believe his older brother could be the Unabomber. Once he sat down and conducted his own analysis of the manifesto and compared it to the known writing and speaking style of his brother, he was less skeptical. However, he was still not entirely convinced. What ultimately tipped the scale for him to the realization of his brother's possible complicity was the use by the manifesto's author of the term *cool-headed logicians* in paragraph 18. He recalled Ted using that distinctive term on numerous occasions. It was at that time that he made the difficult decision to contact an attorney and eventually report Ted to the FBI.

When I returned to San Francisco and the UTF, I was met with a flurry of activity. I tracked down ASAC Turchie, and I asked him what my role was in this new phase of the investigation. He immediately responded that I was to be in charge of the comparative analysis project. Although I was pretty sure of what he wanted me to do, I decided to ask him for specific instructions. He told me that he wanted me to lead a team of agents and analysts. I could request anyone in the FBI that I wanted, and I was to take the fourteen U-Docs and compare them to the ever-increasing number of documents provided by the Kaczynski family. I was told that I was to attempt to compare the writings and determine whether both sets of documents were written by the same person, that being Ted Kaczynski. I responded that I would be glad to assist in this type of project, but since I was not a forensic linguist (thinking of Roger Shuy) at the time, perhaps we should consider hiring one to participate in this process. ASAC Turchie stated that too much of a learning curve would be needed to be overcome for someone new in that role. He also felt that no one knew the manifesto and the other U-Docs as well as I did and that my investigative and behavioral science experience would suffice for this purpose, even without (at the time) any formal linguistic training. I nervously agreed to accept the tasking (I am not really sure that I had a choice), and the comparative analysis project began that night.

THE COMPARATIVE ANALYSIS PROJECT

Since Ted's mother lived in Chicago, Illinois, and his brother in the Albany, New York, area, there were two separate FBI divisions responsible for maintaining contact with them and attaining the various documents. Once attained, copies were made, and the originals were sent to the FBI laboratory in Washington, DC, for evidentiary analysis. Among other examinations, this included the comparison of the typewriter strokes on these new documents with the typewriter strokes on the U-Docs. Throughout all these checks, a match of the make and model of typewriter between two sets of documents was never made. If Kaczynski was the Unabomber, he apparently kept one typewriter for his personal communications and another one for his criminal communications.

The copies of the documents then made their way to the UTF. Once there, they were recopied and distributed accordingly, including to the newly formed comparative analysis team. They were also retyped by a full-time stenography pool, occasional mistake and all, and entered into the Zy-Index program for data retrieval purposes. At the start of the project, there were sixty-nine documents of Ted's that the family had turned over to the FBI.

My first order of business was to treat these documents in the same way the U-Docs had been treated, beginning with setting up a categorization system. I designed this one as simply as I did the first one. These documents were to be alpha-designated as the T-Docs, and they would be numbered chronologically. The sixty-nine T-Docs the UTF had in late February were numbered accordingly. The previously referenced twenty-three-page document was numbered T-2, since there was only one document found to predate it. The rest were ordered by date of letter or envelope accompanying it. Some were undated, making up the last ten or so, the last one being T-69.

What appeared to be a smoothly running numbering system did not last very long. Within a week, another batch of T-Docs arrived at the UTF. They comprised communications from many different dates. My orderly categorization methodology was now skewed. I briefly considered renumbering the original T-Docs to include these and put them all into a new chronological order, but before I could move along with that notion, yet another batch was received at the UTF. It seems the Kaczynskis were finding hidden or forgotten collections of Ted's communications everywhere. Copies were being received sporadically at the UTF as they were received at the FBI divisional level. Sometimes they would come in batches of two or three, other times, it was ten or more. In the end, my alpha-numeric system was simply based upon the date that the UTF received them and not the dates they were written and/or mailed by Ted. While the first sixty-nine maintained their date order, the remainder were numbered with no regard for their original composition dates or postmarks.

The T-Docs themselves were of a mixed variety. Some were typed, some were handwritten. Some were only one or two pages, at least one was seventy-nine pages (Ted's dissertation for his PhD), but the average length was approximately seven pages. Some T-Docs contained drawings and cartoonlike characters. Some were written in Spanish.

The topics of the T-Docs included personal, touching letters to Ted's parents and brother. Still other letters to the family were filled with anger and resentment for the perceived wrongs they committed toward him. Other letters consisted of extensive mathematical formulae and original short stories; yet others were requests for money. Many of the letters included the topics, as found in the U-Docs, of power, technology, society, and individual freedoms. In writing to his brother, Ted seemed obsessed with these notions, much like the author of the manifesto. Content-wise, the following themes were mentioned most commonly in the T-Docs:

a) society—50 times
b) power—38 times
c) technology—47 times

d) freedom, autonomy, and/or liberty—42 times

e) psychology—53 times

In various places, the T-Docs also contained the British variant and alternate spelling forms of the four words found in the manifesto—*analyse, licence, wilfully, instalment*. They were not spelled otherwise throughout the T-Docs.

There were several dozen documents written by Ted in Spanish. Some were long stories composed to David. Others were to a short-term pen pal that David knew from his time living in south Texas in the late 1970s. David's neighbor back then was Mexican-American, and he gave Ted his address. The two wrote to each other for a while in Spanish. David later told the FBI that Ted had never received any formal training or education in Spanish. He was self-taught, mostly from books he attained from the local library or bookstore. When the FBI translators read these specific T-Docs, they were amazed to learn that Ted had never traveled to or lived in a Spanish-speaking country, nor was he ever formally trained in the language. Like the rest of his writings, his Spanish text was impeccable. It was written in formal Spanish, with little slang or vernacular included.

From a text-analysis perspective, and when any translation from one language into another is required, I found it prudent to have a few basic rules:

a) The translators should be highly rated in their respective language skills. They should be able to demonstrate to the courts, if necessary, that they are proficient in both of the languages required for translation.

b) The same team of translators (and not too many) should be maintained for all the translated documents. This is especially true when a later comparative analysis between writings in the two different languages for authorship purposes is undertaken. All language translation involves some degree of interpretation. If the L2 (second language) letters are to be compared accurately to other Us, and just as importantly, to Ll (first language) documents, a consistency of translation must be present and demonstrable.

c) The translators and the analysts should work in two separate areas and have no professional linkage. Any authorship analysis project involving two or more languages should have the two processes bifurcated so as to preclude any possibility of tainting between the two teams. It must be assured that any comparisons between writings in the two languages are done in a linguistically sterile environment. Otherwise, there might be admissibility issues at the time of trial.

As the T-Docs began adding up, I requested additional assistance. Eventually, at the peak of the project, I had twelve people working with me. Each new team member was given a several-hour training block of what was to be accomplished in the project and a consistent methodology of how to go about it. Mostly, we were working seven days a week and at least twelve hours a day. After all, there was no guarantee that the Unabomber would not start bombing again. If it was Kaczynski, the UTF wanted to make sure that we worked as effectively and efficiently as possible in determining whether he was involved. The team knew that our findings would be instrumental in determining his level of involvement and whether he would eventually be arrested for the related bombings. I assigned team members certain batches of T-Docs as they arrived. At any given time, one team member would have as many as ten documents assigned to him or her. Team members were then instructed to read each document carefully and look for individual topics, words, phrases, literary references, names, et cetera that seemed distinctive and/or was repeated throughout the document. They were to then highlight each item and run it through Zy-Index for any similarities with the U-Docs.

It was important in this type of text-analysis project, one in which there is a voluminous amount of documents, to maintain a master log of all the documents as they arrive. It was imperative to note the assigned number, the date of the document, to whom it was addressed, the postmark, the general topic, how many pages, what language, whether it was typed or handwritten, and to which analyst it was assigned. Forms were designed that accurately recorded each letter and each specific entry. They were kept readily available for quick referral.

In addition, individual accountability is important in a project such as this one. Each team member knew that he or she was responsible for approximately ten to twenty documents and any salient findings therein. As a way of cross-checking everyone's work, toward the end of the project, sets of documents were switched to other analysts for their review. Proper notice was given in advance for the analysts who were originally assigned the documents, so they could double-check their work and not miss anything. This teamwork method was a positive way to assure that little, if anything, of value was missed in terms of items of textual significance.

As my team members reported various phrases, sentences, and topic areas of great similarity between the two sets of documents, I realized that I had to devise a method to clearly and cogently illustrate these findings. I wanted to be very careful, as I knew that whatever I put on paper would be scrutinized later by a team of defense attorneys and experts in terms of its validity, reliability, and admissibility. While I was not necessarily being pressured by ASAC Turchie, I knew that he was soon hoping to have a written report of some kind that summarized my findings. I had kept him abreast of many of the findings that the team produced, but nothing was in report form at this point. The FBI wanted to see my findings in written format so it could begin adding it to the probable cause to attain a search warrant to get inside of Kaczynski's mountain cabin. At this time, the target date for the search, and hopeful arrest, of Kaczynski was mid-April 1996.

In view of this, I decided on my project report strategy. As with most people, when measured over a sufficient amount of textual material, Kaczynski could not help but write in a consistent format and style regardless of under which persona he was communicating. This style, fortunately, remained consistent over the course of several decades. The analysis team started a computer-generated side-by-side chart of the findings with the T-Docs in one column and the U-Docs in the other. This was just a working format until I could decide the best way to accurately represent all the positive comparisons that we were finding.

As I was not a forensic linguist at the time, I did not feel comfortable rendering an official written opinion as to the probability that the authors were, in fact, one and the same. I decided then that I would keep any report elementary in design and merely replicate the present working report into the official report. The report would list page after page of these topic, phrase, and word comparisons, including the reference point for each item, with the key words/phrases emboldened in both examples. It would be constructed for the common man, or lay person, to understand. After all, it would be a federal judge who would read the probable cause affidavit, and it was likely that he or she was not a linguist. So by mid-March, this was the process the UTF had agreed upon, and the report was to be made available shortly.

As in any major investigation, especially one in which an arrest or search is imminent, there was a prosecutor assigned to it. This particular assistant United States attorney (AUSA), Stephen Freccero, had an excellent prosecutorial reputation, was intelligent, and was a veteran of numerous successful criminal investigations and prosecutions. However, the type of work I was doing in this case was new to him. He had never depended on a text-analysis project to further one of his criminal cases. Quite frankly, he was unsure of exactly what my team was doing or if it would hold any value at all to him in a court of law. So an education process had to be implemented. Once or twice a week, I brought examples to him of what we were doing. I showed him some of the samples my team had uncovered of almost identical sentences between the two sets of T-Docs and U-Docs. He seemed impressed by this process, but he still did not see a smoking gun among the items listed. He was not sure how useful our project or our report would be. He did some legal research and determined that at that time, text-analysis evidence had not been permitted in federal court. In spite of my attempting to convince him otherwise, he remained supportive but steadfast in that he did not know if this element of the investigation would bear fruit. It was only a matter of time before he was to change his mind.

The total number of T-Docs in mid-March was up to 178. I was the one who initially received them, numbered them, and then assigned them to my team members. However, although I had an analytical team assembled around me, there was not a T-Doc that was not read by me at some stage of the investigation.

One day, while reviewing a batch of documents recently provided by Mrs. Kaczynski, I began reading what eventually came to be numbered as T-137. It was a letter that Ted had sent to the *Saturday Review* magazine in the early 1970s. It dealt with numerous environmental issues and how modern society is responsible for the damage to our ecosystems. Buried in one of the paragraphs near the end of the two-page letter-to-the-editor was the following sentence: "[W]e will be sacrificing some of the materialistic benefits of technology, but there just isn't any other way. We can't eat our cake and have it too."

There was something vaguely familiar about that last sentence. I quickly reached for my copy of the manifesto. I was not exactly sure where I had seen this before, but I started thumbing through it until I found a paragraph high-lighted in red. I noticed that there were hardly any red highlighting, since that was my color for mistakes, and the manifesto contained very few. I was now at paragraph 185, and there was that statement again. It was the same proverb, with the verbs *eat* and *have* transposed. In this, I found what I believed to be yet another mistake among the writings of the Unabomber, whom I firmly believed at this point to be Ted Kaczynski. And now I had a viable linguistic connection between the two, in a very distinct way.

It turns out that although I was right that the documents were connected, I was wrong, at least in one respect. While this phrase, and the distinctive usage incorporated by this writer, was valuable in an evidentiary sense and served to further link the two sets of documents in terms of common authorship, I learned shortly afterwards through my own research that it was not really a mistake. In fact, if anyone was making a mistake, it was virtually everyone, myself included, who states or writes the same proverb as "You can't have your cake and eat it too."

The latter form is the generally accepted usage in modern American English and the form that has been used for several hundred years now in the United States. However, the historically correct form, and the form based in fifteenth-century Middle English, is the one the Unabomber and Ted Kaczynski used. And when one thinks about it, it actually makes more sense to state it this way. (You *can* have your cake and eat it too. You cannot "have" the cake after you "eat" it though.) So, linguistically speaking, at least from an historical sense, he had it right, and the majority of American English speakers had it wrong. But his having it right in a very uncommon way added greatly to the value of this finding and the project. When the doubting AUSA Freccero was presented with this comparative example shortly after it was uncovered, he immediately realized its importance and the potential importance of the rest of the comparative analysis project.

Toward late March of 1996, the project was running well. The final U-Doc/T-Doc comparative analysis report was being typed, and it was to be incorporated into a comprehensive report that detailed all the ancillary findings relating to the collection of documents. However, the compilation of this master report was put on hold on March 31, as the UTF had a bombshell of its own with which to deal.

The fact that the UTF was in existence was no secret. The public was aware of this because of occasional media coverage, whether welcomed or not. However, it was a well-kept secret that we had developed a very good suspect in Ted Kaczynski. The press had no idea of this fact, at least not until about March 31.

It was at that time that CBS News unexpectedly contacted the UTF. The reporter advised ASAC Turchie that he had a very reliable and high-placed source in the federal government who told him many of the details of what the UTF had been working so diligently to keep from the public and the media all these months. CBS knew that we had a viable suspect; that he lived in Lincoln, Montana; and that we had teams of undercover agents there already in place. CBS was correct on all counts. The reporter informed us that news anchor Dan Rather was going to broadcast the story on the 6:30 news that night, March 31.

The FBI was not prepared to arrest Kaczynski that day. The affidavit was simply not ready yet. And if CBS went public with this information, and Kaczynski was not under arrest, he would surely attempt to flee into the Montana woods and mountains. Even though he had no television, it would only be a matter of hours before an enterprising CBS reporter would have most likely knocked on his cabin door, stuck a microphone in his face, and asked him a question similar to, "What does it feel like to be the Unabomber?"

In an effort to stall for time, then–FBI director Louis Freeh contacted the president of CBS News, and a compromise was reached. CBS would give us three days, no more, no less, and then it would broadcast the story whether or not the FBI was ready. That meant the Unabomber had to be under arrest in less than seventy-two hours. (This scenario is referenced, in part, in the 1999 film *The Insider*.)

THE SEARCH AND ARREST

The plans of the UTF remained essentially the same as they were all along, but we now had to greatly expedite them. We were in the process of assembling all our data, information, and evidence and incorporating it into a probable cause affidavit. We hoped to obtain a signed federal search warrant in the district of Montana and proceed to Kaczynski's cabin on the morning of April 3, 1996. At that time, there was simply not enough probable cause to arrest Kaczynski, but it was felt that there was enough to legally obtain entry into his cabin to search it. It was hoped that enough evidence would be found in his cabin so that he could then be arrested. The next three days were quite dynamic. Additional teams of agents were flying to Helena, Montana; renting sport utility vehicles (SUVs); and driving the rest of the way to Lincoln. Available SUVs and hotel space in the Helena/Lincoln area were becoming quite scarce in early April of that year. No doubt, CBS personnel were renting them, too.

Our team was assigned to finalize the comparative analysis report and get it ready to attach to the probable cause affidavit. At this point, it was fifty pages long, and there were nearly seven hundred examples of linguistic similarities, if not exact matches, of the T-Docs in a column on the left side of the page to the U-Docs on the right side of the page. There were no opinions asked for in this document, nor were any offered. The document stood on its own linguistically. Either the probable cause was there for the judge to determine, or it was not.

On April 2, the UTF comparative analysis project team, still in San Francisco, learned that a federal judge in Montana read the entire search warrant application, including our report. He determined there was probable cause, signed it, and the search was about to begin.

The next day, Kaczynski's cabin was approached on foot by two FBI agents and a US forest service officer. Other agents were hiding in the woods in case Kaczynski tried to flee. The agents knocked on the cabin door, and the focus of an eighteen-year-long serial bombing investigation met his adversaries for the first time. He did not know this yet, as the FBI agents at his door did not immediately identify themselves. Initially, they asked him questions relating to his property line. This was done in an attempt to distract him, get him out of his doorway, and away from any potential weapons. Within a minute or two, Kaczynski warily stepped outside of his doorway and the agents identified themselves. He attempted to run into the woods but was wrestled to the ground and handcuffed. The terror campaign of the Unabomber was now officially over. The UTF was monitoring the agents' telephone and radio traffic transmitted from Montana into our workstation in San Francisco. When we heard the words "Kaczynski is in custody," a sigh of relief was expressed by all. And most importantly, everyone was safe. Now, the logical question was, what would be found inside the cabin?

It took several days to fully examine Kaczynski's cabin because the bomb technicians had to sweep it first for any working bombing devices and/or booby traps. Once safely inside his ten-foot by twelve-foot cabin, it was found to be a virtual treasure trove of evidentiary materials. In fact, I received a phone call from ASAC Turchie, who was in Lincoln, and he advised me that along with at least one fully assembled bomb and numerous bomb parts, there were also reams of new documents for my team to review. So, based on that phone call, the day after Easter Sunday 1996, my team and I headed northeast to Montana.

All of us in the UTF were naturally hoping we would find something of evidentiary value in the cabin. We were conservatively optimistic that perhaps a copy of the WP's printed manifesto or even some newspaper articles about the UNABOM case would be found. Those of us who were truly positive thinking hoped that the U-Doc typewriter itself would be located there. Within several days, the evidence team recovered all the mentioned items. In addition, the team found original handwritten versions of the manifesto, handwritten versions of practically every U-Doc, Kaczynski's personal journal, his personal notes, his autobiography, books in which bombs were described, details of bombing events, potential victim lists, and much more.

The UTF's comparative analysis team's next project was to read and categorize all the now-called Cabin Documents (C-Docs). There were more than a thousand of these documents, entailing several thousand pages in total. This project took place in Helena and took over two weeks to complete. No linguistic analysis of these documents was necessary, just the reading and reviewing of them to prepare for Kaczynski's trial. At this time, there was no doubt as to the complicity of Kaczynski in the sixteen bombings. He told us in his own words via his writings. (However, he never did give an oral statement to any investigator. Once in custody, he was polite, but he refused to answer any questions relating to his cabin or the bombings.)

The Montana aspect of the investigation was about to end. My days at the UTF in this phase were soon numbered. I returned to Quantico in early May to resume my regular duties. But my role in the Unabom case was still not complete.

TRIAL PREPARATION

I was called back to San Francisco months later to assist in the trial preparation for *U.S.* v. *Kaczynski*. Since he had no money, the government appointed him a team of lawyers to assist in his defense. The lawyers, in turn, hired their own experts to dispute various aspects of the UNABOM investigation and Kaczynski's arrest. If they could get a ruling from the judge during the pretrial stage that the search warrant was obtained by the FBI improperly, and that there was not enough probable cause to support the search, the entire case against Kaczynski could conceivably be dismissed. One of the primary areas they contested was our team's fifty-page report in the probable cause affidavit. This was certainly expected, but the methodology employed to attack it, and the person they hired to attack it, surprised many people.

A. DEFENSE TEAM'S EXPERT WITNESS

After at least one rejection from another expert, the Kaczynski defense team hired Dr. Robin Lakoff of the University of California at Berkeley as their linguistic expert. Her affidavit was received by the UTF in March 1997. After noting her academic and professional achievements, she wrote that the FBI's findings regarding the textual analysis were flawed. She then listed seven categories of errors made by the FBI in its report.

The first of Lakoff's categories was "Allegations of identity of authorship based on the double use of content-linked lexical choices in the T-Docs and the U-Docs." Her passage continued, "In many instances the FBI analysis alleges similarities between passages in the T-Docs and the U-Docs of two types, where in fact only one type of similarity exists. In each instance, the similarity in topic or *content* necessitates similarity in wording or *diction*." (Lakoff's italics.) Thus, each instance is counted twice in the FBI's analysis, where it should only count as an instance of one type or the other. Several examples are then listed.

Category two reads, "Allegations of identity of authorship based on similarities in diction, i.e., the use in both the T-Docs and the U-Docs of very common words. Since these words would be expected to appear in documents of any length written in contemporary English, their appearance in the texts of both documents cited [do] not argue for identity of authorship." Examples are then included.

Category three reads, "Allegations of identity of authorship of T-Docs and U-Docs based on the use in both categories of documents of words that, while less common than those cited in above, nevertheless are of frequent occurrence in scientific, formal, or scholarly prose (such as presented in the 1971 essay and the UNABOM manuscript); or are especially apt to be prevalent in writing on topics dealt with by both the essay and the UNABOM manuscript, e.g., technology and society."

Category four deals with lexical similarities in which the comparisons "are used in different senses, or in different contexts."

Category five deals with "claimed idiosyncrasies in spelling and/or usage, while not the most common, [are] nonetheless a common secondary form as listed in dictionaries and manuals of English usage."

Category six deals with Spanish/English miscomparisons.

Category seven deals with typographical errors.

Lakoff ended the declaration with, "On the basis of the foregoing findings, I find the FBI claims of authorial identity of the T-Documents and the U-Documents to be untenable and unreliable at best."

B. FBI'S RESPONSE

I was asked to draft a report challenging every one of Lakoff's categories and clarifying the FBI's position in its findings. While I acknowledged the several typographical errors referenced in category seven, the rest of my report responded to every one of her allegations point by point.

At least one aspect of the FBI's fifty-page report that Lakoff apparently did not comprehend was the concept of totality. It was clearly recognized by the FBI that no one comparison or example would link the two sets of documents. Instead, it was the almost seven hundred comparisons, including many virtually identically written sentences, each discussing such divergent topics as technology, mass entertainment, psychology, and freedom, in their entirety, which made for the strongest argument. This was an argument that Lakoff somehow failed to grasp or chose to ignore.

It was mutually decided between the prosecutors and the rest of the UTF management that we would need to respond to Lakoff's declaration from the same arena in which she challenged the FBI's.

C. PROSECUTION TEAM'S EXPERT WITNESS

The prosecution team felt it would be appropriate to hire its own expert, a move that I fully supported, to review my UTF report, my response, and Lakoff's declaration and to respond to the defense affidavit accordingly. The team hired Dr. Donald Foster, a professor of English at Vassar College, in Poughkeepsie, New York, who, at the time, had recently gained notoriety by his identification of the author of the book *Primary Colors*. Coincidentally, he was the person that the defense team had initially attempted to hire. However, he had turned them down upon reviewing the FBI report. He knew he could not assist the defense in this regard, as based on the documents and reports they provided him, he could not dispute the FBI report.

Foster's first declaration, after being provided to the defense team, was attacked in a second subsequent declaration by Lakoff. Foster, in rebuttal to Lakoff, prepared his second declaration, addressing each of her issues in a cogent and well-founded manner. He sums up his findings best in the conclusion of his forty-eight-page report. It reads, "In a computer-assisted study extending to thousands of writers, hundreds of thousand of texts, and millions of words, I find no individual whose writings more closely match those of the UNABOM subject than Theodore J. Kaczynski. I find throughout the T- and U-Documents the same linguistic habits, the same patterns in diction, phrasing, spelling, grammatical accidence, and customary syntax—even the same distinctive punctuation. I find throughout the documents the same anarchist and neo-Luddite ideology; similar reference or allusion to many of the same secondary sources." The last sentence reads, "I consider the authorial identity of the T-Docs and the U-Docs to be a virtual certainty, the truth of which I am convinced beyond any reasonable doubt."

Foster's two affidavits were submitted to the court, and the motion to suppress the evidence filed by the defense was denied by the judge. In other words, the FBI's report stood on its own merit, and contrary to Lakoff's opinion, it was tenable and reliable. A detailed overview of this aspect of the Unabom case is found in chapter 3 of Foster's book, *Author Unknown: On the Trail of Anonymous*.

In retrospect, Lakoff's problems were seemingly twofold. First, while she has a demonstrated expertise in the area of linguistics, specifically gender and language issues, she has little, if any, known training or experience in the field of forensic linguistics or authorship attribution. Second, and most important, she did not read most of the documents associated with this case, which she readily admits in her own signed affidavit. She never read the manifesto or any of the U-Docs or T-Docs. She read only the FBI reports relating to them and a report assembled by the defense team. It is unclear how anyone could render an expert linguistic opinion having never read the most pertinent documents in a particular case. I believe that because of this, in part, and Foster's salient rebuttal to her affidavit (he is reported to have read all the U-Docs and T-Docs), the defense motion was unsuccessful.

In view of the above, there are at least two issues potential expert witnesses should consider before providing linguistic opinions, especially for court-related purposes:

1. One should deliberate very carefully when venturing outside of his or her field of demonstrated expertise or professional/academic experience.
2. One should read every document directly associated with the particular analysis at hand. Merely reading someone else's summary report, or only some of the documents, severely handicaps the expert from rendering a tenable opinion.

In 1999, Theodore J. Kaczynski pleaded guilty to numerous federal charges related to his role in the deaths of three people as the result of his bombings. This was after he was found to be legally competent to stand trial. He is presently serving multiple life sentences in a maximum-security prison in Florence, Colorado. In March 2002, the United States Supreme Court denied Kaczynski's appeal. He has no remaining options in the appellate process.

Why did the Unabomber send his bombs? Why did he choose certain victims? Time and space do not permit discussion of this matter in great detail. However, suffice it to say, the reasons for Kaczynski wanting to kill people were rooted in his somewhat conflicted psychological makeup. Yet the reasons were actually quite basic in nature. These were learned upon reading his personal documents found inside his cabin subsequent to his arrest.

Primarily, Kaczynski was very frustrated with the fact that he never had a successful relationship with a woman. He was heterosexual, yet he had never engaged in a relationship of any duration or significance with a woman. His writings indicated that this notion frustrated him greatly, and he linked this fact with his penchant for wanting to kill people. He also knew the vast shortcomings of his own personality. He knew he was brilliant, yet he was aware that he had limited social skills. That is why he chose to get as far away as he possibly could from other humans, living in a remote cabin in the woods of Montana.

Why some of the targets? While investigators put much thought into the rationale for the Unabomber's target selection, as it turned out, his selection process was very elementary in design. Kaczynski chose representational targets—that is, targets that were not necessarily directly associated with him but that represented an issue problematic to him in some way. He bombed universities and/or professors because he could not succeed professionally in his short stint as a mathematics teacher at the University of California at Berkeley. While he knew his subject matter, he did not function well within the faculty ranks or with his students. So he ultimately attempted to destroy people similar to them years later.

The computer industry represented one of the advances of technology that Kaczynski so much despised. A modern computer could calculate in seconds a mathematical problem that used to take him hours, if not days, to resolve. This explains several of his early bombings. Also, twice a day, Kaczynski heard commercial aircraft flying over his cabin. The noise of the jet engines, even at over twenty thousand feet, and this "violation" of his vertical property rights disturbed him immensely. So in the early 1980s, he bombed various entities associated with the airline industry. The forestry lobbyist was killed because a sawmill opened approximately a half mile from Kaczynski's cabin. The noise offended him, and he decided to make a randomly chosen lumber company advocate, living and working over a thousand miles away, pay with his life. Other victims were chosen for similar reasons. All reasons very personal to Kaczynski and difficult to understand by others.

Why he chose to begin writing letters and mailing them to the various recipients was also based on very personal reasoning on the part of Kaczynski. Quite frankly, if he remained as careful as he had been in the construction and mailing of his bombing devices, and he chose never to begin writing to others, he may have still been a free man to this day. Upon the review of all his writings, he never clearly answers this question. Apparently, something compelled him to go public with his ideology, and he obviously did it in a grandiose way. Ultimately, as is now seen, it led to his personal downfall.

It is hoped that I will have the opportunity to interview Kaczynski in prison one day as part of an ongoing serial bomber research project being undertaken in the FBI. If and when I do, the issue of why he started writing will be one of the first questions I ask him.

CONCLUSION

Being involved in an integral way in the UNABOM case was a once-in-a-lifetime opportunity. I feel very fortunate to have been asked to participate in one of the most interesting and challenging criminal investigations of the twentieth century. Forming and supervising the comparative analysis project in this case was even more rewarding. In that fourteen-month period, I learned more about the practical application of forensic linguistics, at least in terms of authorial attribution, than in my entire career up to that time. Furthermore, I was encouraged to pursue academic studies in the field of linguistics, a process in which I am now well engaged and fully committed.

The FBI and the UTF did not necessarily invent anything or any process in its implementation of the text-analysis aspect of the UNABOM investigation. Most applications had been used previously in one investigation or another. However, the totality of these practices had never been used in an investigation of this scope and scale in the past. The bottom line: it worked.

While I see the successful resolution of this case as a victory for the FBI and the UTF, I also see it as a victory for the field of forensic linguistics. The day the federal judge in Montana signed the search warrant, the probable cause of which was substantially derived from the text-analysis aspect of the investigation, the field of forensic linguistics took a giant step forward in the criminal justice process. The denial of the defense motion to suppress the fifty-page report provided an even stronger endorsement.

It is hoped that this article will aid and assist the other investigators/analysts, whether in the public or private sector, in law enforcement or academics, in managing and preparing for their next case in the area of forensic linguistics. There may never be another investigation quite like the UNABOM case. However, the experiences of that investigation, and what the US courts reviewed and upheld as admissible evidence, has set the legal precedent for continued use of this process in future criminal and civil court proceedings.

REFERENCES

1979. Webster's New Collegiate Dictionary. Springfield, MA: G. and C. Merriam.

1996. *The American Heritage Dictionary of the English Language*, 3rd ed. Boston: Houghton Mifflin.

De Man, Paul. 1983. *Blindness and Insight*, 2nd ed. Minneapolis: University of Minnesota Press.

Foster, Donald W. 2000. *Author Unknown: On the Trail of Anonymous*. New York: Henry Holt.

Johnson, Edward D. 1982. *The Handbook of Good English*. New York: Pocket Books.

Lakoff, Robin T. March 2, 1997. Written Declaration to United States District Court, Eastern District of California.

Zy-Index, a product of ZyLAB, Germantown, Maryland.

Chapter 15

CRIMINAL PROFILING
THE FBI USES CRIMINAL INVESTIGATIVE ANALYSIS TO SOLVE CRIMES

Mary Ellen O'Toole

Mary Ellen O'Toole, PhD, is a supervisory special agent at the National Center for the Analysis of Violent Crimes, located at the Federal Bureau of Investigation Academy in Quantico, Virginia.

Violent crime scenes tell a story—a story written by the offender, the victim, and the unique circumstances of their interactions. Behavioral "clues" left at a crime scene can provide insights not only into the crime itself but also into the type of person responsible for the crime and his or her motivation, lifestyle, fantasies, victim selection process, and preoffense and postoffense behavior.[1]

Criminal profiling is a process now known in the Federal Bureau of Investigation (FBI) as criminal investigative analysis. Profilers, or criminal investigative analysts, are highly trained and experienced law enforcement officers who study every behavioral aspect and detail of an unsolved violent crime scene in which a certain amount of psychopathology has been left at the scene. Psychopathology is an offender's behavioral and psychological indicators that are left at a violent crime scene as a result of his physical, sexual, and, in some cases, verbal interaction with his victim(s). Violent crimes can be profiled only if residual offender psychopathology can be identified. Such crimes include homi-

Published in a slightly different form in *Corrections Today* 61 (February 1999): 44–46. Copyright © 1999. Reprinted with permission of the American Correctional Association, Lanham, MD.

cides, sexual assaults, kidnappings, extortions, bombings, product tampering, and threats. A profile, or criminal investigative analysis, is an investigative tool, and its value is measured in terms of how much assistance it provides to the investigator.

Police reports, crime scene photographs, witness statements, forensic laboratory reports, and, if the case is a homicide, autopsy photographs are provided by the investigating law enforcement agency and are carefully examined for the smallest behavioral detail or nuance. Through this intense review process, a "behavioral" blueprint of the crime and the offender can be constructed. This blueprint allows a profiler to re-create what happened at the scene.

A profile can provide a wide range of information concerning the offender and his or her lifestyle, including race and gender, emotional age (rather than his chronological age), marital status, level of formal education or training, and occupation and work history. It also can include details about the offender's ability to relate and communicate with others, the likelihood of prior criminal activity, the presence of mental deterioration, feelings of remorse and/or guilt concerning the crime or the victim, the likelihood of committing a similar crime again, and sexual dysfunctioning,[2] which is an impairment either in the desire for sexual gratification or in the ability to achieve it.[3]

When beginning to construct a profile, one must complete a comprehensive review and a close examination of case materials, which include police reports; witness and victim statements; the victimology, or extensive background information on the victim; results of the neighborhood investigation; the medical examiner's report, if applicable; forensic reports; and a comprehensive series of photographs of the crime scene, including autopsy photos if the case is a homicide. This in-depth review allows the profiler to begin to reconstruct how the crime most likely occurred and the interaction between the offender and the victim.[4] The profiler then examines the crime scene to identify all the behaviors, which, taken as an aggregate, can be interpreted and extrapolated into investigative suggestions and profile characteristics.

PROFILER CHARACTERISTICS

What qualities or traits constitute a good profiler? Contrary to the current television and movie depictions in which a profiler can "just see it happening," a successful profiler is not psychic. An experienced and well-trained profiler is intuitive, has a great deal of common sense, and is able to think and evaluate information in a concise and logical manner. A successful profiler also is able to suppress his or her personal feelings about the crime by viewing the scene and the offender-victim interaction from an analytical point of view. Most important, a successful profiler is able to view the crime from the offender's perspective rather than his or her own.[5]

In addition, the successful profiler possesses an in-depth understanding of human behavior, human sexuality, crime scene investigation, and forensics and has extensive training and experience in studying violent crimes and providing interpretations of his or her insights and observations to investigators.

Profiling is not a new concept. Variations of profiling have been used for many years in an effort to understand particularly heinous individuals, such as Adolf Hitler, or to attempt to resolve a baffling crime or series of crimes. During the 1950s, several bombings occurred in New York City, and the unknown offender ultimately became known as "The Mad Bomber." Despite intense investigative efforts, law enforcement officials were unable to identify this individual. Dr. James A. Brussel, a New York psychiatrist, was brought into the case to "profile" the personality of this unknown offender. Brussel studied the facts surrounding this series of bombings and from this review developed an assessment of the offender's personality. His assessment was remarkably accurate.

In addition to other characteristics, Brussel opined that the offender would be between forty and fifty years old, of Eastern European heritage, and living in Connecticut with a maiden aunt or sister, and he would have a paranoid personality. However, the most remarkable characteristic that Brussel offered investigators was that when they identified their offender, not only would he be dressed in a double-breasted suit, but all the buttons on his suit coat would be properly buttoned. When police eventually arrested George Metesky, not only did he fit the profile provided by Brussel, but also he was wearing a double-breasted suit with every button properly buttoned.[6]

It was not until the mid 1970s that profiling started to become a more refined process. Research conducted by the FBI into serial murderers and rapists provided a much greater understanding of these offenders and the often complex, curious, and unique behavior they display at their crime scenes.[7]

BEHAVIORAL CHARACTERISTICS

Several behavioral characteristics that can be gleaned from dynamics identified at the scene include the 1) amount of planning that went into the crime, 2) degree of control used by the offender, 3) escalation of emotion at the scene, 4) risk level of both the offender and victim, and 5) appearance of the crime scene (disorganized versus organized).

Level of Planning. One of the behavioral indicators that can suggest that the offender planned out some or many aspects of the crime is the lack of physical evidence found at the scene. The lack of physical evidence suggests that the offender considered what precautions to take so he or she would not leave a forensic trail, such as fingerprints, semen, hairs, and so forth. A well-planned crime can suggest a sophisticated and/or experienced offender.[8]

Level of Control. The amount of control the offender exercises over the victim can often be seen in markings or impressions found on the victim's body left by bindings and/or ligatures used to restrain the victim. If the bindings or ligatures appear to be excessive and/or unnecessary, experience with prior similar bondage behavior suggests the offender could be a sexual sadist and looking for other indicators or "red flags" of this paraphilic behavior becomes extremely important.[9]

Level of Emotion. Injuries and physical trauma suffered by the victim can suggest the amount of emotion the offender brought to the crime scene or the anger he or she developed once at the scene. For example, if the offender is extremely angry at the victim during the assault, the resulting injuries to the victim will frequently appear to be excessive, extensive, and even lethal. *Overkill*, which is "excessive trauma or injury beyond that necessary to cause death," frequently is the result of a very angry offender.[10]

Escalation of an argument or fight also can be detected at a crime scene. Battery to the victim's face and trauma to other parts of the body, including defensive injuries on the victim, can indicate there was an escalation of emotion during the crime. Escalation suggests the offender and victim began their interaction with a verbal altercation, followed by a physical assault, in some instances resulting in death. Knowing how to interpret escalation from the scene becomes very important for the investigator because the reason for the argument becomes a critical part of understanding the motive for the crime.[11]

Offender and Victim Risk Levels. Both the victim and the offender's risk levels are important components in a crime scene and important for the profiler to understand when assessing or profiling the crime. Victimology is the study of the victim(s) of a violent crime or crime series. The premise in developing a victimology is that the more that is known about the victim, the greater insight investigators will have about the offender.[12] The profiler must ask how likely it is, considering the victim's lifestyle, family, friends, habits, behaviors, and environment, that this person would have become the victim of a violent crime. To answer this question, the risk level of the victim must be assessed to determine whether the victim is a high-, medium-, or low-risk victim. A low-risk victim, for example, is the homicide victim with an ordinary background who works during the day inside his or her secured home located in a low-crime area, with a protective dog in the backyard. The likelihood of this victim randomly encountering a murderer in this environment is very low. It is much more likely this victim knew his or her offender.[13]

A high-risk victim can be a prostitute, drug dealer, hitchhiker, or anyone whose lifestyle exposes him or her to exponential dangers. Crimes involving high-risk victims are extremely difficult to profile because these people could be victimized by any number of people.

Understanding the risk level of the offender also is important. How much risk did the offender take in committing this crime, in terms of where the crime occurred, the time of day it occurred, and the type of victim the offender selected? If a review of these variables suggest there is a high level of risk for identification and apprehension to the offender, the question must be asked, "Why did this offender take this kind of risk?" especially if other aspects of the crime suggest that he or she planned the crime well. Two possible explanations are that 1) the offender targeted that particular victim, or 2) this offender needed an element of high risk/high thrill in the crime to be emotionally or psychologically satisfied. Either conclusion reached by the profiler can be extremely helpful to investigators. If the first determination is made, that is, this offender wanted and targeted a particular victim, an even more intense investigation of the victim and his or her background would be extremely important, since some type of relationship likely existed between them before the crime occurred. On the other hand, if the offender needs a sense of risk or thrill in his or her crimes, that "need" could be present in other unrelated crimes in his or her background, which might otherwise be overlooked by investigators.[14]

Organized and Disorganized Homicide Crime Scenes. Homicide scenes are behaviorally categorized according to whether they are an organized or disorganized scene. No homicide scene is exclusively one way or the other. It is based on a preponderance of the behavioral characteristics observed at the scene. An organized homicide scene suggests "a semblance of order existed prior to, during and after the offense." An organized scene suggests a carefully planned crime that is aimed at deterring detection. A disorganized homicide scene gives the impression that "the crime has been committed suddenly and with no set plan of action for deterring detection."

The degree of organization or disorganization can provide tremendous insights into the level of sophistication of the offender, including the approach used in accessing the victim, the style of attack, the relationship of the victim to the offender, and the type of interaction that likely took place at the scene between the offender and the victim.[15]

INTERPRETATION PROCESS

The interpretation of behavior observed at a crime scene is extremely difficult. It is not a science or psychic guess, but rather a process. Profiling is based on research and years of experience in reviewing similar cases with similar psychopathology and offender characteristics. A successful profiler must be able to read all the behavior and behavioral clusters present at the scene in order to understand the dynamics that took place there. This is the only way a profiler can make behavioral interpretations, which will help the investigator to limit the suspect pool and structure investigative strategies. The experience of the FBI's research of violent offenders strongly suggests that "similar crimes committed for similar reasons generally are perpetrated by similar offenders."[16] In other words, "If you want to understand the artist, you have to look at the painting," and "To know the offender, you have to look at the crime."[17]

NOTES

1. R. Ressler, A. Burgess, and J. Douglas, *Sexual Homicide: Patterns and Motives* (Lexington, MA: Lexington Books, 1988).

2. R. Hazelwood and A. Burgess, eds., *Practical Aspects of Rape Investigation: A Multidisciplinary Approach* (New York: Elsevier Books, 1987).

3. J. C. Coleman et al., *Abnormal Psychology and Modern Life*, 6th ed. (Glenview, IL: Scott, Foresman, 1980).

4. J. Douglas, Ann Burgess, Allen Burgess, and R. Ressler, *Crime Classification Manual* (New York: Lexington Books, 1992).

5. Hazelwood and Burgess, *Practical Aspects of Rape Investigation*.

6. A. Pinizzotto, "Forensic Psychology: Criminal Personality Profiling," *Journal of Police Science and Administration* 12, no. 1 (1984): 32.

7. Douglas, Burgess, Burgess, and Ressler, *Crime Classification Manual*.

8. Ibid.

9. Hazelwood and Burgess, *Practical Aspects of Rape Investigation*.

10. Douglas, Burgess, Burgess, and Ressler, *Crime Classification Manual*.

11. Ressler, Burgess, and Douglas, *Sexual Homicide*.

12. R. Hilley and M. O'Toole, *In Search of a Kidnapper—Through the Eyes of a Child* (San Francisco: US Department of Justice, Federal Bureau of Investigation, Crimes Against Children Task Force, 1996).

13. Ressler, Burgess, and Douglas, *Sexual Homicide*.

14. Ibid.

15. Ibid.

16. Hazelwood and Burgess, *Practical Aspects of Rape Investigation*.

17. J. Douglas and M. Olshaker, *Mind Hunter* (New York: Scribner, 1995).

ASSAULTIVE EYE INQUIRY AND ENUCLEATION

Alexander O. Bukhanovsky, Anthony Hempel,
Waseem Ahmed, J. Reid Meloy, Alan C. Brantley,
Daniel Cuneo, Roman Gleyzer, and Alan R. Felthous

An especially dangerous behavior observed in some forensic and security hospital populations is assaultive eye gouging. Although a number of case reports in the literature concern auto-enucleation, gouging out the eyes of another is virtually unmentioned. We present a case series of eye gougers (n = 10) gathered through clinical contributions from several forensic populations in the United States and Russia. Four subjects were psychotic during the eye-gouging episode; one was only mentally retarded; and five, who were neither psychotic nor retarded, deliberately injured victims' eyes during acts of extreme sexual violence.

> *Lest it see more, prevent it. Out, vile jelly! [said Cornwall as he plucked out Gloucester's other eye.] Where is thy luster now?*
> —Shakespeare, *King Lear* 3.7

Assaultive ocular injury and enucleation, the deliberate injury or complete gouging of another person's eyeball(s), is a serious and dangerous behavior, a form of mayhem resulting in mutilation or permanent deprivation of vision and/or causing disfigurement and pain and grief for the victim if he or she survives. We include in this concept the mutilation of a murdered victim's eyeball(s)

Published in a slightly different form in *Journal of the American Academy of Psychiatry and the Law* 27, no. 4 (1999): 590–602. Copyright © 1999. Reprinted by permission.

when perpetrated by the murderer himself. Curiously, this alarming behavior has received virtually no attention in the professional research. Why would someone want to enucleate the eyes of another person? In what psychopathological conditions can such behavior occur? These are some of the issues addressed by our case examples derived from several forensic populations and representing various psychopathologies and other possible predisposing conditions.

In contrast to the assaultive enucleation of other people, *self*-enucleation has been presented and discussed in the literature, at least through individual and series case reports.[1] Subjects reported in the psychiatric literature were typically psychotically disturbed at the time of the self-enucleation. In some cases, a mind-altering substance was involved. In several cases, the self-enucleator felt driven to obey a familiar Biblical injunction (Matthew 5:29: "And if thy right eye offend thee, pluck it out") within the context of a very concrete and personalized interpretation. In some cases, self-enucleation involved guilt over sexual issues, reminiscent of the myth of Oedipus.

Felthous and Meloy contributed several unusual case reports of men accused of violent offenses, including murder.[2] Before the violent act, each had experienced bizarre perceptions and/or delusions involving cats or dogs. In a few of these cases, psychotic thinking regarding the animal involved the perception that the animal was staring at the individual and the animal's eyes were visibly changing in some manner. In a few cases, the subject was thought to have killed the animal before allegedly committing murder, but eye gouging of animals or homicide victims was not involved. Meloy discussed this phenomenon in the context of scopophilia, oral sadism, and the Cyclopean glaring eye.[3]

Assaultive enucleation is referenced in myth, legend, and history. According to Egyptian mythology, the sky god Horus, representing Lower Egypt, took the incarnate form of a falcon, whose right eye was the sun and left eye, the moon. Seth, a god representing Upper Egypt, was defeated by Horus, whose eye was damaged in the battle.[4] According to another version, Horus either wounded Seth's testicles or Horus lost his testicles in the struggle for the throne of Egypt, and Seth damaged one or both of Horus's eyes. In a third version of this myth, Seth, incarnate as a black boar, either shredded the moon eye of Horus or ingested it. According to a fourth version, Seth gouged out the eyes of Horus, but his eyesight was restored by rubbing with the milk of a gazelle.[5] Salient in the Horus and Seth myths is the close association between sexual aggression and eye gouging.

A recurrent belief among peoples of various cultures and ages is in the mysterious, puissant ability of the eyes to express evil and cause harm. For a thorough treatise on this topic, the reader is referred to the classic contribution of Frederic Elworthy, *The Evil Eye.*[6]

From ancient times in Russia, cutting off part of the body (hand, finger, foot, ear, nose, tongue) was a fairly common form of punishment, and eye gouging played a historical role in several struggles for political power.[7] Vasily II Vasilevich, Tiomny (1425–1462), the Grand Duke of Moscow and Vladimir and grandfather of Ivan the Terrible, was a central figure in one such struggle.[8] His uncle

Yury and Yury's sons, Vasily Kosoy and Dmitry Shemiaka, did not want ten-year-old Vasily to become the Grand Duke. In the ensuing conflict, lasting years and into his adulthood and dukedom, Vasily II's minions abducted and blinded Vasily Kosoy, his cousin. Vasily II, in turn, was captured by Dmitry Shemiaka and blinded (hence, his sobriquet *Tiomny*, which means "dark").[9] With the help of other intelligent and energetic supporters, Grand Duke Vasily II, although blind, continued to rule and was known for his capacity for cruelty.[10]

Russian Orthodox Bishop Feodorets in the city of Vladimir was known for various cruelties, including burning out the eyes of his victims.[11] The ruling metropolitan punished Bishop Feodorets for his atrocities by sentencing him to have Ins his tongue cut out, his right hand cut off, and his eyes removed.

Ivan Vasilyevich, Ivan IV, known in the West as Ivan the Terrible and in Russia as Ioann Grozny (1530–1584), was the first official Tsar of Russia and undoubtedly the most notorious. Ivan's young mother was poisoned when he was only eight years old. As a child, he had been cruel to animals. By age fifteen, he proclaimed himself ruler of Russia and began persecuting the boyars (aristocrats ranked below princes in early Russia). He threw one into a cage with guard dogs and killed many himself. Also at fifteen years, together with peers, he amused himself by riding through the city and injuring children and elderly women.[12] As Tsar of Russia, his alleged cruelties were many and diverse. An especially sadistic method of torturing and killing his victims was termed "sitting on a stick"; death came only after hours of agony from impalation. After discovering that his first wife, Vasilisa Melentievna, had been unfaithful, Ivan had her bound, gagged, placed in a coffin, and buried alive.[13]

Ivan ordered the construction of the Cathedral of St. Basil the Blessed (1555–1560), today the oldest building in Moscow's Red Square. According to legend, he intended for this commemoration of the Russian conquest of a Tatar city, Kazan, to be unique and the most beautiful cathedral in the world.[14] To ensure the edifice would never be replicated nor its magnificence surpassed, he had the architects who designed it enucleated and blinded.

Historically, eye gouging has been used as a method of terrorism and as a punishment to enforce social norms. In nineteenth-century America, Irish gangsters used eye gouging against Englishmen, especially in large cities. Settlers on the American frontier mutilated Native Americans in this manner.[15] In the 1870s, gangster Dandy Johnny Dolen invented a copper instrument specifically for eye gouging. In Africa, members of several tribes (Pokot, Turkana, and Karamojong) wear a wrist knife (*abaret*) specifically for assaultive enucleation, typically in protection of their cattle.[16]

EYE GOUGERS REPORTED IN THE NEWS MEDIA

We first turned to popular news media for secondary reports of eye gougers because this phenomenon has not been previously addressed in the professional literature. Because we had not examined these individuals directly, for both ethical and clinical reasons, we cannot establish or rule out specific diagnoses. We handle these cases separately from those subjects who had been interviewed and evaluated by one of us directly, and we acknowledge that there undoubtedly are others reported in the popular media that have not come to our attention.

A case reported by several newspapers in 1994 involved three sisters who consulted a "hoodoo man" in Louisiana to help solve a family conflict, hoodoo representing a mixture of religious practices from Africa, Haiti, and Christianity.[17] Two of the sisters later reported that the third underwent mysterious changes. They believed that she had been overcome by an evil spirit. They beat their sister, pressed garlic cloves into her eyes, and then one of the sisters proceeded to gouge out her eyes while quoting Matthew 5:29. From the popular news accounts, the motivation for this eye gouging was fear within the context of religious beliefs.

Another newspaper account reported that a thirty-six-year-old man had been accused of attacking a woman on a jogging trail.[18] He allegedly. dragged her from the trail, attempted to sexually assault her, and forced his thumbs into her eyes, which resulted in permanent blindness of one eye.[19]

A third account was reported in a book about Charles F. Albright, a known serial killer who had a long-standing fascination with eyes.[20] Skilled in taxidermy, he stuffed a number of animals that remained eyeless, even though he reportedly had a jar filled with artificial animal eyes. He was eventually sentenced to life for killing at least. three women, all of whom had been mutilated and had had both eyes skillfully excised.

Other examples could be listed, but popular news accounts have limited clinical information, and the authenticity of secondhand and thirdhand reports is questionable. We now turn to our series of case reports ($n = 10$), whose subjects are grouped as psychotic, mentally retarded, and psychopathic, respectively.

PSYCHOTIC EYE GOUGERS

Case A. Mr. A., a twenty-three-year-old single Caucasian male, employed as an electrician, was found not guilty by reason of insanity (NGRI) of aggravated assault and kidnapping, the assault involving the enucleation of his girlfriend's right eye.

At the age of twenty-two, while working as an electrician, Mr. A. called his girlfriend of six months and asked her to give him a ride home. While in her car, he reported, "I saw angels in her eyes." At her apartment, after drinking one or two glasses of wine and having sexual intercourse with her, he was overtaken by the paranoid delusion that his girlfriend was the devil. He exclaimed, "I could see the devil coming from her eyes." He began choking her. He punched her, and then he totally enucleated his girlfriend's right eye and blinded her left eye with his thumbs. While gouging her eyes, Mr. A. chanted, and he seemed to believe that he was expelling evil from her. Once the police arrived, Mr. A.'s statements reflected his belief that they had come to reward him for his good deed.

Following the NGRI verdict for the instant offense, Mr. A. was hospitalized for evaluation and treatment. The final diagnoses were schizoaffective disorder, bipolar type, and polysubstance abuse. His paranoid delusions responded promptly to olanzapine, fifteen milligrams every evening. Further benefit was achieved with depakote, 1,250 milligrams per day in divided doses. He presented no behavioral management problems on the unit. He demonstrated great remorse for his act of assaultive enucleation. After successful treatment, Mr. A. no longer experienced psychotic symptoms and was released to a less restrictive hospital. Although he was completely free of psychotic symptoms, the court returned Mr. A. to the security hospital because of concern for public safety.

Case B. Mr. B. was a thirty-two-year-old married African-American man who was remanded to a maximum security hospital after having been found incompetent to stand trial. He had a history of assaultive enucleation.

When Mr. B. was seventeen, while on furlough from the hospital, he enucleated an eye of a woman with a sharp object. He was both angry and acting in response to his perception that evil was in her eyes. The act occurred in a bar while others were present, but Mr. B. acted completely alone. At the time of the enucleation, Mr. B. had consumed some alcohol, and his mental condition was considered to be both psychotic and mentally retarded.

As a psychiatric inpatient, Mr. B.'s eye-gouging behavior was persistent and recurrent. Although his motivation was difficult to discern clearly, he stated, "I attack devil eyes." He frequently threatened others with his fingers or scissors. Despite his poor concentration, Mr. B. was able to answer questions about why he attacked people's eyes. He explained that when he becomes upset, he goes for the eyes. "I attack the devil eyes," he said, laughing repeatedly. "I want to kill the evil." Prior to the diagnostic interview, the evaluator was warned that Mr. B. could become labile, and he typically focused on the interviewer's eyes. When evaluated in the security hospital, Mr. B. was very difficult to interview because of his stuttering and disorganized thought processes. Psychiatric disorders diagnosed were organic delusional disorder, polysubstance abuse, mild mental retardation, and antisocial personality disorder. Despite intensive inpatient treatment, including pharmacotherapy with various mood stabilizers and antipsychotic medicines, and current management with fluphenazine decanoate, Mr. B. remains psychotically disturbed, and his aggressive behaviors, including eye-gouging gestures, persist.

Case C. Ms. C., a single, unemployed, thirty-six-year-old Vietnamese-American woman was remanded to a security hospital after she was determined to be manifestly dangerous. At a nonforensic, nonsecurity hospital, a patient informed the staff that Ms. C., then thirty-four, was having sex with another patient. When the incident was investigated, it was discovered that Ms. C. had gouged out a female patient's eyes with her fingers immediately after performing oral sex on this other patient. The third patient witnessed the event but did not participate in either the sexual or mutilative behavior. Ms. C. was thought to have ingested both eyeballs.

Ms. C. was psychotic. When queried, she admitted having committed the enucleations. She said, "Oh, that was my daughter. She wants to die, so I was helping her," adding that her daughter "requested I kill her." She further believed that her daughter was thousands of years old. Ms. C. was thought to have been experiencing auditory hallucinations at the time. The victim was blinded but not killed. Other eye-gouging attempts in the hospital did not result in serious injury.

Ms. C. experienced her initial psychotic break at twenty-seven years of age, resulting in the first of approximately eight psychiatric hospitalizations prior to her present admission to the forensic security hospital. During these hospitalizations, her behavior was erratic and often bizarre. She was preoccupied with sexual themes and manifested psychotic symptoms, including delusions and both auditory and visual hallucinations. She commonly exhibited public nudity, extreme bisexual promiscuity, and open masturbation. She frequently ate fecal matter, cigarette butts, and sanitary napkins and drank urine.

Assessment in the security hospital yielded the following diagnoses: schizophrenia, undifferentiated type; polysubstance abuse (alcohol, marijuana, cocaine, and amphetamines); and a history of conduct disorder in childhood. An abnormal electroencephalogram showed multifocal epileptiform activity. Spike and wave complexes were noted in the frontal areas, and polyspikes in the right temporal region. During her hospitalization, she was extremely assaultive. Ms. C. was resistant to various combinations of typical and atypical antipsychotic medications together with anticonvulsants and different mood stabilizers. At times she believed that others practiced "voodoo" on her. To this day she remains delusional, violent, and sexually inappropriate.

Case D. Mr. D. was a thirty-seven-year-old Caucasian man who was twenty-three years old when admitted to the security hospital after having been found to be manifestly dangerous at another state hospital where he had enucleated both eyes of another patient.

Mr. D. expressed, and the referring hospital records documented, his belief that the other patient was the devil at the time of the enucleation. On the day of his assaultive enucleations, he reported having seen "things like the devil, snakes, and pills." Around this same time, he believed that he was Jesus. With little planning, he used only his fingers to pluck out both eyeballs of the victim.

Diagnoses in the security hospital included bipolar disorder with psychotic features, polysubstance abuse in institutional remission, and antisocial personality disorder. Sometimes he believed he was Jesus Christ and contemplated concepts of good and evil. On several occasions, he planned assaults on much weaker patients. His moods fluctuated rapidly from suicidal states to manic states to euphoria. Multiple medications were used in the course of his present hospitalization. His affective and psychotic symptoms abated, and his assaultiveness decreased substantially. Nonetheless, Mr. D. remains mildly to moderately paranoid.

These four cases (table 16.1) illustrate subjects whose mental illness can be

Table 16.1
Data on a Series (N = 10) of Eye Gougers Grouped as Psychotic, Mentally Retarded, and Psychopathic

Subjects	Sex	Age (years) at Time of First Assaultive Eye Injury	Planned (P) or Unplanned (U) Assault	Instrument Used in Assault	Sexual Component to Event	Mutilation of Other Body Parts	Victim Killed in Assault	Affective Motive	Apparent Desired Result
Psychotic									
A	M	22	U	Finger	Yes	No	No	Fear	Self-protection
B	M	17	U	Sharp object	No	No	No	Fear	Self-protection
C	F	34	U	Finger	Yes	No	No	Compassion	Help victim
D	M	23	U	Finger	No	No	No	Fear	Self-protection
Mentally retarded									
E	M	23	U	Fingernail	No	No	No	Frustration	Communication
Psychopathic									
F	M	13	U	Knife	Yes	Yes	Yes	Anger	Kill victim
G	M	14	U	Sharp instruments	Yes	Yes	Yes	Anger	Kill victim
H	M	40	P	Sharp instruments	Yes	Yes	Yes	Anger	Avert victim's gaze
I	M	34	P	Knife	Yes	No	No	Anger	Revenge
J	M	25	P	Knife	Yes	Yes	Yes	Anger	Avert victim's gaze

classified as psychotic. They were psychotic at the time of the eye assault, and the enucleations appear to have resulted from psychotic exacerbation. All but one were youthful (under twenty-five years of age) men. In all but one exception, the act was unplanned and accomplished with only the assailant's fingers. A sexual component to the assault was present in two cases. Other body parts were not mutilated, and none of the victims was killed.

MENTALLY RETARDED EYE GOUGER

Case E. Mr. E. was a thirty-nine-year-old, never married, African-American man with no formal education. He had been continuously hospitalized since age six, except for a five-month period in 1994 when he lived in a group home. At twenty-three, he was transferred to a maximum security hospital as he had become "unmanageable [injuring both staff and patients' eyes] at that facility." The event that precipitated the transfer was his gouging out the eyes of another patient with his fingernail and causing blindness. A letter accompanying Mr. E. noted his "ability to skillfully injure the eyesight of other recipients despite being on heavy medication." His admitting diagnoses at that time were moderate mental retardation (IQ 43), organic personality disorder, and seizures.

It was then hypothesized that Mr. E.'s aggression may be linked to his not having a vocabulary to express his feelings; thus, he resorted to physically acting out that which he could not verbally express. A methodology of individual, twice-a-day teaching sessions employing shaping, fading, modeling, role playing, and positive and negative reinforcement was used. A baseline of previous acting-out behaviors was taken. After an initial increase in aggressive acting-out behaviors along with attempts at eye scratching, within two months these behaviors began to subside. After six months, his aggressive acting out dropped to one to two incidents a month. After a year, he was incident free. Eight months later, he was transferred to an open hospital. He has had no aggressive behavior or eye-gouging behavior since. He was continued on carbamazepine, lorazepam, and thioridazine HCl.

Although but a single example, this mentally retarded individual shared several commonalities with most psychotic subjects: a young man whose acts were unplanned and accomplished with his own fingers (table 16.1). Other body parts were not targeted, and the victim was never killed. Unlike the psychotic subjects, Mr. E. was not psychotically motivated. His acts appear to have resulted from frustration at his poor ability to communicate, and an effective treatment plan was formulated accordingly.

PSYCHOPATHIC EYE GOUGERS

Case F. Mr. F. was a thirteen-year-old Hispanic boy who lived alone with his divorced mother at the time of the incident. The victim of his assaultive enucleation was a fourteen-year-old girl who was a family friend and known to the perpetrator for at least ten years. There was no evidence of sexual or romantic involvement before the incident.

The eye gouging occurred during the course of a homicide and was not planned by Mr. F. He used a knife, which he obtained from the kitchen in the course of dragging the victim into the backyard of her home; they were in the home of the victim's parents, who were out having a drink with Mr. F.'s mother.

Mr. F. attempted to fondle the victim's breasts while she was asleep in her bed. When she awoke, he attacked her, choking her and dragging her into the kitchen and then into the backyard. Afterward, Mr. F. went to his own house and burned in his backyard various *Playboy* magazines, a spiral notebook, and a brown paper bag.

The victim was stabbed in the face and head thirty-seven times, and both eyes were completely destroyed. The kitchen knife had an approximately six-inch blade, of which the distal end was broken off and recovered from the victim's left eye during autopsy. The eye stabbing was judged to be ego syntonic in the sense that it served Mr. F.'s goal of attempting to murder the victim by penetrating her brain.

Diagnoses included on Axis I: conduct disorder, childhood onset, mild; obsessive-compulsive disorder, with poor insight (OCD); dysthymic disorder, early onset; Axis II: developing psychopathic and sadistic personality traits; Axis III: history of asthma and enuresis; Axis IV: loss of father and brother (father had died six months before the homicide); and Axis V: global assessment of functioning (GAF) 50. His intelligence was measured at over 130 full-scale IQ (very superior range). With no neuropsychological impairments, no further neurological testing was indicated.

Mr. F. was sentenced to the state youth authority until age twenty-five. He was involved in ongoing individual and group treatment at that facility.

One interesting finding is that an hour before the homicide, Mr. F. watched the movie *Demolition Man*, which has two eye-gouging death scenes in it that are quite explicit. He denied that this movie (which he had seen twice) shaped his behavior in any way. Psychological testing confirmed the diagnostic findings, especially the OCD and developing psychopathy. As an adult, he is expected to meet the criteria for sexual sadism, and he hinted at such fantasies when evaluated. He also stated to the evaluator, "It has always been clear to me that one day I would kill somebody. . . . I've had the thought since I was seven. Never told anyone. I'd tell my friend I'm dangerous, I'm insane, crazy, but not one they can find, not one a psychiatrist can find." He was not sure if he would kill again.

Case G. Mr. G. was a fourteen-year-old Caucasian boy who acted alone at the time of the eye gouging and concurrent homicide. Earlier on the day of the attack, he met a thirteen-year-old girl for the first time and lured her to an isolated area in proximity to where they met.

Although the girl appeared to have been a victim of opportunity and the occurrence unplanned for the specific time and date, rehearsal in the form of fantasy was evident. Printed materials were recovered from Mr. G.'s residence that revealed a history of fantasies consistent with the violent behavior displayed at the crime scene.

Once isolated from public view, Mr. G. forced the victim to remove her clothing and attempted to rape her. According to his self-report, which was later corroborated forensically, he was unable to have sexual intercourse with the victim. Frustrated by his sexual failure, he became angered and struck the victim repeatedly with a blunt object. Two separate slender saw blades (for drywall construction) penetrated the length of the brain and both were left protruding from the eye sockets. In addition, her body had been posed, and she had received numerous postmortem lacerations to her breasts, torso, vagina, rectum arms, and legs. There was no evidence the victim was tortured prior to death; however, the eye gouging was done antemortem and, in all likelihood, after she became unconscious.

Approximately one week before the homicide, Mr. G., reportedly after watching the movie *Natural Born Killers*, shaved his head and purchased sunglasses in an effort to mimic the appearance of the movie's protagonist. He also reported that his favorite movie was *Hellraiser*, which depicts graphic scenes of mutilation and eroticism.

Diagnoses included on Axis I: attention deficit hyperactivity disorder; polysubstance abuse: amphetamines, hallucinogens, cannabis; Axis II: conduct disorder, reading disorder; and Axis III: asthma, migraine headaches. Notwithstanding previous diagnoses, Mr. G. currently clearly meets all the criteria for the diagnosis of antisocial personality disorder and had manifested the most salient traits and features of this disorder far in advance of age eighteen. All treatment efforts were unsuccessful.

Case H. Mr. H., a fifty-four-year-old white male teacher, was accused of fifty-two murders. Of these, twelve victims were subjected to severe eye injuries. Mr. H. began killing at the age of forty and was not stopped until his arrest at the age of fifty-four.

His twelve separate eye injury victims, who were also killed after torture, included prepubertal and adolescent boys and girls, as well as adult women. Body parts subject to torture included the face, upper body, and abdomen but not the eyes. Other injuries and mutilations inflicted on the victims were multiple, up to fifty-four on a single victim, with heavy disfigurement of the face. Specific mutilations included cutting off the tip of the tongue, cutting off the end of the nose, simultaneous excision of the sternum and ribs, and excision of internal genitalia (including uterus and adnexa), rectum, and external genitalia, including the vaginal wall. Victims died from lethal trauma to vital organs, exsanguination, and shock.

After torturing the victims and attempting but failing at sexual intercourse, Mr. H. typically stabbed the victim's heart, cutting into the heart and then quickly pumping the knife in and out, but without completely removing the knife, a rapid repetitive movement very similar to the fortissimo of coitus and the paraphilia of piquerism. Once the victim was deceased, the apparent "stare" of the corpse was sufficiently disturbing to Mr. H. so that he would then pierce the victim's eyes and rapidly thrust the knife back and forth as he had just done to the victim's heart.

Diagnoses made prior to his criminal trial included obsessive-compulsive necrosadism, obsessive-compulsive vampirism, necrophilia, organic personality disorder, and schizoid personality disorder. He was not provided psychiatric treatment. Following his conviction, he was sentenced to death and executed.

Case I. Mr. I. was a thirty-four-year-old married Caucasian man with one child. He was employed as a plumber at the time of his arrest. He injured the eyes of seven of thirteen young women and girls whom he attacked sexually. During a rape attempt, Mr. I. would press his fingers against the victim's eyes to gain compliance by inflicting pain. However, the more serious ocular injuries were inflicted immediately after his rape attempt was interrupted or ended in his failure to complete the sexual act. Motivated by a desire for revenge and to punish his victim for his own humiliating sexual failure, he would use a knife to cut the victim's superciliary region above the eye, down across the eye and the face below, bilaterally (six cases); one victim was instead cut horizontally through neighboring facial tissues and the eye. Ocular injuries did not blind the victim, but facial trauma resulted in unattractive scarring.

None of the victims was tortured or killed; however, resulting injuries, beyond the above described ocular and facial traumata, included hematoma, cerebral concussion, and unattractive scars resulting from the facial lacerations.

When evaluated forensically, the diagnoses were dissocial personality disorder (ICD 9) and organic personality disorder. Mr. I. underwent no psychiatric treatment.

Case J. Mr. J., a twenty-five-year-old single male cattle rancher, was accused of two separate sexual homicides, during which he gouged out the eyes of both of his victims.

He raped two older women, seventy-three and eighty-one years of age. After each rape, he killed the victim by chopping the victim's head with a spade. With a knife, Mr. J. then inflicted multiple stab wounds on the breasts and body. The ultimate cause of death in each case was damage to vital organs and exsanguination. He gouged both eyes of one victim and one eye of the other. Eyes, eyelids, and superciliary arches were traumatized but without complete ocular enucleation. In each case, Mr. J. injured the victim's eye(s) after killing her. All these offenses were committed in a state of intoxication after consuming home-distilled vodka.

Mr. J. had no history of prior psychiatric hospitalizations. At the age of twenty-one, he was convicted of rape and subsequently served four years of imprisonment. He recidivated within three months of his release from prison. Mr. J. had a history of animal cruelty, with a pattern, begun in childhood, of torturing animals.

Diagnoses established from the forensic examination included organic personality disorder (likely caused by maternal drinking during pregnancy), gerontophilia, dissocial personality disorder, alcohol dependence, and behavioral disorder secondary to alcohol abuse. He received no psychiatric treatment, and he displayed no compassion for his victims or their relatives.

The rubric *psychopathic* does not mean that a diagnosis of antisocial personality disorder was made; rather, it captures the observation that eye assaults invariably occurred in the context of another criminal act by an individual who had neither a psychotic disorder nor mental retardation but who showed signs of beginning psychopathy or fully developed character pathology.

All five psychopathic subjects inflicted eye injury as only one component of a violent sexual act (table 16.1). All appeared to have been angry but not psychotic at the time of the act, and all five inflicted eye injuries with a sharp instrument. In all but one case, the victims were killed during the assault. In two of these cases, the assailants were youthful, they apparently did not plan the eye injuries in advance, and the eye injuries were secondary to an attempt to kill the victim by piercing the brain. The other three, representing an older age span, were serial sexual offenders who planned their ghoulish acts in advance.

DISCUSSION

Assaultive enucleation is an important, dangerous, and rare behavior that warrants further study. From this multicenter review of cases in the United States and Russia, two initial typologies are suggested. First, the psychotically disturbed subject impulsively uses his or her fingers to gouge another person's eye(s) because he is terrified and believes he is acting in self-defense. Although assaultive enucleation is dangerous and mutilative, these psychotic subjects did not appear homicidal, and their eye-gouging behavior subsided when acute symptoms of psychosis were brought under control with effective treatment. Where psychotic symptoms persist, however, eye-gouging behaviors can continue unabated.

Five of the eye gougers were treated in a security hospital, four with mental illness and one with mental retardation. Four of the five were men. Ages of these five mentally disturbed assailants ranged from seventeen to thirty-four years at the time of the assault. All four with mental illness were psychotically disturbed at the time of the enucleation and typically perceived the victim to represent the devil or evil, especially through the victim's eyes. The eye gougings were impulsive and unplanned. In two cases, assaultive enucleation was associated with a sexual act, and in one case, the perpetrator inflicted additional mutilation. Most of the psychotic eye gougers were motivated out of fear. None of these individuals committed homicide. Only one attacked the eyes of more than one person. In contrast to the psychopathic eye-gouging behavior, enucleations committed by psychotic individuals were discovered immediately after the act.

Although one psychotic eye gouger (Mr. B.) was also mentally retarded, another patient (Mr. E.) was predominantly retarded and did not have a psychotic disorder. In Mr. E.'s case, a behavioral therapeutic program tailored to his specific needs was remarkably effective in curbing eye-gouging behaviors and permitting his eventual discharge from the security hospital. It was postulated at his eye-gouging behaviors resulted in large part from the frustration he experienced because of poor communicative and socializing abilities.

Five other eye-gouging subjects, representing the psychopathic category, did not suffer from a psychotic disorder or mental retardation. Rather, they showed signs of significant character pathology; sexual paraphilias, including sadism; and various degrees of alcohol or drug abuse. Psychopathic personality was suggested by other signs of violent behaviors and preoccupations.[21] Three of the five psychopathic eye gougers had histories of cruelty to animals, a behavior that has been associated with deviant aggression and psychopathic or antisocial personality disorder.[22] The temporal association between the violent, mutilative acts and viewing an especially violent movie in two individuals is remarkable and suggests imitative behavior. All psychopathic eye-gouging acts involved both sexual and violent or homicidal behavior. All these subjects inflicted eye injuries or enucleations by piercing with a sharp instrument, and in four of these psychopathic cases, the enucleations were only one component of a more generalized act of beating, mutilating, and/or killing the victim. Two of these assailants injured their victims' eyes as part of the lethal attack; two inflicted ocular injury after killing their victims; and one sadistically inflicted ocular trauma without killing his victims. Psychopathic assailants were not apprehended during or immediately after the act.

These five psychopathic cases compare with other apparently nonpsychotic eye gougers in popular media accounts who are typically men engaged in sexual violence with a female victim. Violence involving enucleation in this group is associated with a sexual act, other mutilations, and, with the exception of Mr. I., who attempted to rape but did not kill his victims, homicide, even if there is no physical evidence of sexual consummation. In three of these cases, the assailant mutilated his victim's eyes after he attempted but failed to rape her. In some cases, the subjects were known to have killed several to many victims, and their eye gouging involved multiple victims as well. The behaviors and personal histories of these psychopathic eye gougers are similar to the known research concerning single and serial sexual murderers.[23]

Our gross categorization of those who enucleate others—whether psychotic or psychopathic—needs to be replicated on larger samples and further explored from social, biological, and psychological perspectives. The apparent desired results of assaultive eye injury includes self-protection, based on psychotic perceptions, and a paradoxical desire to help the victim, based on psychotic perceptions, communication, revenge, death of the, victim, and aversion of the deceased victim's gaze. Nonetheless, the affective motivation of such abhorrent behavior appears to be sadly plebeian: fear, compassion, frustration, and anger.

NOTES

1. B. I. Kennedy and T. B. Feldmann, "Case Presentations and a Literature Review," *Hospital and Community Psychiatry* 45 (1994): 470–74.
2. A. R. Felthous, "Psychotic Perceptions of Pet Animals Accused of Violent

Crimes," *Behavioral Sciences and the Law* 2 (1984): 331–39; J. R. Meloy, *The Psychopathic Mind: Origins, Dynamics, and Treatment* (Northvale, NJ: Jason Aronson, 1988).

3. Meloy, *Psychopathic Mind*.

4. *The New Encyclopedia Britannica*, vol. 6 (Chicago: Britannica, 1986), p. 76.

5. J. Baines and G. Pinch, "Horns and Seth: The Struggle for the Throne of Osiris," in *World Mythology*, ed. R. Willis (New York: Henry Holt, 1993), pp. 36–55; P. Clayton, *Great Figures in Mythology* (New York: Crescent Books, 1990), pp. 103, 170.

6. F. T. Elworthy, *The Evil Eye* (New York: Julian Press, 1958).

7. N. Evreinov, *History of Corporal Punishment in Russia*, vol. 1 (St. Petersburg: Typography of V. K. Ilinchik, 1913), pp. 20, 26–32, 45.

8. V. M. Behterev et al., eds., *New Encyclopedic Dictionary* (Leningrad: Vesaik-Znanie Publishing House of PP Soikina, 1926–27), p. 426.

9. Ibid.

10. N. I. Kostomarov, *Russian History: Biographies of its Most Significant People*, 3rd ed., vols. 1–2 (St. Petersburg: Typography of L. M. Stanolevich, 1880), pp. 248–50.

11. Evreinov, *History of Corporal Punishment in Russia*.

12. P. I. Kovaleysky, *Psychiatric Essays from History*, ed. L. Grozny, vol. 1 (St. Petersburg: Typography of M. I. Akinfiev, 1901; repr., Moscow: Tara, 1995), p. 59.

13. Evreinov, *History of Corporal Punishment in Russia*.

14. A. A. Zimin and A. L. Horoschivitch, *Russia in the Times of Ivan Grozny* (Moscow: Nauka, 1982), p. 58.

15. C. Sifakis, *Encyclopedia of Crime* (New York: Facts on File, 1982).

16. A. Fisher, *Africa Adorned* (New York: Harry N. Abrams, 1984), p. 63.

17. J. Bachman, "Women Get Probation in Sister's Eye-Gouging," *Fort Worth Star Telegram*, September 23, 1994, p. 1A; Bachman, "Eye-Gouging Jury Mulling Punishment, Two Sisters Are Convicted in Demon-Ridding Effort," *Fort Worth Star Telegram*, September 22, 1994, p. 23A; S. Scott, "Women Get Probation for Gouging Sister's Eyes," *Dallas Morning News*, September 23, 1994, p. 23A; Associated Press, "Gouging Trial about to Begin, Blinded School Teacher Seeks Release of Sisters," *Fort Worth Star Telegram*, September 20, 1994, p. 19.

18. "Sanders K. Man Jailed in Assault, Eye Gouging in Park," *Fort Worth Star Telegram*, August 9, 1995, p. 22.

19. "Sanders K. Man Accused in Sex Assault, Eye Gouging," *Forth Worth Star Telegram*, August 9, 1995, p. 23.

20. J. Matthews and C. Wicker, *The Eyeball Killer* (New York: Kensington, 1996).

21. R. D. Hare, *The Psychopathy Checklist-Revised Manual* (Toronto: Multihealth Systems, 1991).

22. A. R. Felthous and S. R. Kellert, "Violence against Animals and People: Is Aggression against Living Creatures Generalized?" *Bulletin of the American Academy of Psychiatry and the Law* 14 (1986): 55–69; R. Gleyzer, A. R. Felthous, and C. E. Holzer, "Psychiatric Disorders and Animal Cruelty," paper presented at the 29th Annual Meeting of the American Academy of Psychiatry and the Law, New Orleans, October 22–25, 1998.

23. J. R. Meloy, "The Nature and Dynamics of Sexual Homicide: An Integrative Review," *Aggression and Violent Behavior* 5 (2000):1–22.

Chapter 17

A MULTIDISCIPLINARY APPROACH TO SOLVING COLD CASES

Michael R. King

Mike King was born in Salt Lake City, Utah, in 1958. He has been a police officer since 1979, worked in all aspects of police work, and spent the last ten years of his career investigating multijurisdictional serial crimes. He has consulted in hundreds of criminal cases throughout the country and abroad. Mike served in the criminal intelligence section for the 2002 Winter Olympic Games and currently serves as an intelligence supervisor for the Utah Criminal Intelligence Center under the Department of Homeland Security. He is the former chief of staff to Utah Attorney General Jan Graham and retired from the office as a lieutenant.

Mike has a master's degree and a Bachelor of Arts degree in criminal justice and public relations. He is an adjunct professor at Weber State University and the Salt Lake Community College and teaches for police academies and law enforcement agencies throughout America and abroad.

In 1979, while still in his rookie year, Mike had a 49,000-volt power line fall on him. He remained entangled in the current for over twenty minutes, severely burning him. He immediately received the nickname of "Sparky" and "Reddy-King-O-Watt." "That shocking experience changed my whole outlook on life," King recently said.

In 1990, after investigating over a hundred people involved in a large religious cult that was sexually abusing children, Mike became interested in the behavioral sciences. He soon began his study of criminal personalities and was

Written for this anthology.

privileged to learn personally from experts like John Douglas, Kenneth Lan-
ning, Greg Cooper, and other national and international experts. His graduate
studies focused on combining multiple disciplines in the solving of serial, vio-
lent crime. His greatest accomplishment at the Attorney General's Office was
the formation of a multidisciplinary task force used in serial crime investiga-
tions that received state and national accolades.

In his twenty-five-year career, Mike has received numerous departmental
and national awards and citations, including Footprinter National Police
Officer of the Year, National Association of Police Officer National Honorable
Mention, and a personal commendation from President Ronald Reagan.

Mike's favorite escape from daily stress is to sneak out fishing, riding in the
mountains, camping, or listening to his musically gifted children, Whitney, Cliff,
and Skyeler: "There is always a piano, guitar, trumpet, synthesizer, or vocal
number being played or practiced." Late at night, Mike and his close friends can
be found attending "loser movies" where they not only get in for less money but
often times enjoy free popcorn. "If there are more than three people in the the-
ater when we go, then it's still way too early in the evening! Most importantly,
the movie needs to have action, comedy, and more action—I want the escape!"

Mike credits all his successes to his wife of twenty-five years, Bonnie.
"Without her I would be nothing. She has taught me patience, consistency, for-
giveness, faith, and commitment."

Police agencies across America are as different as the people, lifestyles, and communities they serve. From the visibly quiet settings of our rural farmlands to the hustle and bustle of our metropolitan areas, law enforcement challenges are ever changing. In today's mobile society, a criminal can commit a crime in one part of the United States and within hours be hundreds, even thousands, of miles away, planning the next crime.

Traditionally, when a violent felony occurs, little, if any, information is shared among our law enforcement agencies. With the benefits of complex databases and the ever-evolving world of computing, our chances of identifying and apprehending criminals are improving. Often, our lack of attention to information sharing, communicating effectively with each other, and coordinating efforts causes a reduction in our ability to effectively respond to, investigate, and solve the incidents. Another major problem facing law enforcement today is training and experience as it pertains to major case management. With the introduction of younger retirement ages, shifts in administrative focus, or declining policing budgets, some agencies are left with fewer experienced investigators than at any other time in our history.

Most individual policing agencies lack expertise in specialized areas of enforcement, such as financial or computer crimes. If, or when, a repetitive crime such as serial robbery, rape, or murder strikes these communities, most agencies lack the ability to provide specific services in the area of criminal investigative analysis, offender profiling, personality assessments, interview and interrogation strategies, search warrant assistance, forensic needs, or prosecution strategies.

The United States of America has over seventeen thousand police agencies, with nearly nine hundred thousand police officers serving within those jurisdictional boundaries. Each agency, whether a city police department or a county sheriff, generally has its own patrol, investigations, and administrative divisions. When a violent crime is committed that the agency resources cannot handle, the demand that the crime places on it, the agency must rely on neighboring jurisdictions to assist them. Sometimes, arrogance and pride prevent the individual investigator, or the agency, for that matter, from asking for help when it is desperately needed. When the crime is too difficult to solve, the agency may look beyond local support to the Federal Bureau of Investigation's Behavioral Science Unit to provide a criminal analysis and offer a profile of the offender. Too often though, the agency may choose to handle the investigation on its own or may be forced to do so because of the amount of time it must wait for the FBI to be able to consider its particular case.

When this happens, officers and agencies involved can become frustrated and even lose interest as other pressing issues come to the forefront. While every agency suggests that it continues to "look into the matter," in reality, the case becomes lost, as more violent crimes are committed, surface in the public eye, and demand law enforcement response.

Yet amid this doom and gloom, law enforcers are emerging with better, more capable investigators and techniques than at any time in American history. We have discovered that training and information sharing are paramount to bridging the gap that has resulted. One of the benefits of this information sharing is the combined efforts and synergy that can be realized when multiple agencies, disciplines, and backgrounds come together in a common goal of solving unsolved crime.

The FBI's Behavioral Science Unit has led the way in understanding criminal behavior and the method and manner employed by some personality types in the commission of criminal acts. One perceived shortcoming of the bureau's unit though is the lack of a multidisciplinary approach to the investigation. This chapter deals primarily with the organization of a multidisciplinary team and reflects on the lessons learned in the formation of one of the country's most successful programs, the Utah Criminal Tracking and Analysis Project (UTAP).

In spring 1997, the Strategic Planning Committee for Utah Law Enforcement opened discussions to determine a way to speed up the investigative support process for unsolved crimes. Provo, Utah, Police Chief Greg Cooper, a former FBI profiler, and I, a lieutenant in the Utah Attorney General's Office, were tasked with developing Utah's own behavioral science unit. The chiefs and sheriffs of Utah felt that the unit was necessary because the FBI was often backlogged with requests for assistance, and local enforcers had to wait for periods of time longer than they consider reasonable.

In approaching the concept, it was determined that broad-based support was needed from across the state, extending to police chiefs, sheriffs, and other law enforcement leaders from the city, county, state, and federal level. The purpose of the unit would be to provide case support in difficult, unsolved crimes through the process of case reviews by a board of experts, evaluation of the traditional forms of evidence collected by investigators, and investigative suggestions based on behavioral analysis of a crime.

Police officers, county attorneys, chiefs, and sheriffs were asked to identify the best investigators and scientists in the state in the areas of forensics, behavioral science, medical science, psychiatric science, and crime scene investigations. With their recommendations, a laudable "board of experts" was organized. The original board included seasoned investigators who were unquestionable experts in the area of sexual assault and homicide investigations. A physician from the medical examiner's office joined the team, as did psychiatrists and psychologists from the department of corrections and the state mental hospital. Forensic scientists from the state crime lab and a major university joined experts in the process of instruction and training from the state police academy and neighboring academic institutions. In all, sixteen people were called together to form the first team.

Shortly after UTAP became operational, additional benefits were realized. Soon, Cooper and I were entering the Utah State Correctional System on a regular basis to interview violent repeat offenders. Those meetings developed a great deal of information about the manner and method in which serial predators selected their victims and avoided police detection and equally important, what motivated them to commit crimes. As time went on, UTAP recognized a need to share that information with other investigators, and the training arm of UTAP was born. Training soon became a surprise benefit of the UTAP project, and that training revolutionized violent crime investigation techniques, as shown in these *Salt Lake Tribune* articles dated August 20, 2000.

"Delving into the Dark Side"

Sitting with legs crossed at the front of a hotel conference room, John talks of the summer of 1988 with its open windows and lacy drapery, cool night walks through tree-lined neighborhoods and women who sleep in the nude.

John is calm and occasionally cheeky with his audience. But he is precise with details: A small pocketknife, plastic toys in a yard and the tears of some 85 women in 11 states who John . . . not his real name . . . stalked and raped.

"He's the expert," says Utah Attorney General investigator Mike King, while a videotape of John's presentation plays in his Salt Lake City office. "You get the sense that talking about it is cathartic for him."

Three months ago, 400 New Mexico police officers gathered in an Albuquerque conference room to hear John recount his crimes. For the officers, it was a rare opportunity to be tutored by an expert in the methodology of serial rape.

John is part of a program designed to help law officers learn firsthand what makes a criminal tick. Devised in Utah by King, Utah Chief Deputy Attorney General Reed Richards and Provo Police Chief Gregory Cooper, the program went national earlier this year at the request of the U.S. Department of Justice.

Since then, King and Cooper have shared their interview methods and profiling models of selected inmates with police agencies in New York, New Jersey, New Hampshire, New Mexico, Arizona, Massachusetts, Texas, Wyoming and Montana.

"What the inmate does is provide a great example of a certain profile, whether that be cockiness or self-consciousness," says Jeff Pierce, deputy director of the Rocky Mountain Information Network, an agency that collects criminal intelligence for eight Western states under a grant from the Justice Department.

"The law enforcement professionals who are involved in this never forget," says Pierce, who encouraged federal support for Utah's efforts. "It is a sobering, eye-opening event, a real-life validation of the principles that are being taught. After listening to these guys, the officers chasing leads in the field are just a little more wise, a little more attuned to what's going on in the criminal mind."

John is one of six Utah inmates each a prototypical offender who have agreed to participate. They are promised nothing but the chance to air their dark ruminations before an audience.

King's stock of inmates includes a hermaphrodite who molested some 500 boys and girls over 35 years, a religious cult leader/child abuser, a rapist who targeted professional women, a flimflam artist who took millions through pyramid schemes and murderous polygamist Dan Lafferty, the only inmate who agreed to the use of his name for this story.

"In most cases we found the inmates were not only willing but eager," says King. "For some of them, it's the first opportunity to be really honest about what they've done."

Next month, John, now serving up to life in prison at Utah State Prison, will speak at a seminar on serial rapists in Duchesne County. In October, King, Cooper and Richards will present a conference on "The Making of a Serial Killer" to officers at the Utah prison.

The October session is based on interviews with a 21-year-old transient whose ritualistic slaying of a 9-year-old California boy shocked even hardened investigators. The confessed killer, now awaiting execution in California's San Quentin Prison, was caught before he could kill again. But King says he had all the makings of a mass murderer.

"This was his first killing and he found it to be more thrilling than anything he had ever done," King says. "He was a boy with incredible confidence problems, but no prior record that we could find. And suddenly he kills one person and the next day nearly kills another. It was about having total dominion and control."

King recently interviewed California mass murderer Richard Ramirez, the so-called Night Stalker. He hopes to include the Ramirez profile in the training that is part of the Utah criminal Tracking and Analysis Project (UTAP). The program, which sponsors the inmate interviews, also acts as Utah's clearinghouse for unsolved homicides, missing persons and unidentified bodies and is teamed with the FBI's Violent Criminal Apprehension Program.

Much of UTAP's mission centers on forming agency partnerships and providing training for local law enforcement. King, a former Weber County investigator, directs the programming based on working relationships with convicted criminals.

"This is about understanding why they do it. That doesn't mean you have to like it, or them. But there is a very meaningful exchange here, empathy if you will," he says. "When the officers start realizing it's not a hunk of meat out there, that there's fear and disgust and anger and all these other emotions, that turns them."

While UTAP's program is the first of its kind in the nation, the idea of teaching detectives to become amateur psychologists is not new. Long the grist of pulp fiction, criminal psychology became the focus of an elite team of FBI detectives in the 1980s.

From those interviews, the FBI developed a "profiling" database and went on to crack numerous unsolved crimes by matching characteristics of a crime with the profiled traits of the criminal, such as age, race, profession and marital status.

Profiling is by no means an exact science, but as a teaching model the skills are invaluable, says Provo's Cooper, who studied under the most famous profiler of all, John Douglas.

Douglas, who retired from the FBI five years ago, found certain killing fetishes tended to reveal personality traits. Details of his interviews with Ed Gein, a mass murderer who liked to preserve the skin of his victims and look at himself in feathered masks made from their faces, were popularized in the book and movie "Silence of the Lambs."

Douglas amassed a gruesome list of prison interviews with Gein, Ted Bundy, Charles Manson, David "Son of Sam" Berkowitz and Richard Speck.

Five years before Douglas retired, Cooper joined the FBI's profiling unit. The two became friends and, later, partners in a police consulting firm. Now Cooper is extending the legacy of Douglas' program by casting workaday cops in the role of forensic profiler.

"Instead of trying to theorize about what these criminals are thinking, it's going right to the source," says Cooper. "You can see the lightbulbs go off in the heads of the audience."

In the New Mexico presentation, the serial rapist spends two hours detailing his transformation from long-haul truck driver and part-time burglar with a cocaine addiction into a voyeur fixated on women who sleep in the nude.

John tells how he profiled his victims, targeting single women with children living in poorly kept homes. He recounts how he watched nearby as officers arrived to investigate his rapes.

"He was never violent with any of his victims, but he used the threat [to the children] to get his way. Only one victim ever resisted," King says. "He would look for the type of vehicle, children's toys. He looked at mail to see if it was just delivered to a female's name. He was a voyeur who became an opportunist who would rape."

The ultimate goal of UTAP's program is to teach officers how to catch perpetrators like John. When John leaves the stage, King and Cooper return to guide the officers through the thicket of lies or half-truths he has planted.

King tells the audience that John demanded oral sex from his victims. When rebuffed, he would commit a second rape within two hours. Knowing this, Weber County detectives put hundreds of officers on alert to look for a rape victim who refused oral sex. When that victim suddenly came forward, detectives were ready and John was arrested not far from the crime scene.

"It's the kind of detail you can teach detectives to look for," King says. "Cops know how to investigate. Looking at behavior is the new twist."

*   *   *

"Lafferty to Sheriff's Deputy: 'If God Asked Me to, I'd Kill You Right Now'"

UTAH STATE PRISON—Sixteen years after he slit the throats of his sister-in-law and her daughter in their American Fork home, Dan Lafferty remains tormented by his past.

Not by the murders, but an unpaid debt.

As a young man, Lafferty backed his vehicle into another car owned by a friend. The collision damaged her fender.

"I never fixed her car for her, and that torments me. Things like that," the Utah State Prison inmate told The Salt Lake Tribune. As for the killings, Lafferty remains convinced he was following God's instructions and feels no remorse.

"I'm not going to offend God by saying something inappropriate like, 'I wish I'd never done it.' I'll never say that. If you're a child of God, it'll make sense to you someday. I'll never say I'm sorry I did it."

Lafferty's cold-blooded candor and use of religious beliefs to justify his crimes make him a compelling subject for homicide investigators seeking insight into the criminal mind. During the past year, Lafferty has told his story several times to groups of law enforcement officers as part of the Utah criminal Tracking and Analysis Project (UTAP), a new program that assists agencies in investigating ritualistic violent crimes.

"We looked at Lafferty and thought, 'Here's a guy we can really learn from,'" said state UTAP coordinator Mike King, a criminal investigator with the Utah Attorney General's Office. "My job is to find the truth. And the only real expert [on ritual crime] is the person who's done it."

Lafferty needs little prompting to spin his tale of biblical prophecy and bloodshed. He is soft-spoken, thoughtful and polite, all while revealing chilling glimpses of his skewed morality.

In April, King brought Lafferty before a class on religious-based homicides at a law enforcement conference in Phoenix. When one angry sheriff's deputy confronted the convicted murderer about his lack of remorse, Lafferty calmly replied, "With all due respect, if God asked me to, I'd kill you right now."

"That kind of mindset frightens me," said King, who has established an unusual friendship with the longtime inmate. "I have many things I like about Dan Lafferty, but I don't ever want to see him on the street."

That won't happen soon if ever. Lafferty, who narrowly avoided being sentenced to death, is serving two consecutive life terms for his role in the July 24, 1984, slayings. He has little chance of parole. His older brother, Ron Lafferty, is on death row for the same crimes. Speaking with unnerving matter-of-factness, the younger Lafferty appears remarkably untroubled by having taken the lives of a young woman and her child.

"Just recently I had a [new inmate] come to my [cell] door and call me a baby killer. It was sort of humorous. I'm not sure how else to respond to these kinds of things. I find myself smiling in their face," Lafferty said. "He came up and pushed this other guy away from my door and said, 'Do you realize this guy killed a baby? He cut her throat so deep her head nearly fell off!' And I said, 'So what's your point?' Don't call anybody a fool for what they feel led to do."

The grisly facts are undisputed: On Pioneer Day afternoon, Dan and Ron Lafferty pushed their way into the home of 24-year-old Brenda Wright Lafferty while her husband, Allen Lafferty, was away. As she pleaded for her daughter's life, the two men beat her and throttled her with a vacuum cord. Dan then stepped into the bedroom and, as the girl cried out for her mother, slashed the throat of Brenda's 15-month-old daughter, Erica. That done, he used the same knife to finish off Brenda.

"School of Prophets": By the time of the murders, Ron and Dan Lafferty had been excommunicated from The Church of Jesus Christ of Latter-day Saints for their radical views. Both had joined a renegade polygamist cult called "School of Prophets," whose members sought to receive and share revelations from God.

In March 1984, Ron claimed to have received a revelation ordering the killings of Brenda Lafferty and her daughter because the woman stood in the way of the cult's work.

"It was a cold-blooded murder for sure," Dan Lafferty told The Tribune last week. "I wasn't anxious, I wasn't vengeful, I wasn't hateful. It was just business, that's all. I had a calm peacefulness when I did it. I was being led by the Spirit."

Dan was convicted of the murders in January 1985 but spared the death penalty by a lone holdout juror. Ron was convicted in a separate trial later that year, but the verdict was overturned in 1991 by a federal appeals court on the grounds that attorneys never established whether he was mentally fit to stand trial. Ron was sentenced to death after a retrial in 1996.

Allen Lafferty now is remarried and living in California. He and Dan have not spoken since the trials in 1985, and Dan Lafferty's letters to his brother have gone unanswered. "I've told him, I don't expect you to understand this completely, but I don't feel like I've done wrong and one day it'll all make sense," Dan Lafferty said. "I tell him it'll have a happy ending."

This "happy ending" relates to the evolution of Dan Lafferty's religious views during the 16 years he has been incarcerated. About four years ago, Lafferty says, he began receiving revelations casting him as a modern-day Elijah, a prophet whose role is to prepare the world for the Second Coming of Christ. Lafferty believes the events of his life, including the murders, are part of a divine plan that will somehow spring him from prison upon Jesus' return.

"I believe there's an unseen hand, guiding everything that takes place. It all just feels right. To prepare the way for Christ . . . yes, I believe that's what I was born into the world to do."

"Comforting Delusion": "That's a very comforting delusion," said David Tomb, a professor of psychiatry at the University of Utah Medical School. Criminals cling to delusions to explain their actions, he said. "They're often using delusions to combat a sense of inferiority. Their life has gone down the tubes. It's the only way they can live with themselves."

Despite his loyalty to God, Lafferty no longer believes in organized religion. He has nothing but contempt for the Mormon religion in which he was raised, and, after committing much of it to memory, he tore up his Bible eight years ago. In Lafferty's mind, everyone is either a child of God or a child of the devil. Brenda and Erica Lafferty were children of the devil, so they needed to be killed. At the Second Coming of Christ, Lafferty believes, all the devil's children will be wiped from the earth.

"He's a religious nut," said investigator King. "This is a guy who knew what society's standards were. He knew what he was doing was wrong, but he'd rather offend society than offend God."

Lafferty now believes his brother Ron is a child of the devil. He also claims Ron tried repeatedly to kill him in 1984 while the pair were being held at the Utah County Jail.

"He was being told by voices to take my life," said Lafferty, who claims Ron tried to stab him with a sharpened pencil and later choked him with a towel. Lafferty said he surrendered willingly to the choking, passed out and awoke some time later on the floor. "I was not afraid to die. If I'm willing to take life, I guess I should also be willing to give my life."

Ron Lafferty, 58, declined to comment for this story.

At 52, Dan Lafferty is a graying, prison-savvy version of the twinkle-eyed defendant who repelled and riveted Utahns during court appearances more than 15 years ago. He hasn't shaved his beard since the day he was sentenced in January 1985; it now hangs, rope-like and bound by rubber bands, to his waist. On his left elbow is a spider-web tattoo commemorating his first 10 years in prison.

Lafferty's cellmate in the prison's maximum security wing is Mark Hofmann, who killed two Salt Lake City residents in much-publicized 1985 pipe bombings Hofmann hoped would divert attention from a forgery scheme he was attempting to perpetuate on the LDS Church.

"We are the arch typical opposites," Lafferty said of his notorious cellmate, with whom he has become friends. "I'm a religious fanatic. You might call him an atheist. But we are brothers, which has been so valuable to me."

In turn, King believes Lafferty is valuable to the UTAP program. Lafferty lends his services to UTAP in part because he likes King, who treats him with respect. "I consider Mike King a friend. I call him my manager, setting up gigs."

Lafferty also believes his UTAP appearances give him a platform for spreading his religious views.

"They always have me run through the gory details, and that's fine. They seem to think [I can help]. I doubt it. The truth is, I feel like I'm using them."

Brenda Lafferty's father agrees. Jim Wright sees Lafferty as a manipulator whose rationale for committing the murders is bogus. By inviting Lafferty to speak in public, authorities are playing into his hand, he said.

"He thrives on telling his story," Wright said by phone from his Idaho home. "He's supposed to be in there to be punished for what he did. It's probably rewarding him more than it's helping them."

Wright has long since stopped hoping for an apology from Lafferty for the loss of his daughter and grandchild. And Lafferty is not inclined to offer one since he believes God has assured him he did nothing wrong.

Wright's response is "absolutely understandable," said King. "The secret here is that in order to understand the mind of these people you've got to give officers the opportunity to talk to them."

Lafferty denies his religious views are an elaborate justification for languishing behind bars as a scorned child-killer. But he concedes the convoluted path he claims to be following on behalf of God, to kill two people, go to prison, become a prophet and pave the way for Jesus' return, sounds far-fetched.

"It doesn't make a whole lot of sense, no, to be honest. Sometimes I think to myself, 'Am I crazy?' And I might be. And if I am, that's OK, too. It's all just survival. Do whatever it is that enables you to survive the best you can. If you feel the need to play the game of religion, play it.

"If I had known when I first came that I was going to be here 16 years, I don't think I could have handled it. I've always believed I've only got a few more weeks to go. I still hope. It's like a carrot sitting in front of me. That's the way I do time. I don't think my mind could comprehend the thought of never getting out.[1]

The UTAP mission is similar to that of the FBI Violent Criminal Apprehension Program (ViCAP), to facilitate cooperation, communication, and coordination between law enforcement agencies and provide support in their efforts to investigate, identify, track, apprehend, and prosecute violent offenders and assist in successfully resolving any major case. A major difference though is the multidisciplinary approach used in solving cases. Parts of this chapter are adapted from the FBI program, but they are enhanced through adding other professional disciplines into investigative process. By doing so, investigative decisions are based solely not on the opinions of investigators but also on those of psychological, medical, and forensic backgrounds.

The services of this type of unit should be supportive in nature and initiated exclusively at the prompting of the requesting agency. In addition, services will be offered primarily in the form of suggestions, recommendations, observations, and references based upon a review and analysis of cases presented by submitting agencies. To develop this type of unit any other way would probably prove futile. If a law enforcement agency feels that anyone is looking over its shoulder or critiquing its work, it will dismiss any offers to assist.

A unit of this nature must be able to provide assistance to any legitimate law enforcement agency confronted with unusual, bizarre, and/or repetitive violent crimes without being tied down by politics or personality conflicts. Through the expertise of its staff of crime analysts, sociologists, forensic scientists, political scientists, computer scientists, and police specialists, the unit brings a multidisciplinary approach to a wide variety of investigative problems and is ultimately prepared to provide several types of crime analysis assistance to any law enforcement agencies.

Once organized, the unit may conduct a crime analysis of particular crimes for several purposes. Criminal investigative analysis (CIA) is simply a tool for law enforcement to assist in the solution of unsolved crimes. It involves a method of reviewing and assessing the facts of a criminal act by individuals who have investigative experience and specialized academic training. It often includes interpreting the offender's behavior and interaction with the victim, as exhibited during the commission of the crime or as evidenced by the subsequent crime scene. CIA should be viewed as a process of reviewing crime(s) from a law enforcement perspective.

In the crime analysis phase, an independent analyst, who is uncluttered with various on-scene stresses and extraneous information, reviews initial crime scene information and preliminary investigative efforts. Through this examination, possible motives may be detected as well as a determination of the sequence of the events occurring during the offense.

The unit can be helpful in providing a profile of the unknown offender by analyzing the way a crime was committed. Often, personality and behavioral characteristics of an individual can surface by more closely examining the crime scene, the disposal site, the initial contact site, and many other factors. Generally, the person's basic patterns of behavior exhibited in commission of a crime will also be present in that person's lifestyle.

The unit or key members of the unit can provide insight into the subject's strengths, weaknesses, and vulnerabilities from a law enforcement perspective. Identifying these strengths and weaknesses can assist the investigator in preparing for and conducting an interview. The information gained may also provide insight into the subject's motivation for the crime and assist the investigator in gaining a better understanding of the offender's reasons for committing the crime.

Because each crime and each request is unique, the assessment process requires a detailed submission of data about the person targeted and demands extensive review and consultation by the analyst. The availability of this material is considered essential to constructing appropriate interview strategies. As the investigator gains this unique insight into the offender's personality type, he is better equipped to develop an interview strategy.

One of the major hurdles in conducting interviews and interrogations is being able to identify verbal and nonverbal behavior in an untruthful person. This ability is often considered to be an art, while some consider it a science. It is my belief that the ability to identify detection during an interview is a combination of both disciplines. My experience has shown that the preparatory efforts of the investigator make the defining difference in a successful interview or interrogation. Too often, investigators become overwhelmed with the facts of the case. They may be experiencing stress based on external and internal factors. In preparing for an interview, an investigator must be able to separate his or her personal feelings, sense of morality, experiential background, and education from the task at hand, which is ultimately understanding the motivation and methodology of the criminal act.

Law enforcers generally are more concerned with the "whodunnits" in a crime scene than the many other factors that exist there. Instead of focusing on who the offender is, we should first focus our attention on victimology—the study of who the victim is. Why was this particular victim selected? What motivated the suspect to choose her? As we focus our attention on the victim, often we are led to a better understanding of who the offender might be and what his individual characteristics are.

An interview is considered to be more inquisitive than the interrogation. We interview witnesses and victims of crime to paint a clearer picture of what occurred. On the other hand, the interrogation is more specifically directed toward the thoughts, feelings, and emotions of the suspect in the case.

By directing our focus and investigative and interrogative attention on the most probable suspect in a case, we can more quickly move the investigation along without wasting valuable time or putting other victims in jeopardy of a suspect's continued criminal activity.

For the purpose of this discussion, deviant behavior is that which contrasts or changes, especially from expected or such acceptable standards as a law, rule, or custom. It usually represents a significant departure from the norm and is often described by such terms as *abnormal*, *aberrant*, or *atypical*.

Criminal behavior is defined as behavior that is in violation of the law. It also fits the definition of *deviant behavior*; however, the standard of measurement applied is defined by the law as *criminal*. There are three forms of behavior that are found either in part or whole at all crime scenes: verbal, nonverbal, and sexual. The verbal can be easily explained by the things said by the offender during the commission of the crime. The nonverbal could be a bizarre action(s) made or taken by the offender. Finally, the sexual would be any peculiar fantasies or actions required by the offender.

All criminals are motivated by physiological and learned motives. Physiological motives are activities that are characteristic of, or appropriate to, a person's healthy or normal functioning. Learned motives might be aggression, affiliation, and achievement. Aggression in this example is a forceful action or procedure (as an unprovoked attack), especially when intended to dominate or master another person. It is generally hostile, injurious, and destructive behavior that occurs out of anger or frustration. Affiliation, or motivation because of belonging to a gang or group, can lead to motive, just so the criminal can belong to something. Affiliation can give a person living an otherwise mundane life a special feeling of superiority or partnership in something. The desire to achieve, to be the best at something, to have power or dominion, is a terrific motivator for good or evil.

A member of the Chicago dynasty of psychologists and sociologists, Abraham Maslow published his theory of human motivation in 1943. Its popularity continues unabated. Like his colleague Carl Rogers, Maslow believed that actualization was the driving force of human personality, a concept he captures in his 1954 book, *Motivation and Personality*: "A musician must make music, an artist must paint, a poet must write, if he is to be ultimately at peace with himself. What a man can be, he must be." Maslow's great insight was to place actualization into a hierarchy of motivation. Self-actualization, as he called it, is the highest drive, but before a person can turn to it, he or she must satisfy other, lower motivations like hunger, safety, and belonging.[2]

James K. Van Fleet described fourteen human motivators that affect our decision making. They are a sense of personal power and mastery of others; a sense of pride and importance; financial security and success; a reassurance of self-worth and recognition of efforts; peer approval and acceptance; the desire to win, to excel, to be the best; a sense of belonging to either a place or a group; an opportunity for creative self-expression; the accomplishment of something worthwhile; new experiences; a sense of individual liberty and freedom; a sense of self-esteem, dignity, and self-respect; the experience of love in all forms; and emotional security.[3]

The elements of personality are affected by our biological makeup, that is, our genes and gender, and the experiences we have in our lives, that is, family, culture, and environment. Personality can be best described as an individual's characteristic pattern of behavior, thought, and emotion.

If we, as investigators, are to understand what truly motivates the offender and gain valuable insight into her mind, personality characteristics, values, and more important her emotional strengths and weaknesses, we must take the time to understand "who" and "what" she truly is. Once we have determined her strengths and weaknesses, we can adjust our interview style, manner, questioning, and environment in a way that will enhance our chances of success.

In October 2001, Greg Cooper and I interviewed serial killer Daniel Troyer in a prison system outside of Utah. Troyer, a confessed serial killer, stated that on several occasions, he undressed the victims, placed them in their beds, and masturbated over them. Research of his background showed that he had a feeling of inferiority around older women because his mother had been very demeaning and verbally hostile toward him as he grew up. At age seventeen, he left home and joined the Navy, only to go AWOL after a couple of years of service. During his AWOL, he committed a rape and physical assault of an elderly woman. He was dishonorably discharged from the Navy.

As we prepared for the interview, we had the choice of interviewing him in a small room at the prison or in the much larger, "Board of Pardons" room. Based on the information gained by researching his past, we set the interview for the Board of Pardons room and arranged the room in the following manner (with explanations added).

> We moved the Board of Pardons large "bar" to the back of the room and took the Chairman of the Board of Pardons's chair from behind the bar and placed it against the southern-most wall. The chair was a high-backed, cushioned chair. We placed a small working desk in front of the chair and then placed two plastic stacking chairs on the other side of the interview table. On the northern-most wall we placed a standing American flag and in the eastern end of the office, we turned a computer monitor toward the high-back chair. We accessed the Internet and brought up a photograph of an unsolved murder of an elderly woman and left the monitor turned on so that Troyer could see the picture of the elderly victim.[4]

When Troyer entered the room, we thanked him for allowing us to interview him *and learn from him*. We told him that his crimes were intriguing and that we thought we could learn a great deal from exploring his victim selection processes and his crime motivation. We assured him that *he* was in charge of the interview and that we were the *students*, there to learn. (This initial move was carefully planned out and later proved to be very successful. Based on Troyer's terrible self-image and inability to feel confident, we empowered him with confidence right from the start.)

We invited Troyer to sit down. He immediately started to sit in the smaller, plastic chair. We stopped him and motioned toward the much more "powerful" high-backed and padded chair, which was usually occupied by the chairman of the Board of Pardons. We then took our seat in the plastic chairs, remaining the student, while he basked in the more prominent position of teacher. His eyesight immediately glanced at the American flag. Acting as though we hadn't noticed his gaze on the flag, we commented about our appreciation for guys like him who volunteered to protect our American soil. He spoke of his dishonorable discharge, and we changed the event from a violation of law to an unfortunate misunderstanding that occurred during a time of great confusion for him. We then spoke of the heroes in today's military and how valuable their, as well as his, service to America was.

When Troyer looked at the picture of the elderly woman on the computer, we didn't say anything. After a few restless moments, he turned back and the interrogation began. At the conclusion of eight hours (over two days) of interrogation, Troyer changed his story about the murders being an accident to a full confession of premeditation, fantasy, and experiences of reliving the murders. Through the process of gaining a better understanding of his personality, childhood, background, and strengths and weaknesses, the interrogation was successfully concluded.

In the winter of 1994, the seven-week-old son of Mark and Cara Wing was found dead in his crib at 8:00 a.m. The city police department investigated the case and after consultation with the medical examiner determined that the child had twenty-nine rib fractures, two broken legs, and a broken arm. The medical examiner could not offer a cause of death in the investigation. It was clear that the child had suffered some abuse, but no other leads were established beyond that initial hypothosis.

In the course of the city police investigation, five people were identified as possible suspects in the case. They were the child's father, mother, brother, baby-sitter, and maternal grandmother. After a year of investigation, the city concluded that it couldn't take the case any further and couldn't identify any one individual as the prime suspect in the case. While each of the possible perpetrators had some opportunity, even means and theorized motive, no one surfaced as the most probable suspect.

The county sheriff's office took the case for several more years and afterwards concluded that it too was unable to develop the case any further. Thus, the case was placed inactive and not pursued for several more years. In 1998, the case was examined by the Utah Child Fatality Review Board, which was troubled with the circumstances of the case and lack of activity on it. The case was referred to the Attorney General's Office, specifically me. After nine months of investigation, the case was closed with a confession by the father of squeezing the child to death. The difference in the investigative methods boiled down to reviewing the evidence in the case in an entirely different manner to gain a better understanding of motive and methodology of the killer.

In traditional investigations, there are four forms of evidence that law enforcement officers and criminal prosecutors deal with, in part or whole, on every criminal case they handle. How the court deals with this evidence affects the type and length of sentence (if any) that the defendant receives.

These traditional forms of evidence may be clearly manifested, or they may take closer observation to detect, but they are there: physical or forensic, circumstantial, eyewitness accounts, and participant confessions. In American courtrooms, these forms of evidence are introduced in every civil and criminal case that is heard by a court of law.

The effective interviewer uses what is now classified as the newest form of evidence—behavior. Once an in-depth understanding of behavior is gained, the doors of opportunity open for the investigating officer, who must look at the traditional forms of evidence and use behavior to recognize the strengths and weaknesses to obtain not only admissions to crimes but confessions.

A service such as providing interviewing techniques can provide investigators with suggestions regarding how to interview a subject, particularly when the agency may only have one opportunity for a successful interview. These techniques may include suggestions on the most appropriate type of interview, the desired approach, and the best environment in which to conduct the interview.

Studies have shown that certain types of offenders are more apt to feel comfortable or threatened based on the type and manner of interview technique. Using the appropriate approach can make the defining difference in obtaining a confession or having an interview prematurely terminated.

Likewise, the location of the interview can lend to its success. Some interviews may need to be conducted in the controlled environment of a police station by investigators who represent a great deal of authority. In other circumstances, a quiet interview in an offender's home or place of work may prove to be the best strategy.

An effective multijurisdictional team offers suggestions based on the evaluation of the crime scene and the assessment of the offender. The suggestions might range from conducting additional interviews to gathering and testing additional pieces of evidence. Other suggestions may deal with media campaigns or accessing outside disciplines.

In addition, assisting the prosecutor in the development of the case, including trial strategies, can involve considerations regarding jury selection, possible cross-examination techniques for offenders and/or witnesses (requires personality assessments), overall prosecutorial theme development, and crime analysis/crime motivation evaluation.

In other cases, such as threats, when verbal or written communications are received, a multidisciplined unit can assist in determining whether the author of threats has the intent, knowledge, or means to carry out the threats. A behavioral description of the author may be provided to assist in identification and apprehension. In light of the many national and local tragedies that have occurred by both domestic and foreign terrorists, this service could be one of the most valuable yet least used of all services.

A major component of criminal investigative analysis is research showing that certain behavior and personality traits are commonly possessed by specific types of offenders (i.e., child molesters). This information can be highly beneficial in search warrant affidavits in order to describe the types of evidence that "can be expected to be found" (i.e., souvenirs from victims, seemingly innocuous items that may have evidentiary value). Timeliness (staleness) issues might be alleviated through the appropriate use of data gained from current research.

One of the most difficult areas for police investigators to understand is that of forensic evidence. Very few officers have sufficient technical training to properly interpret bloodstain patterns, DNA results, and so forth. A multidisciplinary unit could help determine which analytical tools would be most beneficial and whom to call for the best support and/or advice.

Nearly all law enforcement agencies have access to state-of-the-art technology and electronic databases to assist them. AFIS, CODIS, NCIC, DRUG-FIRE, and ULEIN offer online search capabilities that can greatly enhance an investigation. Most recently, programs like the Multistate Anti-Terrorism Information Exchange (MATRIX) provide law enforcers with a data-mining capability that can streamline access to information for which police have had to search multiple databases and locations. Originally developed as a tool to fight terrorism, MATRIX gives police officers information more quickly than at any time in history. Such programs are not without detractors though. The ACLU has questioned the appropriateness of such a program, and open discussion will only help law enforcement in the long run. According to MATRIX executives, "The Matrix does not make any predictive analysis of anything. It is not an intelligence database. We do not put raw intelligence into it. We do not have access to that."[5] Having had the opportunity to be trained on MATRIX, to see its effectiveness in every type of criminal investigation from narcotics trafficking to homicide, I hope that it is here to stay. While open discussion is necessary and a key component of our society, we cannot be afraid to examine and even to be examined.

One of the greatest hidden benefits of multidisciplinary approaches to the investigation of unsolved crime can also come in the form of cutting-edge training not only in crimes against persons but also in financial crimes and threat assessment. Additional resources, like a Web site accessible to law enforcement and the general public and used to solicit information from the public on unsolved homicides, unidentified bodies, and missing persons where foul play is suspected, has untapped potential.

After years of examining and studying criminal cases from all across America, I have had the pleasure of putting these concepts into play as I have worked alongside my longtime friend and mentor, Gregory M. Cooper. One of the things we discovered early on was that together we were better than when we are alone when dealing with the profiling process. We have had the chance to consult on, teach, and implement these principles all around the world. In our final analysis though, we have discovered that the profiling process can be effectively narrowed down to our patented "Ten Filters of Profiling." Greg deserves the majority of the credit for the creation of the filters, although I have taken great joy in the joint development of the technique.

The profiling process is similar to the dentist's approach in diagnosing a patient's condition accurately before prescribing the cure. Another analogy is akin to a miner who pans for gold. The prospector patiently probes while sifting through granulate debris to separate the dross. Finally rewarded, the refuse is discarded, leaving only the valuable yellow metal. Like the prospector, the investigator purges the least valuable data through a filtering process while unearthing the gold nuggets of truth. This approach allows the examiner to focus by "process of elimination" on the most probable or informative material rather than the least possible and distracting data. The end result leads the investigation instead of reacts to it. The remainder of this chapter briefly focuses on each of the ten filters, which can be examined in greater detail in our book *Analyzing Criminal Behavior II*.

The ten filters are 1) victimology, 2) initial contact site, 3) crime scene, 4) disposal site, 5) physical assault, 6) sexual assault, 7) M.O. versus signature, 8) organized versus disorganized crime scenes and crimes, 9) offender risk, and 10) suspect information.

VICTIMOLOGY: FILTER 1

The ultimate aim of an investigation is to solve the mystery, answer the questions, and reveal the truth. Revelation of the truth is the primary and critical foundation to final resolution. For without the truth, the indisputable facts, a conclusion will never be reached to precisely solve the mystery. Otherwise, hasty conclusions may be drawn; unless they are based on accurate and reliable data, the answer remains open to conjecture, fallibility, and false claims.

Among the most serious follies of an investigator is to develop theory before acquiring sufficient data. Gathering accurate, articulable data and infallible facts is the keystone to developing a reasonable hypothesis that will lead the investigation to a successful, certain, and reliable conclusion. Otherwise, we stand the risk of adjusting the facts to satisfy our theory (ego), which can lead to the most serious of consequences, including false accusation and conviction of an innocent person. Another misfortune is that a case may remain unsolved because of the failure to first accurately diagnose before prescribing on impulse and prejudices.

The key to crime analysis is victimology—the study of the victim. By examining who the victim is, we begin to unravel and eliminate an often perplexing web of misguided leads. A thorough understanding of the victim can often lead the investigation toward a probable suspect rather than to a reaction to an endless pool of less likely possible candidates. According to the *Crime Classification Manual*, written by the FBI:

> Victimology is often one of the most beneficial investigative tools in classifying and solving a violent crime. It is a crucial part of crime analysis. Through it the investigator tries to evaluate why this particular person was targeted for a violent crime. Very often, just answering this question will lead the investigator to the motive, which will lead to the offender. Victimology is an essential step in arriving at a possible motive. If investigators fail to obtain complete victim histories, they may be overlooking information that could quickly direct their investigations to motives and to suspects.

INITIAL CONTACT SITE: FILTER 2

Much can be learned from the initial contact site, or the place where the victim and the suspect first meet each other. Questions surrounding why this particular location was used, how it assisted the offender in accessing the victim, and other related questions can often be answered by an analysis of this filter. Close detail should be noted in the description of the general neighborhood. Is this location a business area, industrial, commercial, farm land, agricultural, or uninhabited? Is the actual site in a residential area, a shopping district, or near a school or playground? Other areas might be public streets, "vice" areas, wooded or open fields, a vehicle, or public transportation vehicles.

When considering the contact site, crime scene, or disposal site, it is necessary to determine what the last known location of the victim was. Did the victim end up in that particular location because the predator chose it, or is it a place where the victim visited or stayed in regular circumstances? The answers to these questions will help determine the level of familiarity the victim had with the particular site. More important, it can also lead the investigator to surmise the level of familiarity the predator had with the site.

CRIME SCENE ANALYSIS: FILTER 3

The location of the crime scene is significant. It may reveal an immediate supposition about a personal versus stranger relationship between this location and the victim and offender. Consideration should be given to the exact location and date and the approximate time of the crime. It is necessary to include information about the city, the county, the state, and the date and time. If the date and time coincide with any religious or remarkable holidays, that is, supremacist historical events, occult holidays, and such, additional information surrounding the event should be included.

As in filter 2, similar questions must be asked: "What is the description of the general area of the crime scene?" (rural, suburban, urban, or other); "What is the general description of the crime scene?" (residential, shopping district, at or near a school or playground, public street, vice area, wooded area, open field, in a vehicle or public transportation, or other); "Is this site the victim's residence? Is this site the victim's place of employment? Were there other people present or in the immediate area? Is there evidence that the suspect disabled the telephone, utilities, or security devices?" (If so, these should be identified); and "Was the property at the crime scene(s) ransacked, vandalized, or burned?"

DISPOSAL SITE: FILTER 4

The disposal site is relevant to the offender's thought process during the phases of the crime. It may further reveal his association to the area, site, and victim and the degree of planning taken in the formulation of the crime.

The first question asked in regard to the disposal site should be, "What is the relationship between the offender, the initial contact/abduction site, the crime scene, and the disposal site?" By gaining the answer to this lengthy but extremely important question, we can gain valuable insight into the offender's personality, which can help us determine the sophistication level of the disposal. Did the offender get frightened and just dump the victim or body off at the earliest point of convenience, or was there forethought and planning involved? Did the offender take the time to adequately plan the crime and the disposal in order to ensure success? What is the relationship between the victim and the offender? If this can be determined, it can help greatly in determining the level of preplanning and motivation for the crime.

PHYSICAL ASSAULT: FILTER 5

By studying the nature and degree of the physical assault against a victim, or the body disposition and the cause of death and/or trauma, we can glimpse the personality and emotional state of the predator responsible for the crime. It also suggests the degree of planning, impulsiveness, and mental condition of the offender.

Early consideration should be given to whether there is reason to believe that the offender moved the victim's body from the crime scene, the death site, or other major assault site to the disposal or recovery site. This information may lead the investigator to theorize about the offender's level of comfort with the location of death or injury or the perceived probability of discovery in a time frame that is not desired by the offender. Certain criminal personalities may desire the victim's body to be discovered sooner rather than later to satisfy some internal desire of the offender.

At many crime scenes, especially those in which there are multiple injuries, the investigator can theorize what the offender's emotions were at the time of the assault or murder, evaluate the type of weapon used and the association between the offender and the weapon, and combine this information with all the elements of the physical assault to begin painting a picture of the offender's personality.

SEXUAL ASSAULT: FILTER 6

The sexual assault committed against the victim may reveal criminal intent. The method and manner of sexual assault (e.g., rape) may reflect certain characteristics consistent with a specific personality type. This particular filter involves close examination of many elements, including type of and body location of the assault, scripting, and so forth. In cases of rape and sexual assault, typologies have been developed to assist the investigator in determining the type of offender, the best interview strategy, and other helpful suggestions.

M.O. VERSUS SIGNATURE: FILTER 7

The M.O. (modus operandi) and signature of an offender play a crucial role in an investigation. The M.O., or the offender's practical actions during the crime, can reveal clues about his identity. M.O. can be very dynamic and can be modified as the offender gains experience and learns from previous mistakes or crimes.

The *signature* of an offender likewise will reveal a great deal about his identity. When an offender goes beyond the actions necessary to perpetrate his crime, his signature is reflected. The signature composes a unique part of the behavior while committing the offense; it often demonstrates an expression or ritual based on the offender's fantasies. Unlike the M.O., the core of an offender's signature will not change. It can, however, evolve or possibly be modified because of interruptions or unexpected victim response.

There are three purposes of M.O., and consideration should be given to the manner in which the suspect first approached the victim. This information may be available by questioning the victim or witnesses. Some common methods of approach may be by deception or by the open and tricky approach. A good example of this type of M.O. would be to recall the manner in which Ted Bundy approached his victims. Recall the way in which Bundy feigned injuries or the need for help to disarm his victims. Then, when Bundy's victims least expected any action, Bundy sprung into a violent attack, gaining control over his victims.

Another common tactic is the blitz attack. In this tactic, the perpetrator attacks the victim by immediate physical assault. The Capitol Hills Rapist in Salt Lake City, Utah, used this M.O. to gain control over his victims. After watching his victims for weeks, and sometimes months, convicted rapist Bobby Lee Boog would gain enough familiarity with his intended victims that he could plan his assaults around their late-night work schedules or other habitual behavior. When his victims returned to their homes, Boog (while waiting inside) would jump them as they came through the door. With blinding speed and while brandishing a knife, Boog would quickly subdue his victims and then rape them.

The third common M.O. would be the deceptive approach. Generally, this offender would pose as an authority figure, a business professional, and such. Some examples have been fraudulent modeling agencies wherein the perpetrator uses the guise of photographing women for future modeling opportunities. During the course of the photo shoot, the perpetrator becomes more deviant in his modeling requests and in some cases may even forcibly assault the victim. Other examples may be the offering of a ride, interviews for employment opportunity, money, treats, or implied family emergencies or illnesses. Convicted serial rapist Michael Blake Jensen reported that he used his position as a deputy fire marshal to forcibly compel women to have sex with him. Jensen's favorite target was the single or divorced mother of a juvenile who was suspected of starting fires. Jensen offered to forget the incident if the mother succumbed to his sexual advances, a tactic that reportedly worked many times.

ORGANIZED VERSUS DISORGANIZED CRIMINAL BEHAVIOR: FILTER 8

During the commission of a crime, an offender will reflect certain behavioral traits often associated with his personality characteristics. Any one crime may reveal characteristics of both the organized and disorganized personalities (mixed). Generally though, a crime may transform from organized to disorganized; however, the reverse of this is rarely observed.

Consider this example: Many people in the United States enjoy hunting deer. Each year as the deer season approaches, and the green leaves of summer begin to change color, announcing the beginning of fall, the hunter starts to think about the annual ascent into the mountains to stalk the elusive deer. Prior to the hunt, the hunter may begin practicing his marksmanship to ensure that his weapon of choice is accurate and deadly. As the season nears, he may purchase hunting magazines or rent hunting videos in order to tune up his skill of stalking. He may purchase new camouflage clothing or pull out all his hunting clothes to make sure that everything is in order. He begins to think about the big "bucks" that have gotten away in the past or the bigger buck that he dreams about bagging this year. As he fantasizes about the hunt, he becomes more and more excited. Soon, as the hunt begins, he is physically and emotionally ready to stalk his prey.

Once the hunter bags his buck, he generally goes through an interesting ritual of taking photographs of the slain animal. The photo almost always includes the hunter in order to prove the conquest to anyone who may hear the hunter's story or see the hunter's photo or trophy. Some hunters even save the head of their trophy buck and have it stuffed and mounted on the wall of their home or office, again to prove their conquest and to remind them of a very favorable and happy experience.

Like the legal hunter of big game, the predator who murders humans goes through similar emotions. Thus, we see the value in beginning to think like the criminal, and as we begin to recognize that crime is the "pursuit of legitimate needs through illegitimate means," as Cooper says, we can begin to better understand the motivation of the criminal.

OFFENDER RISK LEVEL: FILTER 9

An analysis of the offender's risk level to identification and apprehension during the commission of the crime may reveal a number of considerations for the investigator. That an offender risks exposure to identification and apprehension may suggest such things as a lack of concern or a lack of sophistication. The lower the risk, the more consideration may be given to increased criminal sophistication, thorough preplanning, or premeditation. The offender risk level can be evaluated in light of each of the filters while gaining insight into the criminal's thought process. Any suspect behavior that elevates the risk level to identification and apprehension should be determined and evaluated.

When considering the level of risk taken by the offender, the investigator must consider whether the victim was allowed to live. A living victim becomes a witness and elevates the offender's risk of apprehension. Thus, we must also discover whether the suspect attempted to conceal his own identity by wearing a mask or blindfolding the victim. If the victim was bound, to what extent did the suspect go to maintain control of the victim? The longer the suspect stays with the victim, the more time the victim has to examine identifying marks like scars or tattoos or imprint the sound of the offender's voice or peculiar body odors, and such. When reviewing the amount of time the offender spends with the victim, consideration should be given to the time spent at the initial contact site, the crime scene, and the location of the disposal. Further examination should be made regarding the method of disposal, what communication was initiated by the suspect regarding the crime and whether there was any communication from the suspect before or after the crime, and a thorough review of the approach that the suspect used to confront the victim should be conducted.

When criminals repeat criminal behavior, they demonstrate that their thought patterns have not changed, and there is a high probability that there will be a new victim. Violent crimes represent the highest risk of dangerousness and have high recidivism rates. Thus, when dealing with repeat or experienced offenders, it is clear that the experienced offender recognizes the increased risk level and will attempt to compensate or reduce the level of risk in several ways.

SUSPECT INFORMATION: FILTER 10

Accurate suspect information is invaluable to any successful investigation. The more accurate the information obtained about the suspect, and the sooner it is available for the investigators and public awareness, the more quickly effective leads can be generated. Specific and distinguishable characteristics will effectively eliminate the "possible" and focus on the "probable." The sooner the public knows about the offender, the more quickly identification and apprehension can be achieved.

"Suspects" include arrestees, perpetrators, or persons the investigator has reasonable cause to believe are responsible for the commission of the crime. In every investigation, the number of suspects that have been identified as possible and probable must be evaluated.

Suspect identification should include name, aliases, address, social security number, state and federal ID numbers, physical description, vehicle description and availability during the crime in question, and any other identifying characteristics or behavior.

CONCLUSION

Law enforcers in America are consistently examining the protocols and methodology of investigative and solving crime. Over the years, some incredible programs have developed into very useful tools, such as behavioral profiling. It is refreshing to know that the profiling process, or the system of evaluating behavior at a crime scene, does not have to be reserved for the offices of the FBI unit. Police officers across the country have the expertise, experience, and education to develop similar, locally based units. Within nearly every community in America, there are psychological experts, criminologists, forensic scientists, and medical examiners who would welcome the opportunity to delve into the unsolved crimes that sit dormant in our detective divisions nationally. Family members of the deceased or missing, often at the hands of criminals, would be thrilled that another attempt is being made in solving their particular crime. Today's advancements in forensics are helping police solve cases that are decades old. Introducing behavioral analysis into those investigations will help direct the investigator from the often huge pool of possible suspects to the most probable suspect. As the investigator becomes more aware of a suspect's strengths and weaknesses, the investigator is armed with the understanding of what type of interview or interrogation approach to take. Most importantly, as a multidisciplinary approach to solving crime is taken, fresh perspectives, strategies, and solutions can be formed and more crimes can be solved.

I often think about seven-week-old Ian Wing, murdered at the hands of his father. For years, his killer got away with murder. Without the introduction of behavior and its comparative association with the traditional forms of evidence, his killer would be walking the streets today. Perhaps there is some solace in that.

NOTES

1. Greg Burton, "Delving into the Dark Side," *Salt Lake Tribune*, August 20, 2000; Brandon Griggs, "Lafferty to Sheriff's Deputy: 'If God Asked Me to, I'd Kill You Right Now," *Salt Lake Tribune*, August 20, 2000. Copyright © 2000 Salt Lake Tribune. Reprinted by permission.

2. Abraham Maslow, *Motivation and Personality* (1954; repr., New York: Harper, 1970).

3. James K. Van Fleet, *Conversation Power: Communication Skills for Business and Personal Success* (abridged, 2 CDs) (New York: Simon & Schuster Audio, 2002).

4. Taken from my notes.

5. Multistate Anti-Terrorism Information Exchange (MATRIX), "Frequently Asked Questions" (online), http://www.matrix-at.org/faq.htm (accessed July 9, 2004).

SEXUAL HOMICIDE OF ELDERLY WOMEN

Mark E. Safari, John Jarvis, and Kathleen Nussbaum

Mark E. Safarik is a supervisory special agent and serves in the Federal Bureau of Investigation's National Center for the Analysis of Violent Crimes' (NCAVC) Behavioral Analysis Unit. He specializes in the behavioral analysis of violent crime with an emphasis on homicide and has conducted extensive research on the sexual homicide of elderly women. He works closely with law enforcement agencies throughout the United States as well as internationally. Prior to becoming an FBI special agent, he was a detective with the Davis, California, Police Department. His law enforcement career spans twenty-eight years.

John Patrick Jarvis has been employed with the FBI since July 1991. He has served in both the Headquarters's Program of the Uniform Crime Reports and, since 1995, in the Training Division, Behavioral Science Unit (BSU), at the FBI Academy in Quantico, Virginia. He has seventeen years of experience in criminal justice analysis, serving with the Virginia Department of Corrections, the Virginia Department of Criminal Justice Services, and the Federal Bureau of Investigation. He holds a PhD in sociology from the University of Virginia in Charlottesville.He is currently conducting research in the area of lethal and no-lethal violence, deception in written statements, quantifying homicidal injury, and elderly and child homicide.

Kathleen E. Nussbaum is a graduate student in investigative psychology at the University of Liverpool. She holds an undergraduate degree from New York University and has served as a research intern with the Federal Bureau of Investigation's National Center for the Analysis of Violent Crime.

he FBI consults regularly on the investigation of extraordinarily violent and unusual cases. Although overall awareness of elderly victimization throughout the United States has greatly increased over the past decade, little attention has been focused on elderly female victims of sexual homicides and the offenders who commit these crimes. Law enforcement agencies are often faced with rarely seen and excessively violent crime scenes as they attempt to solve these homicides. This in-depth study examines the characteristics of 128 elderly women who were murdered by 110 offenders as well as the characteristics of the attendant crime scenes. An empirical analysis of crime scene attributes, victim characteristics (including severity of victim injuries), and offender demographics produces significant predictive information about offender characteristics that may assist law enforcement investigation of such cases.

CASE 1

A seventy-seven-year-old widow was sexually assaulted and murdered in her bedroom. The medical examiner identified three separate causes of death. The offender strangled the victim into unconsciousness, severely fractured her skull using a nearby clock he removed from the bedroom dresser, and then repeatedly stabbed her in the face, chest, and vagina with a butcher knife he obtained from the kitchen. A twenty-year-old man living two blocks away was arrested.

CASE 2

A nineteen-year-old offender, while walking by the apartment of a seventy-six-year-old woman at 2 a.m., noticed a light on and began peeping through the windows. He saw her sitting alone watching television. He smashed out the front door window, reached in, and unlocked the door. He blitz attacked the victim, shattering her jaw as he knocked her unconscious to the floor. He ripped off her clothing, raped her vaginally, then anally, and finally assaulted her vaginally with an umbrella lying nearby. He used a piece of glass from the broken window to cut her throat. He returned to a friend's house covered in blood and told him he had just killed an "old lady." He was convicted and sentenced to life in prison.

CASE 3

A seventy-year-old woman was found dead, lying on her bed in a blood-spattered bedroom of a rural farm house. She suffered twenty-eight stab wounds to the face, neck, and chest. The offender had pushed her night clothes above her breasts and spread her legs. She was nude except for the night shirt. After killing her, he placed a pillow over her face. No semen was located at the scene. Ten years later, investigators still pursue leads in this woman's death, and her daughters are haunted on a daily basis because the offender remains unidentified.

INTRODUCTION

Most law enforcement agencies in the United States seldom face the unenviable task of investigating the brutal sexual assault–homicide of an elderly female member of their community. However, this crime does occur, and its prevalence may increase as the nation's population ages. Although law enforcement agencies respond to violent criminal behavior on a daily basis, even the most experienced homicide investigator is rarely prepared for the extreme brutality and sexual degradation that is sometimes unleashed on one of the most vulnerable and fragile community citizens: the elderly woman.

That an elderly woman has been viciously sexually assaulted appears, on its surface, to be incongruous with what the public at large and even most law enforcement officers associate with a sexual assault offense. Sexual assault, in the minds of many lay and professional people, is believed to be motivated by sexual arousal and desire on the part of the offender (Groth and Birnbaum 1979). Rape and sexual assault are in fact distortions of human sexuality (Groth 1978). When the victim is an elderly woman, these distortions cause us to question the more traditional avenues of investigating these types of homicides. This perception can pose serious difficulties as law enforcement attempts to establish initial investigative directions for solving these cases.

Because of the relative infrequency of these cases and the lack of research in this area, investigators often encounter difficulties when trying to investigate a sexual homicide involving an elderly female victim.[1] Complicating this is a lack of knowledge with respect to offenders who perpetrate these heinous crimes. Empirical research, perhaps leading to investigative decision support systems, is needed to assist law enforcement in rapidly identifying and apprehending these offenders. Specifically, analysis and study of readily obtainable crime scene, victim, and demographic variables may be useful in supporting such goals. The research offered here examines cases of elderly female sexual homicide to identify patterns in the behavioral aspects of the victims, offenders, and their interactions within the context of the crime and to link offender characteristics to victim and crime scene attributes. Thus, the goal is to distinguish factors that are specific to these cases and then to examine their usefulness in guiding the investigative efforts to identify these offenders. Before examining the elderly sexual homicide data, a review of the research surrounding the scope and nature of crimes against the elderly, with special attention to sexual assault and homicide, is necessary to insure a fuller understanding of these difficult cases.

CRIMES AGAINST THE ELDERLY

Both Bureau of Justice Statistic studies and the National Crime Survey reflect that crimes against the elderly tend to be more serious in nature than those against younger persons (Bureau of Justice Statistics 1994). Older victims of violent crimes are more likely to be attacked by total strangers (Kennedy and Silverman 1990; Muram, Miller, and Cutler 1992) and are most likely to be victimized in their own homes. They are less likely to try to protect themselves during a crime and are more likely to sustain injuries. These findings are confirmed by numerous studies that discuss the general problem of victimization of the elderly and by specific research addressing violent offenses (Antunes, Cook, Cook, and Skogan 1977; Faggiani and Owens 1999; Fox and Levin 1991; Lent and Harpold 1988; Nelson and Huff-Corzine 1998).

These studies also demonstrate that in particular ways elderly women are inherently more vulnerable to crime than younger women. First, they are more likely to live alone. Nearly 80 percent of elderly persons who live alone are female due in large part to an increased risk of widowhood and longer life expectancy (Taeuber and Allen 1990). Second, "Vulnerability is related to physical size and strength; elderly females are less capable of fleeing or resisting a physical attack than a younger person" (Nelson and Huff-Corzine 1998, p. 135). As women age, they experience skeletal, neuromuscular, and other systemic changes (Davis and Brody 1979). These age-related changes restrict mobility and reduce women's abilities to escape or defend themselves against an assailant. As Moen (1996) noted, this may be particularly true of the older members of the aged population (seventy-five years and older), who are disproportionately female and living alone.

This notion of vulnerable victims is also characteristic of the routine activities perspective offered in criminology (Cohen and Felson 1979). That is, considering the interaction of available victims, motivated offenders, and the lack of guardianship may offer an understanding of how these incidents occur. Elderly women, perhaps as a consequence of widowhood, are more likely than younger females to lack the guardianship common to children and younger women with parents, boyfriends, and husbands and thus are more likely to be perceived by motivated offenders as suitable targets.

This vulnerability conception is further supported by the work of R. E. Longo and C. Gochenour (1981), which indicates that some rapists select elderly victims because of their vulnerability (see also Davis and Brody 1979). Furthermore, the idea that predators often choose prey for particular reasons based on some set of criteria is not unique to criminal behavior. In nature, predators continually assess a victim's vulnerability (chance of successful capture and killing) and accessibility (likelihood of detection and deterrence) in the course of their daily activities (Boudreaux, Lord, and Jarvis 2001). Our contending theory in these cases of sexual homicide is that offenders are no different and engage in similar decision-making assessments.

However, an abundance of definitive literature is lacking, perhaps largely due to an emphasis on broad categories of both violent and property offenses and an inability to adequately distinguish between crimes against men and women. A thorough search of the literature found that any extensive focus on violence against elderly women was limited. However, some discussion of the few studies that were found is merited.

SEXUAL ASSAULT OF THE ELDERLY WOMAN

The sparse research literature relative to sexual assault of the elderly woman reveals that these victims are much more likely to be injured or killed compared to other victims of similar crimes (Davis and Brody 1979; Gerry 1983; Kerschner 1976; Pollock 1988). Some studies examine rapists (Hazelwood and Burgess 1995; Warren et al. 1998), but few focus specifically on those who rape the elderly (Fletcher 1977; Groth 1978; Muram et al. 1992; Pollock 1988). Pollock (1988) conducted the only study to date that was found to contrast those who commit sexual offenses against older women with those who victimize younger women. His findings clearly identify predatory rapists who purposefully select older women. According to this study, when a rapist attacks an older woman, the rape or sexual assault is likely to be "a particularly brutal act largely motivated by rage or sadistic intent" (p. 530). He also suggested that apparently motiveless violent attacks on elderly women may be cases of sexual assault.

Many elderly women are unaware of their vulnerability to sexual assault and perceive sexual assault as a sexually motivated crime, directed primarily at young and promiscuous women who somehow contribute to being selected as victims through their actions and behaviors (Groth 1978; Hazelwood 1987). More recent research suggests that sexual assault is motivated by the need to express power or anger or a combination of both (Groth, Burgess, and Holmstrom 1977; Hazelwood and Warren 1990, 2000; Pollock 1988). This power or anger may be expressed as a need to punish, dominate, and control the victim. The offender is rarely seen as seeking sexual gratification from his assaults. Consistent with this notion, Groth's (1978) examination of case files of sexual assaults of older victims found that offenders use physical force, including beating, stabbing, and killing their victims, in 60 percent of the cases. Groth suggested that the elderly female represents an authority figure or is the actual woman over whom the assailant wants power. Sexuality is the method used to affect revenge or express his hostility and anger. Groth, like Pollock (1988), noted that the sexual assault of older victims is often an exceptionally violent crime that is "more an issue of hostility than sexual desire" (Groth 1978, p. 213). For the moment, however, consider the information noted above relative to sexual assaults and the following research findings relative to homicides involving elderly female victims.

ELDERLY FEMALE HOMICIDE

According to the FBI (2000), 15,553 homicides in the United States were reported to the police in 1999. Of these homicide victims, 812 were determined to be elderly (sixty years or older), and more than half of this total (499) were identified as females. Elderly female homicides that became known to the police constituted just more than 3 percent of all homicides in the United States in 1999 (FBI 2000). According to the annual publication FBI Uniform Crime Reports (UCR), this percentage has been fairly stable over the past decade. Although homicide may result from a confrontation between an offender and a victim in the course of another crime, most homicide studies do not focus exclusively on the elderly. Many of the studies cited in this research are largely limited to aggregate analyses regarding both male and female victims with little attention to the importance of both qualitative and quantitative analyses. Conversely, the studies that have examined homicide of the elderly concentrate on the types of homicide, which, in most cases, do not exhibit an identifiable sexual component.

ELDERLY FEMALE SEXUAL HOMICIDE

There are many difficulties in obtaining reliable statistics relative to the number of elderly sexual homicides. One of the most problematic of these involves the identification of the offense as a homicide without note of the subordinate offense of rape or sexual assault (Brownmiller 1975).[2] Other difficulties include the lack of necessary investigation to identify the sexual behavior, poor communication between investigators and other personnel relative to understanding the sexual nature of the offense, and classification errors in official data entries (see Burgess, Hartman, Ressler, Douglas, and McCormack 1986). Although official statistics are elusive, one demographic fact is inescapable: Census data show that an increasing proportion of the baby boom generation will be aging into the elderly population in the coming years (US Bureau of the Census 1999). Coupled with people living longer, this suggests that the incidence of violent victimization of elderly women may also increase. This is further evidenced by nearly 75 percent of people older than the age of sixty-five being women (US Bureau of the Census 1999).

As with all criminal behavior, examination of any factors that may assist law enforcement in rapidly identifying and apprehending responsible offenders and protecting potential victims has merit. In addition, because cases of the type described here are generally uncommon, when such cases occur, law enforcement must be cognizant of and use the most effective investigative tactics and strategies available.

From a practitioner's perspective, the current body of knowledge regarding elderly female sexual homicide is derived principally from experiential patterns observed by homicide investigators. Their experience and collective training have helped them form a consensus regarding these kinds of cases. In particular, it is believed that the age of the victim and offender appear to be quite disparate. The excessive violence exhibited in a number of these cases, the excessive injury that results from this violence, and a perceived ambiguity between burglary or robbery and sexual homicide as motivations are attributes that may be distinct from other violent crimes. To further investigate these contentions, as well as for the reasons stated earlier, cases of elderly female sexual homicide are examined.

DATA AND METHOD

Data were collected from two sources. First, we examined the data available from the Supplementary Homicide Reports (SHR) as collected by the FBI UCR from 1976 to 1999. These data served to provide a brief statistical description of the 604 cases that were identified during that period. However, many details of the crime scene, the nature and extent of victim injuries, and similar case attributes were not available from the SHR. Therefore, we turned to the ongoing data collection efforts of the National Center for the Analysis of Violent Crime (NCAVC) to acquire data on incident, victim, and offender details in cases of this nature that are not available in the SHR. This NCAVC data, therefore, serve as the principal data source for the research conducted here. The NCAVC case data reflecting the types of cases examined here were identified through various sources. Cases were identified through the FBI's Violent Criminal Apprehension Program, brought forward by law enforcement through their participation in the FBI's National Academy Training Program, and through the operational activities of the FBI's NCAVC. The cases represent submissions from thirty states, with California, Georgia, Washington, Florida, New York, New Jersey, and Texas providing a large number. These sources identified 128 solved cases involving a woman sixty years or older who was determined to be a victim of a sexual homicide.[3] The 110 offenders in these cases have been convicted and are responsible for at least one sexual homicide of an elderly female.[4]

Following A. W. Burgess et al. (1986), this study involved a comprehensive review of the behavioral and psychological details of the 128 sexual homicides through analysis of the offenders' physical, sexual, and, when known, verbal behavior with the victim (see also O'Toole 1999). This also includes a complete study of the victim, a thorough evaluation of the crime scene, and an in-depth investigation of the nature and scope of the interactions between the victim and the offender.

These records were very comprehensive and usually contained investigative, autopsy, and forensic and evidence analysis reports; crime scene and autopsy photographs, diagrams, sketches, and maps; victimology information; offender background; and any confessions or admissions by the offender. Psychological evaluations of the offender were provided in a number of the cases. In addition, investigators who worked on these cases were contacted to clarify or provide supplemental information not identified in the police reports.

Clearly, for both statistical and methodological reasons, it would be impossible to fully examine every aspect of these incidents with the relatively small number of cases available. Nonetheless, examination of the data was conducted in two stages. First, the descriptive information available from these incidents was examined in an effort to fully depict the relative frequencies of specific victim, offender, and offense attributes that comprise the behavior evident in these cases. Typical variables examined included, but were not limited to, demographics, injury, weapon use, and so forth. Through this analysis, links between the attributes are suggested.

Second, for the purposes of this research, we narrowed our focus to four dependent variables: race of offender, age of offender, relationship of victim to offender, and distance of offender's residence (in blocks) from that of the victim. These dependent variables were selected for analysis because these attributes are most likely to assist law enforcement investigators confronted with solving such cases (Safarik, Jarvis, and Nussbaum 2000). Each dependent variable was then examined separately using logistic regression models. Particular attention was given to the degree of probability to which each independent variable could contribute to the explanation of variance in the dependent variable. The set of independent variables represents crime scene and victim characteristics and specific offender behavioral attributes.

RESULTS

Initial analyses of the SHR data revealed 604 cases reported to law enforcement over the twenty-four-year period.[5] The data associated with these SHR cases showed 81 percent of the victims to be white; offender race, when known, to be approximately 45 percent white and 55 percent nonwhite; a predominate use of personal weapons (hands, fists, and feet) rather than firearms (2.8%); and when it could be established, a stranger was most often, 54 percent of the time, found to have been the assailant. Further analysis of the circumstances of these incidents reported in the SHR showed that 92 percent of the cases involved a rape of the victim, with just 8 percent involving some other sexual offense. Finally, the age of the offender was found, on average, to be twenty-seven years. Although these demographic results are useful for describing the overall nature of these cases, virtually no further detailed investigative information about these cases is available to explore potential relationships between crime scene, victim, and offender attributes. Therefore, analyses of the NCAVC data were undertaken to extend the demographic results available from the SHR.

Analyses of NCAVC case data examined the descriptive statistical properties of all candidate variables to be included in the analysis. These results, as shown in table 18.1, are largely consistent with findings from the SHR and suggest that the average offender was more likely nonwhite, age twenty-five or older, living within six blocks of the victim, and not known to the victim. These demographics depict an average offender in these data; however, it is important to note that variation in these attributes was also evident as shown by the standard deviations in table 18.1.

TABLE 18.1: Descriptive Statistics for Dependent and Independent Variables

Variable	% of Cases	M	SD
Offender race		0.41	0.49
Nonwhite	59		
White	41		
Took items		0.72	0.45
Took items	69		
No items taken	26		
Neighborhood composition		0.58	0.50
Primarily White	57		
Less than 80% white	42		
Offender age		1.60	0.50
Between 15 and 24 years old	43		
25 or older	57		
Victim's state of dress		3.09	7.91
Fully dressed	5		
Partially nude	77		
Nude	16		
Injury Severity Score[a]		47.40	16.93
Offender distance		0.42	0.50
Within 6 blocks	54		
More than 6 blocks	39		
Homicide Injury Scale[b]		4.58	7.87
Neighborhood composition		0.58	0.50
Primarily white	57		
Less than 80% white	42		
Offender knew victim		0.55	0.50
Knew victim	52		
Did not know victim	42		
Victim's body left		1.02	5.78
Uncovered	57		
Covered	33		
Altered	9		
Method of entry		0.40	0.49
No force used	56		
Force used	37		
Time of day		0.20	0.13
Between 8 p.m. and 8 a.m.	66		
Between 8 a.m. and 8 p.m.	22		

NOTE: Offender race, 0 = nonwhite, 1 = white; took items (from crime scene), 0 = none taken, 1 = items taken; neighborhood composition, 0 = 79% or less white, 1 = 80% or more white; offender age, 1 = between 15 and 24 years old, 2 = older than 25; victim's state of dress (when found at crime scene), 1 = fully dressed, 2 = partially dressed, 3 = nude; offender distance (from victim's residence), 0 = 6 blocks or less, 1 = more than 6 blocks; offender knew victim, 0 = victim unknown to offender, 1 = victim known to offender; victim's body left (at crime scene), 0 = uncovered, 1 = covered, 2 = altered; method of entry, 0 = no force, 1 = forcible entry; time of day, 0 = 8 p.m. to 8 a.m., 1 = 8 a.m to 8 p.m.

THE OFFENDERS

The offender population includes forty-eight white (44%), forty-six black (42%), fourteen Hispanic (13%), and 1 percent others.[6] Of note is the absence of Asian offenders. The offenders range in age from fifteen to fifty-eight. Blacks offend interracially 77 percent of the time, Hispanics 80 percent, and whites only 4 percent. Of the offenders, 56 percent live within six blocks of the victim, with nearly 30 percent living on the same block. Of Hispanic offenders, 85 percent live within six blocks of the victim. Overall, 81 percent of the offenders travel to the scene on foot. And 93 percent of blacks and 85 percent of Hispanics were on foot.

The offenders in many respects are found to be quite similar. For instance, 90 percent have criminal records, with burglary (59%) making up the highest proportion. However, property and violent offenses are found to be approximately equally represented among those with criminal histories. It should be noted that just 21 percent are found to have sex offenses in their criminal histories, a key point for law enforcement when considering the background of potential suspects. In terms of their employment skill levels, 93 percent are unskilled, with nearly 70 percent unemployed. Of the offenders, 93 percent have twelve years or fewer of formal education, and 19 percent of that group have eight years or fewer. Of those who attended high school, the majority had spotty attendance records and poor academic performance. Many simply dropped out after a couple of years. Also, 93 percent had a history of substance abuse, with no race or age trends noted. The drug abused most often was alcohol (85%), followed by marijuana (54%) and cocaine (44%).

Finally, 45 percent of the offenders confessed to the crime subsequent to their arrest, and 19 percent made some kind of an admission relative to the crime yet continued to deny responsibility for the homicide. In terms of racial differences, whites were observed to have confessed nearly twice as often as blacks, and blacks made some sort of admission more than twice as often as whites.

THE VICTIMS

Analysis of the victims revealed several important observations. The mean age was seventy-seven. Although the victim population was disproportionately white (86%), both blacks (9%) and Hispanics (4%) were also victimized. Similar to the offender data, Asian victims were rare: Only a single Asian victim was identified. Of the victims, 94 percent were killed in their own residences. Although 14 percent of the victims had lived in their neighborhoods from four to nine years, 73 percent had lived there at least ten years, and many had lived there substantially longer. Contributing to their vulnerability, 81 percent of the victims had no additional home security beyond locks normally found on doors and windows.

Qualitative analyses of these cases suggests the possibility that variation in the degree of injury suffered may be a useful measure to analyze offender behavior. In an effort to identify a way these cases could be compared using the severity of the victim's injuries, a scale was created to quantify the severity of injuries directly related to the cause(s) of death. This scale, called the Homicide Injury Scale, draws on available medical examiner data and ranks injury severity from internal injuries only (1) to multiple excessive external injuries with multiple causes of death (6). Not relying solely on this convention, a second measure, the Injury Severity Score, is also used by adapting an injury scale developed by S. P. Baker, B. O'Neill, W. Haddon, and W. B. Long (1974). The Injury Severity Score is currently used by the Centers for Disease Control.[7] Both of these derived measures, the Homicide Injury Scale and the Injury Severity Score, are then applied to the victim data. It should be noted that the correlation between these measures was determined to be .77. Mean injury levels were 4.6 and 47.4, respectively, and reflect more rather than less severe injury. These measures are then used in subsequent analyses in an effort to further the examination of offender characteristics.

Turning to cause of death (COD) determinations, strangulation (63%) was found to be the most frequent, followed by blunt force trauma (38%). Death by a firearm (1%) was the least frequent. Variations in this pattern by race were also examined, but no significant differences were found.

THE INCIDENTS

Some of the limited findings relative to violent victimization of the elderly were also found in the data. In particular, there are some consistencies in the dynamics of the victimization. Of the offenders, 40 percent gained entrance through unlocked doors or windows, and 20 percent were freely admitted to the residence. Close to 40 percent used force on a door or window to gain entry. Of white offenders, 38 percent entered through unlocked windows or doors, and 36 percent gained entry through admittance by the victim or by the use of a ruse or con scheme. Of black offenders, 48 percent used force, and only 10 percent were admitted by the victim through use of a ruse or con. White offenders were either admitted by the victim or used a ruse/con almost four times as often as black offenders. In contrast, black offenders were nearly twice as likely as white offenders to use force to gain access to their victims.

Analysis of offender behavior at the crime scene indicates that 77 percent of the offenders brought nothing with them to the scene. When they did bring something, the items consisted mostly of weapons (10%) or tools (8%). In contrast, they removed property 72 percent of the time, mostly small easily accessible items such as cash and jewelry. Offenders left the body of the victim uncovered 57 percent of the time. White and Hispanic offenders were most likely to leave the victim uncovered (64%), in essence, discarding her body where they last interacted with her. Black offenders were more likely to cover the body (43%), and white offenders were least likely (21%). The approach used by 82 percent of the offenders was found to be a blitz attack (the immediate and overwhelming use of injurious force to physically incapacitate the victim). Nearly 70 percent killed their victims between 8 p.m. and 4 a.m., with the greatest percentage (39%) occurring after midnight.

Offenders were found to have sexually assaulted their victims vaginally (65%) and anally (24%). Black offenders sexually assaulted both vaginally (71%) and anally (29%) more often than white offenders, who assaulted at 58 percent and 16 percent, respectively. Hispanic offenders ($n = 14$) assaulted anally 36 percent of the time, more often than either blacks or whites, but the significance of this finding is hampered by consideration of the small sample ($n = 5$). Overall, these offenders inserted foreign objects into the victim's body 22 percent of the time, with white offenders responsible for just more than half of those cases. Of note, more than half of all foreign object insertions were perpetrated by offenders younger than twenty-four years of age.[8] Finally, semen was identified in only 48 percent of the cases, with no differences noted for race or age. Sexual activity, without the presence of semen, was noted in the remaining 52 percent of cases. This sexual activity in addition to vaginal, anal, and oral assault included fondling the sexual areas of the body, foreign object insertion, and posing the victim to expose sexual areas, among others.

LINKING OFFENDER CHARACTERISTICS

These results provide a baseline for judging the degree to which various independent variables may increase the likelihood of accurately assessing offender characteristics. In more complex analyses, following J. Warren et al. (1999), logistic regression models are employed to examine the performance of various independent variables in predicting four offender characteristics as shown in table 18.2 (offender race, offender age, distance from offender's residence to victim's residence, and victim-offender relationship). The percentage correctly classified in these models represents the degree of accuracy that was obtained using the indicated independent variables. Our results are encouraging, with each model resulting in about 60 percent to 70 percent classification accuracy. Particular attention should be given to the improvement of prediction accuracy that results from inclusion of crime scene or victim attributes as explanatory variables. Using this approach, the model classification accuracy and performance of various independent variables for the demographic attributes in question are shown in table 18.2.

Our results demonstrate that by considering the independent variables shown in table 18.3, items taken from the crime scene and neighborhood com-

TABLE 18.2: Logistical Regression Results for Dependent Variables of Interest

Variable	B	Odds Ratio	x^2	% Corrected Classified	Adjusted R^2
Offender race			21.630**	69.4	.219
Took items*	-0.97	0.38			
Neighborhood composition**	1.70	5.51			
Constant	-0.78	—			
Offender age			20.180**	65.6	.196
Victim's state of dress**	-1.90	0.15			
Injury Severity Score*	-0.02	0.98			
Constant	0.53	—			
Offender distance			13.251**	72.3	.141
Homicide Injury Scale**	-0.30	0.74			
Neighborhood composition**	1.23	3.40			
Constant	0.09	—			
Offender knew victim			5.063**	61.0	.054
Victim's body left*	-0.51	0.60			
Constant	0.51	—			

NOTE: For variable definitions, see table 20.3. In all analyses reported here, the predictors were entered as single blocks. Stepwise procedures yielded slightly different parameter estimates, but the overall fit of the models did not vary significantly.
*$p < .10$. **$p < .05$.

position, the ability to predict offender race increases. Prediction likelihood of an offender's race increases from 0.60 (not reported in the table) to 0.69. Thus, determining the racial homogeneity of the neighborhood where the crime took place increases the odds by 5.5 of correctly predicting offender race. Although other candidate variables and diagnostics (including autocorrelation, specification errors, multicollinearity, etc., as in all analyses in table 20.2) were examined, this model was found to be adequate for predicting offender race. A similar analysis of offender age improved classification accuracy from 0.57 to 0.66. The independent variables of the victim's state of dress (clothed, unclothed, etc.) and the Injury Severity Score were found to have significant influence on predicting the offender's age category.

Analysis of the distance between the offender's residence and the victim's was also conducted, with the independent variables of neighborhood composition and the Homicide Injury Scale improving classification accuracy from 0.57 to 0.72, or approximately 25 percent. This suggests that the proximity of the offender's residence to the crime scene is significantly influenced by the racial homogeneity of the neighborhood. Interracial offending of blacks against whites (77%) occurs more in heterogeneous communities. White against black offending was found to be virtually nonexistent in heterogeneous communities. Recognizing the intraracial nature of these crimes only appears to be applicable if the victim is black. If the victim is white, the intraracial aspect of violent offending does not appear to be as germane.

Finally, an analysis of the relationship between the offender and the victim revealed an increase in classification accuracy from 0.55 to 0.61. The variable of how the victim's body was left at the crime scene (uncovered, covered, or altered) had statistical significance in the prediction of victim-offender relationship. Stronger findings in this particular analysis may have been found if not for a lingering difficulty defining relationships between offenders and their victims, as will be discussed later.

DISCUSSION AND CONCLUSION

Pollock (1988), among others, noted that there have been few studies that systematically examine those who commit sexual offenses against older women. This study responds to this scarcity of knowledge by examining sexual homicides of elderly women.

To understand the importance of these results, it is also necessary to look beyond the statistically significant findings and correlations and look at the other substantive findings that may be important for understanding these cases. Through an exhaustive and detailed examination of each crime scene, an attempt was made to relate the criminal behavior exhibited in these scenes with the known characteristics and behavioral patterns of the offenders. Many of the descriptive findings here are also consistent with other studies that have explored violent victimization of the elderly (Faggiani and Owens 1999; Fox and Levin 1991; Kennedy and Silverman 1990; Nelson and Huff-Corzine 1998). Although some of the observations of the data cannot be applied to all cases (for primarily methodological reasons), there are others that may support law enforcement efforts to gain investigative direction.

This analysis reveals several points that merit further elaboration, the most important of these being the comparison of the results to law enforcement's anecdotal beliefs, victim location and routine activities theory, defining stranger versus acquaintance, community composition and interracial offending, levels of homicidal injury, classifying sexual homicide offenders, and financial gain versus sexual/homicide motives.

First, despite that the offenders in these cases are diverse in age and split relatively evenly between black and white offenders (with a less significant contribution by Hispanic offenders), many aggregate demographic characteristics are found to be strikingly similar. These observations are consistent with the experience of investigators who have anecdotally described violent offenders of the elderly as younger offenders, assaulting the victims at or close to the victims' residences, living within proximity to the crime scene, and generally unknown to the victim.

Second, elderly violent crime victims sustain their injuries at their residences anywhere from 82 percent (Hochstedler 1981) to 100 percent (Pollock 1988) of the time for sexual assault and 52 percent for violent crimes overall (Antunes et al. 1977) and 34 percent for robbery of females (Faggiani and Owens 1999). A similar result is identified here with 94 percent of these women killed at home. Although only 56 percent of offenders lived within six blocks, fully 81 percent (higher for blacks and Hispanics) initiated the assault by walking to the scene. This implies that a majority of the offenders had some pretense to be in the vicinity of the victim prior to the crime, thus providing the opportunity to initiate the assault on foot. Although 14 percent of the victims had lived in their neighborhoods four to nine years, 73 percent had lived there at least ten years and many substantially longer. This suggests that in conjunction with longevity in their neighborhoods, these victims were well-known to many residents in the area as well as individuals who routinely engaged in the activities of daily life there. Unfortunately, this longevity may have produced unrecognized risk to the victim. K. D. Rossmo (1999) suggested that motivated offenders may sometimes create "mental maps" of neighborhoods when they identify potentially suitable victims. Mental mapping is the process by which an offender catalogs victim information in a mental "card file" to facilitate a return to that victim in the future (p. 89).

Third, relationship classifications of stranger and acquaintance are particularly problematic (Riedel and Rinehart 1996). Stranger classifications are prevalent in widely used national data sets such as the UCR and the National Crime Victimization Survey, but a gray area may exist between stranger and acquaintance classifications. Stronger findings in this particular analysis may have been found if not for a lingering difficulty defining relationships between offenders and their victims. Many offenders labeled as strangers may, in fact, be marginally acquainted with their victims. This acquaintance may have arisen out of a former service performed by the offender (gardening, lawn care, odd jobs, etc.), from common routine activities engaged in by the victim and offender (e.g., common bus stops, shopping areas, commuting patterns of the victim and offender), or other commonalities that brought them into visual contact, making them acquaintances by sight but more accurately classified as "apparent" strangers. Therefore, although stranger classifications were common in the data and are commonly found in many data sets relative to crimes of violence, it is theorized that this frequency may be overstated (see Safarik et al. 2000). Within this study, few crimes occurred between absolute strangers. This does not imply that a prior relationship existed between the offender and victim but rather that the offender was aware of where the victim lived (prior to the crime) and perceived her to be alone and vulnerable.

Fourth, the paradigm of intraracial offending in violent crimes as identified in UCR data (FBI 2000) has been observed for many years. However, intraracial offending patterns by these offenders appear to depend on specific conditional case factors. The most notable of these seems to be the homogeneity of the neighborhood. This result is not surprising because the racial composition of communities tends to be reflected in residential patterns. Offending patterns appear to be no different. This study reiterates the intraracial nature of offending in homogenous communities shown in existing experiential data (Safarik et al. 2000). In contrast, white victims of black and Hispanic offenders lived in neighborhoods characterized by investigators as transitional. These transitional neighborhoods were thought to have undergone a socioeconomic change from middle to lower class. Often accompanying such a change are other demographic transformations that result in social disorganization and increased criminal activity. The elderly may also experience emotional or economic issues that detract from their willingness to move to a different location. However, because these victims may be cognizant of changes in their neighborhoods and sense more potential dangers as a result, they may also be aware of their vulnerability and more likely to take proactive steps to secure their residences. The intraracial offending pattern among white offenders and the observation that whites are nearly four times as likely as blacks to be admitted by the victim may suggest that because the offenders were the same race, these victims were more easily lulled into a false sense of security and hence dropped their guard. No Hispanic offender either used a ruse or was admitted by the victim.

Fifth, most studies of homicide examine weapon use, or more broadly the COD, as a characteristic of homicidal behavior. UCR data consistently reveal that firearms are the leading cause of homicidal death in all age categories except children ages one to four. Elderly victimization research confirms that firearms are the leading COD among the elderly. Death by strangulation is rarely seen, composing only 4 percent of elderly homicide victims (Fox and Levin 1991). This is in marked contrast to the findings from this study. Firearms (1%) are virtually never seen, but strangulation accounted for 63 percent of these victims' deaths. Despite the extensive examination of weapon use and COD, little if any homicide research has examined the degree of injury. Most studies assume either no variation in injury because every victim suffered a lethal injury, or they consider only the COD. The level of injury exhibited in a number of the cases in this study was found to be excessive and is an attribute believed to be distinct from other violent crimes. As noted earlier, both A. N. Groth (1978) and N. L. Pollock (1988) found similar results in earlier studies. Although the Homicide Injury Scale and the Injury Severity Score metrics are somewhat different, both of these measures provide quantitative evidence supporting the differentiation of levels of homicidal injury as an attribute of these cases. The data examined here also reveal that many of these victims suffered multiple, severe, and excessive injuries. Many died from brutal and horrific injuries in excess of what would be necessary to cause death. This excessive violence is commonly referred to as overkill (Douglas, Burgess, Burgess, and Ressler 1992, p. 254). As noted earlier, the mean for both injury metrics approximated the range of the scale synonymous with overkill.

Sixth, R. R. Hazelwood and J. E. Douglas's (1980) work, which offers a categorization of sexual murderers on a continuum from organized to disorganized, may have relevance here. Applying this typology, these offenders are found to be overwhelmingly consistent with the disorganized typology. In addition, more recent work by Hazelwood and Warren (2000) extends earlier work and establishes a new typology of impulsive and ritualistic offenders. The descriptive assessment of the impulsive offender is remarkably consistent with the majority of the offenders in this study. G. C. Salfati (2000) and Salfati and D. V. Canter (1999) offered a model of homicide behavior that appears to provide empirical support for categorizing patterns or themes of behavior at the crime scene into either an expressive or instrumental style or a combination of the two. These offenders and their crime scene behavior suggest consistency with the instrumental classification. The collective attributes of these offenders and their crime scenes, as found in table 18.3, manifest the characteristics associated with the disorganized, impulsive, and instrumental offender typologies. Such classifications may provide investigative direction to law enforcement.

Seventh, the literature on violent crime suggests that elderly women are simply the unfortunate victims of nonviolent offenders, primarily motivated by financial gain, who have randomly targeted their residences for the commission of either a property crime (e.g., burglary) or a robbery (Faggiani and Owens 1999; Falzon and Davis 1998; Fox and Levin 1991; Hochstedler 1981; Nelson and Huff-Corzine 1998; Lent and Harpold 1988). In the process of committing this purported financial crime, the offender inadvertently discovers an elderly

TABLE 18.3: Contrasts of Incident Characteristics with Descriptive Typologies

Attribute	Disorganized[a]	Impulsive	Instrumental	Elderly Sexual Homicide Offender
	Crime scene attributes			
Body disposition	Left at death scene, Not transported, Left in view, Partially undressed or naked.		Left at death scene, Not transported, Left in view, Partially undressed or naked.	Left at death scene, Not transported, Left in view, Partially undressed or naked.
Criminal sophistication	Criminally unsophisticated	Criminally unsophisticated		Criminally unsophisticated
Planning	Little or no planning, spontaneous offense	Little or no planning, spontaneous offense		Little or no planning, spontaneous offense
Evidence consciousness	Leaves evidence at scene	Leaves evidence at scene		Leaves evidence at scene
Organization	Scene appears random and sloppy with no set plan for deterring detection	Scene appears random and sloppy with no set plan for deterring detection		Scene appears random and sloppy with no set plan for deterring detection
Protects identity	No measures taken to protect identity	No measures taken to protect identity		No measures taken to protect identity
Approach	Sudden violence to victim (blitz attack) to gain control	Sudden violence to victim (blitz attack) to gain control		Sudden violence to victim (blitz attack) to gain control
Sexual activity	Sexual activity at scene, usually postmortem		Sexual activity at scene	Sexual activity at scene, usually postmortem
Weapon	Weapon used from scene and often left		Weapon used from scene	Weapon used from scene and often left
Forensic Evidence	Leaves forensic evidence	Leaves forensic evidence	Leaves forensic evidence	Leaves forensic evidence
Cause of death	Most often death results from strangulation and blunt force trauma	Most often death results from strangulation and blunt force trauma	Most often death results from strangulation and blunt force trauma	Most often death results from strangulation and blunt force trauma
Use of restraints	Minimal	Minimal		Minimal
Other activity			Property taken, financial gain	Property taken, financial gain
Level of force	Often excessive or brutal	Often excessive or brutal		Often excessive or brutal

TABLE 18.3: Contrasts of Incident Characteristics with Descriptive Typologies (*continued*)

Attribute	Disorganized[a]	Impulsive	Instrumental	Elderly Sexual Homicide Offender
Crime scene attributes				
Paraphilic behavior		Absence of paraphilic behavior (e.g., bondage or sadism)		Absence of paraphilic behavior (e.g., bondage or sadism)
Motivation		Underlying theme of anger		Underlying theme of anger
Offender attributes				
Work history	Poor work history			Poor work history
Skill level	Unskilled work			Unskilled work
Employment			Unemployed	Unemployed
Criminal history		Arrest history diverse and generally antisocial; Depending on age, history will reflect a multiplicity of crimes with no specific theme	Criminal histories with both property and violent offenses, Burglary or theft convictions	Arrest history diverse and generally antisocial; Depending on age, history will reflect a multiplicity of crimes with no specific theme; Criminal histories with both property and violent offenses; Burglary or theft convictions
Intelligence	Lower intelligence	Lower intelligence		Lower intelligence. Most have only some high school
Travel and search patterns	Lives or works near death scene	Travels shorter distance to offend, Offends over smaller area		Lives or works near death scene, Association with area, Travels shorter distance to offend, half live within 6 blocks.
Social skills	Socially incompetent			Socially incompetent
Substance abuse		Abuse of alcohol		Abuse of drugs and/or alcohol.

SOURCE: Hazelwood and Warren (2000) and Salfati (2000).

NOTE: Although certain attributes under the three headings are shown by an empty cell, this does not mean that the attribute is not applicable to that categorization. The attributes listed were only those identified in the literature.

a. "This disorganization may be the result of youthfulness of the offender, lack of criminal sophistication, use of drugs and alcohol" (Douglas, Burgess, Burgess, and Ressler 1992, p. 128). The offenders in this study are usually characterized by at least one of these attributes.

woman. He then changes his primary motive resulting in him not only sexually assaulting her but also murdering her. The observation that 72 percent of the offenders in this study removed something from the crime scene may appear on the surface to support earlier research. However, from both a behavioral and experiential perspective, such a scenario stands in stark contrast to what has been observed in detailed reviews of these cases. The suggestion of a financially motivated crime gone awry is contradicted by the observation that the preponderance of the behavior was directed at the victim in furtherance of not only the sexual assault but also the effort required to kill her. Not only was the majority of the interaction occurring with the victim, but chronologically, it was occurring first. The removal of property occurred subsequent to the homicide. In addition, there was a lack of balance between the effort expended to sexually assault and murder the victim and the subsequent search for and theft of property. The items taken were generally located after a cursory search in the immediate vicinity of the victim and consisted mostly of cash and jewelry. The theft of property was, in most cases, an afterthought. This was supported by forensic examination of the crime scenes, admissions to uninvolved third parties, and admissions or confessions to police.

Clearly, offenders can have more than one motive when they engage in a specific criminal activity. They can also change the motive or add other criminal objectives that they had not thought of previously. Although this appears to be the case with some of these offenders, this study provides support contrary to the literature and suggests that the selection of these women was premeditated. The majority of the offenders fully intended to sexually assault and murder these women prior to the initiation of the crime, and this intent superseded their intent to steal. Supporting this interpretation, Groth's (1978) earlier work relating to elderly rape victims revealed that one third of the offenders who sexually assaulted elderly women reported their intention was to physically injure the victim.

We have shown that empirical support for linking offender characteristics with victim and crime scene attributes has merit. The application to the sexual homicide of elderly women was evident in this data set. Although this study was limited to some of the basic elements of behavioral assessments of these types of criminals, other data collection efforts and analyses may yield different results (Muller 2000; Salfati 2000; West 2000). Nonetheless, this effort shows specific support for the potential to identify offender characteristics from incident, victim, and crime scene variables.

The failure to carefully review and analyze all the behavioral interactions of elderly female homicides may contribute to at least some cases being improperly classified as nonsexual homicides without note of the subordinate offense of sexual assault. Consideration of the totality of the offense behavior, including the sexual components, rather than simply noting whether the victim was raped or semen was forensically identified, will likely result in more accurate classification of these cases as sexual homicides. The homogeneity of many of the crime scene attributes and the consistency with characteristics of the disorganized, impulsive, and instrumental offender should provide law enforcement with a well-informed position from which to start their investigation. In addition, analysis of readily available victim and crime scene attributes can provide statistically significant contributions for discerning important offender characteristics.

NOTES

1. Sexual homicide is defined as "the killing of a person in the context of power, sexuality, and brutality with evidence or observations that include a sexual nature. These include: victim attire or lack of attire; exposure of the sexual parts of the victim's body; sexual positioning of the victim's body; insertion of foreign objects into the victim's body cavities; evidence of sexual intercourse (oral, vaginal, or anal); and evidence of substitute sexual activity, interest, or sadistic fantasy" (Ressler, Burgess, and Douglas 1988, p. 1).

2. This hierarchy rule of official reporting may be more common in historical Uniform Crime Reporting data than will be so in the future. The redesigned Uniform Crime Reporting Program known as the National Incident-Based Reporting System (NIBRS) suspends such rules and allows for full reporting of collateral offenses (see Chilton and Jarvis 1999a, 1999b).

3. One fifty-five-year-old victim was included because she was found to be the victim of an offender who specifically targeted elderly females for sexual homicide. Despite this victim's age, she had the physical appearance of a significantly older woman.

4. One offender was positively identified through DNA analysis but fled to Mexico to avoid apprehension.

5. The Supplementary Homicide Reports data, although limited in investigative case details, do provide an opportunity to examine trends. Examination of the reported cases since 1976 suggests a marked decline in the number of elderly female sexual homicides that came to the attention of law enforcement by the late 1990s. However, as we have noted, these statistical data must be viewed with caution, as it is not uncommon for sexual behavior in homicide cases to sometimes remain unidentified or undetected until much further investigation.

6. Although comparable national estimates for offenders are not collected, arrest information by race is available through the FBI Uniform Crime Reports. Examination of these data shows more involvement of whites (53%) among all arrestees for murder/nonnegligent manslaughter. Similar involvement of other races (47%) was found. Caution should be taken relative to these Uniform Crime Reports data, however, because this information reflects all homicide arrests rather than just those committed against the elderly. Contrasts are further clouded by the inability of these data to show which of these cases may have involved a sexual component to the crime. The Supplementary Homicide Reports analysis, however, was consistent with the demographic composition reported here.

7. Original scoring is based on location and severity of the injury on the body, with scores ranging from 1 (minor) to 6 (unsurvivable). Modifications to this scoring scheme were required when coding cause of death injuries in homicides with a resulting minimum value of 25 (a single body region sustaining a critical/fatal injury) and a maximum of 75

(at least three body regions receiving critical/fatal injuries). A full discussion of the original scoring scheme can be found by referencing Baker, O'Neill, Haddon, and Long (1974); Baker and O'Neill (1976); and Yates (1990). The authors are continuing work examining the merit of scoring injuries in homicides, and further details on the scoring scheme adopted here are available on request.

8. This corresponds with the analysis of Ressler et al. (1988), which suggested that sexual homicide offenders that engage in foreign object insertion do so as a form of sexual substitution or sexual exploration, which may correspond with a sexually inadequate or immature offender. Such a description would suggest a younger offender, as found here.

REFERENCES

Antunes, G. E., F. L. Cook, T. D. Cook, and W. G. Skogan. 1977. Patterns of Personal Crime against the Elderly: Findings from a National Survey. *Gerontologist* 17: 321–27.

Baker, S. P., and B. O'Neill. 1976. The Injury Severity Score: An Update. *Journal of Trauma* 16: 882–85.

Baker, S. P., B. O'Neill, W. Haddon, and W. B. Long. 1974. The Injury Severity Score: A Method for Describing Patients with Multiple Injuries and Evaluating Emergency Care. *Journal of Trauma* 14, no. 3: 187–96.

Boudreaux, M. C., W. D. Lord, and J. P. Jarvis. 2001. Behavioral Perspectives on Child Homicide: The Role of Access, Vulnerability, and Routine Activities Theory. *Trauma, Violence and Abuse* 2, no. 1: 56–76.

Brownmiller, S. 1975. *Against Our Will: Men, Women, and Rape.* New York: Simon & Schuster.

Bureau of Justice Statistics. 1994. *Elderly Crime Victims: National Crime Victimization Survey.* Washington, DC: US Department of Justice, Office of Justice Programs.

Burgess, A. W., C. R. Hartman, R. K. Ressler, J. E. Douglas, and A. McCormack. 1986. Sexual Homicide: A Motivational Model. *Journal of Interpersonal Violence* 1: 251–72.

Chilton, R., and J. Jarvis. 1999a. Using the National IncidentBased Reporting System (NIBRS) to Test Estimates of Arrestee and Offender Characteristics. *Journal of Quantitative Criminology* 15: 207–24.

———. 1999b. Victims and Offenders in Two Crime Statistics Programs: A Comparison of the National Incident-Based Reporting System (NIBRS) and the National Crime Victimization Survey (NCVS). *Journal of Quantitative Criminology* 15: 193–205.

Cohen, L. E., and M. Felson. 1979. Social Change and Crime Rate Trends: A Routine Activity Approach. *American Sociological Review* 44: 588–608.

Davis, L. J., and E. M. Brody. 1979. Rape and Older Women—A Guide to Prevention and Protection (DHEW publication no. ADM 82111195). Washington, DC: US Government Printing Office.

Douglas, J. E., A. W. Burgess, A. G. Burgess, and R. K. Ressler. 1992. *Crime Classification Manual: A Standard System for Investigating and Classifying Violent Crimes.* New York: Lexington Books.

Faggiani, D., and M. G. Owens. 1999. Robbery of Older Adults: A Descriptive Analysis Using the National Incident-Based Reporting System. *Journal of the Justice Research and Statistics Association* 1, no. 1: 97–117.

Falzon, A. L., and G. G. Davis. 1998. A 15-Year Retrospective Review of Homicide in the Elderly. *Journal of Forensic Sciences* 43, no. 2: 371–74.

Federal Bureau of Investigation. 2000. *Crime in the United States*. Washington, DC: US Government Printing Office.

Fletcher, P. 1977. Criminal Victimization of Elderly Women—A Look at Sexual Assault. Syracuse, NY: Rape Crisis Center of Syracuse.

Fox, J. A., and J. Levin. 1991. Homicide against the Elderly: A Research Note. *Criminology* 29: 317–27.

Gerry, D. P. April 1983. The Effects of Rape on Three Age Groups of Women: A Comparison Study. Paper presented at the Southern Gerontological Association Meeting, Atlanta, Georgia.

Groth, A. N. 1978. The Older Rape Victim and Her Assailant. *Journal of Geriatric Psychiatry* 2: 203–15.

Groth, A. N., and H. J. Birnbaum. 1979. *Men Who Rape*. New York: Plenum.

Groth, A. N., A. W. Burgess, and L. L. Holmstrom. 1977. Rape: Power, Anger, and Sexuality. *American Journal of Psychiatry* 134: 1239–43.

Hazelwood, R. R. 1987. Analyzing the Rape and Profiling the Offender. In *Practical Aspects of Rape Investigation*, ed. Hazelwood and A. W. Burgess. New York: Elsevier NorthHolland, pp. 169–99.

Hazelwood, R. R., and A. W. Burgess, eds. 1995. *Practical Aspects of Rape Investigation: A Multidisciplinary Approach*, 2nd ed. Boca Raton, FL: CRC.

Hazelwood, R. R., and J. E. Douglas. 1980. The Lust Murderer. *FBI Law Enforcement Bulletin* 49, no. 4: 18–22.

Hazelwood, R. R., and J. Warren. 1990. The Criminal Behavior of the Serial Rapist. *FBI Law Enforcement Bulletin* 59 (September): 1–17.

———. 2000. The Sexually Violent Offender: Impulsive or Ritualistic? *Aggression and Violent Behavior* 5, no. 3: 267–79.

Hochstedler, E. 1981. *Crime against the Elderly in 26 Cities*. Washington, DC: U.S. Department of Justice, Bureau of Justice Statistics.

Kennedy, L. W., and R. A. Silverman. 1990. The Elderly Victim of Homicide: An Application of Routine Activity Theory. *Sociological Quarterly* 31: 305–17.

Kerschner, P. A. October 1976. *Rape and the Elderly: An Initial Analysis*. Paper presented at the Annual Meeting of the Gerontological Society, New York.

Lent, C. J., and J. Harpold. 1988. Violent Crime against the Aging. *FBI Law Enforcement Bulletin* 57, no. 7 (July): 11–19.

Longo, R. E., and C. Gochenour. 1981. Sexual Assault of Handicapped Individuals. *Journal of Rehabilitation* 47, no. 3: 24–27.

Moen, P. 1996. Gender, Age, and the Life Course. In *Handbook of Aging and the Social Sciences*, ed. R. Binstock and L. George. San Diego: Academic Press, pp. 171–87.

Muller, D. 2000. Criminal Profiling: Real Science or Just Wishful Thinking. *Homicide Studies* 4, no. 3: 234–64.

Muram, D., K. Miller, and A. Cutler. 1992. Sexual Assault of the Elderly Victim. *Journal of Interpersonal Violence* 7, no. 1: 70–76.

Nelson, C., and L. Huff-Corzine. 1998. Strangers in the Night: An Application of the Lifestyle-Routine Activities Approach to Elderly Homicide Victimization. *Homicide Studies* 2: 130–59.

O'Toole, M. E. 1999. Criminal Profiling: The FBI Uses Criminal Investigative Analysis to Solve Crimes. *Corrections Magazine* 61, no. 1 (February): 44.

Pollock, N. L. 1988. Sexual Assault of Older Women. *Annals of Sex Research* 1: 523–32.

Ressler, R. K., A. W. Burgess, and J. E. Douglas. 1988. *Sexual Homicide: Patterns and Motives*. Lexington, MA: Lexington Books.

Riedel, M., and T. A. Rinehart. 1996. Murder Clearances and Missing Data. *Journal of Crime and Justice* 19: 83–102.

Rossmo, K. D. 1999. *Geographic Profiling*. New York: CRC Press.

Safarik, M. E., J. P. Jarvis, and K. E. Nussbaum. 2000. Elderly Female Serial Sexual Homicide: A Limited Empirical Test of Criminal Investigative Analysis. *Homicide Studies* 4, no. 3: 294–307.

Salfati, G. C., and D. V. Canter. 1999. Differentiating Stranger Murders: Profiling Offender Characteristics from Behavioral Styles. *Behavioral Sciences and the Law* 17: 391–406.

Salfati, G. C. 2000. The Nature of Expressiveness and Instrumentality in Homicide: Implications for Offender Profiling. *Homicide Studies* 4, no. 3: 265–93.

Taeuber, C. M., and J. Allen. 1990. Women in Our Aging Society: The Demographic Outlook. In *Women on the Front Lines: Meeting the Challenge of an Aging America*, ed. J. Allen and A. J. Pifer. Washington, DC: Urban Institute, pp. 11–46.

U.S. Bureau of the Census. 1999. *1999 Census of Population: Characteristics of the Population*. Washington, DC: Government Printing Office.

Warren, J., R. Reboussin, R. R. Hazelwood, A. Cummings, N. A. Gibbs, and S. L. Trumbetta. 1998. Crime Scene and Distance Correlates of Serial Rape. *Journal of Quantitative Criminology* 14: 35–59.

Warren, J., R. Reboussin, R. R. Hazelwood, N. A. Gibbs, S. L. Trumbetta, and A. Cummings. 1999. A Crime Scene Analysis and the Escalation of Violence in Serial Rape. *Forensic Science International* 100: 37–56.

West, A. 2000. Clinical Assessment of Homicide Offenders: The Significance of Crime Scene in Offense and Offender Analysis. *Homicide Studies* 4, no. 3: 219–33.

Yates, D. W. 1990. Scoring Systems for Trauma. *British Medical Journal* 301: 1090–94.

Chapter 19

GEOGRAPHIC PROFILING UPDATE

D. Kim Rossmo

While instances of the use of spatial analysis in criminal investigations go back many years, geographic profiling as we know it today began in the late 1980s in Vancouver, British Columbia, Canada. This was the start of a research program at Simon Fraser University's School of Criminology that culminated in 1995 in the development of a robust computer algorithm (CGT, for Criminal Geographic Targeting) and a formalized methodology for geographic profiling. That year, the Vancouver Police Department established the world's first Geographic Profiling Section, with a mandate to provide the service to the international police community. Since then, substantial progress in the field has been made thanks to the efforts of dedicated individuals, visionary police agencies, and supportive scholars. I would like to summarize the main areas of advancement as an update to this chapter (first written in 1996 and published in 1997).

The Royal Canadian Mounted Police (RCMP) and the Federal Bureau of Investigation (FBI) were two of the first agencies to support geographic profiling. Their national mandates helped spread awareness and acceptance of this then-new criminal investigative methodology across North America. The Bureau of Alcohol, Tobacco and Firearms (ATF), through the National Center for the

Analysis of Violent Crime (NCAVC) at the FBI Academy in Quantico, Virginia, currently provides geographic profiling services in the United States for major crime investigations, while the RCMP and the Ontario Provincial Police (OPP) do the same in Canada. Successes in several high profile European cases, such as the Mardi Gras Bomber and Operation Lynx (the largest police manhunt in Britain since the Yorkshire Ripper case), established a strong interest in the technique across the Atlantic. The National Crime and Operations Faculty (NCOF) is now the source for all geographic profiling in the United Kingdom. And since the late 1990s, the Interpol procedure for intelligence-led DNA screens has recommended geographic profiling where appropriate.

To date, geographic profiles have been provided to police agencies on five continents. In addition to the ATF, RCMP, OPP, and NCOF, the system has been adopted by the German *Bundeskriminalamt* (BKA) and the Limburg Police in The Netherlands. A modified system for property crime is in use by several law enforcement agencies in Wales, California, Florida, North Carolina, Tennessee, South Carolina, and Ontario. A comprehensive training and certification program was developed, and qualified geographic profilers now become members of the International Criminal Investigative Analysis Fellowship (ICIAF), a professional organization originally begun by the FBI for psychological profilers. This integration is appropriate, as geographic profiling is one component of the criminal investigative behavioral science repertoire, a triad that also includes linkage analysis and psychological profiling.

All qualified geographic profilers are required to keep statistics and performance results on solved cases. The performance of a geographic profile is measured by what is termed the *hit score percentage* (defined as the ratio of the area searched in the prioritized order given by the geoprofile before the offender is located to the total area covered by the crimes). A recent review of all solved operational geographic profiles from four different police agencies (covering cases in several different countries), combined with the findings from the initial research project at Simon Fraser University, resulted in a mean hit score percentage of 4.7 percent and a median of 3.0 percent, with a standard deviation of 4.4 percent (N = 1,426 offenses and 1,726 crime locations).

The volume of research in the area of environmental criminology has grown significantly over the last decade (judging by the number of papers presented at academic conferences on the topics of geography of crime, routine activity theory, and crime mapping), adding an important dimension to criminological theory and practice. Recent research efforts specifically related to the field of geographic profiling include studies on geo-demographics and stranger rape, geographic patterns of illegal land border crossings, and causes of criminal investigative failures. Scholars have also begun to express an interest in the intersection between geographic and behavioral profiling. One Canadian project, for example, found criminals with high psychopathy scores were more mobile, with a history of criminal charges from a larger number of cities and provinces across the country.

Rigel, the software program used in geographic profiling, has grown from an original five hundred lines of code to more than five hundred thousand. The current version contains powerful three-dimensional visualization tools, a sophisticated analytic engine, flexible geographic information system (GIS) infrastructure, and database connectivity. It includes an expert system and animation routines, next-crime prediction and date/time analysis modules, orthodigital photography, GIS and image map import options, and other features. Geographic profilers continuously provide suggestions for software enhancements and improved functionality based on their operational needs.

On the negative side, growing use by police of behavioral science, its popularization in feature films, and an increasing number of twenty-four-hour news programs interested in crime have led to the emergence of pseudoprofilers (both psychological and geographic)—individuals better known for their television appearances and self-promoting Web sites than for their scholarly contributions or concern for public safety. These "profilers" often attempt to insert themselves into active investigations, usually through the media or families of victims. Their actions can interfere with the police investigation, as such individuals typically are reckless regarding the impact their media statements have on the offender's behavior. Fortunately, they are easy to spot, as they usually possess some combination of the following characteristics: (1) lack of police investigative experience, (2) little empirical research and few peer-reviewed publications to their credit, (3) no recognized professional association (e.g., ICIAF), (4) dialogue that is highly critical of the responsible police agencies, and (5) pontifications of firm conclusions based on limited public information. It is important for law enforcement, the public, and the media to be aware of these individuals and the risks they pose.

As for the future, we continue to need more research, enhanced training, commitment to professional certification, and heightened awareness of the capabilities and utility of geographic profiling. Significant potential exists in hybrid approaches, such as those that combine forensic and behavioral sciences. Most critical is an ongoing commitment to professionalism, which obligates us to learn more about criminal behavior so we can continue to improve the effectiveness and efficiency of the police investigative response.

INTRODUCTION

When the throat of Victorian prostitute Polly Nichols was slashed in Buck's Row on August Bank Holiday, 1888, horrified London newspapers warned of a "'reign of terror" (Rumbelow 1988). Jack the Ripper was certainly not the first or last of his type, but the unsolved mystery of the Whitechapel murders still symbolizes our lack of understanding of such dangerous predators. Equally important, the very nature of their crimes makes these criminals difficult and challenging to apprehend.

One of the most problematic aspects of predatory violent crime is the volume of tips and suspects generated through their investigation. Traditional police methods are not always sufficient, and detectives need alternative tactics to assist them in these types of cases. Geographic profiling, a strategic information management system designed to support investigative efforts in cases of serial murder, rape, and arson, is one such approach.

INVESTIGATIVE DIFFICULTIES

For heaven's sake catch me before I kill more. I cannot control myself.
—Message written in lipstick on the living room wall of Frances Brown,
victim of serial murderer William Heirens (Kennedy 1991)

The investigation of serial violent and sexual crime is complex and difficult. Most murders are solved because they involve intimates, and the search for the offender begins with the victim's family, friends, and acquaintances. There is no such victim-offender relationship, however, in stranger sexual crime.

The police therefore must delineate likely groups of potential suspects, a process referred to as "framing" (Kind 1987) or establishing the "circle of investigation" (Skogan and Antunes 1979). Such an effort typically involves the inspection of those parties with relevant criminal or psychiatric records, the accumulation of intelligence, and the collection of suspect tips from members of the public. Because these investigative efforts can produce large numbers of potential suspects, often totaling into the hundreds and even thousands, problems with information overload usually develop. "Although a modern police force can fill rooms with details of possible suspects, they still have the enormous problem of finding the vicious needle in their haystack of paper" (Canter 1994).

The Green River Killer case in Seattle, Washington, involved the murder of forty-nine prostitutes. In 1993 the police had only the resources to investigate two-thirds of the eighteen thousand names in their suspect files (Montgomery 1993). Detectives have gathered eight thousand tangible items of evidence from the crime scenes, and a single television special on the case generated thirty-five hundred tips. In Britain, the nationwide search for the Staffordshire serial murderer amassed details on 185,000 people over the course of eleven years before the child killer was finally caught (Canter 1994). The Narborough Murder Enquiry, a massive four-year manhunt, obtained close to four thousand blood samples for DNA testing prior to eventually charging Colin Pitchfork with the deaths of two teenage girls (Canter 1994; Wambaugh 1989). The Yorkshire Ripper inquiry accumulated 268,000 names, visited 27,000 houses, and recorded 5.4 million vehicle registration numbers (Doney 1990; Nicholson 1979).

A corollary to the problem of information overload is the high cost associated with any extensive, long-term investigation. The final tally for the Atlanta child murders case was more than $9 million (Dettlinger and Prugh 1983), while the Yorkshire Ripper inquiry cost an estimated £4 million (Doney 1990). The Green River Task Force has so far accumulated expenses of approximately $20 million (Montgomery 1992).

It is important for police detectives to know which crimes are connected so that information between related cases can be collated and compared. An inability to recognize connections and confusion over which crimes should form part of a series has occurred in several investigations. This problem has been termed *linkage blindness* (Egger 1984).

Several other investigative difficulties exist that complicate efforts to connect linked crimes and to identify and apprehend serial killers, rapists, and arsonists (Egger 1990; Holmes and De Burger 1988; James 1991; O'Reilly-Fleming 1992). Such problems include (a) the learning process inherent in serial offending; (b) false confessions; (c) copy cat crimes; (d) public fear, media interest, and political pressure; (e) personnel logistics; (f) multiple agency coordination; and (g) resource and cost issues.

GEOGRAPHIC PROFILING

Several investigative approaches to these problems have been developed by police agencies, including psychological profiling and computerized crime linkage analysis systems (Copson 1995; Johnson 1994). Geographic profiling is an information management strategy designed to support serial violent crime investigation (Rossmo 1995a). This service is provided by the Vancouver Police Department's Geographic Profiling Section to police forces and prosecuting offices (MacKay 1994; Thompson 1996). The first such profile was prepared in 1990, and to date, requests have come from a variety of federal, provincial, state, and local law enforcement agencies across North America and Europe, including the Royal Canadian Mounted Police, the Federal Bureau of Investigation, and New Scotland Yard. The cases have involved crimes of serial murder, serial rape and sexual assault, serial arson, bombings, bank robbery, sexual homicide, and kidnapping.

The location of a crime site can be seen as an important clue, one that can provide valuable information to police investigators. Geographic profiling focuses on the probable spatial behavior of the offender within the context of the locations of, and the spatial relationships between, the various crime sites. A psychological profile provides insight into an offender's likely motivation, behavior, and lifestyle and is therefore directly connected to his or her spatial activity. Psychological and geographic profiles thus act in tandem to help investigators develop a "picture" of the person responsible for the crimes in question. It should be noted that not all types of offenders or categories of crime can be geographically profiled. In appropriate cases, however, such a spatial analysis can produce practical results.

A psychological profile is not a necessary precursor for a geographic profile, though the insights it may provide can be quite useful, particularly in cases involving a small number of offenses. Geographic profiling has both quantitative (objective) and qualitative (subjective) components. The objective component uses a series of scientific geographic techniques and quantitative measures to analyze and interpret the point pattern created from the locations of the target sites. The subjective component of geographic profiling is based primarily on a reconstruction and interpretation of the offender's mental map.

The main quantitative technique used in geographic profiling is a computerized process termed *criminal geographic targeting* (Rossmo 1993, 1995b). By examining the spatial information associated with a series of crime sites, the CGT model produces a three-dimensional probability distribution termed a *jeopardy surface*, the "height" of which at any point represents the likelihood of offender residence or workplace (see fig. 19.1). The jeopardy surface is then superimposed on a street map of the area of the crimes (see fig. 19.2); such maps are termed *geoprofiles* and use a range of colors to represent varying probabilities. A geoprofile can be thought of as a fingerprint of the offender's cognitive map.

The system's underlying algorithm was developed from research conducted at Simon Fraser University in the area of environmental criminology (Rossmo 1995c). The process relies on the model of crime site selection proposed by P. J. Brantingham and P. L. Brantingham (1981) and is also informed by L. Cohen and M. Felson's (1979) routine activities approach. The CGT algorithm employs a distance-decay function $f(d)$ that simulates journey to crime behavior. Each point (x, y), located at distance d from crime site i, is assigned a probability value $A(d)$.

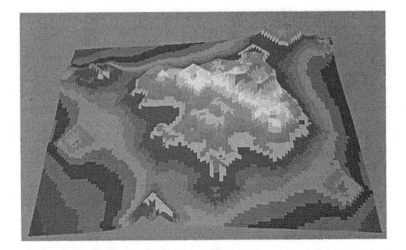

Figure 19.1. Jeopardy surface for series of armed robberies in Vancouver, Canada.

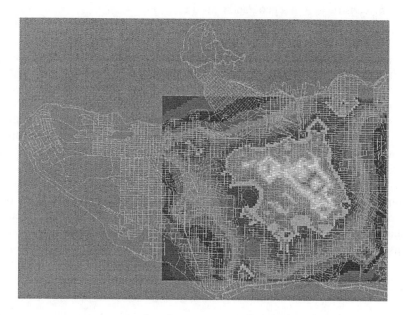

Figure 19.2. Geoprofile for series of armed robberies in Vancouver, Canada.

A final value for point (x, y), representing the likelihood of offender residence, is determined by adding the n values for that point produced from the n different crime sites. The predictive power of the model is related to the number of crime sites—the more locations, the better the performance.

By establishing the probability of the offender residing in various areas and displaying those results on a map, police efforts to apprehend criminals can be assisted. This information allows police departments to focus their investigative activities, geographically prioritize suspects, and concentrate patrol efforts in those zones where the criminal predator is most likely to be active.

THE PROFILING PROCESS

A geographic profile fits into a typical criminal investigation in the following sequence:

1. occurrence of a crime series
2. employment of traditional investigative techniques
3. linkage analysis determining which crimes are connected
4. preparation of a psychological profile

5. construction of a geographic profile
6. development of new investigative strategies.

The preparation of a geographic profile involves the following operational procedure: (a) examination of the case file, including investigation reports, witness statements, autopsy reports, and, if available, the psychological profile; (b) inspection of crime scene and area photographs; (c) discussions with investigators and crime analysts; (d) visits to the crime sites when possible; (e) analysis of neighborhood crime statistics and demographic data; (f) study of street, zoning, and rapid transit maps; (g) analysis; and (h) report writing (Holmes and Rossmo 1996).

In addition to the offense locations and times involved in a crime series, some of the other elements that need to be considered in the construction of a geographic profile include crime location type, target backcloth, and offender hunting style. These three considerations are the most important and are discussed in detail below. Other factors include location of arterial roads and highways, presence of bus stops and rapid transit stations, physical and psychological boundaries, zoning and land use, neighborhood demographics, routine activities of victims, and displacement.

CRIME LOCATIONS

Most of the geography of crime literature treats the concept of crime site as a single location. Depending upon the type of crime, however, there may be various locations connected to a single offense. Each of these has a potentially different meaning to the offender and, consequently, distinctive choice properties (Newton and Swoope 1987; Ressler and Shachtman 1992). In homicide, for example, such location types include victim encounter, attack, murder, and body dump sites. While these particular actions could all occur at one place, in many cases they are divided up between two or more different locations.

Eight possible crime location sets can result from combinations of these four different crime site types. For example, Canadian sex killer Paul Bernardo encountered and attacked his victims on the street, strangled them in his home, and then dumped their bodies at remote sites (Burnside and Cairns 1995; Pron 1995).

The specific location set for a given crime is a function of victim selection and encounter site characteristics, but it also implies something about the offender, how he or she searches for victims and the associated level of organization and mobility. Generally, the greater the organization and mobility of the offender, the greater the potential complexity (i.e., the more separate locations) of the crime location set. Research has also shown a high level of consistency in the geographic modus operandi of serial offenders, as most repeatedly employ the same crime location set (Rossmo 1995a). This implies that the concept of crime location set could be used as an assessment characteristic for the linking of serial offenses.[1]

While all crime scene types are important in the construction of a geographic profile, every site type may not possess an equal degree of relevance in all cases. Some locations, particularly in homicides, are not known to investigating police officers. Prior to the apprehension of the offender, these places can only be determined through evidence recovery or witness statements. In a typical unsolved homicide, the police know the body dump site (which may or may not be the murder scene) and the place where the victim was last seen. In some circumstances, they may only know one of these locations.

TARGET BACKCLOTH

Brantingham and Brantingham (1993) suggest that the structure of the target, or victim backcloth, is important for an understanding of the geometric arrangement of crime sites. The target backcloth is equivalent to the spatial opportunity structure. It is configured by both geographic and temporal distributions of "suitable"—as seen from the offender's perspective—crime targets or victims across the physical landscape. The availability of such targets might vary significantly according to neighborhood, area, or even city and can also be influenced by time, day of week, and season (Brantingham and Brantingham 1984).

Because victim location and availability play key roles in the determination of where offenses occur, nonuniform or "patchy" target distributions can distort the spatial pattern of crime sites. Victim selections that are nonrandom, or based on specific and rare traits, will require more searching on the part of the offender than those that are random, nonspecific, and common (Canter 1994; Davies and Dale 1995a; Holmes and De Burger 1988). For example, if an arsonist prefers to select warehouses as targets, their availability and distribution, geographically determined by city zoning bylaws, will have a strong influence on where the crimes occur. If the arsonist has no preferences, then the target backcloth will probably be more uniform as houses and buildings abound, at least in urban areas. The target sites of a predator who seeks out prostitutes will be determined primarily by the locations of "hooker strolls," while the attack sites of an offender who is less specific could well be found anywhere.

A uniform victim spatial distribution means that the locations of the crimes will be primarily influenced by the offender's activity space; otherwise, crime geography is more closely related to the target backcloth. In the extreme cases of an arsonist for hire or a contract killer, victim location totally determines crime site. The consideration of victim characteristics thus plays an important role in the development of an accurate geographic profile.

The target backcloth is influenced by both the natural and built physical environments, as these affect where people live. Housing development is determined by such factors as physical topography, highway networks, national boundaries, city limits, land use, and zoning regulations. The Werewolf Rapist, Jose Rodrigues, lived in Bexhill on the south coast of Britain during his series of sixteen sexual assaults. With no potential victims situated in the English Channel to the south, he was forced to confine his attacks to locations north of his residence, resulting in a distorted target pattern. Such problems could be compensated for through the appropriate topological transformation of the physical space within and surrounding the offender's hunting area.

HUNTING TYPOLOGY

> Throughout accounts of serial murders run themes of adventurous risk in the stalking of human prey by stealth or deception, the excitement of the kill. . . . The egoism of the hunter permits the degradation of potential victims to the level of wild game. The planning, excitement, and thrill of the hunt overrides all other considerations except eluding capture (Green 1993).

Predatory criminals employ various hunting styles in their efforts to seek out and attack victims. These, in turn, affect the spatial distribution of the offender's crime sites, suggesting that any effort to predict offender residence from crime locations must consider hunting style. It was therefore important to ascertain those methods of hunting that produce target patterns inappropriate for this type of spatial analysis. Previous classifications of serial crime geography have only been descriptive of the final spatial pattern and not of the processes that produced those outcomes. It was therefore necessary to develop a hunting typology relevant to serial offenders. While this scheme was constructed from an exploratory data analysis of serial murderers, it is informed by geography of crime theory and is applicable, for the purposes of geographic profiling, to certain other types of predatory crime.

While a murder can potentially involve several different types of crime locations, experience has shown that victim encounter and body dump sites are most important in terms of an investigation-oriented geographic analysis. These are the location types most likely to be discovered by the police; attack and murder scenes, if different from encounter and dump sites, are usually known only to the murderer. The hunting typology is therefore concerned with offender behavior vis-à-vis these particular crime locations.

SEARCH AND ATTACK METHODS

The serial killer hunting process can be broken down into two components: the search for a suitable victim and the method of attack. The former influences selection of victim encounter sites and the latter, body dump sites. The proposed hunting typology results from the categories produced by the combination of these elements.

The following four victim search methods were isolated:

1. Hunter—A *hunter* is defined as an offender who sets out specifically to search for a victim, basing the search from his or her residence.
2. Poacher—A *poacher* is defined as an offender who sets out specifically to search for a victim, basing the search from an activity site other than his or her residence or who commutes or travels to another city during the victim search process.
3. Troller—A *troller* is defined as an offender who, while involved in other nonpredatory activities, opportunistically encounters a victim.
4. Trapper—A *trapper* is defined as an offender who assumes a position or occupation or creates a situation that allows him or her to encounter victims within a location under his or her control.

The following three victim attack methods were isolated:

1. Raptor—A *raptor* is defined as an offender who attacks a victim upon encounter.
2. Stalker—A *stalker* is defined as an offender who first follows a victim upon encounter and then attacks.
3. Ambusher—An *ambusher* is defined as an offender who attacks a victim once he or she has been enticed to a location, such as a residence or workplace, controlled by the offender.[2]

Hunters are those criminals who specifically set out from their residence to look for victims, searching through the areas in their awareness space that they believe contain suitable targets.[3] The crimes of a hunter are generally confined to the offender's city of residence. Conversely, *poachers* travel outside of their home city, or operate from an activity site other than their residence, in the search for targets. The differentiation between a hunter and a poacher, however, is often a difficult and subjective task.

The terms *hunter* and *poacher* are similar to the "marauder" and "commuter" designations used by D. Canter and P. Larkin (1993) in their study of serial rape in England. *Marauders* are individuals whose residences act as the focus of their crimes. *Commuters*, on the other hand, travel from home into another area to commit their offenses. It was hypothesized that marauders would have homes situated within their offense circle, while commuters would have homes located outside. Only 13 percent of the forty-five British serial rapists were found to have their home base situated outside of the offense circle (pp. 67–68).

The FBI, however, observed that 51 percent of seventy-six US serial rapists lived outside of the offense circle (Warren, Reboussin, and Hazelwood 1995; Reboussin, Warren, and Hazelwood 1993). Alston (1994) had similar findings in a study of thirty British Columbia stranger sexual assault series; in 43 percent of the cases, the offense circle did not contain an offender activity node. The inconsistency in these findings may be attributable to differences between European and North American urban structure, neighborhood density, and travel behavior (Warren et al. 1995).

One of the problems with the circle hypothesis is its determination of hunting behavior solely from crime site point pattern (see Alston 1994 for a discussion of other associated problems). In cases involving large numbers of offenses, the rapist may have commuted to several different areas in various directions, creating an offense circle that contains his residence. And in cases involving small numbers of crimes, a marauder may have found all of his victims through traveling by chance in the same direction, resulting in an offense circle that excludes his home base. Offense circles could therefore lead to both commuter and marauder designations, depending upon what point in a serial rapist's career they were generated.[4]

This happened in both the Yorkshire Ripper and the Boston Strangler cases (Burn 1984; Davies and Dale 1995a; Frank 1966). In other instances, a nonuniform target backcloth may force a commuter pattern regardless of the offender's hunting style. A. Davies and A. Dale warn "that the commuter and marauder models may just be extremes of a continuum of patterns determined by topography and target availability" (1995b). Because of these problems, a more subjective interpretation of offender hunting style is used here to classify serial criminals as either hunters or poachers.

Trollers are those offenders who do not specifically look for victims but rather encounter them during the course of other, usually routine, activities. Their crimes are often spontaneous, but many serial sex offenders have fantasized and planned their crimes in advance so that they are ready and prepared when an opportunity presents itself ("premeditated opportunism").

Trappers either assume positions or occupations where potential victims come to them or entice them by means of subterfuge into their homes or other locations under their control. This may be done through entertaining suitors, placing want ads, or taking in boarders. Black widows, "angels of death," and custodial killers are all forms of trappers, and most female serial murderers fall into this category (Hickey 1986; Pearson 1994; Segrave 1992; Scott 1992).

Raptors, upon encountering a victim, attack almost immediately. *Stalkers* follow and watch their targets, moving into the victim's activity space, waiting for an opportune moment to strike. The attack, murder, and body dump sites of stalkers are thus strongly influenced by their victims' activity spaces. *Ambushers* attack those they have brought or drawn into their "web"—someplace where the offender has a great deal of control, most often his home or workplace. The victims' bodies are usually hidden somewhere on the offender's property. While victim encounter sites in such cases may provide sufficient spatial information for analysis, many ambushers select marginalized victims whose disappearances are rarely linked, even when missing person reports are made to the police.

HUNTING STYLE

Target patterns are determined by offender activity space, hunting method, and victim backcloth. One of the main purposes of the hunting style typology was the identification of those situations where an analysis of the relationship between offender activity space and crime location geography is appropriate. This allows for the elimination of those cases where such an analysis is impossible or redundant. Poachers, for example, who live in one city and commit their crimes in another may not reside within their hunting area. Stalkers, whose crime locations are driven more by the activity spaces of their victims than by their own, will not usually produce target patterns amenable to this type of spatial investigation.

Table 19.1 shows the matrix produced by a cross-tabulation of the search and attack methods and the suitability of the resultant cells for a geographic analysis based on encounter and body dump sites. The matrix uses a sliding scale of designations (*yes, possible, doubtful,* and *no*) to refer to suitability likelihood. A designation of *redundant* refers to a situation where such an analysis is possible but trivial. For example, the offender's address could be accurately determined from an analysis of the body dump site locations of a trapper serial killer (e.g., one who entices victims into his or her home, murders them, and then buries their bodies in the backyard or basement), but such a circumstance negates any need for a spatial analysis. The cases of Belle Gunness, who poisoned her suitors, and Dorothea Puente, who murdered her elderly tenants, are examples of this type of situation.

Table 19.1. Serial offender hunting typology and geographic analysis feasibility

Attack Method	Search Method			
	Hunter	Poacher	Troller	Trapper
Encounter sites				
Raptor	Yes	Doubtful	Yes	Redundant
Stalker	Yes (if known)	Doubtful	Yes (if known)	Redundant
Ambusher	Yes	Doubtful	Yes	Redundant
Body-dump sites				
Raptor	Yes	Doubtful	Yes	Redundant
Stalker	Possibly	No	Possibly	No
Ambusher	Redundant	Redundant	Redundant	Redundant

As there appears to be a correlation between search and attack methods, actual serial criminals tend to fit into some cells more often than others. For example, hunter/raptors and trapper/ambushers are much more common than hunter/stalkers or trapper/raptors. Also, the suitability ratings in table 19.1 are only suggestive, as individual cases may vary significantly from one another in terms of their spatial details.

INVESTIGATIVE STRATEGIES

Various investigative strategies can be employed in a more effective and efficient manner through a geographic profile, and some examples are discussed (Rossmo 1995c, 1996). The choice of a given tactic depends on the specific circumstances in a particular case. As most of our public and private record systems contain address data, it is probable that additional investigative techniques will be developed over time. Indeed, several of the approaches presented below were proposed by police detectives themselves.

SUSPECT PRIORITIZATION

Geographic and psychological profiles can help determine which suspects, leads, and tips should be prioritized during a major crime investigation. This is particularly important in cases suffering from information overload. More than one murder inquiry identified the correct suspect but failed to realize it at the time.

PATROL SATURATION AND STATIC STAKEOUTS

Areas in the geoprofile most probably associated with the offender can be used as the basis for establishing directed or saturation patrolling efforts and static police stakeouts. This tactic is most viable in those cases where the crimes are occurring during specific time periods. Barrett (1990) describes how Kentucky police, correctly anticipating the movements of a serial killer though the pattern of his crimes, set up road blocks in a park to question late-night motorists. This tactic gathered more than two thousand names for the purpose of cross-comparison with other investigative information.

Through a geographic analysis of the crime sites in the Atlanta child murders, C. Dettlinger came to the conclusion that the killer was commuting along certain city routes (Dettlinger and Prugh 1983). But his suggestion that stakeouts be established at the crucial points in this spatial pattern went unheeded by police, and five more bodies would be dumped near these locations before task force officers staking out a Chattahoochee River bridge pulled over Wayne Williams.

NEIGHBORHOOD CANVASSES

A geoprofile can be used for optimizing door-to-door canvasses in urban areas and grid searches in rural areas. Similarly, information requests have been mailed out to target areas established through the prioritization of postal carrier walks. For example, J. L. LeBeau (1992) notes the case of a serial rapist in San Diego who was arrested through canvassing efforts in an area targeted by analysis of the crime locations. The Vampire Killer, serial murderer Richard Trenton Chase, was caught in the same manner after a psychological profile predicted that he would be living near a recovered vehicle stolen from one of his victims (Biondi and Hecox 1992; Ressler and Shachtman 1992).

POLICE INFORMATION SYSTEMS

Police computerized dispatch and record systems often contain information of potential importance to an investigation. Offender databases, records management systems (RMS), parolee lists, computer-aided dispatch (CAD) systems, and the like can be strategically searched by address or location with a geoprofile (Brahan, Valcour, and Shevel 1994; Fowler 1990; Pilant 1994; Rebscher and Rohrer 1991; Skogan and Antunes 1979).

OUTSIDE AGENCY DATABASES

Parole and probation offices, mental health outpatient clinics, social services offices, and certain commercial establishments are often useful sources of information. Determining which of these are located in the area where the offender most likely lives can assist police investigations.

POSTAL CODE PRIORITIZATION

Postal or zip codes can be prioritized with a geoprofile and then used to conduct searches and rankings of address databases. The following case illustrates one example of how this tactic has been used. During the investigation of a sexual murder, police learned of a suspicious vehicle seen prowling the area of the attack on the evening of the crime. The only information witnesses could provide concerned the make and color of the automobile. A geographic profile was prepared, postal codes ranked, and this information then used to optimally search Department of Motor Vehicles computer records.

Even with just a three-parameter search—vehicle make, vehicle color, and registered owner address postal code—this procedure still served as an efficient discriminating method, resulting in only a few dozen records from hundreds of thousands of vehicles. Offender description, and zoning and socioeconomic data, further refined the suspect search.

TASK FORCE COMPUTER SYSTEMS

A major crime inquiry may lead to the creation of a task force involving dozens of police officers investigating tips and following up leads. The resulting information is often entered and collated on some form of computerized database such as the Home Office Large Major Enquiry System (HOLMES), used by British police forces for managing large volumes of investigative case data (Doney 1990; US Department of Justice 1991).

These operations usually suffer from information overload and require some form of data prioritization (Keppel and Birnes 1995). A geoprofile can determine the street addresses, postal codes, and telephone numbers from those areas where the offender most likely resides. This process can also be linked to information available in CD-ROM telephone directory databases listing residential and business names, telephone numbers, addresses, postal/zip codes, business headings, and standard industrial classification codes.

SEX OFFENDER REGISTRIES

Sex offender registries, such as exist in Washington State (Popkin 1994; Scheingold, Olson, and Pershing 1992), are a useful information source for geographic profiling in cases of serial sex crimes. By providing a list of addresses of known violent sex criminals, such registries can be used with a geographic profile to help prioritize suspects. The US Violent Crime Control and Law Enforcement Act of 1994: "requires states to enact statutes or regulations which require those determined to be sexually violent predators or who are convicted of sexually violent offenses to register with appropriate state law enforcement agencies for ten years after release from prison," or risk the reduction of federal grant money (US Department of Justice, 1994).

PEAK-OF-TENSION POLYGRAPHY

In suspicious missing persons cases presumed to be homicides, with known suspects, polygraphists have had success using peak-of-tension tests in narrowing the search area for the victim's remains (Hagmaier 1990; Cunliffe and Piazza 1980; Lyman 1993; Raskin 1989). By exposing the suspect to questions concerning the type of location where the victim's body might have been hidden (e.g., cave, lake, marsh, field, forest, etc.), a deceptive response can help focus the search. The process often involves the use of maps or pictures. The utility of peak-of-tension polygraphy is enhanced when the procedure is directed by a geographic profile.

BLOODINGS

During certain sexual murder investigations, the British police have conducted large-scale DNA testing of all men from the area of the crime ("How the DNA Database," 1995). The first such case was the Narborough Murder Enquiry, when "all unalibied male residents in the villages between the ages of seventeen and thirty-four years would be asked to submit blood and saliva samples voluntarily in order to 'eliminate them' as suspects in the footpath murders" (Wambaugh 1989).

Close to four thousand men from the villages of Narborough, Littlethorpe, and Enderby were tested during the investigation. Considerable police resources and laboratory costs can therefore be involved in such "bloodings." A geographic profile could efficiently direct the testing process through the targeting and prioritization of residents by address or postal code. The use of such a systematic strategy would result in a more effective and less expensive DNA mass screening sampling procedure.

TRIAL COURT EXPERT EVIDENCE

In addition to analyzing the geographic patterns of unsolved crimes for investigative insights, the spatial relationship between the locations of a crime series and a suspect's or accused offender's activity sites can be assessed in terms of the probability of their congruence (Rossmo 1994). When combined with other forensic identification findings (e.g., a DNA profile), such information can increase evidential strength and therefore the probability of guilt. Geographic profiling thus has application in both the investigative and criminal trial stages.

CONCLUSION

> *We were just hunting humans. I guess because we thought they were the hardest things to hunt, but humans are the easiest things to hunt. . . . Sad to say, but it's true.*
> —convicted Canadian murderer (Boyd 1988)

The ease with which such offenders hunt humans has its roots in the basic nature of our society. We simply do not expect to encounter seemingly random violence during the course of our daily lives. Even the offenders themselves may not understand why they do what they do. Albert DeSalvo, the Boston Strangler, could not explain his hunting processes to interviewers: "I was just driving—anywhere—not knowing where I was going. I was coming through back ways, in and out and around. That's the idea of the whole thing. I just go here and there. I don't know why" (Frank 1966). But while we may not understand them, it is still imperative that we know how to catch them.

Geographic profiling is a strategic information management system used in the investigation of serial violent crime. This methodology was designed to help alleviate the problem of information overload that usually accompanies such cases. By knowing the most probable area of offender residence, police agencies can more effectively use their limited resources, and a variety of investigative strategies have now been developed to maximize the utility of this process for unsolved cases: "Some of our [offender profiling] hypotheses . . . seem now to have passed into the general realm of established detective knowledge. . . . It is this gradual building of elements of certainty by scientific rigour that is the object of the researchers" (Copson 1993). But it is also the interaction between academic research and the police field that allows an investigative methodology to grow and develop. The importance of geography for criminal investigation and offender profiling strikes a chord within practitioners, a resonance best explained by an old police truism: "When all else fails, return to the scene" (Barrett 1990).

NOTES

1. ViCLAS, the RCMP computerized linkage analysis system, was designed with certain geographic profiling requirements in mind. It is possible to conduct queries, among other search criteria, based on crime location set similarities.

2. This typology is remarkably similar to Schaller's (1972) description of certain hunting methods used by lions in the Serengeti where he observed ambushing, stalking, driving (direct attack), and unexpected (opportunistic) kills.

3. Westley Allan Dodd, a serial killer executed for the murder of three children in the state of Washington, wrote in his diary, "Now ready for my second day of the hunt. . . . Will start at about 10 a.m. and take a lunch so I don't have to return home." He was worried, however, that if he murdered a child in the park through which he was searching, he'd lose his "hunting ground for up to two to three months" (Westfall 1992).

4. The probability that the n crimes of a marauder will appear to be those of a commuter is approximately

$$\frac{(2n-1)}{(22, -2)}$$

The odds that such a pattern could happen by chance is not insignificant for low values of n. For example, in a series of four crimes the probability is equal to 23 percent.

REFERENCES

Alston, J. D. 1994. The Serial Rapist's Spatial Pattern of Target Selection. Unpublished master's thesis, Simon Fraser University, Burnaby, BC.

Barrett, G. M. 1990. Serial Murder: A Study in Psychological Analysis, Prediction, and Profiling. Unpublished master's thesis, University of Louisville, Louisville, KY.

Biondi, R., and W. Hecox. 1992. *The Dracula Killer*. New York: Simon & Schuster.

Block, C. R., and R. L. Block, eds. 1993. *Questions and Answers in Lethal and Nonlethal Violence: Proceedings of the Second Annual Workshop of the Homicide Research Working Group* (NIJ Publication no. NCJ-147480). Washington, DC: US Government Printing Office.

Block, C. R., M. Dabdoub, and S. Fregly, eds. 1995. *Crime Analysis through Computer Mapping*. Washington, DC: Police Executive Research Forum.

Boyd, N. 1988. *The Last Dance: Murder in Canada*. Scarborough, ON: Prentice-Hall.

Brahan, J. W., L. Valcour, and R. Shevel. 1994. The Investigator's Notebook. In *Applications and Innovations in Expert Systems*. Cambridge: Cambridge University Press.

Brantingham, P. J., and P. L. Brantingham, eds. 1981. *Environmental Criminology*. Beverly Hills: Sage.

———. 1984. *Patterns in Crime*. New York: Macmillan.

———. 1981. Notes on the Geometry on Crime. In *Environmental Criminology*, ed. Brantingham and Brantingham. Beverly Hills: Sage, pp. 27–54.

———. 1993. Environment, Routine and Situation: Toward a Pattern Theory of Crime. In *Routine Activity and Rational Choice*, ed. R. V. Clarke and M. Felsoned. New Brunswick, NJ: Transaction, pp. 259–94.

Burn, G. 1984. *Somebody's Husband, Somebody's Son*. New York: Penguin.

Burnside, S., and A. Cairns. 1995. *Deadly Innocence*. New York: Warner Books.

Canter, D. 1994. *Criminal Shadows*. London: Harper-Collins.

Canter, D., and P. Larkin. 1993. "The Environmental Range of Serial Rapists." *Journal of Environmental Psychology* 13: 63–69.

Clarke, R. V., and M. Felson, eds. 1993b. *Routine Activity and Rational Choice*. New Brunswick, NJ: Transaction.

Cohen, L., and M. Felson. 1979. Social Change and Crime Rate Trends: A Routine Activity Approach. *American Sociological Review* 44: 588–608.

Copson, G. May 1993. *Offender Profiling*. Presentation to the Association of Chief Police Officers Crime Subcommittee on Offender Profiling, London, England.

——— 1995. *Coals to Newcastle? Part 1: A Study of Offender Profiling* (Special Interest Series, paper 7). London: Police Research Group, Home Office Police Department.

Cunliffe, F., and P. B. Piazza. 1980. *Criminalistics and Scientific Investigation*. Englewood Cliffs, NJ: Prentice-Hall.

Davies, A., and A. Dale. 1995a. *Locating the Rapist*. Unpublished MS, Police Research Group, Home Office Police Department, London.

———.1995b. *Locating the Stranger Rapist* (Special Interest Series, paper 3). London: Police Research Group, Home Office Police Department.

Dettlinger, C., and J. Prugh. 1983. *The List*. Atlanta: Philmay Enterprises.

Doney, R. H. 1990. The Aftermath of the Yorkshire Ripper: The Response of the United Kingdom Police Service. In *Serial Murder: An Elusive Phenomenon*, ed. S. A. Egger. New York: Praeger, pp. 95–112.

Eck, J. E., and D. A. Weisburd, eds. 1995. *Crime and Place: Crime Prevention Studies*, vol. 4. Monsey, NY: Criminal Justice Press.

Egger, S. A. 1984. A Working Definition of Serial Murder and the Reduction of Linkage Blindness. *Journal of Police Science and Administration* 12: 348–57.

———. 1990. *Serial Murder: An Elusive Phenomenon*. New York: Praeger.

Fowler, K. 1990. The Serial Killer. *RCMP Gazette* 52, no. 3: 1–11.

Frank, G. 1966. *The Boston Strangler*. New York: Penguin Books.

Green, E. 1993. *The Intent to Kill: Making Sense of Murder*. Baltimore: Clevedon Books.

Hagmaier, B. September 1990. *Ted Bundy, A Case Study*. Lecture presented at the FBI National Academy retraining session, Bellingham, WA.

Hickey, E. W. 1986. The Female Serial Murderer 1800–1986. *Journal of Police and Criminal Psychology* 2, no. 2: 72–81.

Holmes, R. M., and J. E. De Burger. 1988. *Serial Murder*. Newbury Park, CA: Sage.

Holmes, R. M., and S. T. Holmes. 1996. *Profiling Violent Crimes: An Investigative Tool*, 2nd ed. Thousand Oaks, CA: Sage.

Holmes, R. M., and D. K. Rossmo. 1996. Geography, Profiling, and Predatory Criminals. In R. M. Holmes and S. T. Holmes, *Profiling Violent Crimes: An Investigative Tool*, 2nd ed. Thousand Oaks, CA: Sage, pp. 148–65.

How the DNA "Database" and "Caseworking" Units Will Function. 1995 February. *DNA Database*, p. 2.

James, E. 1991. *Catching Serial Killers*. Lansing, MI: International Forensic Services.

Johnson, G. 1994. ViCLAS: Violent Crime Linkage Analysis System. *RCMP Gazette* 56, no. 10: 9–13.

Kennedy, D. 1991. *William Heirens: His Day in Court*. Chicago: Bonus Books.

Keppel, R. D., and W. J. Birnes. W. J. 1995. *The Riverman: Ted Bundy and I Hunt for the Green River Killer*. New York: Simon & Schuster.

Kind, S. S. 1987. *The Scientific Investigation of Crime*. Harrogate: Forensic Science Services.

Kube, E., and H. U. Storzer, eds. 1991. *Police Research in the Federal Republic of Germany: 15 Years Research within the "Bundeskriminalamt."* Berlin: Springer-Velag.

LeBeau, J. L. 1992. Four Case Studies Illustrating the Spatial-Temporal Analysis of Serial Rapists. *Police Studies* 15: 124–45.

Lyman, M. D. 1993. *Criminal Investigation: The Art and the Science*. Englewood Cliffs, NJ: Regents/Prentice Hall.

MacKay, R. E. 1994. Violent Crime Analysis. *RCMP Gazette* 56, no. 4: 11–14.

Montgomery, J. E. 1993. Organizational Survival: Continuity or Crisis? In *Policing in the Global Community: The Challenge of Leadership*, ed. M. Layton. Burnaby, BC: Simon Fraser University, pp. 133–42.

Newton Jr., M. B., and E. A. Swoope. 1987. Geoforensic Analysis of Localized Serial Murder: The Hillside Stranglers Located. Unpublished MS.

Nicholson, M. 1979. *The Yorkshire Ripper*. London: W. H. Allen.

O'Reilly-Fleming, T. 1992. Serial Murder Investigation: Prospects for Police Networking. *Journal of Contemporary Criminal Justice* 8: 227–34.

———, ed. 1996. *Serial and Mass Murder: Theory, Research and Policy*. Toronto: Canadian Scholars' Press.

Pearson, P. 1994. Murder on her Mind. *Saturday Night* (June): 46–53, 64–68.

Pilant, L. 1994. Information Management. *Police Chief* (January): 30–38, 42–47.

Popkin, J. 1994. Natural Born Predators. *US News and World Report* (September 19): 64–68, 73.

Pron, N. 1995. *Lethal Marriage*. Toronto: Seal Books.

Raskin, D. C., ed. 1989. *Psychological Methods in Criminal Investigation and Evidence*. New York: Springer.

Reboussin, R., J. Warren, and R. R. Hazelwood. 1993. "Mapless Mapping" and the Windshield Wiper Effect in the Spatial Distribution of Serial Rapes. In *Questions and*

Answers in Lethal and Nonlethal Violence: Proceedings of the Second Annual Workshop of the Homicide Research Working Group (NIJ Publication no. NCJ-147480), ed. C. R. Block and R. L. Block. Washington, DC: US Government Printing Office, pp. 149–54.

Rebscher, E., and F. Rohrer. 1991. Police Information Retrieval Systems and the Role of Electronic Data Processing. In *Police Research in the Federal Republic of Germany; 15 Years' Research within the "Bundeskriminalamt,"* ed. E. Kube and H. U. Storzer. Berlin: Springer-Velag, pp. 241–51.

Ressler, R. K., and T. Shachtman. 1992. *Whoever Fights Monsters.* New York: St. Martin's Press.

Rossmo, D. K. 1993. Geographic Profiling: Locating Serial Killers. In *Proceedings of the International Seminar on Environmental Criminology and Crime Analysis,* ed. D. Zahm and P. F. Cromwell. Coral Gables: Florida Criminal Justice Executive Institute, pp. 14–29.

———.1994. STAC Tools: The Crime Site Probability Program. *STAC News* (Fall): 9, 14.

———.1995a. Geographic Profiling: Target Patterns of Serial Murderers. Unpublished doctoral dissertation, Simon Fraser University, Burnaby, BC.

———.1995b. Multivariate Spatial Profiles as a Tool in Crime Investigation. In *Crime Analysis through Computer Mapping,* ed. C. R. Block, M. Dabdoub, and S. Fregly. Washington, DC: Police Executive Research Forum, pp. 65–97.

———.1995c. Place, Space, and Police Investigations: Hunting Serial Violent Criminals. In *Crime and Place: Crime Prevention Studies,* ed. J. E. Eck and D. A. Weisburd, vol. 4. Monsey, NY: Criminal Justice Press, pp. 217–23.

———.1996. Targeting Victims: Serial Killers and the Urban Environment. In *Serial and Mass Murder: Theory, Research and Policy,* ed. T. O'Reilly-Fleming. Toronto: Canadian Scholars' Press, pp. 133–53.

Rumbelow, D. 1988. *Jack the Ripper: The Complete Casebook.* Chicago: Contemporary Books.

Schaller, G. B. 1972. *The Serengeti Lion: A Study of Predator-Prey Relations.* Chicago: University of Chicago Press.

Scheingold, S. A., T. Olson, and J. Pershing. November 1992. Republican Criminology and Victim Advocacy: Washington State's Sexual Predator Legislation. Paper presented at the meeting of the American Society of Criminology, New Orleans, LA.

Scott, H. 1992. The Female Serial Killer: A Well-Kept Secret of the "Gentler Sex." Unpublished master's thesis, University of Guelph, Guelph, ON.

Segrave, K. 1992. *Women Serial and Mass Murderers: A Worldwide Reference, 1580 through 1990.* Jefferson, NC: McFarland.

Skogan, W. G., and G. E. Atunes. 1979. Information, Apprehension, and Deterrence: Exploring the Limits of Police Productivity. *Journal of Criminal Justice* 7: 217–41.

Thompson, M. 1996. Zeroing in on the Serial Killer. *RCMP Gazette* 58, no. 3: 14–15.

US Department of Justice. 1991. *Serial Murder Investigation System Conference (Federal Bureau of Investigation).* Washington, DC: US Government Printing Office.

US Department of Justice. October 3, 1994. *Violent Crime Control and Law Enforcement Act of 1994* (fact sheet no. NCJFS000067). Washington, DC: US Government Printing Office.

Wambaugh, J. 1989. *The Blooding.* New York: Bantam Books.

Warren, J., R. Reboussin, and R. R. Hazelwood. 1995. *The Geographic and Temporal*

312   **pRofilers**

Sequencing of Serial Rape (Federal Bureau of Investigation). Washington, DC: US Government Printing Office.

Westfall, B. 1992. Westley Allan Dodd. *Police* 16, no. 7: 58–60, 84.

Zahm, D., and P. F. Cromwell, eds. 1993. *Proceedings of the International Seminar on Environmental Criminology and Crime Analysis*. Coral Gables: Florida Criminal Justice Executive Institute.

Chapter 20

NONFAMILY CHILD ABDUCTORS WHO MURDER THEIR VICTIMS

OFFENDER DEMOGRAPHICS FROM INTERVIEWS WTIH INCARCERATED OFFENDERS

Kristen R. Beyer and James O. Beasley

Dr. Kristen Beyer received her PhD in clinical psychology from the University of Detroit Mercy in 1997. She worked as a clinical neuropsychologist in the Department of Neurosurgery at Children's Hospital of Michigan and The Neurosurgery Group, Inc., evaluating brain-behavior relationships in both pediatric and geriatric populations. Dr. Beyer worked in private practice for several years, specializing in pediatric traumatic brain injury. Dr. Beyer was also an assistant professor at Wayne State University's School of Medicine.

In 1995, Dr. Beyer was selected in a competitive process for the FBI's Honors Internship Program. Dr. Beyer was assigned to the Behavioral Science Unit in Quantico, Virginia. There, she provided research support to the instructors within the unit and was exposed to the overall operation of the FBI. This experience led to the subsequent application for her current position.

Currently, Dr. Beyer works in the FBI's Behavioral Analysis Unit-3 Crimes Against Children, a component of the FBI's National Center for the Analysis of Violent Crime (NCAVC). She is currently the supervisory social behavioral science research coordinator for NCAVC. She has been involved in numerous research projects, including maternal filicide, child abductors who have murdered their victims, domestic violence homicide, Internet sex offenders, and serial murderers. She is also actively involved in the FBI's Employee Assistance Program and provides support to the Undercover Safeguard Unit, administering and interpreting psychological assessments of selected agents.

Published in a slightly different form in *Journal of Interpersonal Violence* 18, no. 10 (October 2003): 1167–88. Copyright © 2003 by Sage Publications, Inc. Reprinted by permission of Sage Publications, Inc.

James O. Beasley II has been with the FBI for more than twenty-one years. As a special agent, he served in three field divisions—Kansas City, Missouri; San Antonio, Texas; and Newark, New Jersey. He also served as a supervisory special agent examiner in the FBI Laboratory in Washington, DC, and as a supervisory senior resident agent in the FBI's Sacramento, California, field division, where he managed violent crime investigations in the division's Fresno, California, Resident Agency. He is currently a supervisory special agent in the FBI's NCAVC, a component of the Critical Incident Response Group, based at the FBI Academy in Quantico, Virginia, where for the past four years he has participated in operational matters relating to violent crimes. He also conducts research on child abduction and serial murder through interviews with incarcerated offenders.

Nonfamily child abductions have a relatively low rate of occurrence despite the intense media attention and public hysteria that these types of cases often attract. Although the incident rate is low, child abduction is an emotionally charged crime that can quickly overwhelm local police agencies with limited resources. Therefore, the need to appropriately allocate resources (e.g., technical, personnel, equipment, and financial and forensic capabilities) early in the investigation is paramount (FBI 1997).

The National Incidence Studies of Missing, Abducted, Runaway, and Thrownaway Children (NISMART) estimated that in 1988, between thirty-two hundred and forty-six hundred nonfamily abductions were known to law enforcement (Finkelhor, Hotaling, and Sedlak 1990). Between two hundred and three hundred of these abductions reportedly met the criteria for "stereotypical" kidnappings, often involving the removal of a child from home for an extended period of time for the purposes of ransom, sexual assault, and/or murder. In 62 percent of these nonfamily child abductions, the perpetrators were strangers (Finkelhor, Hotaling, and Sedlak 1992). Although these statistics are widely cited, they are more than a decade old. The NISMART-2 estimated that in 1999, there were 12,100 nonfamily abductions (Sedlak, Finkelhor, Hammer, and Schultz 2002). However, this estimate should be interpreted with extreme caution, as A. J. Sedlak et al. (2002) stated that the "estimate is based on an extremely small sample of cases; therefore, its precision and confidence interval are unreliable" (p. 6).

The purpose of the present research is to obtain demographic and background history on convicted nonfamily child abductors who have murdered their victims. Data for the study were obtained through interviews with incarcerated offenders and reviews of criminal, medical, and psychological records. This information should provide investigators with insight into offender characteristics and background. The primary goals of the research are to help investigators narrow the focus and scope of their investigations, identify offenders within the earliest stages of the investigations, and supplement the existing literature on child abduction.

Existing research on child abduction is limited (Boudreaux, Lord, and Dutra 1999; Boudreaux, Lord, and Jarvis 2001; Hanfland, Keppel, and Weis 1997). Few studies have specifically examined the characteristics of child abductors who murder their victims. The majority of existing research uses archival data, including federal, state, and local police records and/or telephonic interviews with case detectives.

K. A. Hanfland et al. (1997) telephonically interviewed child abduction and homicide detectives to collect data from 621 cases on initial response of the police agencies, basic investigations, extended investigations, physical evidence, geographical considerations, victim information, and offender information. M. C. Boudreaux et al. (1999) examined offender characteristics in 550 cases of alleged child disappearance.[1] Data were collected on race, gender, motive, and relationship to the victim. Boudreaux et al. also assessed factors involved in victim selection such as victim gender, victim age, motive, cause of death, abduction location, geographic distances between crime scenes and offender frequented locations, and length of time victim was kept after abduction.

OPERATIONAL DEFINITION

The term *abduction* has been inconsistently defined in the literature. This lack of uniformity is further complicated by variations in legal definitions and requirements. For example, *abduction* may be defined as the coercive movement of a person involving a distance as small as twenty-two feet and for a time period as short as half an hour (Finkelhor et al. 1992). This definition may be viewed as significantly different from the stereotypical perception of kidnapping, in which a child is removed from his or her home and held for days for financial gain or sexual assault.

Hanfland et al.'s (1997) definition of abduction includes four possible criteria: (a) The victim was kidnapped; (b) the victim was detained, and his or her freedom of movement was restricted; (c) the victim of domestic violence was reported by the family (or someone else) as a missing child; and/or (d) the police were initially of the opinion that the victim was taken or held against his or her will, whether or not that was determined to be true.

Boudreaux et al. (1999) defined *abduction* somewhat more broadly as the "coerced, unauthorized or illegal movement of a child for the purpose of a criminal act" (p. 540). D. Finkelhor et al.'s (1992) definition of abduction required the "coerced, unauthorized movement of a child, the detention of a child, or the luring of a child for the purposes of committing another crime" (p. 228). NIS-MART-2 further addresses nonfamily child abduction as: "A nonfamily abduction occurs when a nonfamily perpetrator takes a child by the use of force or threat of bodily harm or detains a child for at least 1 hour in an isolated place by the use of physical force or threat of bodily harm without lawful authority or parental permission, or the child is taken or detained by or voluntarily accompanies a nonfamily perpetrator who conceals the child's whereabouts, demands ransom, or expresses the intention to keep the child permanently" (Office of Juvenile Justice and Delinquency Prevention, 2002).

In reviewing previous definitions, it becomes apparent that the core concept of abduction involves the unauthorized movement of the victim, regardless of distance. For the purposes of the present study, FBI researchers determined that Boudreaux et al.'s aforementioned definition would satisfy the inclusion criteria without being too restrictive.

PREVIOUS RESEARCH

Research findings indicate that the majority of child abduction offenders are male (Boudreaux et al. 1999; Finkelhor and Ormrod 2000; Greenfeld 1996; Hanfland et al. 1997; Warren Hazelwood, and Dietz 1996). Hanfland et al. (1997) reported that 98 percent of their child abduction-homicide offender population was male. Similarly, Boudreaux et al. (1999) reported that 87 percent of the offenders in their study were male. L. A. Greenfeld (1996) reviewed cases of violent child victimizers, finding that 97 percent of offenders who committed violent crimes against children were male. Warren et al. (1996) examined records on twenty sexually sadistic serial killers and found that all were male.[2] Data from the National Incident-Based Reporting System were examined in 1997 on 1,214 abductions of juveniles.[3] Of those, 24 percent were reported as nonfamily (stranger) abductions, in which 95 percent of the offenders were male (Finkelhor and Ormrod 2000).[4]

Close comparisons were found among the studies with regard to race, as the majority of offenders were Caucasian, ranging from 66 percent to 71 percent (Boudreaux et al. 1999; Greenfeld 1996; Hanfland et al. 1997). Warren et al. (1996) reported 95 percent of offenders were Caucasian. African Americans represented 20 percent of the populations in Hanfland et al. (1997) and Boudreaux et al. (1999) and only 5 percent in Warren et al. Proportions of other minority groups represented among offender populations were smaller, composing only 9 percent of Boudreaux et al.'s and 13 percent of Hanfland et al.'s studies. Based on these statistics, it appears that Caucasians were slightly underrepresented and African Americans overrepresented, while other minorities were appropriately represented in the offender populations studied by Hanfland et al. and Boudreaux et al. (US census data from the US Department of Commerce 1990: Caucasian 80 percent, African American 12 percent, and other minorities 8 percent). In contrast, in Warren et al.'s study, Caucasians were significantly overrepresented, while African Americans were underrepresented in the sample population. These data should be interpreted with caution given the small sample size (N = 20).

Offender age was an additional variable examined in previous child abduction studies. Hanfland et al. (1997) reported a mean age of twenty-seven, ranging from fifteen to fifty-seven years. The majority (67%) of the offenders in their study were younger than thirty. Fewer than 10 percent of the child abductor murderers were older than forty, with only 2 percent being older than fifty. Boudreaux et al. (1999) reported a mean age of twenty-eight, ranging from eleven to sixty-five years. Similarly, 60 percent of their offender population was younger than thirty.

Hanfland et al. (1997) reported that 73 percent of offenders were single at the time of the offense, and 13 percent were divorced. With only 15 percent of their offenders being married at the time of the offense, Hanfland et al. noted that this may be indicative of a lack of intimate attachments. Warren et al. (1996) studied a different and smaller offender population; however, it was reported that 50 percent of their subjects were married at the time of the offense. Although it is unclear what specifically accounts for the higher rate of marriage at the time of the offense in the Warren et al. study, it is possible that the differences are attributable to variations between offender populations. The extant literature provides little information on offenders' level of education. Warren et al. (1996) reported that 30 percent of their offender population had "post–high school education." It is unclear as to whether this includes college courses or degrees, vocational training, or some other type of educational experience.

In regard to employment history, Warren et al. (1996) found that 75 percent of the offenders in their population had stable employment. However, *stable employment* was not operationally defined by the authors. In contrast, Hanfland et al. (1997) reported that only 50 percent of their offender population was employed at the time of the offense. Of those employed, the majority (60%) of offenders were engaged in unskilled or semiskilled occupations (e.g., construction, truck driving, food industry, service industry, auto maintenance).

The offenders' prior criminal arrest histories were found to be somewhat variable (Greenfeld 1996; Hanfland et al. 1997; Warren et al. 1996). Greenfeld (1996) reported that approximately two-thirds of child victimizers had been arrested prior to the current offense. However, this offender population incorporated individuals arrested for various violent offenses against children (e.g., rape and sexual assault, robbery, assault) rather than solely child abduction and murder. Hanfland et al. noted that 60 percent of their study's child abduction and murder offenders had previous arrests for violent crimes. More specifically, about half (53%) of the offenders had committed crimes against children, with assaults and/or sexual assaults being most frequent. Warren et al. (1996) reported that only 35 percent of their sample had an arrest history. The authors purported that the low percentage of previous arrests may be attributed to specificity of offenders' criminal intent or prowess at avoiding detection, which makes it difficult for law enforcement to identify these offenders early on in their criminal careers.

Although female offenders perpetrate child abductions, they do so with less frequency and less violence and for different motivations than their male counterparts. Hanfland et al. (1997) reported "the killing of children during an abduction is almost a totally male domain of behavior. . . . Female killers in these kinds of child murders are almost nonexistent (1.5%)" (p. 26). Male offenders tend to be motivated by various factors including sexual gratification, profit, ransom, revenge, and/or power (Burgess and Lanning 1995). In contrast, female offenders often perpetrate child abductions for emotion-based reasons (e.g., maternal desire, rage, revenge, retribution, child abuse) (Ankrom and Lent 1995; Boudreaux, Lord, and Etter 2000; Burgess and Lanning 1995). The child abductions that are motivated by maternal desire rarely result in murder. Therefore, female offenders tend to be underrepresented in child abduction homicide studies.

METHOD

Participants in this study were initially identified through FBI case files and the Violent Criminal Apprehension Program, as well as anecdotal reports from law enforcement officers regarding child abduction-homicide offenders who would potentially meet study criteria.[5] In addition, FBI researchers reviewed federal and state prison records to identify participants who met the research criteria. The inclusion criteria for this study were:

1. Victim was less than eighteen years of age.
2. Offender was convicted of the murder.
3. Victim was abducted by the offender.

For the purposes of this research project, *abduction* was defined as "the coerced, unauthorized or illegal movement of a child for the purpose of a criminal act" (Boudreaux et al. 1999, p. 540). This definition is consistent with the basic core components of the definitions of child abduction previously discussed. Offenders meeting either of the two exclusion criteria were eliminated from the potential participant pool: parental abductions (i.e., involving custodial disputes/conflicts) and cases wherein the offenders were processed through the juvenile system.

On identifying appropriate study participants, presentence investigative reports, psychological reports, offense records, autopsy reports, confessions, and/or any other relevant documents were requested and subsequently reviewed by the researchers. After review of each potential participant's collateral records, an interview team consisting of FBI supervisory special agents, special agents, and/or professional support staff traveled to prison facilities to establish contact with the participant and explain the study in greater detail. The interview team reviewed the informed consent form with the inmate and was available to answer any questions. If the offender agreed to participate, he was asked to read and sign an informed consent form.

The inmate was informed prior to beginning the interview process that providing information on criminal activity that had not previously been reported to law enforcement and had not yet exceeded the statute of limitations would result in the immediate discontinuation of the research interview. The offender was also informed that he would be advised of his rights and that the newly obtained information would be reported to the appropriate authorities. The offender did not receive any type of incentive or compensation for participating in the research project. The participation rate for offenders was approximately 20 percent. This low participation rate may be a result of the inmate's sentence, which may involve numerous appeals; attorney disapproval; or lack of financial or material incentive.

To date, interviews with twenty-five child abductors who murdered their victims have been conducted within various prison facilities in the states of Florida, Texas, New Jersey, and New York. (The project remains ongoing and will expand to additional states.) Each offender was interviewed using a structured interview protocol developed by FBI supervisory special agents and professional support staff from the National Center for the Analysis of Violent Crime (NCAVC) and the Child Abduction and Serial Murder Investigative Resources Center in Quantico, Virginia. The protocol covers numerous content areas, including sociodemographic information (e.g., marital and dating history, IQ level, education, employment, military experience, family structure and environment, and religion), psychiatric history (e.g., animal abuse/torture, diagnosis and treatment of mental illness), sexual behavior (e.g., paraphilia history, fantasy development), criminal history (e.g., juvenile and adult), and current offense information (e.g., victim information, geographical information, media involvement, arrest information, and sentencing). The interviews were very comprehensive and somewhat lengthy. Each interview typically lasted between six and eight hours over a period of one to two days. To reduce participant and researcher fatigue effects, the offender was offered several breaks throughout the interview process.

After the interview was completed, FBI analysis reviewed the research protocol and supplement information provided by the offender with data obtained from case records. Offense information provided by the offender during the interview was verified through the use of police and correctional institution records previously obtained by the FBI, in an attempt to minimize confounding variables associated with self-report. Additional records may have been requested depending on the outcome of the interview and any inconsistencies that may have arisen.

For the purposes of this initial study, a limited number of questions from the interview protocol were identified for preliminary analysis. The items were coded, and Statistical Package for the Social Sciences (version 10.0) was used for database maintenance and analysis. Descriptive statistics were generated for various offender characteristics such as gender, age, race, marital history at the time of the offense, education level, employment history, military history, psychiatric disorder, family history, number of offspring, incarceration history, and problem childhood behaviors. In addition, the Hare Psychopathy Checklist–Revised (PCL-R) (Hare 1991) was completed for each offender who was interviewed.[6] The Hare PCL-R is a twenty-item checklist in which the offender receives a score of two, one, or zero based on the degree to which the offender exhibits the personality trait or behavior. After the interview, the research team, in collaboration with an NCAVC clinical psychologist, completed the Hare PCL-R using information gathered from the interview as well as case records.

RESULTS

GENDER

All twenty-five offenders interviewed were male. This is consistent with previous research that found that child abductors who murder their victims are overwhelmingly male (Boudreaux et al. 1999; Hanfland et al. 1997). To date, no female offenders have been identified as meeting inclusion criteria for the present research study. Boudreaux et al.'s (1999) study population included many subjects who abducted but did not necessarily murder their victims. As a result, there was a larger representation of female offenders who abducted but did not murder for maternal desire motives.

AGE

The mean age of offenders in the present study was twenty-seven years, ranging in age from fourteen to fifty-eight years. Approximately 72 percent of offenders in this study were younger than thirty. This is consistent with the findings of Hanfland et al. (1997) and Boudreaux et al. (1999).

RACE

In the present study, the majority of the offenders were Caucasian (76%), with Hispanics and African Americans each representing 12 percent of the population. The research findings from the study were consistent with US census data for adults (Caucasian 75 percent, African American 12 percent, Hispanic 12 percent, and other minorities 1 percent) (US Department of Commerce 2000). This finding should be interpreted with caution given the small sample size of the study population (N = 25). These racial distributions are different from those noted in prior studies. For example, in the offender populations studied by Hanfland et al. (1997) and Boudreaux et al. (1999), Caucasians were slightly underrepresented, and African Americans were overrepresented, while other minorities were appropriately represented (according to US Department of Commerce 1990 census data).

MARITAL HISTORY

Of the offenders, 60 percent were not married at the time of the offense; 24 percent were divorced; 8 percent were married; and 8 percent were involved in common-law marriages. Similarly, Hanfland et al. (1997) reported 73 percent of their offenders were single at the time of the murder, while 15 percent were married and 13 percent divorced.

BIOLOGICAL CHILDREN AND STEPCHILDREN

More than half of the offenders (56%) did not have any biological offspring at the time of the offense, while 16 percent reported having only one biological child, and 20 percent reported having two biological children. None of the offenders had three children. But 8 percent of the offenders had four or more children at the time of the offense. Only one offender reported having a stepchild.

EDUCATIONAL HISTORY

Overall, the participant population reported having little formal education (see fig. 20.1). Of the offenders, 40 percent had less than a high school education. Of those, 12 percent were middle school students at the time of their offenses.[7] In all, 12 percent of offenders attended some high school. Overall, 40 percent of the

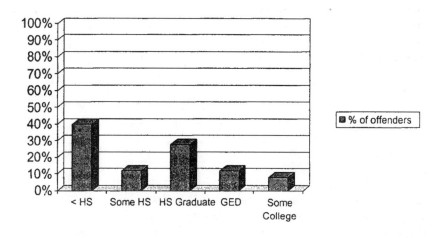

Figure 20.1. Offenders' Education Histories Prior to Incarceration
NOTE: HS = high school; GED = General Educational Development

participants dropped out of school. Approximately 28 percent of the participants graduated from high school. And 12 percent of the offenders earned their high school diploma equivalency through General Educational Development testing.[8] Only 8 percent of the offenders reported having some college education. Offenders' educational levels were not addressed in the previous research; therefore, no comparison to existing literature can be made.

OCCUPATIONAL HISTORY

Most of the child abductors (44%) who murdered their victims were primarily employed at lower level, unskilled jobs (e.g., service industry, fast food, cleaning), while some of the offenders (28%) were employed at semiskilled jobs (e.g., factory worker, construction laborer, truck driver). Of the offenders, 8 percent reported being employed in a skilled position (e.g., electrician, welder, pipe fitter), and 16 percent were students at the time of the offense (see fig. 20.2). Only 4 percent of the offenders reported being unemployed at the time of the offense. With regard to employment, the findings from the present study differ significantly from Hanfland et al.'s (1997) findings, which indicated that 50 percent of their offender sample was unemployed at the time they committed murder. This rate of unemployment is more than ten times that of the present 4.5 percent national unemployment rate for the general population. Hanfland et al. also found that offenders were primarily employed in unskilled and semiskilled labor occupations, with the most common job reported being construction worker.

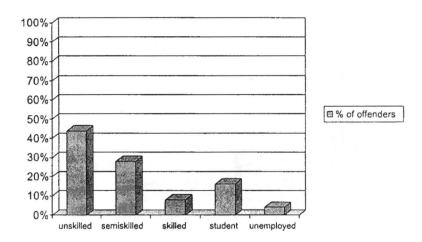

Figure 20.2. Offenders' Occupational Histories Prior to Incarceration.

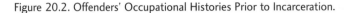

MILITARY HISTORY

The majority of offenders (76%) did not serve in the military. Of those few who did report a military history, all branches of the military including Army, Navy, Air Force, and Marines were represented equally. Offenders' self-reports of military history were verified through police and institutional records. However, military records were not obtained from the central repository.[9]

RELIGION

In the area of religion, the majority of offenders (88%) reported growing up in a Christian household (e.g., Catholic, Lutheran, Protestant, Methodist, or Baptist). As adults, most of the offenders (72%) considered themselves to be Christian. However, 12 percent of offenders reported being atheists as an adult. Gathering data on the offenders' adult religious persuasion was intended to capture the offenders' religiosity at the time of the offense and prior to incarceration. The offenders' religious practices postincarceration were not a focus of this study.

ANIMAL ABUSE

F. Ascione (2001) stated that operational definitions of animal abuse in the literature are inconsistent but provide a general working definition as "socially unacceptable behavior that intentionally causes unnecessary pain, suffering, or distress to and/or death of an animal" (p. 2). Of offenders in the present study, 20 percent reported a history of animal abuse/torture. This finding is similar to S. R. Kellert and A. R. Felthous's (1985) research that found 25 percent of violent, incarcerated felons reported "substantial cruelty to animals" during childhood compared to a group of nonincarcerated men who reported no such behavior. R. K. Ressler, A. W. Burgess, and J. E. Douglas's (1988) study on sexual homicide perpetrators (all men) found that 36 percent of the offenders reported cruelty to animals in childhood and 46 percent in adolescence.

PSYCHIATRIC HISTORY

With regard to psychiatric history, only 36 percent of participants reported a psychiatric diagnosis prior to the offense. These psychiatric diagnoses varied greatly and included anxiety disorders, substance abuse disorders, gender identity disorder, attention deficit hyperactivity disorder, and mood disorders (e.g., bipolar disorder, major depression, dysthymic disorder). It is purported this may be an underestimate due to various difficulties, including poor recollection of childhood and adolescent treatment issues and diagnoses, difficulty obtaining psychiatric records, and low interrater reliability between psychologists and/or psychiatrists in diagnosing patients.

FAMILY BACKGROUND

More than half of the offenders (56%) reported living with both biological parents during childhood, and 20% reported being raised by their biological mother and a stepfather (see fig. 20.3). Some of the offenders (12%) reported being raised by their grandparents, and one reported being raised solely by his biological mother (4%). Also, one participant reported living with his biological father and stepmother (4%), and one reported being raised by adoptive parents (4%). Most child abductors who murdered their victims (64%) reported that their biological father was their primary father figure. Similarly, the majority of the offenders (76%) reported that while they were growing up, their biological mother was their primary mother figure; only 20 percent of offenders reported that their grandmother was their primary mother figure during childhood.

Approximately 40 percent of the offenders reported that during their childhood their mothers were not employed outside the home (i.e., homemakers); the remaining 60 percent of the offenders' mothers were employed in various occupations requiring different skill levels. Of these, 20 percent reportedly worked in unskilled jobs, 16 percent held semiskilled jobs, and 8 percent held jobs in skilled occupations (e.g., office work, secretary). Only one offender (4%) reported his mother's occupation as highly skilled (e.g., teacher). The remaining 12 percent of the employed mothers held jobs with skill levels that were unknown or could not be determined.

Only one offender (4%) reported his father's employment as unskilled. Most of the offenders (48%) reported that their fathers had semiskilled occupations, and 8 percent reported that their fathers worked in highly skilled job positions.

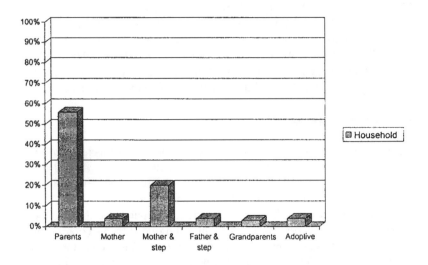

Figure 20.3. Offenders' Family Backgrounds

Many of the offenders (40%) reported that their fathers' occupation was unknown to them. This large percentage of unknown responses may be attributed to a lack of involvement or limited interaction with their biological fathers.

Of the participants, 60 percent reported that their home environment while growing up was "stable" (i.e., *stable* remained intentionally vague as to capture the offender's perspective of his family environment). It should be noted that their responses were based on their subjective experiences and perceptions. Another 24 percent of the incarcerated participants reported being raised in a chronically unstable household environment. Only 16 percent reported having occasional instability and disruption in their household.

FAMILY INCARCERATION HISTORY

Of the offenders interviewed, 24 percent reported at least one parent had been incarcerated. Approximately 12 percent reported their mothers had a history of a least one period of incarceration. Similarly, 12 percent of the participants indicated that their fathers had a previous history of incarceration. Of the twenty-five participants, four (16%) reported biological siblings who had at least one period of incarceration.

OFFENDER INCARCERATION HISTORY

Approximately 40 percent of the offenders in the study reported having a previous incarceration prior to the current offense (e.g., burglary, drug possession or use, driving while intoxicated). Almost half (48%) of the participants reported having a juvenile offense history resulting in some type of contact with law enforcement (e.g., shoplifting, trespassing, vandalism, drugs, disorderly conduct).

CHILDHOOD BEHAVIOR PATTERNS

The offenders were interviewed regarding chronic problem behaviors exhibited from birth to age twelve, including enuresis (bedwetting), isolation, lying, fire-setting, alcohol use, and drug abuse. Of offenders, 44 percent reported a history of childhood enuresis, seven (28%) reported a history of childhood isolation (e.g., few to no friends, limited social interaction), and 32 percent reported chronic lying during childhood. When asked about childhood fire-setting, only 24 percent of the offenders reported demonstrating this type of behavior. In regard to alcohol and drug abuse, 24 percent reported chronic abuse of alcohol and 12 percent reported abusing drugs before age twelve. (The findings are summarized in fig. 20.4.)

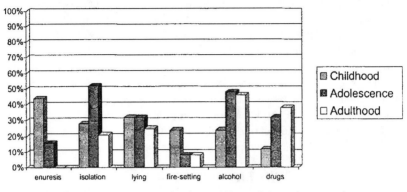

Figure 20.4. Offenders' Developmental Behavior History Prior to Incarceration

ADOLESCENT BEHAVIOR PATTERNS

Offenders were questioned regarding whether the above-mentioned childhood behavior problems existed in adolescence (ages thirteen to seventeen). Fewer offenders experienced enuresis during adolescence (16%) compared to the 44 percent who reported experiencing enuresis during childhood. Of offenders, 44 percent reported feeling isolated, and 32 percent reported chronic lying during adolescence. Only two of the twenty-five offenders reported fire-setting behaviors between the ages of thirteen and seventeen. Both alcohol and drug abuse significantly increased during adolescence: Approximately 48 percent of the offenders reported alcohol abuse, and 32 percent reported drug abuse. (The findings are summarized in fig. 22.4.)

ADULT BEHAVIOR PATTERNS

Finally, the offenders were interviewed regarding the same six problem behaviors experienced at age eighteen and older. Data regarding adult behavior patterns were gathered on all but two, both of which had not yet reached eighteen years of age at the time of interview. None of the offenders reported chronic enuresis as an adult. Only five (21%) reported feeling isolated, which is a significantly lower number than offenders who reported feeling isolated as a teen. This decline may be consistent with isolation being an inherent developmental aspect of adolescence. Only six of the offenders reported chronic lying as adults. The percentage of adult fire setters was also quite low (8%). Alcohol and drug abuse by the offenders continued to be elevated into adulthood, representing 46 percent and 38 percent, respectively. (The findings are summarized in fig. 22.4.)

SEXUAL BEHAVIOR HISTORY

Of offenders, 28 percent reported being sexually molested and/or assaulted as a child. Findings reported by the National Institute of Justice (1998) noted that 14 percent of incarcerated adult male felons (N = 301) reported experiencing childhood sexual abuse. In the present study, only 20 percent of the offenders reported having a printed pornography collection, and none of the offenders reported having a video pornography collection. The majority of the offenders (88%) identified themselves as heterosexuals, and 20 percent identified themselves as pedophiles. Given the stigmatization of certain sexuality issues, and problems with offender self-report, these figures may not be entirely accurate.

PSYCHOPATHY

Data on psychopathy were available for only twenty of the twenty-five offenders due to incomplete records on four of the offenders and one offender who was younger than eighteen at the time of interview. The mean score on the Hare PCL-R for the child abductors who murdered their victims was 17.6. This is significantly below the thirty-point cutoff necessary for classification as a psychopath. The total scores on the Hare PCL-R for child abductors ranged significantly from five to thirty-seven. Only four (19%) of the offenders exceeded the cutoff classifying them as psychopaths. This is consistent with the offenders' behavioral presentations during interviews as well as background histories, as most of the child abductors who murdered their victims did not appear glib or superficial, expressed appropriate affect and remorse, were not overtly conning or manipulative, did not display any grandiose sense of self-worth, and in several cases, even expressed some degree of empathy for their victims. It is important to note, however, that child abductors who meet the criteria for psychopathy may be less likely to volunteer for this type of research.

DISCUSSION

The findings of this study appear consistent with the existing literature. The structured interviews used in the present study, however, provide a more in-depth assessment of the offender's psychosocial background than is found within literature using archival data. These interviews attempt to quantify and analyze not only basic sociodemographic factors but also the offender's development over time, including family structure and environment as well as chronic problem behaviors experienced throughout the life span. Therefore, the present study differs from previous research in that it provides information on offender characteristics that involve the offender's actual input and perception as opposed to obtaining information only through archival means such as case records or law enforcement interviews.

Many of the findings gleaned from the study are consistent with offender characteristics documented in previous research. For example, prior studies have found that offenders are often Caucasian, in their mid- to late twenties, and unmarried with little formal education and employed in unskilled or semiskilled occupations. These traits seem to be consistent with what the general population may perceive to be a stereotypical child abductor. However, society may also believe that child abductors experience severe physical and sexual abuse as children and are raised in single-parent homes with no primary parental figures present. On the contrary, 28 percent of offenders from the study reported being sexually abused. Furthermore, more than half (56%) of the child abductors were raised by their biological parents. The majority of the offenders reported that their biological father was their primary father figure and their biological mother was their primary mother figure during childhood.

More than half of the offenders reported their home environment was stable throughout their childhood. Although the offender's perception of his home environment may be skewed, it is still reflective of how the offender viewed the status of his household as a child and how he reflects on his childhood as an adult. For example, one offender described having a relatively stable home environment while growing up. He reported this despite having an alcoholic mother who habitually used marijuana and was married four times. The accessibility of marijuana within his household resulted in the offender having his first experience with drugs at age eight. In contrast, another offender also reported having a stable household. As an only child, he lived with both biological parents and reportedly received adequate attention to his basic physical and emotional needs. On reflection as an adult, however, the offender admitted to a lack of structure and discipline by his parents, which allowed him to have a significant amount of premature autonomy. Both of the aforementioned examples show the variability in perceived stability among offenders' households. However, the phrasing of the question remains somewhat ambiguous to allow for the offenders' interpretation and perception.

Perhaps the most poignant finding from the present interview study is the lack of identifiable demographic and behavioral indicators during childhood and adolescence. In beginning the interview process, it was hypothesized that the psychosocial background of child abductors would differ significantly from that of the noncriminal population. The preliminary data, however, do not indicate a distinct pattern of childhood or adolescent behavior indicative of violent criminal activity involving child victims. There are no glaring warning signs that would result in predicting that these offenders would ultimately engage in such deviant and antisocial behavior. For example, US census data (US Department of Commerce 2000) indicate that 68 percent of the population grew up in a two-parent household in comparison with 56 percent of the offenders in the present study.

The difference in the two populations is not as dramatic as what was expected by researchers given the nature of the offenders' crimes.

The study does identify and verify some indicators in the offender's level of functioning as an adult. As adults, child abductors who murder their victims are generally not socially integrated within society (e.g., education and personal relationships). For example, compared to US census data (US Department of Commerce 2000), 83 percent of the general population (age twenty-five and older) graduated from high school in comparison to 28 percent of the offender population. In addition, only 8 percent of the offender population was married at the time of the offense as compared to 61 percent of the general population (US Department of Commerce 2000). Furthermore, 60 percent of the offenders in the study were never married compared with 24 percent of the general population (US Department of Commerce 2000). Although these factors alone are not definitive in determining social integration, the differences are dramatic and may require further exploration.

Hanfland et al. (1997) stated that the offenders can be "characterized as social marginals: they are not active, successful in mainstream, conventional social life, but rather they occupy a position in society that is on the 'edge, brink, border, precipice, or margin'" (p. 32). The majority of offenders in the present study reported having less than a high school education. In addition, most of offenders held unskilled or semiskilled jobs. Most of the offenders were never married or were not involved in long-term relationships, suggesting that many of the offenders were unable to develop intimate relationships that require sustained effort and maturity. For example, one unmarried offender was raised with his biological parents and older sister and reported struggling with isolation during childhood and adolescence but reported no other problem behaviors. During adulthood, his reported isolation continued to be an obstacle to his developing healthy relationships with potential mates. His social inadequacy may have played a role in his selection of a nonthreatening seven-year-old girl as an abduction-murder victim.

Despite engaging in highly antisocial behavior, the majority of offenders did not meet the criteria for classification as psychopaths. Some of the offenders did exhibit psychopathic traits such as impulsivity, poor behavioral controls, and irresponsibility. Most notably, three of the five offenders in the study who had murdered more than one victim obtained the highest scores on the PCL-R. Although these offenders are not representative of the study sample as a whole, it is possible that their higher PCL-R scores may somehow correlate with their committing more than one murder. This purported correlation merits further study. In addition, if the finding of few psychopathic offenders in the interviewed population is accurate, an ongoing, parallel archival study on child abduction-homicide by the authors, based on analysis of case materials from offenders who choose not to participate in the interview study or are deceased, should reflect similar findings.

The majority of the offenders, during the structured interview, did not exhibit or report psychopathic traits such as glibness, superficial charm, a grandiose sense of self-worth, promiscuous sexual behavior, or criminal versatility. This observation and self-report was also consistent with the collateral information obtained from case records. Therefore, the majority of child abductors obtained a total score on the Hare PCL-R that was significantly below the cutoff necessary for classification as a psychopath.

The present research does provide some insight into the backgrounds and family environments of child abductors who murder their victims. However, there are several limitations to consider. First, the self-report by the offender raises the issue of the validity and reliability of data obtained. To control for this limitation, the researchers implemented the review of case and correctional records to help verify and corroborate offenders' responses. However, some responses, such as perceived family stability and childhood and adolescent behaviors, could not be cross-referenced in case materials. In addition, much of the information found in the case materials may also have been offender self-report. Those records were useful in determining whether the participant had been providing consistent information over time.

Second, the small sample size limits the generalizability of the findings. However, because nonfamily child abductions are a low base rate phenomenon, a large sample size may be difficult to obtain. As previously mentioned, there was only a 20 percent participation rate. Therefore, the participants included in this study may not be representative of the population of child abductors as a whole. Many of the offenders with the most severe prison sentences declined participation. As a result of this low participation rate, a parallel archival research project is ongoing. In the archival research project, case records from offenders who meet the criteria but have declined participating in the interview process are obtained. A modified version of the interview protocol is completed and entered into a database for statistical analysis. This parallel research project should help to control for any confounding factors that may limit generalizability of the present results.

Finally, the lack of female participants in the study may also affect generalizability and present a slightly skewed image of child abductors. Child abduction is a low base rate phenomenon that rarely occurs in society and even more infrequently involves a female offender. Efforts continue to be made to identify and interview female offenders; however, few meet the study inclusion criterion of having abducted prior to murdering.

The main goal of the child abduction-homicide study is to increase the size of the study population. The size of the participant pool will continue to increase as the study expands to include more states. The preliminary findings will be helpful in identifying offender characteristics and behaviors pertinent to ongoing case investigations.

Future studies will address each offender's criminal history, relationship with victim, precipitating stressors, victimology, and offense information. Interviews with family members, ex-wives, girlfriends, neighbors, and/or employees would be extremely helpful in gaining additional information as well as in verifying data obtained from the offender. This may provide tremendous insight into the overall functioning of the offender. In addition, standardized psychological testing may be added to the interview protocol in the future. Psychological testing would be helpful in obtaining valid test data regarding the offender's level of intellectual functioning (e.g., IQ test), and objective personality measures (e.g., Minnesota Multiphasic Personality Inventory) may provide insight into offenders' personality dynamics. In the present study, the information contained within the psychological evaluations, when available in the institutional records, was found to vary greatly between facilities.

Gaining more accurate and in-depth knowledge of offender characteristics may help law enforcement agencies that investigate nonfamily child abductions to narrow the scope and focus of their investigations. This should ultimately aid in appropriately allocating the limited resources available to law enforcement.

NOTES

1. It is important to note that child abduction cases included in M. C. Boudreaux, W. D. Lord, and R. L. Dutra's (1999) research did not all result in murder. More specifically, the inclusion criteria required that the cases were reported to the FBI as either abductions or alleged abductions or as murders with abduction initially suspected.

2. This study's orientation differs from the other studies cited herein, as it focused on sexually sadistic serial killers. It is included for comparison purposes because 50 percent of the offenders had at least one child victim (younger than fifteen). J. I. Warren, R. R. Hazelwood, and P. E. Dietz (1996) also noted that 80 percent of the offenders used a con or a ruse to abduct their victims.

3. The US Department of Justice began supplementing the Uniform Crime Report with a more comprehensive National Incident-Based Reporting System (NIBRS) in 1988. Because all states have not been mandated to report crime statistics through NIBRS, its data are not yet nationally representative. For example, D. Finkelhor and R. Ormrod (2000) noted that crime data from large urban areas remain underrepresented in NIBRS.

4. It should be noted that only one of the kidnappings in the 1997 National Incident Based Reporting System data resulted in death.

5. The FBI's Violent Criminal Apprehension Program (ViCAP) is a nationwide data information center designed to collect, collate, and analyze crimes of violence, specifically murder. ViCAP's mission is to facilitate cooperation, communication, and coordination between law enforcement agencies and provide support in their efforts to investigate, identify, track, apprehend, and prosecute violent serial offenders. The cases examined by ViCAP include the following: solved or unsolved homicides or attempts, especially those that involve an abduction; homicides that are apparently random, motiveless, or sexually oriented or are known or suspected to be part of a series; missing persons, where the circumstances indicate a strong possibility of foul play and the

victim is still missing; and unidentified dead bodies where the manner of death is known or suspected to be homicide.

6. The Hare Psychopathy Checklist–Revised (PCL-R), developed by R. Hare (1991), is based on twenty-five years of research experience and represents the work of H. Cleckley (1982). The first version of the Hare PCL-R appeared in 1980. The current version of the PCL-R was formally published in 1991. The Hare PCL-R is a symptom-construct rating scale that uses a semistructured interview as well as collateral information to evaluate an individual on twenty items relevant to psychopathy. The Hare PCL-R is intended for clinical and research use in adult male forensic populations.

7. In the United States, middle school typically includes students in sixth, seventh, and eighth grades. These students range, on average, from eleven to fourteen years of age. Some students of this age attend junior high schools, which usually consist of seventh, eighth, and ninth grades. These students range, on average, from twelve to fifteen years of age.

8. The General Educational Development (GED) test dates back to 1942, when it was offered to help World War II veterans finish their high school studies. Approximately one out of seven people who earn their high school diplomas each year does so by passing the GED exam. The GED measures academic skills that should have been acquired through high school. The test measures academic skills in five areas, including language arts (writing), social studies, science, language arts (reading), and mathematics. The average age of GED test takers is approximately twenty-five.

9. The central repository, located in St. Louis, Missouri, is the primary storage facility for military records. For purposes of this study, those records have not been obtained on any participants.

REFERENCES

Ankrom, L. G., and C. J. Lent. 1995. Cradle Robbers. *FBI Law Enforcement Bulletin* 64, no. 9: 12–17.

Ascione, F. 2001. *Animal Abuse and Youth Violence*. Washington, DC: Department of Justice, Office of Juvenile Justice and Delinquency Prevention.

Boudreaux, M. C., W. D. Lord, and R. L. Dutra. 1999. Child Abduction: Age-Based Analyses of Offender, Victim, and Offense Characteristics in 550 Cases of Alleged Child Disappearance. *Journal of Forensic Sciences* 44: 539–53.

Boudreaux, M. C., W. D. Lord, and S. E. Etter. 2000. Child Abduction: An Overview of Current and Historical Perspectives. *Child Maltreatment* 5, no. 1: 63–71.

Boudreaux, M. C., W. D. Lord, and J. P. Jarvis. 2001. Behavioral Perspectives on Child Homicide: The Role of Access, Vulnerability, and Routine Activities Theory. *Trauma, Violence, and Abuse* 2, no. 1: 56–78.

Burgess, A. W., and K. V. Lanning, eds. 1995. *An Analysis of Infant Abductions*. Alexandria, VA: National Center for Missing and Exploited Children.

Cleckley, H. 1982. *The Mask of Sanity*. New York: The New American Library.

Federal Bureau of Investigation. 1997. *Child Abduction Response Plan: An Investigative Guide*. Quantico, VA: Critical Incident Response Group.

Finkelhor, D., G. Hotaling, and A. J. Sedlak. 1990. *Missing, Abducted, Runaway, and Thrownaway Children in America*. Washington, DC: US Department of Justice.

———. 1992. The Abduction of Children by Strangers and Nonfamily Members. *Journal of Interpersonal Violence* 7: 226–43.

Finkelhor, D., and R. Ormrod. 2000. *Kidnapping of Juveniles: Patterns from NIBRS.* Washington, DC: US Department of Justice.

Greenfeld, L. A. 1996. *Child Victimizers: Violent Offenders and Their Victims.* Washington, DC: US Department of Justice, Office of Justice Programs, Office of Juvenile Justice and Delinquency Prevention.

Hanfland, K. A., R. D. Keppel, and J. G. Weis. 1997. *Case Management for Missing Children and Homicide Investigation.* Olympia: Attorney General of Washington.

Hare, R. 1991. *The Hare PCL-R Rating Booklet.* North Tonawanda, NY: Multi-Health Systems.

Kellett, S. R., and A. R. Felthous. 1985. Childhood Cruelty toward Animals among Criminals and Noncriminals. *Human Relations* 38: 1113–29.

National Institute of Justice. 1998. *Early Childhood Victimization among Incarcerated Adult Male Felons.* Washington, DC: Department of Justice

Office of Juvenile Justice and Delinquency Prevention. 2002. *Second Comprehensive Study of Missing Children.* Washington, DC: Department of Justice.

Ressler, R. K., A. W. Burgess, and J. E. Douglas. 1988. *Sexual Homicide: Patterns and Motives.* Lexington, MA: Lexington Books.

Sedlak, A. J., D. Finkelhor, H. Hammer, and D. J. Schultz. 2002. *National Incidence Studies of Missing, Abducted, Runaway, and Thrownaway Children National Estimates of Missing Children: An Overview.* Washington, DC: US Department of Justice, Office of Juvenile Justice and Delinquency Prevention.

US Department of Commerce. 1990. *United States General Population Characteristics: Census of Population.* Washington, DC: Government Printing Office.

———. 2000. *United States General Population Characteristics: Census of Population.* Washington, DC: Government Printing Office.

Warren, J. I., R. R. Hazelwood, and P. E. Dietz. 1996. The Sexually Sadistic Serial Killer. *Journal of Forensic Sciences* 41, no. 6: 970–74.

LETHAL PREDATORS

PSYCHOPATHIC, SADISTIC, AND SANE

Frank M. Ochberg, Alan C. Brantley, R. D. Hare, Peter D. Houk, Robert Ianni, Earl James, Mary Ellen O'Toole, and Gregory Saathoff

Frank M. Ochberg, MD, is clinical professor of psychology and adjunct professor of criminal justice at Michigan State University. Alan C. Brantley, MA, former FBI supervisory special agent for the National Center for the Analysis of Violent Crime, is an owner and executive partner of MAG International, a behavioral science–oriented forensic consulting firm. R. D. Hare, PhD, is emeritus professor of psychology at the University of British Columbia and the president of the Darkstone Research Group. Peter D. Houk, JD, is a retired chief judge for the 30th Judicial Circuit of Michigan. Robert Ianni, JD, is senior deputy attorney general for the state of Michigan. Earl James, PhD, is the president of International Forensic Services, Inc. Mary Ellen O'Toole, PhD, is a supervisory special agent for the National Center for the Analysis of Violent Crime, FBI. Gregory Saathoff, MD, is associate professor of research at the University of Virginia School of Medicine and the executive director for the Critical Incident Analysis Group.

1. INTRODUCTION

In the summer of 1978, police in East Lansing, Michigan, arrested a baby-faced criminal justice student and youth minister named Donald Gene Miller, who had been seen running from the house where he had just raped and nearly

Published in a slightly different form in *International Journal of Emergency Mental Health* 5, no. 3 (Summer 2003): 121–36. Copyright © 2003. Reprinted by permission.

strangled a fourteen-year-old girl and stabbed her thirteen-year-old brother. Miller, then in his early twenties, was no stranger to the Lansing police when he was arrested. He had been a suspect for many months in the disappearance of four area women, beginning with his fiancée, who vanished on the first day of 1977 after spending New Year's Eve with him. Local detectives and prosecutors felt sure Miller was the killer, but despite exhaustive efforts, they had never developed enough evidence to charge him in any of the cases. In three of the four, they had not even found a body.

After Miller's conviction in the case that led to his arrest, prosecutors offered a plea bargain in the other cases. Miller would lead authorities to the bodies of his victims, allowing the cases to be closed and the families to end their anguished uncertainty. In exchange, he would be prosecuted for manslaughter, with sentences to run concurrently with the thirty- to fifty-year term he was already serving. The missing women's families agreed to the deal. So did Miller. Because of statutory sentencing guidelines, including mandatory "good time," Miller was scheduled to be freed in February 1999.

The Ingham County prosecutor who oversaw the plea bargain, who is also one of the coauthors of this article (Houk), remembers Miller this way: "Cunning. Religiously obsessed. Deceptive. He did not look physically threatening or dangerous; anything but." He remained calm and composed during the long investigation; "so composed that he went over to one victim's house on the morning after the murder and offered to help search for her." Twenty years later, the former prosecutor was sure that Miller would still be dangerous if he were freed: "I was positive to a moral certainty that he would kill again."

The authors of this article—four of whom, including the former prosecutor, mounted an effort to keep Miller confined after his sentence was completed— came to see Donald Gene Miller as a representative of a small, identifiable, and exceptionally dangerous group of lethally violent criminals. These are men (in almost every case) who have killed at least once and are likely to keep killing as long as they are free to do so. They are deliberate, sadistic, and often highly intelligent. Their crimes tend to be carried out in a ritualistic manner, have a strong sexual component, and often involve rape or torture. They are hunters. They plan, then pursue, charm, capture, torture, and kill their prey, at times leaving the bodies in poses that express and symbolize the feelings of power and intense pleasure they have achieved in the act of killing. They lack feelings of guilt or remorse. Their violence and cruelty typically escalate over time, driven by fantasies that feed their predatory nature and lead them to compete with themselves in a twisted game of "practice makes perfect." Though mentally abnormal (a term we will attempt to define more fully), they are not legally insane. They understand their misbehavior, know the difference between right and wrong, and can choose when to act upon their urges—and thus are criminally responsible for their acts. As the mother of Donald Miller's first victim put it, they are not insane; "they are evil."[1] Those of us who study them call them "lethal predators."

Many of these killers are skilled at covering their tracks and become more so with each crime. As a result, at times they can be convicted only under plea bargains leading to less severe sentences than their crimes would ordinarily warrant. They have little motivation for treatment and are extremely unlikely to be "cured" by any treatment method now available. When they are released, they are essentially unchanged and, we believe, as likely to kill as they were before their incarceration. For this reason, our subject has more than academic or scientific significance. Developing our understanding of lethal predators—who they are and what they do, how to identify them, and what the criminal justice and mental health systems can and should do with them—has immediate and serious implications for public safety. It is not rhetoric, but literally exact, to say that the questions we raise in this article have life-and-death importance.

In the following pages, we seek to establish a more precise definition of the lethal predator, survey current research and analysis on his characteristic traits (most prominently, psychopathy and criminal sexual sadism), and review the legal issues arising from attempts in a growing number of states to keep dangerous and mentally abnormal predators confined under civil commitment procedures after they have served their criminal sentences. Our effort is to summarize existing knowledge about this small but frighteningly dangerous group of criminals and to contribute to a continuing discussion of the legal, scientific, and public policy issues they present. We also hope to promote further research that will help inform that debate and the decisions facing the medical community, the criminal justice system, and the public at large—decisions for which critical information is now lacking.

We do not know how many lethal predators there are, in prison or out, or how many are serving less than maximum sentences and might be set free with their capacity and need for violence still intact. Nor is there any easy way to develop that information. Crime statistics, court records, and prison data do not distinguish the predators we are concerned with from the rest of the criminal population, or from the more than one hundred fifty thousand inmates now serving time for murder in American prisons.[2] We need to develop sampling or other methods that will help us reach an informed estimate of who and where these predators are.

As we develop and refine a definition of the lethal predator, we also need to develop protocols for evaluating violent felons who may fit the definition. And we must continue to explore the challenging issues of treatment. This means not just how to treat but what treatment means in the context of dealing with these peculiarly dangerous killers: whether it must be something intended to "fix" their abnormality or some form of quarantine, protecting both them and their potential victims from the consequences of their predations, can also be considered a legitimate method of treatment.

In considering the questions surrounding postsentence confinement of these predators, we should remember that it is not only their potential victims who are at risk. When someone is freed from imprisonment and then commits another gruesome, highly publicized crime—a situation that is especially likely when one of these killers is involved it undermines public confidence in law enforcement, the courts, and the mental health professions. In that sense, lethal predators have the capacity to endanger not just the people they stalk and kill but the bond of trust between citizens and government that is essential in a working democracy.

In both the medical and legal areas, the first task is to clarify exactly which offenders we should classify as lethal predators. The following section sets forth the criteria we have developed and that we hope will serve as the basis for future discussion.

2. DEFINITIONS

The lethal predators who are the subject of this article are a small group of killers who form a relatively homogeneous subgroup of the criminal population—cruel, violent, and likely to kill again if released from criminal or civil incarceration, no matter how long they have been confined.

These killers have several overlapping characteristics. They have a history of lethal violence, sexual predation, and certain types of mental abnormality. Law enforcement and mental health professionals agree that each of these factors independently is associated with violence and aggressive behavior. When all three coexist, there is a synergistic effect that greatly increases the probability of violent acts that inflict extreme suffering on others. From a public safety standpoint, the most important facts about lethal predators are that they commit their crimes repeatedly and prey on their victims for personal gratification. At times, their pleasure comes from the prolonged suffering of the victim. This combination of factors is associated with a very strong likelihood of repeat offenses—to the point where policymakers, judicial and law enforcement agencies, and the public may legitimately consider whether criminals of this type are too dangerous to ever be let free.

As the country debates that issue, legislators, the public, the criminal justice system, and the behavioral science community will have to reach a specific, unambiguous understanding of exactly which offenders might be subject to indeterminate confinement. The criteria we will suggest are intentionally narrow, designed to identify a small number of killers who fall at the extreme end of the spectrum of offenders who commit murder or manslaughter. Our definition is based on four elements: lethal violence, multiple acts of sexual predation, mental abnormality, and legal sanity. All four must be present for a criminal to be classed as a lethal predator.

LETHAL VIOLENCE

We define a lethal predator as a person who, as a result of a mental abnormality, has killed at least once in the course of sexual predation.

In setting a standard of one criminal killing committed, our characterization of lethal predation differs from the FBI's current definition of serial killing as "a series of three or more killings in circumstances suggesting a reasonable possibility that the crimes were committed by the same person or persons."[3] It should be noted that the FBI standard defines a crime rather than defining the offender as we are seeking to do here. This reflects the fact that the FBI's primary responsibilities are investigative, and the bulk of its involvement and effort comes before, not after, an offender is arrested and tried. For the same reason, the FBI has defined serial killing without making any reference to underlying motivation, whether sexual or otherwise. Its definition is intentionally broad in order to encompass the full array of serial killers.

This also explains why the FBI's definition uses the term *killing*, instead of murder. Unlike the more general terms of homicide and killing, *murder* has a specific legal meaning. Homicide is the killing of one human being by another, regardless of intent or whether the killing was lawful or unlawful. Murder is the unlawful and deliberate killing of another human being. It requires criminal responsibility. The legal concept of "mens rea," or "guilty mind," meaning that someone knows an act is wrong and commits it with actual, consciously formed intent. Possessing mens rea is ordinarily a requirement for someone to be found legally sane and subject to criminal penalties. Our term *lethal predators* refers to offenders who have killed unlawfully and are criminally responsible for their acts.

Our definition of lethal predation is consistent with, but more restrictive than, the criteria the FBI uses to define sexual homicide. The FBI's National Center for the Analysis of Violent Crime (NCAVC) distinguishes four types of sexual homicide: organized sexual homicide, disorganized sexual homicide, mixed sexual homicide, and sadistic murder.[4] These subclassifications are closely related to the types of criminal acts committed by those we define as lethal predators. According to the FBI, sexual homicide, both organized and disorganized, "involves a sexual element (activity) as the basis for the sequence of acts leading to death. Performance and meaning of the sexual element vary with an offender. The act may range from actual rape involving penetration (either before or after death) to a symbolic sexual assault, such as insertion of foreign objects into a victim's body orifices."

MULTIPLE ACTS OF SEXUAL PREDATION

Sexual violence is defined as "the threat or use of physical force either to coerce another person to submit to sexual behavior or to produce sexual excitement or release in the perpetrator."[5] Predation is not a legal term but denotes an intentional act of selecting, pursuing, and overpowering a person and then inflicting harm on that person for the pleasure of the predator. Sexual predators, whether they kill or not, will escalate their activities over the course of their careers. Typically, they will start with violent sexual fantasies and progress to acting out their imagined scenes with both willing partners and unwilling victims. The lethal predator will also demonstrate increasing skill in preparing the crime; selecting, pursuing, capturing, and controlling the victim; and carrying out the murder.

In analyzing sexual motivation, it should be noted that predators may find sexual gratification in activities that most people would consider nonsexual, such as the infliction of pain, mutilation, or postmortem display of the body and collection of trophies.[6] Sexual predators who murder quite often do things that are unnecessary for the commission of the murder. The victim may be posed, moved, mutilated, or disposed of in an unusual way. These acts may be symbolic and designed to make an impact on others, for the predators' perverse pleasure and enjoyment, or both. In some cases, there will be no evidence of "normal" sexual arousal such as erection and ejaculation. Such seemingly nonsexual behaviors, when they occur repetitively, can also establish the criterion "multiple acts of sexual predation."

These crime scene behaviors should also be considered as indicators that a lethal predator is likely to reoffend. Law enforcement professionals trained in crime scene analysis techniques and who are experienced working with violent offenders are best able to assess evidence of predation, based upon their thorough review of case materials.

MENTAL ABNORMALITY/LEGAL SANITY

Mental abnormality, the most elusive of the four elements in our definition, can be manifested when someone exhibits the traits and characteristics of a variety of mental disorders without reaching the threshold of mental illness necessary for exculpability or diminished capacity based upon legal insanity. At the core will be evidence of severe personality disorder and/or paraphilia as defined by the DSM-IV and Dr. Robert Hare's Psychopathy Checklist–Revised (see part 3). These core problems include, but are not limited to, traits associated with antisocial personality disorder, psychopathy, sexual sadism, pedophilia, and in certain extreme instances, necrophilia. Other disorders may coexist with these but similarly do not rise to the level of mental illness or defect or a legal standard of diminished criminal responsibility. Psychiatrists and psychologists are best able to assess mental abnormality based upon traditional mental health assessment techniques using record reviews, interviews, and psychometric testing.

The Supreme Court, in its ruling in *Kansas v. Hendricks* (see part 4), upheld the language of the Kansas statute, which described mental abnormality as a "congenital or acquired condition affecting the emotional or volitional capacity which predisposes the person to commit sexually violent offenses in a degree constituting such people a menace to the health and safety of others."

The absence of a mental disease or defect makes these offenders unsuitable for traditional mental health treatment. No proof exists that incarceration alone reduces the likelihood that these offenders will continue their pattern of violence after they are released back into society.

In saying that lethal predators are mentally abnormal but legally sane, we recognize that "mental abnormality" and "mental illness" are not precise terms. Anyone who is capable of the extreme acts these predators commit could be called mentally ill in some sense of that phrase. In this article, we use the term *mentally ill* as it is usually used in the legal arena—a condition that diminishes someone's ability to understand the nature of his acts or to commit them with conscious intent. We will use the term *mental abnormality* to describe a mental state that is surely perverse but does not diminish criminal responsibility.

Someone with a mental abnormality may lack the ability to experience guilt and empathy. He may be able to control his predatory behavior in a given circumstance—for example, if witnesses are present, or he is unlikely to escape without being caught—but he will not stop himself when both a victim and a getaway route are available. Mental abnormality can include elements of mental illnesses or severe personality disorders but not necessarily to the point of matching strict clinical diagnostic definitions. Abnormality may include traits of sadism, pathological anger, a sense of entitlement, sexual deviance, and lack of capacity for empathy or remorse.

While the psychiatric community has no uniform definition of *abnormality*, we believe it is a diagnosable condition and that recognized authorities can reach valid, reliable conclusions about its existence when evaluating cases. In the legal world, similarly, there is no commonly accepted meaning for *mental abnormality*. But we believe the concept can be defined and diagnosed clearly enough to represent the "medical justification"—the something more than dangerousness alone—that Supreme Court Justice Sandra Day O'Connor has written must be shown, along with dangerousness, to justify civil commitment after a criminal has completed his prison term (see part 4).[7]

3. PSYCHOPATHY, SEXUAL SADISM, AND LETHAL PREDATION

While lethal predators have not been studied as a group (an important goal of the present article is to call for exactly that research), our accumulated experience and empirical knowledge strongly suggest that nearly all of these killers will satisfy the diagnostic criteria for psychopathy, sexual sadism, and a variety of other personality disorders. To refine our understanding of lethal predators, we should begin by examining those underlying factors. The following section summarizes relevant research on those apparent elements of the lethal predator's personality and their relation to violent crime and recidivism.

PSYCHOPATHY

Psychopathy, as one recent study points out, "was the first personality disorder to be recognized in psychiatry. The concept has a long historical and clinical tradition, and in the last decade, a growing body of research has supported its validity."[8] This tradition is the result of several hundred years of clinical investigation and speculation by European and North American psychiatrists and psychologists. Psychopathy is defined by a cluster of interpersonal, affective, and behavioral/lifestyle attributes. Psychopaths typically are grandiose, egocentric, arrogant, callous, dominant, superficial, deceptive, and manipulative. They are unable to form strong emotional bonds with others and lack anything approaching a normal capacity for empathy, guilt, remorse, or deep-seated emotions. These interpersonal and affective features are typically associated with a socially deviant lifestyle that includes irresponsible and impulsive behavior and a tendency to ignore or violate social and moral conventions and standards.[9]

A new generation of theory and research has provided compelling evidence that there are measurable risk factors for violence and aggression and that one of the most important of these risk factors is the clinical construct of psychopathy.[10] Empirical evidence relating psychopathy to a propensity for violence is one of the key factors in current attempts to identify individuals variously described as "dangerous offenders" in Canada, "sexually violent predators" in the United States, and as having "a dangerous and severe personality disorder" in the United Kingdom.

Recent psychobiological and neuro-imaging research indicates that altered brain functioning may underlie the behavioral and cognitive anomalies associated with psychopathy. In particular, psychopaths appear to have difficulty in modulating goal-directed behavior because of a failure or defect in automatic mechanisms for attending to and evaluating peripheral cues.[11] They also appear to have difficulty in understanding and processing emotional information; emotion does not play the same motivating and directive role for them as it does for normal individuals.[12]

Particularly relevant for present purposes is the ease with which psychopaths engage in instrumental and cold-blooded violence, some of it with cruel and sadistic overtones. Emotionally unconnected to the rest of humanity, psychopaths view others as little more than objects. Thus, they find it relatively easy to dehumanize and victimize the vulnerable. Their world is made up of takers and givers, winners and losers, predators and prey. In that world, their attitudes and behavior are perceived as a rational response to the conditions surrounding them. Charm, manipulation, intimidation, and violence become convenient tools to gain dominance and control over others.

Psychopaths are skilled at deception and camouflage and in locating the "feeding grounds" and "watering holes" of potential victims. When they act violently, their violence lacks the emotional coloring that characterizes the violence of most other individuals. It tends to be straightforward, uncomplicated, businesslike ("a matter of process"), purposeful, and calculated rather than an expression of deep-seated distress or understandable precipitating factors. Psychopaths typically react to the damage and pain they have inflicted with cool indifference, a sense of power, pleasure, or smug satisfaction rather than feeling regret or concern for what they have done.

Unfortunately, we do not know why only a very small percentage of psychopaths evolve into lethal predators, the accounts and explanations contained in popular books on serial killers notwithstanding. Some speculations and hypotheses are worth investigating. For example, some unknown, idiosyncratic experiences may help shape and focus the natural predatory proclivities of certain psychopaths into what ultimately will become lethal predation. They may be very bright, or think they are, and may enjoy outraging and outwitting the authorities. They may also have obsessive and compulsive traits that permit them to perfect their predatory skills. For some, the evolution of their sexual behaviors into criminal sadism might be represented by a drug addiction model in which they become jaded or bored with "normal" sex and need increasingly more variety to experience both sufficient arousal and satisfaction. This variety might easily include sadistic acts, which themselves would need to increase in frequency and intensity to generate a satisfactory level of arousal.

WHO IS A PSYCHOPATH? THE PCL-R ASSESSMENT

The traditional features of psychopathy are reflected in the Hare Psychopathy Checklist–Revised (PCL-R),[13] described in The Twelfth Mental Measurements Yearbook as "the state of the art . . . both clinically and in research use."[14] The PCL-R measures interpersonal and affective characteristics and socially deviant behaviors. Item response theory analyses indicate that the former are more discriminating indicators of psychopathy than are the latter.[15] Total PCL-R scores are highly reliable indices of psychopathy when used with experienced and trained raters.

The PCL-R uses a semistructured interview, case history information, and specific scoring criteria to give an individual zero, one, or two points on each of twenty items. Thus, total scores can range from zero to forty. The higher the score, the more closely an individual matches the prototypical psychopath. The mean score among North American male offenders is about twenty-two to twenty-four, and several points lower for male forensic psychiatric patients; in each case, the standard deviation is about seven or eight. Although dimensional PCL-R scores typically are used for research and predictive purposes, a threshold score of thirty has proven useful for a research diagnosis of psychopathy.

The items in the PCL-R are (1) glibness/superficial charm; (2) grandiose sense of self-worth; (3) need for stimulation/proneness to boredom; (4) pathological lying; (5) conning/manipulative; (6) a lack of remorse or guilt; (7) a shallow affect; (8) callous/lack of empathy; (9) parasitic lifestyle; (10) poor behavioral controls; (11) promiscuous sexual behavior; (12) early behavioral problems; (13) lack of realistic, long-term goals; (14) impulsivity; (15) irresponsibility; (16) a failure to accept responsibility for own actions; (17) many short-term relationships; (18) juvenile delinquency; (19) the revocation of conditional release (because of violation of judicial terms for release on parole, probation, etc.); and (20) criminal versatility.

Although it was developed primarily with data from adult male offenders and forensic patients, the reliability and clinical utility of the PCL-R extend to a variety of other offender and patient populations, including women, adolescent offenders, substance abusers, and sex offenders.[16] Early indications are that the PCL-R can be used across racial and cultural boundaries. A recent analysis of Caucasian and African American offenders indicates that the PCL-R is not racially biased.[17]

PSYCHOPATHY AND CRIME

Although not all psychopaths come into formal contact with the criminal justice system, their characteristics clearly place them at high risk for antisocial behavior, crime, and violence, much of it predatory in nature.[18] The antisocial and criminal activities of psychopaths begin early and continue throughout most of the life span. Although there may be a reduction in overt criminality in middle age, the propensity for aggressive and violent behavior does not appear to diminish appreciably with age.[19]

The connection between psychopathy as measured by the PCL-R and violent crime is well established and powerful. This should not be surprising, considering the list of psychopathic traits. The typical psychopath's cocktail of egocentricity, grandiosity, sense of entitlement, impulsivity, weak inhibitory controls, need for power and control, and lack of empathy, guilt, or remorse makes what could be described as the perfect seedbed for asocial, antisocial, and criminal acts. As one study put it, "psychopathy's defining characteristics, such as impulsivity, criminal versatility, callousness, and lack of empathy or remorse, make the conceptual link between violence and psychopathy straightforward."[20]

The research that is perhaps most relevant to this article is on the association between psychopathy and sexual offending. The offenses of psychopathic sex offenders are likely to be more violent or sadistic or even homicidal than are those of other sex offenders. In extreme cases—for example, among serial killers—comorbidity of psychopathy and sadistic personality appears to be very high.[21] In an analysis of the biographies of serial killers, M. H. Stone indicated that most would meet both the DSM-III-R criteria for sadistic personality disorder and the criteria for psychopathy listed in the Hare Psychopathy Checklist–Revised.[22] (Sadistic personality disorder was dropped from subsequent editions of the DSM, chiefly because of a concern that it might be used by the defense in criminal trials as a mitigating "mental condition" for violent defendants.) Other diagnoses listed by Stone included antisocial, narcissistic, schizoid, obsessive-compulsive, and paranoid personality disorders. In some cases, psychopathy and sexual sadism coexisted with a major mental illness, most often schizophrenia.[23] A particularly potent combination with respect to sexual recidivism is psychopathy and deviant sexual arousal or preferences.[24]

SEXUAL SADISM

Unlike sadistic personality disorder, sexual sadism remains an official diagnosis in DSM-IV. The primary feature of this disorder is that the individual experiences intense sexual arousal from real or fantasized acts that subject another person to physical and psychological suffering. It is the suffering of the victim that leads to sexual arousal. We distinguish here between sexual sadism that technically is not criminal (for example, acts carried out by consenting adults) and sexually sadistic behavior that involves acts that, if detected and prosecuted, would be considered criminal. Of course, the former may lead to the latter, which is the focus of our discussion.

At the extreme end of the spectrum of criminal sexual sadists is the sadistic murderer, described by P. E. Dietz, R. R. Hazelwood, and J. Warren as a "sadist unencumbered by ethical, societal or legal inhibitions."[25] Their study provided a quotation from a sadistic murderer that captures the core of the disorder

> [T]he wish to inflict pain on others is not the essence of sadism. One essential impulse: to have complete mastery over another person, to make him/her a helpless object of our will, to become the absolute ruler over her, to become her God, to do with her as one pleases. To humiliate her, to enslave her, are means to this end, and the most important radical aim is to make her suffer since there is no greater power over another person than that of inflicting pain on her to force her to undergo suffering without her being able to defend herself. The pleasure in the complete domination over another person is the very essence of the Sadistic drive.[26]

Many of the offenders described by Dietz and his colleagues used torture and humiliation to instill morbid fear in their victims; some exercised the ultimate control—the power of life and death—by resuscitating near-dead victims in order to subject them to further torture. The vast majority of these killers were known to be highly organized and to have planned their crimes carefully. They studied law enforcement techniques in order to minimize the possibility of detection, prepared the crime scenes (torture rooms, soundproofed vans with disabled locks), collected tools and supplies necessary for the disposal of the bodies, and acquired tape and video equipment to record their victims' suffering so they could relive their experiences and sharpen their fantasies after the killing. When committing the crimes, they did so in a highly methodical manner, with emotions under control. This is reminiscent of psychopathic violence and contrasts markedly with the extreme emotional states that accompany the violence of most other offenders. For example, M. Woodworth and S. Porter found that homicides by psychopaths were likely to be planned and deliberate, whereas homicides by nonpsychopaths were likely to be reactive or "crimes of passion."[27]

Sexual sadism tends to be a chronic disorder with onset in adolescence or early adulthood. The behavior exhibited by sexual sadists is varied. It may be purely verbal, forcing someone by spoken demands or threats to say words of particular significance to the perpetrator. It may involve compelling the victim to carry out particular acts. The sexual sadist may use physical methods—restraints, whipping, beating, burning, choking, cutting, mutilation, and torture—to terrify and subjugate the victim.

As the sexual offender's fantasies develop, he may lose his ability to generate sufficient sexual arousal.[28] The offender then may begin to engage in "tryouts," turning his fantasies into actual behavior. He may track a woman down a dark street or pretend to bump accidentally into a woman and touch her private parts. Elements of such experiences are incorporated into the fantasies that accompany masturbation and a cycle of progressively more serious tryouts continues. This is a powerful process. As R. A. Prentky et al. have argued, "The selective reinforcement of deviant fantasies through paired association with masturbation over a protracted period may help to explain not only the power of fantasies but why they are so refractory to extinction."[29]

It has been argued that there is a likely association between sexual sadism and psychopathy. This association may be most dramatically illustrated in lethal predators but also is apparent among other offenders. Psychopathy as measured by the PCL-R is also a strong predictor of violent recidivism in both adult and adolescent sex offenders. Research findings on this issue clearly have potential importance for risk assessments.

PSYCHOPATHY, SEXUAL SADISM, AND RECIDIVISM

The significance of PCL-R psychopathy as one of the strongest risk factors for recidivism in general and for violence in particular is well established. R. T. Salekin et al. concluded that the ability of the PCL-R to predict violence among white male offenders was "unparalleled" and "unprecedented" in the literature on the assessment of dangerousness. In a more recent meta-analysis, J. Hemphill et al. found that in the first year following release from prison, psychopaths are three times as likely to commit a new crime, and four times as likely to commit new violent crime, than are other offenders.[30] The predictive power of PCL-R psychopathy, with respect to violence during institutionalization as well as after release, is evident even after more traditional demographic and criminal history risk factors, including prior convictions for violence, and other psychiatric diag-noses have been taken into account.[31] The link between psychopathy and recidi-vism is not confined to adult offenders. Adolescent offenders with a high score on the youth version of the PCL-R (the PCL: YV) are at higher risk for institutional infractions and for recidivism and violence than are other adolescent offenders.[32]

WHAT ABOUT TREATMENT?

While it is clear that psychopaths, particularly those with sexually deviant pro-clivities, are at high risk for recidivism and repeated violence, one might assume that years of incarceration, combined with intensive treatment, would reduce the risk. The reality appears to be otherwise. Not only is there no convincing scien-tific evidence that psychopaths respond favorably to treatment and intervention, but also there is some evidence that psychopaths who have undergone standard prison treatment programs may actually be more likely than untreated offenders to reoffend following release.[33]

There are several possible interpretations of this curious finding. One is that treatment programs may be poorly conceptualized and administered, more suited to the nature and needs of offenders who are not psychopathic. Unlike most offenders, psychopaths do not see much wrong with their attitudes and behavior, experience little subjective distress or concern for what they have done, and are not motivated to change what they consider to be rational behavior. Not surpris-ingly, the group therapy and insight-oriented programs that permeate the correc-tional field have few beneficial effects on psychopaths. Instead of helping them understand themselves, the treatment may help psychopaths develop better ways of manipulating, deceiving, and using people, including the therapists who are treating them.

Psychopaths also may manipulate staff into thinking that they have made progress in therapy and therefore are good candidates for early release. For example, M. C. Seto and H. E. Barbaree found that sex offenders with relatively high PCL-R scores reoffended at a very high rate if their therapists and others thought they had made good therapeutic progress, as rated by seeming changes in the offender's expression of empathy for his victims, understanding of his offense cycle, and the quality of his relapse-prevention plans.[34]

This does not necessarily mean that the attitudes and behavior of all psy-chopathic offenders are immutable, but it does suggest that they are very unlikely to change as a result of current prison programs.[35] The core personality features of psychopathy are very resistant to change and appear to remain stable across most of the life span.[36] The implications are frightening. If prolonged incarcera-tion and current prison treatment programs do not reduce the average psy-chopath's potential for recidivism or violence, the prospects cannot be anything but dismal for those whose attitudes and fantasies have been, and probably still are, deeply ingrained, perverse, and sadistic.

With specific respect to lethal predators, not enough of them have been released into the community for their postrelease likelihood of violence to be determined. But logic suggests that these individuals—whom one former FBI profiler calls "morally unchangeable"—will not become model citizens and that at the very least, they will remain a presumptive risk to society.[37]

Some might argue that prospects are not necessarily that bleak because many years in prison may have involved a variety of treatment programs, periods of self-reflection, personal maturation, "burnout," and the development of a new set of insights, attitudes, and after-the-fact concerns for the rights and feelings of their victims. But here also, the literature on the behavior of psychopathic offenders released after long periods in prison is informative and discouraging.[38]

Obviously, most psychopathic offenders have not committed serial murders, and they may differ in some important qualitative respects from those who have committed such offenses. Nevertheless, extrapolating from our experience with "ordinary" psychopathic offenders, it is reasonable to assume that the propensity for repeated predation, lethal or otherwise, would be at least as high among lethal predators as in nonlethal psychopaths. On that basis, the outlook for lethal predators released into the community must be considered extremely poor.

In conclusion, in spite of the enormous attention paid to some serial killings and other sensational murders by law enforcement, the media, and the public, we are just beginning to accumulate systematic knowledge of the psychological and neurobiological makeup of those who commit these murders. We have scores of descriptive accounts, many by true-crime writers or former homicide investigators, some of which claim to take us "inside the mind of the serial killer." Such accounts at times provide useful descriptive frameworks for making sense of what appear to be senseless, cold-blooded murders. But description is not explanation. There have been no systematic attempts to analyze the killers' nature and motivations in terms of current theories and procedures of cognitive/affective neuroscience.

If we are to even begin to understand what makes and motivates lethal predators, we will have to mount a major interdisciplinary research program. Beyond further study of the killers' traits, two key subjects for research are treatability and how to most reliably identify lethal predators and assess their dangerousness. This research is of much more than theoretical importance. Its findings will bear directly on the problem of defining and evaluating these lethal predators and help determine if they are so dangerous by uncorrectable mental abnormality that they must be indefinitely confined.

4. LEGAL AUTHORITY IN SUPPORT OF THE CIVIL COMMITMENT OF LETHAL PREDATORS

Lethal predators as we have defined them in this article pose a particularly excruciating problem for law enforcement and the courts. From the viewpoint of society, the threat they represent is similar to the threat of deadly violence by killers who are mentally ill. But these predators are legally sane, so the long-standing involuntary confinement procedures that the legal system has created to protect the community from insane killers may not serve to protect against murderers of this type.

As of mid-2003, sixteen states and the District of Columbia had adopted some form of law designed to allow the continued confinement of certain sex offenders who had completed criminal prison sentences and would not otherwise be subject to ordinary civil commitment procedures. A 2002 survey found nearly twenty-five hundred persons confined under those laws in what have come to be called "Sexually Violent Predator" facilities. Of these, 1,632 were under commitment orders, and the rest were held while awaiting commitment hearings.[39]

Several of those laws were challenged in state courts, among them Kansas's Sexually Violent Predator Act. The Kansas law allowed a person to be confined in a mental institution after completing his prison sentence if three conditions were met: the offender had been convicted of a sexually violent crime, had a mental abnormality or a personality disorder, and was found likely to engage in predatory acts of sexual violence in the future. In 1996, the Kansas Supreme Court declared the act unconstitutional, but the following year the US Supreme Court, in a 5–4 decision, upheld it. The court's ruling in the case, *Kansas v. Hendricks*, 521 US 346 (1997), remains the most significant recent decision in this area of law, in the sense that it made clear that confining legally sane offenders who have finished prison terms is not automatically unconstitutional.

In the Hendricks decision, the majority and three of the four dissenters agreed that the Kansas law's standard of a "mental abnormality" could be used to confine someone without violating due process requirements. The majority also found that continued confinement after the end of a prison term was not punitive, under the Kansas procedures, and thus did not unconstitutionally punish someone twice for the same crime. The effect of the ruling was to remove constitutional barriers to state laws that deprive someone of his or her liberty after a criminal sentence has been served, as long as there is clear and convincing evidence that the person is mentally abnormal and dangerous.

Mental abnormality is a broader standard than *mental illness*, as that term has historically been understood. Indeed, in the Supreme Court's hearing on the Kansas law, that state's attorney general explicitly acknowledged that the plaintiff, a sex offender named Leroy Hendricks, was not mentally ill and, under other Kansas laws, would not meet the standard for involuntary civil commitment. The

Hendricks decision was far from exact, however, in defining constitutional standards for states to follow. It gave only imprecise guidelines, for example, on what types of offenders can be subject to continued confinement, the conditions under which they should be confined, and how future dangerousness should be determined. All those would become the subjects of subsequent litigation.

Before the Hendricks case, involuntary commitment laws in the United States had a fluctuating history. For most of our national life, under the broad principle that states had wide latitude to protect the welfare of their citizens, states exercised their power to quarantine or segregate individuals who were considered to pose a serious threat to others or to themselves. The first significant case challenging the involuntary civil commitment of sex offenders was Minnesota, *Ex Rel Perason v. Probate Court*, 309 US 270 (1940). In that case, the Supreme Court upheld a Minnesota statute permitting the involuntary commitment of sex offenders who lacked the power to control their sexual impulses and posed a likely threat of future harm. Rejecting the plaintiff's arguments that the law was unconstitutionally vague and violated equal protection, the court held that a group of people found to be more dangerous to the public than others could be treated differently from the general public, as long as the law provided fundamental procedural protection such as the right to a hearing.

More than three decades later, the court made clear that danger to others or self had to be a condition for confinement beyond the expiration of a prison term. In *O'Connor v. Donaldson*, 422 US 563 (1975), the justices ruled that a Florida mental hospital could not confine a patient, Kenneth Donaldson, against his will after a jury declared he was "neither dangerous to himself nor dangerous to others." The court held that Donaldson must be freed and added the general principle that a "finding of 'mental illness' alone cannot justify a state's locking a person up against his will. . . . There is no constitutional basis for confining such persons involuntarily if they are dangerous to no one and can live safely in freedom." Those words, one analyst wrote, "altered civil commitment throughout the country. By the end of the 1970s, every state had modified or interpreted their civil commitment statutes to include a dangerousness requirement."[40]

Due process and double jeopardy issues continued to arise. In *Addington v. Texas*, 441 US 418 (1979), the court concluded that the requirement of due process in civil commitments could be satisfied by a standard of clear and convincing evidence rather than by the "beyond reasonable doubt" rule applied in criminal cases. In *Allen v. Illinois*, 478 US 364 (1986), the court upheld that state's Sexually Dangerous Persons Act, rejecting the plaintiff's claim that he was undergoing criminal punishment, not civil commitment, because he was confined in a psychiatric center operated by the Illinois Department of Corrections. The justices found that treating a civilly committed person in the same facility as prisoners did not make his confinement unconstitutionally punitive. The court's 5–4 decision also held that while due process was still required, the Fifth Amendment's protection against self-incrimination and other rights of criminal defendants did not fully apply when a state sought to confine someone for treatment rather than punishment. Even though proceedings under the Illinois law resembled a criminal trial and could lead to a long period of incarceration, the court noted that the state "has indicated quite clearly its intent that these commitment proceedings be civil in nature; its decision . . . to provide some of the safeguards applicable in criminal trials cannot itself turn these proceedings into criminal prosecutions requiring the full panoply of rights applicable there."

The most important decision prior to Hendricks was *Foucha v. Louisiana*, 504 US 71 (1992). In that case, the court struck down a Louisiana statute that provided for the involuntary commitment of an individual who was hospitalized after being found not guilty by reason of insanity but was later determined to be no longer mentally ill though still potentially dangerous. The court agreed that the defendant in the case, Terry Foucha, suffered from a personality disorder, but the court ruled that because his condition was neither a "mental illness" nor treatable, he must be freed. The Louisiana law violated due process, the court held, because the defendant no longer met the dual constitutional prerequisites of being dangerous and having a "mental illness."

Like Hendricks, Foucha was decided on a 5–4 vote, with the deciding vote cast by Justice O'Connor. Significantly, although she sided with the majority in setting aside the Louisiana law, O'Connor's concurring opinion suggested a willingness to retreat from the rule that civil commitment always required showing that a person was both dangerous and mentally ill. In declaring that she did not take the decision to mean that Louisiana "may never confine dangerous insanity acquittees after they regain mental health," O'Connor appeared to leave the door open for statutes that would, in different circumstances, permit civil commitment upon a showing of dangerousness and "some medical justification"—clearly, a much broader term than *mental illness*.

The Foucha decision was the basis for the Kansas Supreme Court's 1996 ruling that struck down that state's sexually violent predator act because it did not require a finding of a recognized mental illness, as the Kansas judges believed was necessary under the Foucha ruling. In reversing the state court and upholding the Kansas law, the US Supreme Court set a new standard: that civil commitment can satisfy due process requirements if it is established that those subject to commitment are dangerous and if there is an additional factor involving their mental condition—defined only as "a volitional impairment rendering them dangerous beyond their control."

The court held that the Kansas law's requirement of mental abnormality or personality disorder was constitutional because it applied to people who lacked the capacity to "control their dangerousness." Writing for the majority, Justice Thomas recalled Leroy Hendricks's admission that "when he becomes 'stressed out' he cannot 'control the urge' to molest children." That condition "adequately distinguishes Hendricks from other dangerous persons who are perhaps more properly dealt with exclusively through criminal proceedings," Thomas continued. The court did not go any further in spelling out what kind of mental condition could justify confining someone who is not being punished for a crime. Instead, the Justices left the states free to decide what specific form of abnormality or disorder would meet the new constitutional standard.

The dissenters in Hendricks disagreed with the majority and with the Kansas law on a different question: whether continued confinement under the Kansas law was punishment and thus an unconstitutional ex post facto imposition of a penalty greater than the law would have permitted at the time of the offense. The four dissenting Justices were unconvinced that treatment was truly the goal of the authorities who sought to keep Hendricks confined. The facts in the case, wrote Justice Breyer, "lead me to conclude . . . that the added confinement the act imposes upon Hendricks is basically punitive" and thus violated the ex post facto clause of the Constitution. However, Breyer added, "to find a violation of that clause here . . . is not to hold that the clause prevents Kansas, or other states, from enacting dangerous sexual offender statutes." Thus, the dissenters too appeared to agree that despite the defects they found in the Kansas statute, efforts to keep legally sane but dangerous predators confined beyond their prison terms were not inherently unconstitutional.

The punishment-or-treatment issue that had troubled the dissenting justices in the Hendricks case returned to the Supreme Court three years later. The new case, *Seling v. Young*, 531 US 250 (2001), involved Andre Brigham Young, a six-time rapist who was confined under Washington's Community Protection Act of 1990 after completing the last of his prison terms. The Washington statute, the first of the current generation of state laws aimed at continued confinement of certain sex offenders, survived a challenge in state courts when the Washington Supreme Court upheld its main provisions in 1993. Young then sued in federal court, asking for habeas corpus on the grounds that the conditions he was kept in were so similar to those in prison, and the treatment he received was so minimal, that his confinement was really just another term of punishment and represented illegal double jeopardy. On May 20, 1999, the 9th Circuit U.S. Court of Appeals ruled that Young could pursue his effort to win release on the basis that the law was being unconstitutionally applied.

On January 17, 2001, the Supreme Court reversed the 9th Circuit decision, though on narrowly focused grounds that left the major questions from Hendricks far from settled. Young's lawyers declared that there was enough ambiguity in the decision to permit challenges to the law to continue. But Washington state officials saw the ruling as clearing away the last doubts about the law's constitutionality, as long as the state attempted to treat those confined. The state remained under a federal court order arising from a different case, which required the authorities to improve treatment at the facility, the Special Commitment Center on McNeil Island. Only two and a half months after the Young decision, the Kansas law came back before the Supreme Court. This time, the issue was the standard by which the Kansas authorities could decide that a defendant was likely to commit future crimes and thus dangerous enough to be subject to indefinite confinement. The case, *Kansas v. Crane*, 534 US 407 (2002), involved a sex offender named Michael T. Crane, whose confinement was approved by a lower court but then overturned by the Kansas Supreme Court, which ruled that in order to keep Crane locked up, the state had to prove "that the defendant cannot control his dangerous behavior"—an unqualified formulation suggesting, as one Justice put it during oral arguments before the US Supreme Court, "a total inability" to refrain from dangerous acts.

In her argument to the Justices, Kansas Attorney General Carla J. Stovall called that "an impossible standard." She sought to persuade the Justices that once Crane was determined to have a mental abnormality, that in itself was sufficient to show future dangerousness, and no further proof was needed.

When it handed down its decision on January 22, 2002, the court agreed by a 7–2 majority that the Kansas Supreme Court standard was too rigid. "Most severely ill people—even those commonly termed 'psychopaths'—retain some ability to control their behavior," Justice Breyer noted in his majority opinion. But the court also rejected the state's argument that nothing more had to be proved beyond Crane's mental abnormality. (Supporters on both sides of the case, Breyer observed, were in agreement that "an absolutist approach is unworkable.") Splitting the difference, in effect, the court declared that "proof of serious difficulty in controlling behavior" was required in order to keep a defendant confined.

The Crane decision did not answer all the questions left unresolved in Hendricks, Breyer acknowledged, but he went on to suggest that seeking definitive standards might be an unworkably absolutist approach, too. The ruling "provides a less precise constitutional standard than would those more definite rules for which the parties have argued," he wrote. "But the constitution's safeguards of human liberty in the area of mental illness and the law are not always best enforced through precise bright-line rules."

Because the Supreme Court overturned both the original trial court decision on Crane (which accepted the state's position that no separate proof of dangerousness was needed) and the Kansas Supreme Court's reversal, its order called for a new hearing on Crane's confinement. By then, however, the state's own doctors declared he was no longer a threat, and Crane was freed without another hearing. As if to underscore the uncertainties surrounding such determinations, in June 2003 Crane was arrested for another sexual assault—this one more serious than any of the offenses for which he had previously been sentenced.

From this brief review, we conclude that a law permitting indefinite confinement of lethal predators, as we have defined them, can be tailored to pass constitutional muster. More cases are sure to arise over how law and policy can be made consistent with the Supreme Court's standards—determining just what constitutes "serious difficulty in controlling behavior," for example. But on the fundamental question, the Hendricks ruling and its progeny teach that persons who have been convicted of criminal acts can be civilly committed based in part on those acts without violating concepts of due process and double jeopardy.

If dangerousness is one standard for confinement, there can be no doubt that lethal predators would meet that test. Indeed, they are among the most dangerous people in our society, since under our definition they have already killed and have committed multiple acts of sexual predation. Nor can it be seriously questioned that they satisfy the Supreme Court's requirement of mental abnormality. Hendricks was a pedophile who had killed no one. Nor had Young, though he had committed multiple rapes and was described in part as having the characteristics of a sexual sadist and other paraphilia defined in the DSM. Without minimizing their abnormalities, it can be said that they pale by comparison with those of the lethal sexual predator who kills and mutilates his victim for sexual gratification.

Two important issues need to be addressed: treatability and how reliably dangerousness can be predicted. It may be that modern psychiatry does not have treatment tools that can cure lethal predators. However, mental hospitals provide safe and humane palliative care for many civilly committed persons who have been found to be a danger to themselves or others and are mentally ill but for whom no "cure" has been found. What is legally important with respect to committing lethal predators is that their confinement does not constitute continued punishment or an alternative to punishment. Treatment should be a goal, but it need not be defined as an effort to cure the abnormality that warrants confinement. The most appropriate treatment for the lethal predator may be in preventing the harm to himself that may befall him during or after the commission of another violent act.

Reliability or predictability of future harm is, we believe, the most easily answered of the legal questions. While the scientific community may seek diagnostic approaches that will come close to mathematical certainty, the law, as Justice Breyer commented in the Crane decision, does not. Civil commitment statutes have always been couched in terms of asking a jury (or judge) whether the evidence supports a finding by clear and convincing evidence that the respondent is mentally ill and a danger either to himself or others. The calculus is no different for the lethal sexual predator.

5. CONCLUSION

"What would you do if the latch on the cage of a dangerous animal was loose, and the animal was about to get out?"[41] That's how one observer summarized the discussion at a public forum at Michigan State University when Donald Gene Miller was expected to be released from prison after completing his sentence. Amid growing community anxiety as the release date approached, one of the authors of this article (Ochberg), a former mental health director for the state of Michigan, assembled a group of detectives, judges, legislators, prosecutors, prison psychologists, and victim advocates to explore ways to prevent Miller's release. Those acquainted with Miller strongly doubted that any feasible program of treatment or surveillance after his release could be counted on to keep him from killing again. Under state law, he could not be confined in a mental hospital because he was not insane. In the absence of existing procedures, the group, known as the Committee for Community Awareness and Protection, and other concerned people approached Michigan lawmakers, asking for new legislation consistent with the recently issued *Kansas v. Hendricks* ruling that could be used to keep Miller out of circulation.

Meanwhile, Ochberg's committee was also pursuing a different route: a new prosecution based on an offense Miller had committed in prison. Originally, after guards found a homemade garrote in Miller's cell, prison administrators had simply docked him two years of earned good time. But with his release approaching, prosecutors filed a felony charge of weapon possession while in prison. Because it was Miller's third felony, under Michigan's habitual offender law, he was given an additional sentence of twenty to forty years.

With that outcome, Miller's hometown was spared the fear of having a still-dangerous killer returned to their community. But the circumstances that led to his continued confinement were unique to his case and would not offer protection from other deadly predators. Across the country, other cases have continued to demonstrate the extreme danger that lethal predators can represent—and the loopholes in the criminal justice and mental health systems that sometimes let them remain free despite strong evidence that they are dangerous.

One example was the case of Coral Eugene Watts, who was scheduled to be released from a Texas prison in 2006 after serving just twenty-four years, even though he admitted killing thirteen women and attacking six others between 1979 and 1982 and was a suspect in many more murders.[42] Watts, who explained that he chose his victims because they had "evil eyes," had covered his tracks successfully enough that he was not tried for any of the killings. His confessions came under a grant of immunity as part of a plea bargain after he was caught while trying to drown his last victim in her bathtub. After pleading guilty to burglary with intent to murder, Watts was given a sixty-year sentence. But with "good time" credit, under the state's mandatory formula, he would finish his term and go free in the spring of 2006.

Crime victim advocates and relatives of Watts's victims launched a campaign to find a way to keep Watts confined, and law enforcement officials in several states began searching for evidence that might allow him to be prosecuted for some of the murders he had not admitted and for which he had not been given immunity. But if those efforts failed, an admitted serial killer would walk out of prison, apparently for the first time in US history. As one journalist, who was also a cousin of one of Watts's victims, observed, it was an irony that this would occur in Texas: "A state that has executed more felons than any other could be the first to set a confessed serial killer free."[43]

Another particularly gruesome example is the case of Nathaniel Benjamin Levi Bar-Jonah, who was arraigned January 11, 2001, in Great Falls, Montana, on charges of kidnapping and murdering a fifth-grade boy who had been missing for nearly five years.[44]

According to court documents filed by prosecutors, Bar-Jonah raped and tortured Zachary Ramsay before killing him, then dismembered, cooked, and ate the remains. In Bar-Jonah's garage, detectives dug up twenty-one bone fragments that DNA tests showed belonged to another child, who has still not been identified. In the house, police found other evidence, including photographs and a chilling handwritten list with names and dates that appeared to link him to as many as twenty-seven cases of child abduction and molestation in several states.

The case was horrific enough in itself. But adding to the outrage of Montana residents and officials was that Bar-Jonah (who adopted that name after entering prison under his birth name, David P. Brown) had come to Great Falls following his release from twelve years of confinement in his home state of Massachusetts. The judge who freed him determined he was "not dangerous" even though several evaluations had concluded the opposite and even though his original sentence for the attempted murder and kidnapping of two thirteen-year-old boys in Charlton, Massachusetts, had called for eighteen to twenty years of imprisonment. Evaluations of Bar-Jonah while he was confined in Massachusetts contained such descriptions as "a borderline personality with marked passive-dependent and psychopathic features" and "a dangerously disturbed young man whose prognosis for recovery seems questionable." One psychologist noted that Bar-Jonah's "sexual fantasies, bizarre in nature, outline methods of torture extending to dissection and cannibalism; he expresses a curiosity about the taste of human flesh." Another reported that fantasies of violence appeared to be his primary source of sexual excitement. Those ominous reports were borne out when Bar-Jonah was arrested in another child-molesting incident in Massachusetts barely a month after his release. Yet prosecutors accepted a plea bargain that left him free with two years of probation. Part of the deal, according to Montana authorities, was that he would leave Massachusetts and move with his mother to Montana.

The Montana prosecutors were eventually forced to drop the murder-cannibalism charges because Zachary Ramsay's mother, unable or unwilling to believe her child was dead, was prepared to testify for the defense that she was sure he was still alive. Though they had no doubt about what happened, prosecutors thought her testimony would make conviction impossible. In a separate trial, they succeeded in getting Bar-Jonah convicted and sentenced to 130 years in prison for molesting two other boys.

Like Donald Gene Miller, Coral Eugene Watts, and Nathaniel Bar-Jonah appear likely to fit all or nearly all elements of the definition we have developed for the lethal predator. The grief and loss these men left behind among the families of their victims and the terror they created in their communities stand as compelling reasons for further study of this special type of criminal, and for sober, informed, and careful decisions about how best to guard against the danger they represent. While much further research remains to be done, however, we feel present knowledge (as outlined in this article) clearly establishes the baseline facts: the lethal predator is a psychopath, a sadist, and a relentless hunter who willfully destroys human beings for pleasure; he is dangerous and abnormal and can be defined with reliability and validity.

With respect to the legal and policy issues we have discussed, we believe the baseline is similarly clear: the law permits criminal and civil confinement to be applied consecutively. In pointing this out, we do not intend to say what should be done but what may be done. Our effort is to present the facts that will allow legislators, the criminal justice system, and the mental health community to choose policies that will protect the public while remaining consistent with the legal and moral principles on which our democratic society rests.

NOTES

1. Anne Bond Emrich, "When a Predator Comes Back: Serial/Sexual Predator Conference Update" [online], http://info.jm.msu.edu/serial/home.htm.
2. US Department of Justice, Office of Justice Programs, Bureau of Justice Statistics, *Prisoners in 2001* (July 2002): 13.
3. In 1998, the FBI definition of serial homicide was codified in title 28, chap. 33, of the United States Code: "the term 'serial killings' means a series of 3 or more killings . . . having common characteristics such as to suggest the reasonable possibility that the crimes were committed by the same actor or actors" (28 U.S.C. and 540B (2) 1998). This definition is also contained in the FBI Director's Memorandum to All Special Agents in Charge, dated August 11, 1999, "RE: Serial Killings."
4. J. E. Douglas, A. W. Burgess, A. G. Burgess, and R. K. Ressler, *Crime Classification Manual* (New York: Lexington Books, 1992).
5. A. J. Reiss Jr. and J. A. Roth, *Understanding and Preventing Violence* (Washington, DC: National Academy Press, 1993).
6. K. V. Lanning, "Sexual Homicide of Children," *American Professional Society on the Abuse of Children Advisor* 7, no. 4 (1994): 40–44.
7. *Foucha v. Louisiana*, 504 US 71, 118 L. Ed.2d, 112 S. Ct 1780 (1992).
8. T. Millon, E. Simonsen, M. Birket-Smith, and R. D. Davis, *Psychopathy: Antisocial, Criminal, and Violent Behaviors* (New York: Guilford Press, 1998), p. 28.
9. R. D. Hare, *The Hare Psychopathy Checklist–Revised* (Toronto, ON: Multi-Health Systems, 1991); R. D. Hare, *The Hare Psychopathy Checklist–Revised*, 2nd ed. (Toronto, ON: Multi-Health Systems, 2003); R. D. Hare, "Psychopathy, Affect, and Behavior," in *Psychopathy: Theory, Research, and Implications for Society*, ed. D. J. Cooke, A. E. Forth, and Hare (Dordrecht, The Netherlands: Kluwer, 1998), pp. 105–37.
10. M. Dolan and M. Doyle, "Violence Risk Prediction: Clinical and Actuarial Measures and the Role of the Psychopathy Checklist," *British Journal of Psychiatry* 177 (2000): 303–11; J. F. Hemphill, R. D. Hare, and S. Wong, "Psychopathy and Recidivism: A Review," *Legal and Criminological Psychology* 3 (1998): 141–72; R. T. Salekin, R.

Rogers, and K. W. Sewell, "A Review and Meta-Analysis of the Psychopathy Checklist and Psychopathy Checklist–Revised: Predictive Validity of Dangerousness," *Clinical Psychology: Science and Practice* 3 (1996): 203–15; H. J. Steadman, E. Silver, J. Monahan, P. S. Appelbaum, P. M. Robbins, E. P. Mulvey, T. Grisso, L. H. Roth, and S. Banks, "A Classification Tree Approach to the Development of Actuarial Violence Risk Assessment Tools," *Law and Human Behavior* 24 (2000): 83–100.

11. J. P. Newman, "Psychopathic Behavior: An Information Processing Perspective," in *Psychopathy: Theory, Research, and Implications for Society*, ed. D. J. Cooke, A. E. Forth, and Hare (Dordrecht, The Netherlands: Kluwer, 1998), pp. 81–104.

12. For example, Hare, "Psychopathy, Affect, and Behavior"; S. C. Herpertz, U. Werth, G. Lukas, M. Quanaibi, A. Schuerkens, H. J. Kunert, R. Freese, M. Flesch, R. Mueler-Isberner, M. Osterheider, and H. Sass, "Emotion in Criminal Offenders with Psychopathy and Borderline Personality Disorder," *Archives of General Psychiatry* 58 (2001): 737–45; J. Intrator, R. D. Hare, P. Stritzke, K. Brichtswein, D. Dorfman, T. Harpur, D. Bernstein, L. Handelsman, C. Schaefer, J. Keilp, J. Rosen, and J. Machac, "A Brain-Imaging (Single Photon Emission Computerized Tomography) Study of Semantic and Affective Processing in Psychopaths," *Biological Psychiatry* 42 (1997): 96–103; K. A. Kiehl, A. M. Smith, R. D. Hare, A. Mendrek, B. B. Forster, J. Brink, and P. F. Liddle, "Limbic Abnormalities in Affective Processing by Criminal Psychopaths as Revealed by Functional Magnetic Resonance Imaging," *Biological Psychiatry* 50, no. 9 (2001): 677–84; C. J. Patrick, "Emotion and Psychopathy: Some Startling New Insights," *Psychophysiology* 31 (1994): 319–30; F. Schneider, U. Habel, C. Kessler, S. Posse, W. Grodd, and H. W. Muller-Gartner, "Functional Imaging of Conditioned Aversive Emotional Responses in Antisocial Personality Disorder," *Neuropsychobiology* 42 (2001): 192–201; S. E. Williamson, T. J. Harpur, and R. D. Hare, "Abnormal Processing of Affective Words by Psychopaths," *Psychophysiology* 28 (1991): 260–73.

13. Hare, *Hare Psychopathy Checklist–Revised* and *Hare Psychopathy Checklist–Revised*, 2nd ed.

14. S. M. Fulero, "Review of the Hare Psychopathy Checklist-Revised," in *Twelfth Mental Measurements Yearbook*, ed. J. C. Conoley and J. C. Impara (Lincoln, NE: Buros Institute, 1995), p. 454.

15. D. J. Cooke, and C. Michie, "An Item Response Theory Evaluation of Hare's Psychopathy Checklist," *Psychological Assessment* 9 (1997): 2–13; Cooke and Michie, "Refining the Construct of Psychopathy: Towards a Hierarchical Model," *Psychological Assessment* 13, no. 2 (2001): 171–88; Cooke, Michie, S. D. Hart, and R. D. Hare, "Evaluation of the Screening Version of the Hare Psychopathy Checklist–Revised (PCL: SV): An Item Response Theory Analysis," *Psychological Assessment* 11 (1999): 3–13.

16. Hare, *Hare Psychopathy Checklist–Revised*, 2nd ed.; J. E. Vitale and J. P. Newman, "Using the Psychopathy Checklist–Revised with Female Samples: Reliability, Validity, and Implications for Clinical Utility," *Clinical Psychology: Science and Practice* 9 (2001): 117–32; A. E. Forth, D. Kosson, and R. D. Hare, *The Hare Psychopathy Checklist: Youth Version* (Toronto, ON: Multi-Health Systems, 2003); P. A. McDermott, A. I. Alterman, J. S. Cacciola, M. J. Rutherford, J. P. Newman, and E. M. Mulholland, "Generality of Psychopathy Checklist–Revised Factors over Prisoners and Substance-Dependent Patients," *Journal of Consulting and Clinical Psychology* 68 (2000): 181–86; M. Windle and L. Dumenci, "The Factorial Structure and Construct Validity of the Psychopathy Checklist–Revised (PCL-R) among Alcoholic Inpatients," *Structural Equation*

Modeling 6 (1999): 372–93; M. E. Rice and G. T. Harris, "Cross-Validation and Extension of the Violence Risk Appraisal Guide for Child Molesters and Rapists," *Law and Human Behavior* 21 (1997): 231–41; H. J. Richards, J. O. Casey, and S. W. Lucente, "Psychopathy and Treatment Response in Incarcerated Female Substance Abusers," *Criminal Justice and Behavior* 30 (2003): 251–76.

17. D. J. Cooke, D. S. Kosson, and C. Michie, "Psychopathy and Ethnicity: Structural, Item, and Test Generalizability of the Psychopathy Checklist–Revised (PCL-R) in Caucasian and African American Participants," *Psychological Assessment* 13, no. 4 (2001): 531–42.

18. R. D. Hare, "Psychopathy as a Risk Factor for Violence," *Psychiatric Quarterly* 70 (1999): 181–97. Also see Hare, *Hare Psychopathy Checklist–Revised*, 2nd ed.

19. See A. E. Forth and H. C. Burke, (1998). "Psychopathy in Adolescence: Assessment, Violence, and Developmental Precursors," in *Psychopathy: Theory, Research, and Implications for Society*, ed. D. J. Cooke, Forth, and R. D. Hare (Dordrecht, The Netherlands: Kluwer, 1998), pp. 205–29; R. D. Hare, Forth, and K. Strachan, "Psychopathy and Crime across the Lifespan," in R. DeV. Peters, R. J. McMahon, and V. L. Quinsey, *Aggression and Violence throughout the Life Span* (Newbury Park, CA: Sage Publications, 1992), pp. 285–300; S. Porter, A. Birt, and D. P. Boer, "Report on the Criminal and Conditional Release Profiles of Canadian Federal Offenders as a Function of Psychopathy and Age," *Law and Human Behavior* 25 (2001): 647–62; Hare, L. M. McPherson, and Forth, "Male Psychopaths and Their Criminal Careers," *Journal of Consulting and Clinical Psychology* 56 (1988): 710–14; G. T. Harris, M. E. Rice, and C. A. Cormier, "Psychopathy and Violent Recidivism," *Law and Human Behavior* 15 (1991): 625–37.

20. E. Silver, E. P. Mulvey, and J. Monahan, "Assessing Violence Risk among Discharged Psychiatric Patients: Toward an Ecological Approach," *Law and Human Behavior* 23 (1999): 237–55.

21. R. D. Hare, D. J. Cooke, and S. D. Hart, "Psychopath and Sadistic Personality Disorder," in *Oxford Textbook of Psychopathology*, ed. T. Millon, P. Blaney, and R. Davis (Oxford: Oxford University Press, 1999), pp. 555–84; M. H. Stone, "Sadistic Personality in Murderers," in *Psychopathy: Antisocial, Criminal, and Violent Behavior*, ed. Millon, E. Simonsen, M. Burket-Smith, and Davis (New York: Guilford Press, 1998), pp. 346–58; S. Porter, M. Woodworth, J. Earle, J. Drugge, and D. Boer, "Characteristics of Sexual Homicides Committed by Psychopathic and Nonpsychopathic Offenders," *Law and Human Behavior* 27, no. 5 (October 2003): 459–70.

22. Stone, "Sadistic Personality in Murderers."

23. See ibid.; V. J. Geberth, ed., *Practical Homicide Investigation: Tactics, Procedures, and Forensic Techniques*, 3rd ed. (Boca Raton, FL: CRC Press, 1996); Geberth and R. N. Turco, "Antisocial Personality Disorder, Sexual Sadism, Malignant Narcissism, and Serial Murder," *Journal of Forensic Science* 42, no. 1 (1997): 49–60.

24. M. E. Rice and G. T. Harris, "Cross-Validation and Extension of the Violence Risk Appraisal Guide for Child Molesters and Rapists," *Law and Human Behavior* 21 (1997): 231–41; M. Hildebrand, C. de Ruiter, and M. de Vogel, "Psychopathy and Sexual Deviance in Treated Rapists: Association with (Sexual) Recidivism," *Sexual Abuse: A Journal of Research and Treatment* 16, no. 1 (2004): 1–24. See Hare, *Hare Psychopathy Checklist–Revised*, 2nd ed., pp. 154–57.25. P. E. Dietz, R. R. Hazelwood, and J. Warren, "The Sexually Sadistic Criminal and His Offenses," *Bulletin of the American Academy of Psychiatry and the Law* 18 (1990): 163.

26. Ibid., p. 165.

27. M. Woodworth and S. Porter, "In Cold Blood: Characteristics of Criminal Homicides as a Function of Psychopathy," *Journal of Abnormal Psychology* 111, no. 3 (2002): 436–45.

28. See M. J. MacCulloch, P. R. Snowden, P. J. Wood, and H. E. Mills, "Sadistic Fantasy, Sadistic Behaviour and Offending," *British Journal of Psychiatry* 143 (1983): 20–29.

29. R. A. Prentky, A. W. Burgess, F. Rokous, A. Lee, C. Hartman, R. Ressler, and J. Douglas, "The Presumptive Role of Fantasy in Serial Sexual Homicide," *American Journal of Psychiatry* 146 (1989): 890.

30. Salekin, Rogers, and Sewell, "A Review and Meta-Analysis of the Psychopathy Checklist and Psychopathy Checklist–Revised; Hemphill, Hare, and Wong, "Psychopathy and Recidivism."

31. Dolan and Doyle, "Violence Risk Prediction"; R. D. Hare, D. Clark, M. Grann, and D. Thornton, "Psychopathy and the Predictive Validity of the PCL-R: An International Perspective," *Behavioral Sciences and the Law* 18 (2000): 623–45.

32. Forth, Kosson, and Hare, *Hare Psychopathy Checklist: Youth Version.*

33. See B. Dolan and J. Coid, *Psychopathic and Antisocial Personality Disorders: Treatment and Research Issues* (London: Gaskell, 1993); R. D. Hare, *Without Conscience: The Disturbing World of the Psychopaths among Us.* New York: Guilford Press, 1998); F. Losel, "Treatment and Management of Psychopaths," in *Psychopathy: Theory, Research, and Implications for Society,* ed. D. J. Cooke, Forth, and R. D. Hare (Dordrecht, The Netherlands: Kluwer, 1998), pp. 303–54; P. Suedfeld and P. B. Landon, (1978). "Approaches to Treatment," in *Psychopathic Behavior: Approaches to Research,* ed. R. D. Hare and D. Schalling (Chichester, England: Wiley, 1978), pp. 347–76; S. Wong and R. D. Hare, *Program Guidelines for the Institutional Treatment of Violent Psychopaths* (Toronto, ON: Multi-Health Systems, in press); M. E. Rice, G. T. Harris, and C. A. Cormier, "An Evaluation of a Maximum-Security Therapeutic Community for Psychopaths and Other Mentally Disordered Offenders," *Law and Human Behavior* 16 (1992): 399–412; Hare, Clark, Grann, and Thornton, "Psychopathy and the Predictive Validity of the PCLR."

34. M. C. Seto and H. E. Barbaree, "Psychopathy, Treatment Behavior, and Sex Offenders Recidivism," *Journal of Interpersonal Violence* 14 (1999): 1235–48.

35. See Wong and Hare, *Program Guidelines.*

36. For example, see T. J. Harpur and R. D. Hare, "Assessment of Psychopathy as a Function of Age," *Journal of Abnormal Psychology* 103 (1994): 604–609. For more recent evidence, see Hare, *Hare Psychopathy Checklist–Revised,* 2nd ed.

37. Emrich, "When a Predator Comes Back."

38. For example, see Porter, Birt, and Boer, "Report on the Criminal and Conditional Release Profiles."

39. W. L. Fitch, "Sex Offender Commitment in the United States: Legislative and Policy Concerns," in *Sexually Coercive Behavior: Understanding and Management,* ed. B. J. Winick and J. Q. La Fond (New York: Academy of Sciences, 2003).

40. A. J. Falk, "Sex Offenders, Mental Illness and Criminal Responsibility: The Constitutional Boundaries of Civil Commitment after Kansas v. Hendricks," *American Journal of Law and Medicine* 25, no. 1 (1999): 117–47.

41. Emrich, "When a Predator Comes Back."

42. Material on Coral Eugene Watts is based on these news articles: "Coral Eugene

Watts Murdered at Least 13 Women But Went to Prison Only for Aggravated Burglary; Someday He'll Get Out," *Houston Chronicle*, April 7, 1991; "State May Become 1st to Free Serial Killer," *Houston Chronicle*, July 21, 2002; Pam Easton, Associated Press, "'Evil' Killer to Taste Freedom," *Ottawa Citizen*, August 16, 2002; Larry Werner, "Murder Revisited," *Star Tribune* (Minneapolis), November 10, 2002; Glenna Whitley, "Evil Eyes: Coral Eugene Watts is a Serial Killer. He Says He'll Murder Again. Why Can't Texas Stop Him?" *Dallas Observer*, June 19, 2003. Material from these sources was corroborated in telephone interviews (July 15 and 16, 2003) by Ira Jones of the Harris County (TX) district attorney's office, who prosecuted Watts, and Diane Clements of the organization Justice for All.

43. Werner, "Murder Revisited."

44. Information on Nathaniel Bar-Jonah was culled from the following press accounts: "Bar-Jonah's Life History Full of Tales of Violence," *Boston Herald*, January 7, 2001; "Long History of Dangerous, Bizarre Acts," *Boston Herald*, January 7, 2001; Tragic 'Transfer' to Montana: Mass. Sex Offender Charged in Boy's Death," *Los Angeles Times*, January 9, 2001; "Cannibalism Alleged in Disappearance; Child Molester Held in 5-Year-Old Montana Case," *Washington Post*, January 12, 2001; "Mass. Officials Praise Sex Predator Ruling," *Boston Herald*, January 18, 2001; "Critics Cite Flaws in Sex Predator Lock-up Law," *Boston Herald*, January 14, 2001; "System Stands Accused In a Montana Man's Case," *New York Times*, January 23, 2001; "Mont. Horrors Underlie Sex-Assault Trial," *Denver Post*, February 21, 2002; "Bar-Jonah Sentenced to 130 Years for Assaults," *Boston Herald*, May 24, 2002; "Bar-Jonah Case May Be Dropped," *Boston Globe*, October 2, 2002. Details cited from these accounts were corroborated by Brant Light, county attorney for Cascade County, MT, in a telephone interview conducted July 1, 2003.

CHAPTER 22

FIRE, FILICIDE, AND FINDING FELONS

Timothy G. Huff

Timothy G. Huff works for the Federal Bureau of Investigation, National Center for the Analysis of Violent Crime, FBI Academy, Quantico, Virginia.

The information in the first part of this chapter was developed at the National Center for the Analysis of Violent Crime (NCAVC), located at the Federal Bureau of Investigation Academy in Quantico, Virginia. The NCAVC is a law enforcement–oriented resource center that consolidates research, training, investigative, and operational support functions to provide assistance to law enforcement agencies confronted with unusual, high-risk, vicious, or repetitive crimes. One component of the NCAVC is the Arson and Bombing Investigative Services Subunit (ABIS). ABIS has the primary responsibility to provide assistance in arson, bombing, terrorism, and related violent crimes submitted to the NCAVC by federal, state, local, and foreign law enforcement agencies.

"Local firefighter arrested for arson!" A headline like this in your community's newspaper can be a nightmare come true for any fire chief. What are the

---

Published in a slightly different form as "Fire-Setting Fire Fighters: Arsonists in the Fire Department—Identification and Prevention," *On Scene* 8, no. 15 (August 15, 1994): 6–7, reprinted by permission of the International Association of Fire Chiefs; "Filicide by Fire—The Worst Crime?" [online], http://firechief.com/mag/firefighting_filicide_fire/ [accessed July 1, 1999]; and "The Neighborhood Investigation," a pamphlet of the National Center for the Analysis of Violent Crime.

chances it could happen in your department? That depends on you. This article deals with the phenomenon of firefighters who commit arson, why they commit the crime, and what you can do to prevent it.

The focus is on fire-fighting personnel who betray their comrades, families, and communities by committing arson. No one knows how many firefighters are arsonists. The number of known cases is relatively small, considering the approximately one million paid and volunteer firefighters in this country. Thankfully, the overwhelming majority of firefighters dedicate their lives to serving their communities and richly deserve the hero status they often achieve.

However, the author easily located twenty-five cases of firefighter arson by polling fire investigators in attendance at arson training sessions across the continent. Indeed, every audience produced a few new cases. The data in this article were gleaned from seven states and one Canadian province. The investigators who solved the cases supplied the data. Sixteen of the cases involved lone offenders; the other nine involved multiple offenders amounting to fifty-nine conspirators. In all, there were seventy-five offenders responsible for 182 fires. Using a protocol prepared at the FBI's National Center for the Analysis of Violent Crime (NCAVC) in 1993, the author conducted interviews with the investigators who solved the arson cases.

MOTIVES

There are predictable reasons why firefighters set fires. The author isolated three motives in the twenty-five cases studied. The predominant motive found was excitement. The excitement motive was the driving force for the great majority of the group offender cases analyzed in this study (N = 8 for 89 percent). This is particularly true for the groups of youthful firefighter arsonists. It often was the dominating reason for lone offenders as well (N = 8 for 50 percent). These firefighters put their training and expectations of fire fighting into action by setting the fires themselves.

In another aspect of the excitement motive reported by investigators, the arsonist hoped to be perceived a hero for his fire-fighting efforts. (All reported offenders were men.) The fantasy of being highly regarded by peers, family, friends, and members of the community overwhelms good judgment and common sense, they said.

Some excitement fire setters preferred to set fires in relation to public events such as parades, musters, training days, drills, or holidays to maximize public or peer attention. The sense of belonging and feelings of power and excitement were important to the offender.

Profit was another motive. Some firefighters received considerable overtime pay if kept on beyond their regular shift. Wildland firefighters are included here, too. In some jurisdictions, volunteer firefighters received a fixed sum of money for each call to which they responded.

Revenge was the least common of the three motives used by the firefighter arsonist. A disgruntled employee for any of many reasons may set fires in retaliation for a perceived grievance. In one case, a volunteer torched the fire station. In another case, a group of demoralized firefighters turned fire setters in retaliation for a grievance against their chief.

LONE OR GROUP OFFENDERS

In most serial arson cases (three or more fires set, with a cooling-off period between each), where an NCAVC analysis connects an arsonist with the fire service, a single offender was responsible. This study included sixteen lone offenders. Less common, yet significant, were cases where multiple arsonists from one department were responsible for the fires. Nine such cases are reported here. Frequently, the multiple-arsonist cases were a part of fire department programs connected with younger participants, such as programs designed for apprentice firefighters, youth groups, or some auxiliary firefighter programs for teenagers.

MODUS OPERANDI

Most firefighter arsonists acting alone used material found at the site when setting a fire. It was less common to find one bringing gasoline to the scene or using incendiary devices. To begin their fire-setting careers, many of these arsonists favored targets such as dumpsters, trash piles, or vegetation (so-called nuisance fires). Twenty-five percent of the lone offenders ($N = 4$) and 56 percent of the group offenders ($N = 5$) began this way. Arsonists often escalated over time, setting fires more frequently and selecting targets with more damage potential. These targets often evolved in loss potential from the simple dumpster or trash fires, to vehicles, to abandoned or unoccupied structures. In extreme cases, occupied buildings were targeted. One firefighter selected storage sheds beneath the stairs of occupied apartments, setting his fires at night.

The lone arsonist commonly used matches or a cigarette lighter applied to the available fuel. This is referred to as a *hot set*, as opposed to using a delay incendiary device. Nighttime was the favored period for fire setting, presumably to afford the arsonist the cover of darkness to avoid detection. All the offenders studied set fires at night. Some also occasionally set daytime fires; only one did so frequently.

Arsonists engaged in conspiracy most commonly drove to the scene to set their fires ($N = 7$ or 78 percent). Fifty percent ($N = 8$) of the lone offenders drove, and five (31 percent) walked. The remainder were mixed. For example, one lone arsonist sometimes walked and other times drove. Another one walked or sometimes rode a bicycle. The fires were set within the fire district until the arsonist perceived suspicion directed his way. At that point, some arsonists set fires in adjoining districts to deflect suspicion or ceased setting fires for a period of time.

TELLTALE SIGNS OF FIREFIGHTER ARSON

An increase in nuisance fires within the jurisdiction of the fire department was a common denominator in 38 percent of the twenty-five firefighter arson cases examined. At the same time, few similar fires were found in adjacent jurisdictions.

In two cases, it was found that firefighters in close-knit conspiracies would never call for a fire investigator to come to the scene of the fires they set. This behavior might serve as an indicator when suspicions of firefighter arson are aroused.

The research also revealed offenders were often fairly new members of the department. "Fairly new" is used here because the fires were set by the arsonist after a period of familiarity with the department and fellow firefighters. The average time with the fire department was 2.4 years for the seventy-five arsonists. Most group offenders appeared not to have the inclination to set any fires before joining the department. The idea occurred to them later.

CHARACTERISTICS OF LONE OFFENDERS

There were characteristics and traits common to firefighter offenders who acted alone. This offender, we now know based upon the research, was predictably a white man. All of the lone offenders were white, as were 60 percent of the group offenders. The remaining 40 percent of the group offenders were black. There were no cases involving female arsonists connected with the fire service. All but two of the arsonists were between the ages of eighteen and thirty, with the average age being twenty-three. There were two exceptions involving older men. The oldest was a lone offender of forty-one who set fires for profit.

Often the arsonist who acted alone had a spotty employment record, including frequent job changes, with much absence and tardiness. He may have a criminal record for petty offenses such as theft. The record may also include vehicle code violations, violations relating to alcohol abuse, or other misdemeanors, such as trespassing. He very likely had a poor academic and behavior record in school.

CHARACTERISTICS OF GROUP OFFENDERS

Those instances of multiple arsonists from one department usually involved younger offenders (sixteen to thirty-five years of age, average age nineteen). They too were white men, except as noted above, and exhibited immature behavior in many of their social activities. One member of any group was dominant and became the leader or coleader with another dominant person. The remainder were followers. There was strong peer pressure to cooperate in the fire-setting episodes and even greater pressure not to disclose the activity to others outside the group. All multiple offenders in this study drove to the scenes;

often they were more organized in their fire-setting behavior than the lone offender. The groups did more planning in target selection and often brought a flammable liquid to the scene. They had a middle-class upbringing and no prior criminal records. Many were still in school.

TELLTALE INDICATORS

Typically, there was an evolution of similar events connected with firefighter arson cases. Investigators reported similar thoughts and feelings expressed by fire department personnel during the course of the arson problem.

One similarity in cases was that many nuisance fires were set before serious investigation into the matter was begun. Departments that thoroughly investigate all fires may be exempt from this factor. Indeed, a good investigation policy may deter the firefighter arsonist.

Investigators also reported that initially fire department personnel were perceived as being beyond suspicion. Next, the possibility of fire personnel involvement was briefly considered, then rejected as unlikely. Later, the reluctance to believe a firefighter was responsible for the arsons gave way gradually to genuine suspicion. This suspicion was closely held because of a reluctance to confide in anyone in case the person holding the suspicion was wrong. Further, any suspicion of a peer by rank-and-file firefighters was not expressed to management for the same reason—plus fear of the personal consequences if the suspicion was in error.

WHAT ABOUT THE CHIEF?

The research disclosed some interesting phenomena regarding the departments' chief officers. There is sometimes a reluctance on the part of a fire department's management to report suspicions of firefighter arson to law enforcement authorities. Fire department relations with the police are not always the best, and fire chiefs understandably fear their suspicions being made public. Disclosure could bring shame to the department, whether the suspicions are correct or incorrect. The nagging fear of "What if I'm wrong?" is an extremely powerful deterrent to disclosing suspicions. The impact on employee morale is but one example of the negative result of suspicions becoming known. To focus upon the employee/suspect who is perfectly innocent can have far-reaching negative consequences. It makes good sense from the standpoint of morality, efficiency, and responsibility to eliminate anyone in the fire-fighting ranks from suspicion early in an investigation. The investigation can then concentrate in other potentially more productive areas, and innocent firefighters can be defended from any speculation that they are involved. (The whole case may reveal negligent hiring practices by the department.)

The confrontation with the suspect(s) and the actual arrest(s) may not be nearly as troubling to a department as all the prior stress. The adverse publicity, the dealings with the media, the postarrest investigation, and the judicial proceedings increase the chief's burden. Next come the efforts at face saving, healing, and restoring confidence within the department and beyond.

PREVENTION

Some administrators are interested in grant money so studies of the problem can be conducted. The breadth and depth of the problem has not been studied. While grants are nice, the immediate and apparent answer to prevent firefighter arsons is deceptively simple: applicant screening. The trauma and accompanying problems of having an arsonist in the fire department can be minimized if applicants are screened with a background examination. Screening cannot be one hundred percent effective for a fire department any more than for a police department, but it is the best insurance. There are cases where volunteer firefighters suspected of arson moved from one state to another. A series of arsons took place in the communities shortly after the men's arrival and appointment to volunteer fire companies. The arsonists were suspected of setting fires before they moved. Preappointment telephone calls to the firefighters' previous departments by the new chiefs may have prevented a serious problem for the victimized departments and communities. The previous chiefs, if contacted, might have conveyed their suspicions to the new chiefs.

States have varying restrictions on what can be revealed to a prospective employer. Signed waivers by firefighter applicants permitting the hiring authority to acquire confidential information is an option. Background investigations can be lengthy and labor intensive. More cursory ones need not be. The investigation should be conducted by experienced personnel but does not have to be. The police department has the forms and experience, but perhaps not the time, to conduct fire department personnel background checks. Local law enforcement can provide guidance if fire department personnel intend to conduct the background investigation. Police officials can explain the state's legal restrictions and requirements. Some fire departments use fire investigators or deputy fire marshals as background investigators. Others use administrative personnel. At least some effort must be made to view the personal side of any applicant to the department, whether paid or volunteer. One volunteer chief said he had enough trouble finding volunteers for his department. "A background check might deter potential volunteers," he said. The options must be weighed by the hiring authority.

All factors must be weighed so that an informed decision may be made whether to do no background check, a limited one, or a complete one. The most complete background checks, which include psychological examinations, can predict which applicants are a risk to hire or enroll even if they have never set a fire. Of course, background checks of this caliber are expensive. The most cursory background check should include a review of high school records, credit records, medical records, criminal history, driving record, employment records, and references. It is particularly important to check with previous fire departments the applicant was associated with.

Recruits, particularly younger ones, should be informed about the penalties and consequences of fire setting. A unit of instruction can include what to do if a colleague is suspected of setting fires.

With younger offenders, focused instruction on the criminal aspects of arson, including so-called nuisance fires, may have deterred the activity. Instruction might include obvious dangers arsons pose to firefighters and others, costs in dollars, image to the department, and penalties (fines and prison time). Arson detection training can be given at this time too, in order to correctly channel the recruits, mindset.

SUMMARY

Based upon this research, NCAVC analysts conclude that in the majority of cases involving firefighters who commit arson, the most basic of background investigations before hiring can reveal potential problems. These problems range from criminal records to mere suspicions shared by former fire-fighting colleagues. The suspicions may be that the applicant was responsible for conduct unacceptable for a firefighter. Less obvious are cases where the arsonist was hired as a firefighter and a background check would have revealed indicators of future problems such as a poor driving record, behavior problems in school, petty criminal activity involving theft, or other more serious misdemeanors.

Prompt investigation of the possible telltale signs of firefighter arson can be a deterrent. Many chiefs do not permit even cursory investigation of so-called nuisance fires, concluding these investigations are a waste of time, money, and resources. While there may be rational argument for the policy in this era of tight budgets, it is a fact many arsonists escalate in their fire-setting behavior. That is, they begin their fire-setting careers torching dumpsters or small patches of vegetation but escalate in frequency and selection of targets. Since they were successful in avoiding apprehension for the dumpster fires, they graduate to abandoned buildings, unoccupied buildings, and other targets of increasing value and risk to fire-fighting and civilian personnel.

The earliest possible intervention can be made by demonstrating rapid and thorough investigation of all fires to the extent resources and common sense permit. The most cursory of investigations may eliminate the possibility of firefighter involvement.

It is sad but true that a firefighter gone bad not only discredits his department but also disgraces his profession just as does a dishonest policeman. However, until more departments adopt proactive measures in the firefighter appointment process, whether paid or volunteer, there is little hope of anything but a continuing problem.

FILICIDE BY FIRE—THE WORST CRIME?

It is almost beyond belief that some parents could deliberately set fire to kill their own children. Yet researchers in the United States believe this crime is a growing phenomenon and one that is often overlooked by investigators.

Smoke and flames are seen billowing from the side bedroom window of an occupied dwelling early one morning by a neighbor on his way to work. By the time the fire crews arrive in the lower-middle-class neighborhood, clusters of people are standing in the front yard. Some are watching the spreading fire; others are huddled around a young man and woman, embracing them in turn.

Fire officials soon learn that two children perished in the flames. Their parents—the young couple in the front yard—survived the fire without injury.

This tragic scene is repeated over and over again in the United States every year—a seemingly accidental fire claiming the lives of innocent children. But in some cases, there may be a darker side to the tragedy. Did these parents deliberately kill their children?

One of our society's most heinous entries is murder by fire. When the victims of the fire are children, the cruelty is painful to imagine. And when the killers are the children's parents, it is almost beyond comprehension. Of all the ways to die, death by fire may be the worst.

Filicide refers to cases in which the murderer is a parent of the victim. Filicide by fire (using fire as the instrument of death) appears to be an emerging phenomenon. This hypothesis is based on observations by analysts at the Arson and Bombing Investigative Services program (ABIS), a component of the National Center for the Analysis of Violent Crime (NCAVC), located at the FBI Academy, in Quantico, Virginia.

The ABIS program is staffed by personnel from the FBI and the Bureau of Alcohol, Tobacco and Firearms (ATF). They analyze unsolved serial arsons, bombings, and undetermined fire death cases from departments nationwide.

Although this article is based on eight cases involving death to children, another six cases discussed with field investigators indicates that this phenomenon may be widespread and underreported. Investigators should be alerted to this type of homicide, as it can certainly go undetected.

Currently, the NCAVC receives two or three cases annually that deal with filicide by arson. Analysts agree that only a fraction of the total cases are submitted for analysis and that an undetermined number are undetected. This is based upon the fact that many arsons go undetected and are considered accidental fires. Killing one's own children is such an unnatural and horrendous act that it may leave some guilty parents above suspicion.

MOTIVES FOR FILICIDE

As with any crime, there are various motives for these murders:

- *Unwanted-child filicide.* These murders were committed to remove a perceived obstacle—to get rid of a nuisance. Some parents viewed their children as a wall between them and their spouse or lover. They believed that if the children were removed, the adults could reconcile their difficulties and live happily. In one case, a single mother wanted to marry her boyfriend, but he didn't want to be burdened with her young children. The mother removed the burden to be with her lover.
- *Acutely psychotic filicide.* Some parents were psychotic, such as a single mother who—while severely depressed—stabbed her three small children to death, then set their apartment on fire.
- *Spouse-revenge filicide.* An estranged husband decided to deprive his wife of the object she treasured most—her child. He did so by the use of fire.
- *Murder for profit filicide.* Parents took out large life insurance policies on their children not long before they died in a fire.[1]

With any of these cases, the authorities may not be suspicious for various reasons. The responsible department may not thoroughly investigate the fire, presuming instead that the child was playing with marches and caused the fatal fire. The natural desire of anyone is to feel compassion for the parent and sadness for the children. This reaction could override what might otherwise raise suspicion in the minds of investigators.

COMMON FACTORS OF THE CASES

While no single indicator can be presumptive of a crime, there were common factors in the cases reviewed at the NCAVC. These factors should be shared with investigators who may encounter fire deaths involving children. More cases require study to confirm and add information to the list, and not all statements are true for all offenders. The following represent what the NCAVC cases revealed.

Victims

- The children were young, usually preschool age, but rarely older than seven or eight years. Older children are less likely to share a bedroom than younger children or are more likely to effect an escape and report what happened. Perhaps older children are viewed as being less "disposable" or less vulnerable.
- The fires took place at night or early in the morning, from around 4 a.m.

to 7 a.m., and while the children were still asleep in their beds. In cases where the fire itself was the instrument of death, the children were sleeping. Presumably their killers wanted to be sure the children were trapped in their bedroom. Due to their slumber, the victims would not be alarmed as the fire-setting activity took place.

Crime Scene

- In some cases, the children may have already been shot, stabbed, or strangled to death. The killer staged the scene, positioning the children so they appeared to have died in their sleep. Whatever the scenario, the parent(s) claimed to be awakened by the smoke or sound of the fire.
- Flammable liquid such as gasoline was frequently used to get the fire to do its intended job quickly and efficiently.
- Escape was blocked. Some rearranging of furniture was made to trap the victim(s) by preventing escape through the bedroom door. This was accomplished by placing a mattress or dresser as an obstacle to hinder the victim in attempting to escape.

Parents (May Include Step-Parent or Lover)

- Parents stated they were in bed when the fire occurred. This gave the adult(s) a very logical alibi, accounting for their whereabouts at the critical time when the fire occurred.
- Rescue attempts by the adult were fainthearted. There was little or no sign on the part of the would-be rescuer of prolonged or dangerous exposure to heat. The eyes were not puffy or watering from excessive time spent in a smoke-filled environment. The exposed skin of face and hands was not severely reddened or burned. Hair and eyebrows were not singed. In short, stated heroic or desperate rescue attempts did not match with the appearance of the person.
- There was inappropriate behavior (little or no grief exhibited) by the parents. In conversations with sympathetic neighbors at the scene, the guilty party spoke very little about the victims and instead discussed material losses and made declarations about the future. One must distinguish between grieved parents in shock and disbelief at their tragic loss and those who deliberately killed their children. The latter displayed little personal devastation.
- Careless comments may be made hours or days later by the guilty. Remarks such as "Now we can get on with our lives" or "Now I am free to do as I wish" may be made to friends or neighbors. Similar remarks may be confided to friends before the fire, expressing the wish to be free of the burden of children.

- The parents may not be dressed as one would expect. According to their story, they leapt from bed, tried to rescue their children, and next found themselves in their front yard with a crowd of people. In several cases, the parent(s) were fully clothed when witnesses arrived, in spite of the early hour and the nature of the emergency.
- The family was already known to social services or child protective agencies through previous referrals for neglect or other charges.
- Rarely did the parents own their home. Mobile homes were the most common residences.
- The parents were in their mid-twenties to mid-thirties.

All, or even most, of the factors outlined above may not be present in every case of filicide and fire. Conversely, no single factor alone would necessarily raise suspicion. However, collectively they may be considered indicators of a situation requiring further inquiry.

CONCLUSIONS

Cases examined by the NCAVC and brought to the analysts' attention suggest there are sufficient cases of filicide by fire around the United States to justify alerting investigators.

More cases need to be examined to sharpen profile criteria and perhaps add extra factors. Therefore, the NCAVC is attempting to alert investigators to the phenomenon of filicide by fire so that crimes of this nature are not overlooked and underreported.

Investigators must be alert for other means of child death with fire used to cover up the crime. Examples are stabbing, suffocating, beating, strangling, or shooting. A fire is then set by the killer, hoping it will cover the crime with both the death and fire listed as accidental.[2]

THE NEIGHBORHOOD INVESTIGATION

Criminal investigations are based upon the premise that the offender made mistakes in the perpetration of the crime. Simply stated, if the offender makes no mistakes, he will not be caught. The job of the investigator is to search for any mistakes the offender made. The search may require painstaking effort. A neighborhood investigation (NI) at times falls into this category. The NI is a fundamental method of searching for the witness whom the offender did not consider in the perpetration of the crime. The NI may disclose his big mistake. A less-than-thorough NI may be *your* big mistake.

Definition: A neighborhood investigation is the search for persons who were present in the proximity of a crime to determine if they have information that will advance the investigation.

The term *information*, as used here, may include something seen, heard, or smelled by a witness or referrals to some other person who might possess such information.

One of the basic investigative tools with potentially great dividends, neighborhood investigations are often conducted with little thought, no preparation, and worse, sometimes not at all.

EXAMPLES

Case Study—Arson

Investigators conducted a follow-up investigation on a case involving an arson to a residence that occurred the previous night. They commenced their NI to locate potential witnesses. The two officers went to nearby homes and knocked on doors where someone appeared to be home. When an occupant answered the door, they identified themselves, stated their purpose, and asked if that person had seen anything suspicious the evening before. In every case, the respondents answered they had not. Each encounter was nearly this brief.

The case was solved when an acquaintance of the arsonist who was arrested for an unrelated offense informed on him in an effort to obtain leniency. Detectives did another NI, seeking corroboration for the informant's story. A resident told the detectives that on the night of the fire, she had seen the suspect hurrying down the sidewalk across the street. He was briefly illuminated by the street light and was carrying a gasoline can.

She knew the offender because he grew up in the neighborhood. When asked why she did not report this during the original canvass, she said she had not regarded it as suspicious because she assumed his car had run out of gasoline.

Investigators were lucky in this case; however, no one knows how often solvable cases remain unsolved because leads were missed in a less-than-thorough NI.

Case Study—Bombing Hoax

A hoax bomb was placed on the doorstep of a mobile home at a West Coast mobile-home park late one night. Investigators conducted the NI the next morning. No one was home at two of the neighboring mobile homes, and the investigators did not attempt to locate the absent neighbors. The investigators apparently assumed the neighbors were gone when the offense occurred. When one of the missing occupants returned from a trip three days later, he heard of the crime and contacted the police. He reported that as he was leaving home late the night of the incident, he drove past the mobile home and saw two young adults leaving the porch, one of whom appeared to be placing something there. He thought little of the incident at the time because teenagers frequented that residence. His description of the two was enough to identify them as acquaintances of the intended victim.

If the witness had not come forward, the case might still be unsolved because the investigators had not planned to return to contact neighbors missed in their first canvass.

These and similar scenarios are repeated countless times daily in investigations across the country.

There are lessons to be learned from these cases. In the first instance, if the right questions had been asked, useful information may have resulted. In the second case, investigators assumed that because no one was home at the time of the canvass, the occupants would have no information.

In both incidents no one was injured, and despite the cursory NI, the cases were solved. But in major cases, the cursory is not acceptable, and a less-than-thorough NI is a very serious omission.

Analysts at the FBI's National Center for the Analysis of Violent Crime (NCAVC) in Quantico, Virginia, routinely give investigative suggestions to departments submitting unsolved cases. The NI is a basic investigative tool that is often underused and at times not used at all. A quality NI is fundamental to the investigation of many crimes.

The NCAVC makes the following recommendations when conducting the NI:

- You must be thorough in your approach.
- Prethink questions pertinent to the investigation. Appeal to the potential witnesses' senses of sight, hearing, or in some cases, smell (arson or drug cases).
- Describe the environment at the time of the offense to the potential witness in an effort to enhance memory. For example, remind the person of the weather conditions at the time of the offense and whether it were dark, daylight, sunset, or at about a certain time on the specific day of the week. Consider reminding the person what television programs were on at the time in question.
- Write down the orientation statements and the questions, especially in a case where several investigators canvass designated areas. The information presented to potential witnesses should be consistent and thorough.
- Design pertinent, specific, case-related questions to trigger recollection of information the potential witness would regard as trivial. These queries may include a vehicle of a particular type or color, sounds the investigator can describe to the potential witness, or an infinite variety of factors applicable to a specific case.
- Preplan questions to avoid disclosing too much information and to avoid asking leading questions.

- Find out who lives there and/or was at home during the time in question. If they are not present during this canvass, ask when and where can they be reached.
- Log addresses of neighborhood homes where no contact was made so later contact can be attempted.
- Avoid vague questions such as, "Did you see anything suspicious?" This question evokes different definitions from everyone. It is too subjective. Far better is to ask, as an example, "Did you see anyone on the street (at around a particular time)?" The respondent may have seen persons on the street, perhaps not the offender, but other potential witnesses.
- Ask, if appropriate to the case, if anyone in the home videotaped or photographed the event (a fire or explosion, for example).
- Conduct a precanvass meeting with all participating investigators so all are provided a checklist and reminded of the importance of a thorough NI.
- Although the suggestions imply an urban residential neighborhood, other scenarios also apply. The same principles transfer to commercial or rural areas and must be adjusted to accommodate.
- Other considerations for the NI beyond the door-to-door canvass must not be overlooked.
- Consider delivery persons who might make daily or frequent trips past the crime scene at a time appropriate to the investigation. These include postal employees, newspaper delivery persons, public transportation drivers or passengers, pizza delivery persons, and many other possibilities, including commuters in personal vehicles. Neighborhood children, even those who are quite young, are potential witnesses who may be overlooked in the NI.

CONCLUSION

Neighborhood investigations are often unsuccessful, so investigators, convinced of a low return for the time invested, spend little time and energy on them. The real problem may be the way the investigations are conducted. Certainly, the reward for the invested time can be increased by conducting thorough, well-planned neighborhood investigations.[3]

NOTES

1. Phillip J. Resnick, MD, "Child Murder by Parents: A Psychiatric Review of Filicide," *American Journal of Psychiatry* 126 (September 1969: 73. The first three motives are found in Resnick's paper along with others that are not included here because of a lack of association with fire. The fourth is derived from a single case. A literature search revealed very little on filicide by fire. Dr. Resnick's 1969 paper is the most relevant.

2. The author wishes to thank the following people for their help: Dr. David J. Icove,

FBI, Program Manager, Arson and Bombing Investigative Services Program; Special Agents Gordon P. Gary and Joseph J. Chisholm, Bureau of Alcohol, Tobacco, and Firearms, assigned to ABIS; other members of the National Center for the Analysis of Violent Crime; Barker Davie of Barker and Herbert Laboratories, New Haven, Indiana; Barbara S. Gelband, Assistant Attorney General, State of Arizona, Tucson; and the many cooperating professionals with the California Department of Corrections.

3. The author acknowledges the valuable contributions to this document by SSA Mary Ellen O'Toole, FBI, SA Ronald L. Tunkel, ATF, SA Kevin L. Kelm, ATF, (all three assigned to the NCAVC at Quantico) and Mary Lynne Wolfe, ATF Headquarters.

DATE DUE